10th Anniversary of *Axioms*: Logic

10th Anniversary of *Axioms*: Logic

Editor

Oscar Castillo

MDPI • Basel • Beijing • Wuhan • Barcelona • Belgrade • Manchester • Tokyo • Cluj • Tianjin

Editor
Oscar Castillo
Division of Graduate Studies
and Research
Tijuana Institute of Technology
TecNM
Tijuana
Mexico

Editorial Office
MDPI
St. Alban-Anlage 66
4052 Basel, Switzerland

This is a reprint of articles from the Special Issue published online in the open access journal *Axioms* (ISSN 2075-1680) (available at: www.mdpi.com/journal/axioms/special_issues/10th_Anniversary_of_axioms_logic).

For citation purposes, cite each article independently as indicated on the article page online and as indicated below:

LastName, A.A.; LastName, B.B.; LastName, C.C. Article Title. *Journal Name* **Year**, *Volume Number*, Page Range.

ISBN 978-3-0365-7839-2 (Hbk)
ISBN 978-3-0365-7838-5 (PDF)

Contents

About the Editor

Oscar Castillo

Oscar Castillo obtained his Doctor of Science degree (Doctor Habilitatus) in Computer Science from the Polish Academy of Sciences (with his Dissertation, titled "Soft Computing and Fractal Theory for Intelligent and Manufacturing"). He is a Professor of Computer Science in the Graduate Division, Tijuana Institute of Technology, Tijuana, Mexico. In addition, he is serving as Research Director of Computer Science and is head of the research group focusing on hybrid fuzzy intelligent systems. Currently, he is the president of the HAFSA (Hispanic American Fuzzy Systems Association) and the former president of the IFSA. Prof. Castillo is also the chair of the Mexican Chapter of the Computational Intelligence Society (IEEE). He belongs to the Mexican Research System (SNI Level 3). His research interests are in type-2 fuzzy logic, fuzzy control, and neuro-fuzzy and genetic-fuzzy hybrid approaches. He has published over 300 journal papers, 10 authored books, 60 edited books, 300 papers in conference proceedings, and more than 300 chapters in edited books, totaling more than 1080 publications (according to Scopus), with an h index of 89 and more than 26,000 citations according to Google Scholar. He has been the Guest Editor of several successful Special Issues in the past in the following journals: *Applied Soft Computing, Intelligent Systems, Information Sciences, Soft Computing, Non-Linear Studies, Fuzzy Sets and Systems, JAMRIS*, and *Engineering Letters*. He is currently the Associate Editor of the *Information Sciences Journal, Journal of Engineering Applications on Artificial Intelligence, International Journal of Fuzzy Systems, Journal of Complex Intelligent Systems*, and *Granular Computing Journal and Intelligent Systems Journal* (Wiley). He was elected as an IFSA Fellow in 2015 and an MICAI Fellow in 2016. Finally, he received recognition as a Highly Cited Researcher in 2017 and 2018 from Clarivate Analytics and Web of Science.

Preface to "10th Anniversary of *Axioms*: Logic"

Published for the first time in 2012, *Axioms* is celebrating its 10th anniversary. To mark this significant milestone and celebrate the achievements made throughout the years, we have organized a Special Issue entitled "10th Anniversary of *Axioms*—Logic" in the section "Logic" of *Axioms*.

Mathematical logic is a field of mathematics which has a wide range of various applications. This reprint includes high-quality papers which focus on original research in logic, mathematical logic, and applications, with the main (but not only) focus being on algebraic logic, fuzzy logic, descriptive set theory, decision making, computability and recursion theory, and algorithmic and combinatorial optimization.

We developed this reprint in order to honor the collective efforts of all those who have contributed so far to the success of the journal and the gathering of scientific research in mathematical logic related to current challenges and future innovations.

Oscar Castillo
Editor

axioms

Article

Granular Computing Approach to Evaluate Spatio-Temporal Events in Intuitionistic Fuzzy Sets Data through Formal Concept Analysis

Imran Ali [1,2], Yongming Li [1,*] and Witold Pedrycz [3,4]

1 College of Computer Science, Shaanxi Normal University, Xi'an 710062, China; aliimran@snnu.edu.cn or imran.bhatti@iba-suk.edu.pk
2 Department of Computer Science, Sukkur IBA University, Airport Road, Sukkur 65200, Pakistan
3 Department of Electrical and Computer Engineering, University of Alberta, Edmonton, AB T6R 2G7, Canada; wpedrycz@ualberta.ca
4 Systems Research Institute, Polish Academy of Sciences, 01-224 Warsaw, Poland
* Correspondence: liyongm@snnu.edu.cn

Abstract: Knowledge discovery through spatial and temporal aspects of data related to occurrences of events has many applications in digital forensics. Specifically, in electronic surveillance, it is helpful to construct a timeline to analyze information. The existing techniques only analyze the occurrence and co-occurrence of events; however, in general, there are three aspects of events: occurrences (and co-occurrences), nonoccurrences, and uncertainty of occurrences/non-occurrences with respect to spatial and temporal aspects of data. These three aspects of events have to be considered to better analyze periodicity and predict future events. This study focuses on the spatial and temporal aspects given in intuitionistic fuzzy (IF) datasets using the granular computing (GrC) paradigm; formal concept analysis (FCA) was used to understand the granularity of data. The originality of the proposed approach is to discover the periodicity of events data given in IF sets through FCA and the GrC paradigm that helps to predict future events. An experimental evaluation was also performed to understand the applicability of the proposed methodology.

Keywords: granular computing; formal concept analysis; intuitionistic fuzzy sets; periodicity; spatial and temporal aspects; knowledge discovery

MSC: 74E20; 94D05; 03B52; 03G10; 06D72

Citation: Ali, I.; Li, Y.; Pedrycz, W. Granular Computing Approach to Evaluate Spatio-Temporal Events in Intuitionistic Fuzzy Sets Data through Formal Concept Analysis. *Axioms* **2023**, *12*, 407. https://doi.org/10.3390/axioms12050407

Academic Editor: Hsien-Chung Wu

Received: 9 February 2023
Revised: 29 March 2023
Accepted: 20 April 2023
Published: 22 April 2023

1. Introduction

An event is the occurrence of something at some place and time which involves some actors as objects and spatio-temporal features as attributes. In theliterature, the idea of spatial, temporal, and spatio-temporal co-occurrences can be found. In general, spatial co-occurrence is defined as when two or more events occur at the same place, temporal co-occurrence as when a number of events occur at the same time or in the same time-interval, and spatio-temporal co-occurrence as when events occur at the same place and time. Periodical events are those that occur at the same time intervals, for example, an event that occurs every day, weekend, month, or year. In the application domain, it is important to analyze these aspects of events. In the context of smart video surveillance, it is possible to discover the periodical and same-place movements of pedestrians to predict a crime before it happens. Moreover, in the context of intuitionistic fuzzy (IF) sets, there are some membership and nonmembership values that can be indicated for events occurring at some place and time. Existing approaches only work on occurrences and co-occurrences of events; however, in real life, there can be three aspects: occurrences (and co-occurrences), nonoccurrences, and the uncertainty of occurrences/nonoccurrences. The limitation of focusing only on the occurrences and co-occurrences of events is that it indicates the data related to event occurrences that may be missing the elicitation of complete and important knowledge related to event nonoccurrences, as well as the uncertainty of occurrences/non-occurrences. Motivated by these limitations, this research provides a novel approach based on granular computing (GrC) to discover these three aspects of events at the same places and in the periodical form in the IF sets, where μ (membership), γ (non-membership), and π (uncertainty) values indicate the occurrences (and co-occurrences), nonoccurrences, and the uncertainty of occurrences/nonoccurrences of events, respectively. GrC was used to discover the periodicity in data at various abstraction levels. Moreover, formal concept analysis (FCA) was used to discover the granulation levels and process the granulation measures to understand the IF concepts, where the events indicated as objects and spatio-temporal occurrences showed the attributes of lattices formed by formal concepts. The originality of the proposed approach is to discover the periodicity of spatial–temporal occurrences data of events given in IF sets through GrC and FCA. Moreover, this approach helps predict the occurrence (co-occurrence), nonoccurrence, and uncertainty of occurrence/nonoccurrence of events for spatial and temporal aspects of data through IF sets. The motivation for the use of IF sets instead of fuzzy sets in this proposed approach is the three-tuple nature of the IF sets, which contain the μ (membership), γ (nonmembership), and π (IF set index or indeterminacy, which expresses the degree of uncertainty) values of the elements. Here, π is used in the computation of GrC measures i.e., IG and COV that help in the process of decision making. This paper is organized as follows: Section 2 discusses the related works; Section 3 provides the definitions of IF sets and FCA specifically used in the context of the IF sets data; Section 4 explains the GrC; Section 5 explains the proposed methodology; Section 6 demonstrates the experimental evaluation; Section 7 gives the results and discussion; Section 8 explains the comparison of the proposed approach with existing SOTA (state of the art) approaches; and Section 9 contains the conclusion and future work, followed by the references.

2. Related Works

In the literature, research work related to spatio-temporal and periodical occurrences and co-occurrences can be found. The most important task regarding periodical occurrences is to determine the data blocks in the whole dataset from which suitable views can be analyzed. For example, in a dataset of hundred events, discovering seventy events that always occur on a Sunday may be more interesting than ninety events occurring on the weekends. For this type of task, views are determined by selecting the temporal attributes and adjusting the temporal units in a way that helps to create a temporal zoom operation on data and discover the more interesting data blocks in the form of periodical occurrences. Depending on the data and objective, some data analysis techniques are required to evaluate the data blocks aiming to discover the periodical co-occurrences of events. Based on the GrC paradigm and FCA, different computational approaches are proposed to discover the spatio-temporal co-occurrences for different purposes. As in [1], FCA as a central tool for the proposed method is used to combine time-based granulation and three-way decisions to understand the learned granular structures conceptualizing spatio-temporal events. Moreover, the GrC is integrated with FCA as concept learning via GrC [2], granular rule acquisition in decision formal contexts [3], GrC approach based on FCA in fuzzy datasets [4], granular transformations, and irreducible element judgement [5]. There are two types of granules in FCA, one is the granule made by the set of objects in formal concept and the other is the one formed by the individual objects. Some research studies show that the granule formed by the individual objects play a vital role, with a strong correlation with object granules, object concepts [5], and granular concepts [6]. Additionally, there exist many other types of granules in FCA; however, the classification and the criteria for the classification of information granules in FCA are still an open research direction.

Yang et al. in [7] explained the sequential approach of three-way GrC by a framework of spatio-temporal multilevel granular structure, described with temporality of data and spatiality of parameters. Moreover, in the context of three-way decision approaches in [8], an IF three-way decision model based on IF sets is proposed to improve the ability to process complex fuzzy incomplete information systems. Zhao et al., in [9], proposed a novel spatial–temporal fuzzy information granule (STFIG) model to achieve the multistep forecasting of time series. In [10], the method puts forward research on the optimal route planning of traffic multisource routes based on GrC. GrC is used with set theory, shadowed sets, rough sets, fuzzy sets, etc. In each of these sets' environments, the granules or the granulation processing is defined in different ways, as well as a tentative one to find similarity and bridge the gap between these settings, as described in [11]. Additionally, the IF sets using an FCA algorithm have already been discussed in the literature [12]; for example, in [13], the structure of formal concept forming operators is given in the form of fuzzy dilation and fuzzy erosion operators of bipolar fuzzy mathematical morphology, and in [14], attribute reduction in IF concept lattices is discussed.

This methodology uses the GrC paradigm and FCA with IF datasets as spatio-temporal attributes to realize the granulation or abstraction of data related to the periodical timeslots in temporal attributes of formal contexts, which were formed from the IF datasets; the granules involving spatio-temporal attributes were used to determine the co-occurrences of events with respect to space and time. In addition, the granulation measures of lattices made from the formal contexts of IF sets were discussed, such as information granulation (IG), coverage (COV), specificity (SP), and unique index (Q) value, to evaluate the granule according to its information related to spatio-temporal and periodical co-occurrences.

3. Preliminaries

3.1. Intuitionistic Fuzzy (IF) Sets

In [15], the notion of fuzzy sets is given as

$$C' = \{\langle x, \mu_{C'}(x)\rangle \mid x \in X\}$$

where $\mu_{C'}(x) \in [0,1]$ is the membership function of the fuzzy set C'. The notion of IF set [16–18] is given as

$$C = \{\langle x, \mu_C(x), \gamma_C(x)\rangle \mid x \in X\},$$

where $\mu_C : X \to [0,1]$ and $\gamma_C : X \to [0,1]$, such that

$$0 \leq \mu_C(x) + \gamma_C(x) \leq 1.$$

Here, $\mu_C(x), \gamma_C(x) \in [0,1]$ indicate the degree of membership and the degree of non-membership of $x \in C$, respectively. Each fuzzy set in terms of IF sets can be represented as

$$C = \{\langle x, \mu_{C'}(x), 1 - \mu_{C'}(x)\rangle \mid x \in X\}.$$

In addition to this, the important concept of each IF set C in X is given as

$$\pi_C(x) = 1 - \mu_C(x) - \gamma_C(x).$$

Here, $\pi_C(x)$ is called the "hesitation degree" of $x \in C$, which indicates the uncertainty or the lack of the knowledge of whether $x \in C$ or $x \notin C$. Moreover, it is clear that $0 \leq \pi_C(x) \leq 1, \forall x \in X$. This hesitation degree plays an important role in distance [19,20], similarity [20], and entropy [21,22], which are key measures that are used specially in the information processing tasks. Additionally, hesitation degree also plays a significant role in image processing [23], multicriteria group decision making [24], IF decision trees [25], genetic algorithms [26], and many other situations. In addition to this, let $C_1, C_2 \in IF(U), C_1 \subseteq C_2 \Leftrightarrow \mu_{C_1}(x) \leq \mu_{C_2}(x)$ and $\gamma_{C_1}(x) \geq \gamma_{C_2}(x), \forall x \in U$. If both $C_1 \subseteq C_2$ and $C_2 \subseteq C_1$ then, $C_1 = C_2$ and $C_2 = C_1$. The universe set U and null set $\emptyset$ are the special type of IF sets, where $U = \{\langle x, 1, 0\rangle \mid x \in U\}$ and $\emptyset = \{\langle x, 0, 1\rangle \mid x \in U\}$.

3.2. Formal Concept Analysis (FCA)

The FCA method was proposed in early 1980 by R. Wille for when a set of objects share a set of attributes. The foundation of FCA is built on the notions of lattice and set theory. This method outputs two sets of data. The first one provides the hierarchical relationship of constructed concepts in the form of a diagram called "Concept Lattice". The second set of data provides the list of the interdependencies among all the attributes in a formal context.

Definition 1. *In FCA, the relation $K = (G, M, I)$ is called a formal context, where G and M denote the set of objects and set of attributes, respectively. In addition to this, $I \subseteq G \times M$ shows the relationship between G objects (extents) and M attributes (intents). Moreover, the relation $(g, m) \in I$ shows that the object g has attribute m, which can also be written as gIm.*

Definition 2. *For a subset $A \subseteq G$ of objects then, the subset of the attributes common to all the objects in A is given as*

$$A \uparrow = \{m \in M \mid \forall g \in A, gIm\}.$$

Likewise, given a subset $B \subseteq M$ of attributes, the subset of objects having all the attributes in set B is given as

$$B \downarrow = \{g \in G \mid \forall m \in B, gIm\}.$$

Definition 3 ([26])**.** *A formal context $K = (G, M, I)$ is defined as a pair (A, B), where $A \subseteq G$, $B \subseteq M$ and $A \uparrow = B, B \downarrow = A$, where A denotes the objects (extents) and B indicates the attributes (intents) of the pair (A, B). Let (A_1, B_1) and (A_2, B_2) be the two formal concepts of a formal context $K = (G, M, I)$; (A_1, B_1) is called a superconcept of (A_2, B_2), and (A_2, B_2) is called a subconcept of (A_1, B_1) if it satisfies the equivalent condition given as*

$$(A_1, B_1) \leq (A_2, B_2) \Leftrightarrow A_1 \subseteq A_2 \Leftrightarrow B_2 \subseteq B_1$$

The set of all the superconcept and subconcept interrelations construct a design structure known as a lattice. The lattice is an abstract structure with join (denoted by "$\vee$") and meet (denoted by "$\wedge$") operations. The above expression in this definition, in the form of join and meet, is

$$(A_1, B_1) \vee (A_2, B_2) = ((A_1 \cup A_2) \downarrow\uparrow, B_1 \cap B_2),$$

$$(A_1, B_1) \wedge (A_2, B_2) = (A_1 \cap A_2, (B_1 \cup B_2) \downarrow\uparrow)$$

where "$\vee$" and "$\wedge$" indicate the supermum and infimum operations, respectively.

For any $\forall g \in G$, the pair $(g \uparrow\downarrow, g \uparrow)$ is called the object concept, and $\forall m \in M$, the pair $(m \uparrow\downarrow, m \uparrow)$ is called the attribute concept. In a lattice diagram, when two branches join below, it is called a join operation "$\vee$", and the point where two branches meet above is known as a meet operation "$\wedge$". This interprets the relationship among the concepts, objects, and attributes. The nodes in this diagram express the concepts. However, this diagram is a type of directed acyclic graph. In IF sets, FCA is used for decision making, data analysis, knowledge discovery, and especially for forecasting purposes.

Definition 4. *Let $C_1, C_2 \in IF(U)$ be the two IF sets, given as*

$$C_1 = \{(x, \mu_{C_1}(x), \gamma_{C_1}(x)) \mid x \in U\},$$
$$C_2 = \{(x, \mu_{C_2}(x), \gamma_{C_2}(x)) \mid x \in U\}.$$

where $\mu_{C_1}(x), \gamma_{C_1}(x) : U \to [0,1]$ and $\mu_{C_2}(x), \gamma_{C_2}(x) : U \to [0,1]$ such that

$$0 \leq \mu_{C_1}(x) + \gamma_{C_1}(x) \leq 1,$$

$$0 \leq \mu_{C_2}(x) + \gamma_{C_2}(x) \leq 1.$$

Here, $\mu_{C_1}(x), \gamma_{C_1}(x) \in [0,1]$ *indicate the degree of membership and nonmembership of* $x \in C_1$*, and* $\mu_{C_2}(x), \gamma_{C_2}(x) \in [0,1]$ *indicate the degree of membership and nonmembership of* $x \in C_2$ *IF sets, such that* $\forall x \in U$*.*

Definition 5. *Let* $C_1, C_2 \in IF(U)$ *be the two IF sets given in Definition 4, then these two sets through FCA algorithm are evaluated as*

$$C_{1,2} = \{(x, min(\ \mu_{C_1}(x), \mu_{C_2}(x)\ ), max(\ \gamma_{C_1}(x), \gamma_{C_2}(x)\ )) \mid x \in U\}.$$

These are the basic mathematical definitions which define the FCA and its operations with respect to IF sets. Moreover, later sections explain it more in detail by means of the GrC approach.

4. Granular Computing (GrC)

GrC is an emerging field for information processing [27,28] through the basic building blocks of information, named granules. In the data science literature, the granule is defined as the cluster or set of objects extracted or grouped together by similarity, uniformity, proximity, predictability, resemblance, physical adjacency, or functionality. These granules can be represented in interval values, rough sets, neutrosophic sets [29], fuzzy sets [30], IF sets, etc. Moreover, these granules can be partitioned into finer or smaller granules called subgranules. In order to compose and decompose the granules, specific measures called granulation measures are employed.

In this study, the GrC approach is used with FCA by considering the IF datasets containing various events as objects having spatio-temporal attributes. Moreover, different GrC measures are used, including IG, COV, SP, and Q value for the IF datasets. Here, for the first decomposition, IF datasets are decomposed in different granules, while each granule consists of the set of events as objects having spatio-temporal attributes. In the first decomposition, the IG of each granule is determined, and the granule (having more IG) is selected for further granulation measures i.e., COV and SP. For the second decomposition, the granule determined in the first decomposition (for the further granulation measures) is further decomposed into subgranules, the IG of each subgranule is found, the subgranule (with higher IG) for further granulation measures is determined, and so on. This process is performed until the granules/subgranules are obtained, with interesting granulation measures having more COV, less SP, and higher Q value.

5. Proposed Methodology

5.1. Periodic Occurrences (Co-Occurrences), Nonoccurrences, and Uncertainty of Occurrences/Nonoccurrences of Events in the Form of IF Datasets

In real life, an event can be represented by spatio-temporal occurrences and co-occurrences. Based on the specific time unit, different timelines can be assumed for the temporal information related to the occurrences and co-occurrences of events [31]. For example, the time unit is a day or a month, considering the timeline based on the day or the month, respectively. A timeslot is the sequence of time units (days or months); if the timeline is considered based on the days, then each day corresponds to a timeslot. Hence, different timelines can provide temporal granularity.

In the literature, spatial and temporal events data are evaluated through FCA and the GrC paradigm using classical single-attribute value in FCA data [31]. This proposed methodology uses the IF datasets, in which events occur at a certain place (spatial aspect) and time (temporal aspect) with certain membership and nonmembership values.

Definition 6. *Let* G_i *be the set of objects having* M_j *set of attributes, where* $i = 1,2,3,\cdots$ *and* $j = 1,2,3,\cdots$ *denote the number of objects and attributes, respectively, such that each* M_j

attribute has IF set values $\mu_{i,j}$ and $\gamma_{i,j}$ as membership and nonmembership of the G_i object in the M_j attribute, respectively.

$$M_j = \{(x, \mu_{i,j}(x), \gamma_{i,j}(x)) \mid \forall x \in M_j\}$$

Definition 7. *Formally, consider an IF formal context $K_{i,j} = (G_i, M_j, I)$ such that G_i, M_j, and I indicate the objects, attributes (given in Definition 6), and relation between the objects and the attributes, respectively, as shown in Table 1, where*

$$G_i = \{\mathtt{G}_1, \mathtt{G}_2, \mathtt{G}_3, \cdots\},$$
$$M_j = \{\mathtt{M}_1, \mathtt{M}_2, \mathtt{M}_3, \cdots\}.$$

Definition 8. *Let a subset $G_i \subseteq G$ of the objects, then the subset of the attributes to all the objects in G_i is given as*

$$G_i \uparrow = \{m \in M \mid \forall g \in G_i, gIm\}$$

Likewise, given a subset $M_j \subseteq M$ of attributes, the subset of objects having all the attributes in set M_j is given as

$$M_j \downarrow = \{g \in G \mid \forall m \in M_j, gIm\}$$

Definition 9. *According to FCA, for an IF formal concept of a formal context $K_{i,j} = (G_i, M_j, I)$, let there be a pair (G_i, M_j), where $G_i \subseteq G, M_j \subseteq M$ and $G_i \uparrow = M_j, M_j \downarrow = G_i$, where G_i denotes the objects (extents) and M_j indicates the attributes (intents) of the pair (G_i, M_j).*

Definition 10. *Let the IF concept lattice $L_{i,j} = (G_i, M_j, I)$, constructed with all the concepts of IF formal concepts of $K_{i,j} = (G_i, M_j, I)$, such that $(\mathtt{G}_1, \mathtt{M}_1)$ and $(\mathtt{G}_2, \mathtt{M}_2)$ are the two IF formal concepts of the IF formal context $K_{i,j} = (G_i, M_j, I)$, where $(\mathtt{G}_1, \mathtt{M}_1)$ is called a superconcept of $(\mathtt{G}_2, \mathtt{M}_2)$, and $(\mathtt{G}_2, \mathtt{M}_2)$ is called a subconcept of $(\mathtt{G}_1, \mathtt{M}_1)$ if it satisfies the equivalent condition given as*

$$(\mathtt{G}_1, \mathtt{M}_1) \leq (\mathtt{G}_2, \mathtt{M}_2) \Leftrightarrow \mathtt{G}_1 \subseteq \mathtt{G}_2 \Leftrightarrow \mathtt{M}_2 \subseteq \mathtt{M}_1$$

Definition 11. *The set of all the IF superconcept and the subconcept interrelations construct a lattice. The lattice is an abstract structure with join (denoted by "$\vee$") and meet (denoted by "$\wedge$") operations. Hence, the above expression of the IF superconcept and subconcept in this definition, in the form of join and meet, is*

$$(\mathtt{G}_1, \mathtt{M}_1) \vee (\mathtt{G}_2, \mathtt{M}_2) = ((\mathtt{G}_1 \cup \mathtt{G}_2) \downarrow\uparrow, \mathtt{M}_1 \cap \mathtt{M}_2),$$

$$(\mathtt{G}_1, \mathtt{M}_1) \wedge (\mathtt{G}_2, \mathtt{M}_2) = (\mathtt{G}_1 \cap \mathtt{G}_2, (\mathtt{M}_1 \cup \mathtt{M}_2) \downarrow\uparrow)$$

In this mathematical form, "$\vee$" and "$\wedge$" indicate the supermum and infimum operations of IF formal concepts, respectively.

Definition 12. *The IF formal concept of the given set of G_i objects with M_j attributes having the IF values $(\mu_{i,j}, \gamma_{i,j}) \rightarrow [0,1]$ in $K_{i,j} = (G_i, M_j, I)$ formal context is evaluated as*

$$(min(\mu_{i,j}), max(\gamma_{i,j}))$$

where $i \in G, j \in M$.

Example 1. *Let the IF formal concept for $\mathtt{G}_1$ and $\mathtt{G}_2$ objects having M_j $(j = 1,2,3,\cdots)$ attributes (given in Table 1) be computed as*

$$\mathtt{G}_{12} = [(min(\mu_{1,1}, \mu_{2,1}), max(\gamma_{1,1}, \gamma_{2,1})), (min(\mu_{1,2}, \mu_{2,2}), max(\gamma_{1,2}, \gamma_{2,2})), (min(\mu_{1,3}, \mu_{2,3}), max(\gamma_{1,3}, \gamma_{2,3})), \cdots, (min(\mu_{1,j}, \mu_{2,j}), max(\gamma_{1,j}, \gamma_{2,j}))]$$

In this prposed methodology, the objects G_i indicate the events, and the attributes M_j indicate the occurrence of those events at a certain place and time, with certain membership μ (occurrence/co-occurrence), nonmembership γ (nonoccurrence), and uncertainty π (uncertainty of occurrence/nonoccurrence) values provided in the IF datasets. For example, in Table 1, let $\mathtt{G}_1$ be one of the events, $\mathtt{M}_1$ and $\mathtt{M}_2$ be two places, and $\mathtt{M}_3, \cdots, M_j$ be the number of times an event has occurred with some μ membership of occurrence and γ nonmembership of nonoccurrence values; then, it can be said that the event $\mathtt{G}_1$ has occurred at $\mathtt{M}_1$ and $\mathtt{M}_2$ places at $\mathtt{M}_3, \cdots, M_j$ different times with μ happening and γ not happening values of events.

Table 1. Objects having attributes in the form of IF sets.

	$\mathbf{M_1}$	$\mathbf{M_2}$	$\mathbf{M_3}$	$\cdots$	M_j
$\mathtt{G}_1$	$\mu_{1,1}, \gamma_{1,1}$	$\mu_{1,2}, \gamma_{1,2}$	$\mu_{1,3}, \gamma_{1,3}$	$\cdots$	$\mu_{1,j}, \gamma_{1,j}$
$\mathtt{G}_2$	$\mu_{2,1}, \gamma_{2,1}$	$\mu_{2,2}, \gamma_{2,2}$	$\mu_{2,3}, \gamma_{2,3}$	$\cdots$	$\mu_{2,j}, \gamma_{2,j}$
$\mathtt{G}_3$	$\mu_{3,1}, \gamma_{3,1}$	$\mu_{3,2}, \gamma_{3,2}$	$\mu_{3,3}, \gamma_{3,3}$	$\cdots$	$\mu_{3,j}, \gamma_{3,j}$
$\vdots$	$\vdots$	$\vdots$	$\vdots$	$\vdots$	$\vdots$
G_i	$\mu_{i,1}, \gamma_{i,1}$	$\mu_{i,2}, \gamma_{i,2}$	$\mu_{i,3}, \gamma_{i,3}$	$\cdots$	$\mu_{i,j}, \gamma_{i,j}$

Example 2. *Let* $\mathtt{M}_3$ *be the one-year temporal attribute showing the events occurring in the* $\mathtt{M}_3$ *year. For the temporal granulation of the* $\mathtt{M}_3$ *year attribute, let* Q_1, Q_2, Q_3, *and* Q_4 *be the four quarters, indicating data for January, February, and March; April, May, and June; July, August, and September; and October, November, and December, given that each month's data are a basic granule. Hence, for the first decomposition, there will be four granules containing data for events occurring in the four quarters of the year. For example,* E_1 *event's data in the* Q_1 *quarter of the* $\mathtt{M}_3$ *year in the form of IF sets is given as* $(0.3, 0.6)$, *where* $\mu = 0.3$, *(membership) indicates the* E_1 *event's occurrence (co-occurrence) and* $\gamma = 0.6$ *(nonmembership) indicates the* E_1 *event's nonoccurrence. Moreover,* $\pi = 0.1$ *(IF set index or indeterminacy) indicates the* E_1 *event's uncertainty of occurrence/nonoccurrence, which is used to compute the IG later in this section.*

Existing approaches only work on the periodical occurrences and co-occurrences of events using the GrC paradigm and FCA by considering single-value attributes for formal concepts. However, in the proposed approach, three aspects of the phenomenon of events are considered: event occurrence (co-occurrence), nonoccurrence, and the uncertainty of occurrence/nonoccurrence using GrC and the FCA algorithm by considering the IF datasets. Furthermore, the events data are represented in the form of three-tuple IF datasets as μ (membership), γ (nonmembership), and π (IF set index or indeterminacy), indicating the event occurrence (co-occurrence), nonoccurrence, and the uncertainty of occurrence/nonoccurrence, respectively. This timed granulation of occurring event data is further explained and analyzed for the knowledge discovery in Section 6.

Here, the IF datasets (containing the objects and attributes relationship) are divided into multiple parts, and each part is considered as the IF granule. Moreover, the lattice of each IF granule is designed for the data analysis using FCA and IF granulation measures.

5.2. Computation of an IF Granule

In [32], fuzzy information granules and the hierarchical structures of IF rough sets from the viewpoint of GrC are presented. In addition to this, FCA is also widely used in IF sets, such as the research study in [33], which mainly focuses on the FCA in an IF formal context. Moreover, in [33], the primitive notions in concept lattice theory are also extended to the IF environment. In this research, the idea of IF granule evaluation is performed by calculating IG, COV, SP, and the Q value of the IF concept lattice, where each concept lattice is treated as an individual granule.

5.3. Information Granulation (IG)

IG $(IG) : IG = |1 - IE|$ provides the information on the granule within the lattice by taking into account the extensional parts (objects) included in the granule [31]. Information entropy (IE) is an important measure to evaluate the uncertainty in data [34,35], which is why the term $|1 - IE|$ gives the total IG obtained from the data granule or the concept lattice. According to Shannon's theory, IE is the key information measure in data analysis. Based on the IF sets, different types of IE measures may be needed, depending upon the evaluation. In [36], the authors introduce IE into the field of FCA to quantify the weight of the concepts' intent. A type of nonprobabilistic entropy measure for IF is proposed in [37]. Here, in [37], the entropy measure is the result of the IF sets' geometric interpretation, and it uses the ratio of distances between them, defined in terms of the ratio of the IF sets' cardinalities of $F \cap F^c$ and $F \cup F^c$, where F^c is the complement of the F IF set. Two methods to determine the attribute weights are proposed in [38]. The first is when the information regarding the attributes is completely unknown, and the second is when partial information about attribute weights is known. Moreover, in [38], the attribute weights' identification based on the IF entropy is offered in the context of IF sets. In the literature, every type of uncertainty measure, such as information Shannon entropy, information granularity, rough entropy, and IE, is called by a common name: information granularity. The distance-based information granularity for IF and multigranulation IF granular spaces is presented in [39]; moreover, the author used this distance-based information granularity to construct a novel hierarchical structure on such spaces. In [40], the authors compute the information granularity by taking into account the number of objects (extensional parts) included in the granule; hence, in this study, IG and IE provide the framework to evaluate the set of granulation. Let $K = (G, M, I)$ be the IF formal context of IF granule and $L = (G, M, I)$ be its corresponding lattice. The first granulation measure for the designed lattice of IF formal context is given as

$$IG(L) = \frac{1}{G}\sum\left[\frac{1}{n}\sum_{j=1}^{n} 1 - \left(\gamma_j + \frac{\pi_j}{2}\right)\right], \tag{1}$$

where "G" is the number of objects involved in the IF granule, "n" is the number of attributes of each object, $j = 1, 2, 3, \cdots$ shows the number of attributes, and "γ_j" and "π_j" are the nonmembership and hesitancy degree of the "jth" attribute. For the different IF formal contexts from the IF datasets, $K_x = (G_x, M, I_x)$ and $L_x = (G_x, M, I_x)$, where K_x indicates the formal contexts, L_x indicates their corresponding lattices, and $x = 1, 2, 3, \cdots$ denotes the number of formal contexts and their lattices. If the IG of lattice $L_1 = (\mathtt{G}_1, \mathtt{M}, \mathtt{I}_1)$ is greater than that of $L_2 = (\mathtt{G}_2, \mathtt{M}, \mathtt{I}_2)$, then the K_1 formal context contains more IG and is more interesting with respect to providing spatio-temporal information in the IF GrC perspective.

Let E_1, E_2, E_3, and E_4 be the four events as objects; $Place_1, Place_2, Place_3$, and $Place_4$ be the four spatial attributes; and Q_1 and Q_2 be the two parts of one-year data, such that Q_1 consists of Jan, Feb, Mar, Apr, May, and June and Q_2 consists of July, Aug, Sep, Oct, Nov, and Dec temporal attributes data in the form of IF sets, as given in the Table 2. Furthermore, let the events E_1, E_2, E_3, and E_4 occur at the given spatiality, with Q_1 temporality in the K_1 formal context and with Q_2 temporality in the K_2 formal context.

Table 2. Four Events as Objects with Four Spatial and Two Temporal Attributes Data.

	$Place_1$	$Place_2$	$Place_3$	$Place_4$	Q_1	Q_2
E_1	(0.9, 0.1)	(0.6, 0.2)	(0.3, 0.7)	(0.8, 0.1)	(0.3, 0.6)	(0.9, 0.0)
E_2	(0.3, 0.5)	(0.5, 0.5)	(0.8, 0.2)	(0.2, 0.5)	(0.7, 0.2)	(0.8, 0.1)
E_3	(0.8, 0.2)	(0.6, 0.2)	(0.7, 0.1)	(0.2, 0.7)	(0.4, 0.6)	(0.1, 0.8)
E_4	(0.2, 0.6)	(0.3, 0.6)	(0.6, 0.3)	(0.1, 0.6)	(0.2, 0.8)	(0.7, 0.2)

Hence, the IG of K_1 and K_2 formal contexts is given as

$IG(K_1) =$

$$\frac{1}{4}\sum\Big\{\tfrac{1}{5}\Big(1-\Big(0.1+\tfrac{0}{2}\Big)\Big)+\Big(1-\Big(0.2+\tfrac{0.2}{2}\Big)\Big)+\Big(1-\Big(0.7+\tfrac{0}{2}\Big)\Big)+\Big(1-\Big(0.1+\tfrac{0.1}{2}\Big)\Big)+\Big(1-\Big(0.6+\tfrac{0.1}{2}\Big)\Big)\Big\}+$$
$$\Big\{\tfrac{1}{5}\Big(1-\Big(0.5+\tfrac{0.2}{2}\Big)\Big)+\Big(1-\Big(0.5+\tfrac{0}{2}\Big)\Big)+\Big(1-\Big(0.2+\tfrac{0}{2}\Big)\Big)+\Big(1-\Big(0.5+\tfrac{0.3}{2}\Big)\Big)+\Big(1-\Big(0.2+\tfrac{0.1}{2}\Big)\Big)\Big\}+$$
$$\Big\{\tfrac{1}{5}\Big(1-\Big(0.2+\tfrac{0}{2}\Big)\Big)+\Big(1-\Big(0.2+\tfrac{0.2}{2}\Big)\Big)+\Big(1-\Big(0.1+\tfrac{0.2}{2}\Big)\Big)+\Big(1-\Big(0.7+\tfrac{0.1}{2}\Big)\Big)+\Big(1-\Big(0.6+\tfrac{0}{2}\Big)\Big)\Big\}+$$
$$\Big\{\tfrac{1}{5}\Big(1-\Big(0.6+\tfrac{0.2}{2}\Big)\Big)+\Big(1-\Big(0.6+\tfrac{0.1}{2}\Big)\Big)+\Big(1-\Big(0.3+\tfrac{0.1}{2}\Big)\Big)+\Big(1-\Big(0.6+\tfrac{0.3}{2}\Big)\Big)+\Big(1-\Big(0.8+\tfrac{0}{2}\Big)\Big)\Big\},$$

$IG(K_1) = 0.53$
$IG(K_2) =$

$$\frac{1}{4}\sum\Big\{\tfrac{1}{5}\Big(1-\Big(0.1+\tfrac{0}{2}\Big)\Big)+\Big(1-\Big(0.2+\tfrac{0.2}{2}\Big)\Big)+\Big(1-\Big(0.7+\tfrac{0}{2}\Big)\Big)+\Big(1-\Big(0.1+\tfrac{0.1}{2}\Big)\Big)+\Big(1-\Big(0+\tfrac{0.1}{2}\Big)\Big)\Big\}+$$
$$\Big\{\tfrac{1}{5}\Big(1-\Big(0.5+\tfrac{0.2}{2}\Big)\Big)+\Big(1-\Big(0.5+\tfrac{0}{2}\Big)\Big)+\Big(1-\Big(0.2+\tfrac{0}{2}\Big)\Big)+\Big(1-\Big(0.5+\tfrac{0.3}{2}\Big)\Big)+\Big(1-\Big(0.1+\tfrac{0.1}{2}\Big)\Big)\Big\}+$$
$$\Big\{\tfrac{1}{5}\Big(1-\Big(0.2+\tfrac{0}{2}\Big)\Big)+\Big(1-\Big(0.2+\tfrac{0.2}{2}\Big)\Big)+\Big(1-\Big(0.1+\tfrac{0.2}{2}\Big)\Big)+\Big(1-\Big(0.7+\tfrac{0.1}{2}\Big)\Big)+\Big(1-\Big(0.8+\tfrac{0.1}{2}\Big)\Big)\Big\}+$$
$$\Big\{\tfrac{1}{5}\Big(1-\Big(0.6+\tfrac{0.2}{2}\Big)\Big)+\Big(1-\Big(0.6+\tfrac{0.1}{2}\Big)\Big)+\Big(1-\Big(0.3+\tfrac{0.1}{2}\Big)\Big)+\Big(1-\Big(0.6+\tfrac{0.3}{2}\Big)\Big)+\Big(1-\Big(0.2+\tfrac{0.1}{2}\Big)\Big)\Big\},$$

$IG(K_2) = 0.58$

Hence, the IG of the K_2 IF formal context is greater than the IG of the K_1 IF formal context, implying that the events with given spatial and Q_2 temporal attributes are more interesting with respect to providing more spatio-temporal information in the periodical IF GrC perspective. Moreover, for the further process, the K_2 IF formal context will be decided for the computation of granulation measures, which is discussed in Section 6.

5.4. Granular Computing Measures for the Interestingness Level of IF Lattice

In the literature, there are various proposed granular measures based on FCA which identify the interestingness level of the granule. The GrC and FCA measures defined in [41] and [42], respectively, include COV, SP, stability, robustness, probability, separation, etc. The most important granular measures are COV and SP, which are used in the GrC approach based on FCA. In this study, COV, SP, and Q value are used to analyze the interestingness level of the IF lattice.

5.5. Coverage (COV)

COV is the most important granulation measure to evaluate the granule within the spatial, temporal, or spatio-temporal granulation perspective [31]. COV indicates the data granule to represent or cover the given data. The main objective of calculating the COV in this study is to find the IF lattice granule data objects' COV which contains the interesting information. Generally, the larger the data objects being covered the higher the COV of the interesting information granule. In [43], the concept of COV with invariability and its interconnections are analyzed from the viewpoint of algebraic properties of a fuzzy system, including membership function, inclusion, union and intersection, and support and fuzzy relation. Depending on the nature of granule, the definition of COV can be properly expressed, as in [44], where the concept of COV is defined with the fuzzy perspective of GrC. Here, the COV for the IF concept lattice objects using membership values in the perspective of GrC approach is computed as

$$COV(C) = \left[\left(\frac{D}{G} \times \frac{1}{N}\sum_{i=1}^{N} C\left(x_{\mu_j}\right)\right) + \frac{\pi_j}{2}\right], \tag{2}$$

where "N" is the number of elements in the IF concept lattice C granule, μ_j, where $j = 1, 2, 3, \cdots$, is the number of membership values, and π_j is the hesitation degree of each attribute involved in the granule. Here, D shows the involved objects, and G indicates the total number of objects in the granule. In the above Equation (2), $(\frac{\pi_j}{2})$ is used because the uncertainty can be membership or nonmembership of the IF set value.

The motivation behind the use of Equation (2) is the computation of COV for the formal concept granule containing the event's spatio-temporal information in the form of IF sets. The COV for the IF formal concept as a granule C for the involved objects (events) $\frac{D}{G}$ [31] is the sum of membership grades [44] $\frac{1}{N}\sum_{i=1}^{N} C\left(x_{\mu_j}\right)$ in the IF formal concept. Additionally, the term $\frac{\pi_j}{2}$ indicates the membership value in the π degree of indeterminacy. The illustration to compute the COV is given in Example 3.

Example 3. *Let* $X = \{x_1, x_2, x_3, x_4, x_5\}$ *and* $\widetilde{C}(x)$ *be the IF formal concept of IF formal context, consisting of* E_1 *event as an involved object with* Q_1 *temporal data given in Table 2, such that*

$$\widetilde{C}(x) = \{(0.9, 0.1, x_1), (0.6, 0.2, x_2), (0.3, 0.7, x_3), (0.8, 0.1, x_4), (0.3, 0.6, x_5)\}.$$

Let $D = 1$ *and* $G = 4$*, because the object involved in the* $\widetilde{C}$ *IF formal concept is one, i.e.,* E_1*, and the total number of objects is four, i.e.,* E_1, E_2, E_3*, and* E_4*, respectively. Moreover,* $N = 5$ *is the number of IF attributes in the data, and* π_j *is the total degree of indeterminacy in all the attributes of the* $\widetilde{C}$ *IF formal concept.*

$$COV(C) = \left[\left(\frac{1}{4} \times \frac{1}{5}\sum_{i=1}^{5} 0.9 + 0.6 + 0.3 + 0.8 + 0.3\right) + \frac{0.4}{2}\right] = 0.34.$$

5.6. Specificity (SP)

The SP measure is the fundamental granulation measure used to find the abstract, precise, or specific level of the granule in GrC. SP's role in IF sets is similar to the role of entropy in probability theory, as entropy estimates the probability of the specific event under consideration, which encapsulates the information about the fundamental probability distribution. The author of [45] states that in expert- and knowledge-based systems, SP plays a fundamental role in determining the usefulness of the information provided by these systems. Moreover, an increase in the abstract level of the SP of the information provided increases the information's usefulness. For example, a system shows the prediction of tornado storm occurrences in different states at different times. Additionally, this system, in most cases, will correctly predict the situation of the tornado's occurrence in both spatial and temporal perspectives. This system will not be of much use if it does not determine which type of precautionary measures should be taken at particular states at a particular time. This scenario points out a very important uncertainty principle of information theory, which is called the specificity–correctness trade-off.

An important idea to note is that the higher the SP, the lower the granule level of abstraction. In this study, the concept of SP is used for the spatio-temporality (two perspectives) of the IF concept lattice granule measure by using the $len(d)$ and $range$ concepts. As explained in [31], $len(d)$ and $range$ indicate the length of the involved temporal slot and the sum of the lengths of all temporal slots, respectively. According to refs. [31,45], SP is measured as follows:

$$SP(C) = \left[1 - \frac{len(d)}{range}\right] \times \left[\alpha - \frac{1}{n-1}\sum_{x \in X \neq X^*} G(x)\right]. \quad (3)$$

Here, the IF set's concept lattice is considered. Let $X = \{x_1, x_2, x_3, \cdots, x_n\}$ be the set of attributes in set X and C be the IF set with $(C^+(x), C^-(x))$ membership and nonmembership of the IF ordered pair. In Equation (3) $\alpha = Max_x[C^+(x)]$, assuming that it occurs at x_m such that $\alpha = C^+(x_n), \forall x_n \neq x_m$, calculate $G(x) = \alpha \wedge (1 - C^-(x))$ to compute the SP of IF set C [45]. The illustration of calculating SP is given in Example 4.

Example 4. *Let* $X = \{x_1, x_2, x_3, x_4, x_5\}$ *and* $\widetilde{C}(x)$ *be the IF formal concept, such that*

$$\widetilde{C}(x) = \{(0.9, 0.1, x_1), (0.6, 0.2, x_2), (0.3, 0.7, x_3), (0.8, 0.1, x_4), (0.3, 0.6, x_5)\}.$$

Here, the value of $\alpha = 0.9$ *occurs in* x_1*, then* $G(x) = \alpha \wedge (1 - C^{-}(x))$ *is computed for the* $x \neq x_1$ *as*

$$\begin{aligned} G(x_2) &= 0.9 \wedge (1 - 0.2) = 0.8, \\ G(x_3) &= 0.9 \wedge (1 - 0.7) = 0.3, \\ G(x_4) &= 0.9 \wedge (1 - 0.1) = 0.9, \\ G(x_5) &= 0.9 \wedge (1 - 0.6) = 0.4. \end{aligned}$$

For example, $\widetilde{C}(x)$ is one of the IF formal concepts of the IF formal context, with Q_1 temporal data given in Table 2; then, $len(d) = 6$ and $range = 12$.

$$SP(\widetilde{C}(x)) = \left[1 - \frac{6}{12}\right] \times \left[0.9 - \frac{1}{5-1}\sum(0.8 + 0.3 + 0.9 + 0.4)\right] = 0.15.$$

The SP of individual IF concept lattice granules is calculated in Section 6.

5.7. Unique Index (Q) Value

In ref. [31], the authors define the aggregation of COV and SP as the Q value. In the Q value, the COV(C) determines the objects representing the IF concept lattice granule COV; on the other hand, SP(C) indicates the SP for the IF concept lattice granule in the perspectives of spatial and temporal attributes using the GrC approach. The mathematical measure to compute the Q value is given as

$$Q(C) = COV(C) \times (SP(C))^{\zeta} \tag{4}$$

Here, the exponent on SP, "ζ", is the aspect of the SP. It shows the change in the partition level of the data. Moreover, the higher the value of "ζ", the more important the aspect of the SP. The idea of "ζ" is more understandable later in the experimental analysis. In ref. [31], the authors also propose the average Q value of data granules; here, the IF concept lattice granule average Q value can be computed as follows:

$$\overline{Q}(L) = \sum_{(A,B) \in L} \frac{Q(C)}{n} \tag{5}$$

In this expression, the IF concept lattice granule C shows the object or the set of objects A, which contains the attributes in the form of membership and nonmembership B of the IF set.

To assess different hierarchical levels of data, granulation measures can be compared by checking which granulation level provides more interesting results. To assess the hierarchical levels, a particular attribute is decomposed to check whether the data granulation provides improved results over the previous ones. Here, the focus was spatial and temporal attributes. Suppose that temporal attributes are decomposed, such that T denotes the temporal attribute, and after decomposing T in n attributes $\{T_1, T_2, T_3, \cdots, T_n\}$, it can be determined through the granulation measures which temporal decomposition provides more interesting results. Additionally, the formal context related to the T temporal attribute is shown as $K = (G, M, I)$, while that related to the decomposed temporal attributes, i.e., $T_1, T_2, T_3, \cdots, T_n$, is given by $K' = (G', M', I')$. Moreover, the granulation measures are expressed for different hierarchical levels accordingly. With this, the COV for different granularity levels can be shown as

$$COV(C) \geq COV(C') \tag{6}$$

In addition to this, the SP for the different granular levels can also hold the following statement:

$$SP(C) \leq SP(C') \quad (7)$$

To check the granularity level of interestingness for a particular timeslot, [31] can be computed as

$$\overline{Q}(T) = \sum \frac{Q(C)}{n_T} \quad (8)$$

where n_T is the cardinality of the set of IF formal concepts having T temporal attributes. It is obvious that the granulation through the decomposition of temporal attribute may lead to better results, such as

$$Q(C) \geq Q(C') \quad (9)$$

In this way, the level of interestingness is assessed in different hierarchical granule levels by checking that the greater $Q(C)$ value is the more suitable granule in terms of interestingness.

6. Experimental Evaluation

In this section, experimental analysis for the proposed IF concept lattice granule through GrC methodology is discussed. The objective of this study is to analyze the spatio-temporal perspectives of the IF granule. The results may be used to predict the spatiality and periodicity of the information granule, particularly when the data are provided in the IF sets. The datasets used in this experiment consist of the four activity records of providing information related to spatiality and temporality of the activities executed by a specific actor or user. Here, the activities are indicated as four events, E_1, E_2, E_3, and E_4; four places, $Place_1, Place_2, Place_3$, and $Place_4$, denoting spatiality; and four quarters, Q_1, Q_2, Q_3, and Q_4, of the year, denoting temporality, where events indicate objects, and places and quarters of the year indicate the attributes. The main focus of this experiment is the periodical granulation of the IF concept lattice granules. There may be hundreds of events indicating object occurrences at different spatio-temporal attributes, but here, four events as objects and four spatial and four temporal attributes for the experimental analysis are considered, as presented in Table 3. In the temporal perspective of attributes, annual periodicity of time granulation is decomposed into four quarters, Q_1, Q_2, Q_3, and Q_4, where these timed granulation quarters consists of Jan, Feb, and Mar; Apr, May, and June; July, Aug, and Sep; and Oct, Nov, and Dec, respectively. Additionally, the GrC approach is performed by considering the periodicity of the temporal attribute, in which the first decomposition of periodicity is set to months.

Table 3. Four Events as Objects with Four Spatial and Four Temporal Attributes Data.

	$Place_1$	$Place_2$	$Place_3$	$Place_4$	Q_1	Q_2	Q_3	Q_4
E_1	(0.9, 0.1)	(0.6, 0.2)	(0.3, 0.7)	(0.8, 0.1)	(0.3, 0.6)	(0.9, 0.0)	(0.7, 0.2)	(0.4, 0.3)
E_2	(0.3, 0.5)	(0.5, 0.5)	(0.8, 0.2)	(0.2, 0.5)	(0.7, 0.2)	(0.8, 0.1)	(0.8, 0.2)	(0.5, 0.4)
E_3	(0.8, 0.2)	(0.6, 0.2)	(0.7, 0.1)	(0.2, 0.7)	(0.4, 0.6)	(0.1, 0.8)	(0.7, 0.3)	(0.2, 0.7)
E_4	(0.2, 0.6)	(0.3, 0.6)	(0.6, 0.3)	(0.1, 0.6)	(0.2, 0.8)	(0.7, 0.2)	(0.8, 0.1)	(0.1, 0.6)

The IF concepts of the given four objects with spatial attributes in the Q_1 quarter of time granule are $(1, \widetilde{C}_1^1)), (2, \widetilde{C}_2^1), (3, \widetilde{C}_3^1), (12, \widetilde{C}_4^1), (13, \widetilde{C}_5^1), (23, \widetilde{C}_6^1), (24, \widetilde{C}_7^1), (123, \widetilde{C}_8^1), (124, \widetilde{C}_9^1)$, $(234, \widetilde{C}_{10}^1), (U, \widetilde{C}_{11}^1) and (\emptyset, \widetilde{C}_{\emptyset}^1)$ where:

$$\widetilde{C}_1^1 = \{(0.9,0.1), (0.6,0.2), (0.3,0.7), (0.8,0.1), (0.3,0.6)\}, \widetilde{C}_2^1 = \{(0.3,0.5), (0.5,0.5), (0.8,0.2), (0.2,0.5), (0.7,0.2)\}$$
$$\widetilde{C}_3^1 = \{(0.8,0.2), (0.6,0.2), (0.7,0.1), (0.2,0.7), (0.4,0.6)\}, \widetilde{C}_4^1 = \{(0.3,0.5), (0.5,0.5), (0.3,0.7), (0.2,0.5), (0.3,0.6)\}$$
$$\widetilde{C}_5^1 = \{(0.8,0.2), (0.6,0.2), (0.3,0.7), (0.2,0.7), (0.3,o.6)\}, \widetilde{C}_6^1 = \{(0.3,0.5), (0.5,0.5), (0.7,0.2), (0.2,0.7), (0.4,0.6)\}$$
$$\widetilde{C}_7^1 = \{(0.2,0.6), (0.3,0.6), (0.6,0.3), (0.1,0.6), (0.2,0.8)\}, \widetilde{C}_8^1 = \{(0.3,0.5), (0.5,0.5), (0.3,0.7), (0.2,0.7), (0.3,0.6)\}$$
$$\widetilde{C}_9^1 = \{(0.2,0.6), (0.3,0.6), (0.3,0.7), (0.1,0.6), (0.2,0.8)\}, \widetilde{C}_{10}^1 = \{(0.2,0.6), (0.3,0.6), (0.6,0.3), (0.1,0.7), (0.2,0.8)\}$$

$\widetilde{C}^1_{11} = \{(0.2, 0.6), (0.3, 0.6), (0.3, 0.7), (0.1, 0.7), (0.2, 0.8)\}, \widetilde{C}^1_{\emptyset} = \{(1, 0), (1, 0), (1, 0), (1, 0), (1, 0)\}$

The IF values of the IF formal concepts are evaluated according to the expression $(min(\mu_{i,j}), max(\gamma_{i,j}))$, given in Definition 12. The IF concept's lattice design of the given four objects with spatio-temporal attributes with the Q_1 quarter of time granule is given in Figure 1.

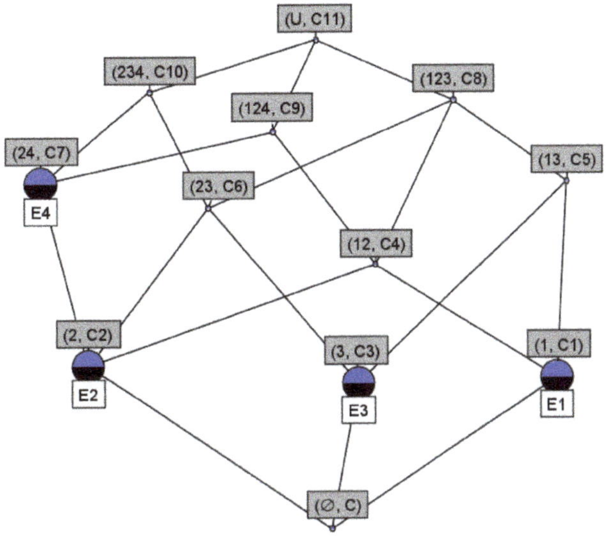

Figure 1. IF concept's lattice diagram of four objects with spatial and Q_1 quarter of time granule attributes.

Similarly, the IF concepts of the given four objects with spatial attributes in the Q_2 quarter of time granule are$(1, \widetilde{C}^2_1), (2, \widetilde{C}^2_2), (3, \widetilde{C}^2_3), (12, \widetilde{C}^2_4), (13, \widetilde{C}^2_5), (23, \widetilde{C}^2_6), (24, \widetilde{C}^2_7), (123, \widetilde{C}^2_8),$ $(124, \widetilde{C}^2_9), (234, \widetilde{C}^2_{10}), (1234, \widetilde{C}^2_{11}), (\emptyset, \widetilde{C}^2_{\emptyset})$ where:

$\widetilde{C}^2_1 = \{(0.9, 0.1), (0.6, 0.2), (0.3, 0.7), (0.8, 0.1), (0.9, 0.0)\}, \widetilde{C}^2_2 = \{(0.3, 0.5), (0.5, 0.5), (0.8, 0.2), (0.2, 0.5), (0.8, 0.1)\}$
$\widetilde{C}^2_3 = \{(0.8, 0.2), (0.6, 0.2), (0.7, 0.1), (0.2, 0.7), (0.1, 0.8)\}, \widetilde{C}^2_4 = \{(0.2, 0.6), (0.3, 0.6), (0.6, 0.3), (0.1, 0.6), (0.7, 0.2)\}$
$\widetilde{C}^2_5 = \{(0.8, 0.2), (0.6, 0.2), (0.3, 0.7), (0.2, 0.7), (0.1, 0.8)\}, \widetilde{C}^2_6 = \{(0.3, 0.5), (0.5, 0.5), (0.7, 0.2), (0.2, 0.7), (0.1, 0.8)\}$
$\widetilde{C}^2_7 = \{(0.2, 0.6), (0.3, 0.6), (0.6, 0.3), (0.1, 0.6), (0.7, 0.2)\}, \widetilde{C}^2_8 = \{(0.3, 0.5), (0.5, 0.5), (0.3, 0.7), (0.2, 0.7), (0.1, 0.8)\}$
$\widetilde{C}^2_9 = \{(0.2, 0.6), (0.3, 0.6), (0.3, 0.7), (0.1, 0.6), (0.7, 0.2)\}, \widetilde{C}^2_{10} = \{(0.2, 0.6), (0.3, 0.6), (0.6, 0.3), (0.1, 0.7), (0.1, 0.8)\}$
$\widetilde{C}^2_{11} = \{(0.2, 0.6), (0.3, 0.6), (0.3, 0.7), (0.1, 0.7), (0.1, 0.8)\}, \widetilde{C}^2_{\emptyset} = \{(1, 0), (1, 0), (1, 0), (1, 0), (1, 0)\}$

The IF concept's lattice design of the given four objects with spatio-temporal attributes with the Q_2 quarter of time granule is given in Figure 2.

Moreover, the IF concepts of the given four objects with spatial attributes in the Q_3 quarter of time granule are $(1, \widetilde{C}^3_1), (2, \widetilde{C}^3_2), (3, \widetilde{C}^3_3), (4, \widetilde{C}^3_4), (12, \widetilde{C}^3_5), (13, \widetilde{C}^3_6), (23, \widetilde{C}^3_7), (24, \widetilde{C}^3_8),$ $(123, \widetilde{C}^3_9), (124, \widetilde{C}^3_{10}), (234, \widetilde{C}^3_{11}), (1234, \widetilde{C}^3_{12}), (\emptyset, \widetilde{C}^3_{\emptyset})$ where:

$\widetilde{C}^3_1 = \{(0.9, 0.1), (0.6, 0.2), (0.3, 0.7), (0.8, 0.1), (0.7, 0.2)\}, \widetilde{C}^3_2 = \{(0.3, 0.5), (0.5, 0.5), (0.8, 0.2), (0.2, 0.5), (0.8, 0.2)\}$
$\widetilde{C}^3_3 = \{(0.8, 0.2), (0.6, 0.2), (0.7, 0.1), (0.2, 0.7), (0.7, 0.3)\}, \widetilde{C}^3_4 = \{(0.2, 0.6), (0.3, 0.6), (0.6, 0.3), (0.1, 0.6), (0.8, 0.1)\}$
$\widetilde{C}^3_5 = \{(0.3, 0.5), (0.5, 0.5), (0.3, 0.7), (0.2, 0.5), (0.7, 0.2)\}, \widetilde{C}^3_6 = \{(0.8, 0.2), (0.6, 0.2), (0.3, 0.7), (0.2, 0.7), (0.7, 0.3)\}$
$\widetilde{C}^3_7 = \{(0.3, 0.5), (0.5, 0.5), (0.7, 0.2), (0.2, 0.7), (0.7, 0.3)\}, \widetilde{C}^3_8 = \{(0.2, 0.6), (0.3, 0.6), (0.6, 0.3), (0.1, 0.6), (0.8, 0.2)\}$
$\widetilde{C}^3_9 = \{(0.3, 0.5), (0.5, 0.5), (0.3, 0.7), (0.2, 0.7), (0.7, 0.3)\}, \widetilde{C}^3_{10} = \{(0.2, 0.6), (0.3, 0.6), (0.3, 0.7), (0.1, 0.6), (0.7, 0.2)\}$
$\widetilde{C}^3_{11} = \{(0.2, 0.6), (0.3, 0.6), (0.6, 0.3), (0.1, 0.7), (0.7, 0.3)\}, \widetilde{C}^3_{12} = \{(0.2, 0.6), (0.3, 0.6), (0.3, 0.7), (0.1, 0.7), (0.7, 0.3)\}$
$\widetilde{C}^3_{\emptyset} = \{(1, 0), (1, 0), (1, 0), (1, 0), (1, 0)\}$

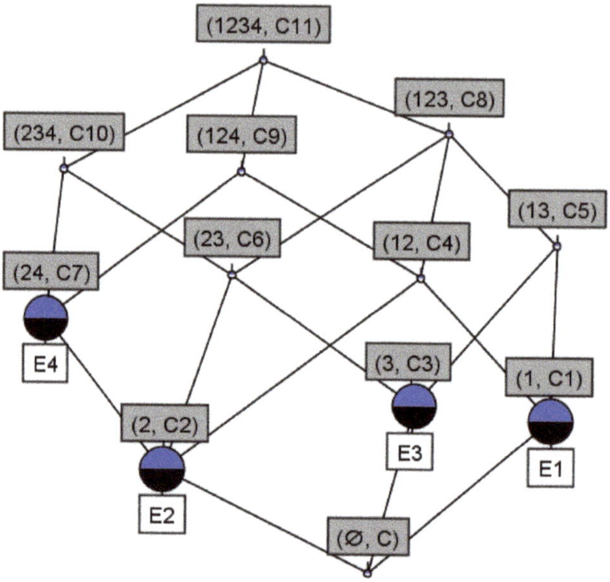

Figure 2. IF concept's lattice diagram of four objects with spatial and Q_2 quarter of time granule attributes.

The IF concept's lattice design of the given four objects with spatio-temporal attributes with the Q_3 quarter of time granule is given in Figure 3.

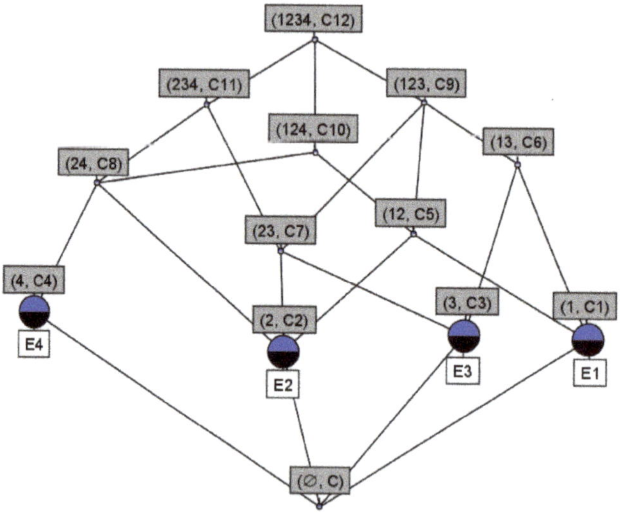

Figure 3. IF concept's lattice diagram of four objects with spatial and Q_3 quarter of time granule attributes.

Similarly, the IF concepts of the given four objects with spatial attributes in the Q_4 quarter of time granule are $(1,\widetilde{C}^4_1)$, $(2,\widetilde{C}^4_2)$, $(3,\widetilde{C}^4_3)$, $(12,\widetilde{C}^4_4)$, $(13,\widetilde{C}^4_5)$, $(23,\widetilde{C}^4_6)$, $(24,\widetilde{C}^4_7)$, $(123,\widetilde{C}^4_8)$, $(124,\widetilde{C}^4_9)$, $(234,\widetilde{C}^4_{10})$, $(1234,\widetilde{C}^4_{11})$, $(\emptyset,\widetilde{C}^4_{\emptyset})$ where:

$\widetilde{C}_1^4 = \{(0.9, 0.1), (0.6, 0.2), (0.3, 0.7), (0.8, 0.1), (0.4, 0.3)\}, \widetilde{C}_2^4 = \{(0.3, 0.5), (0.5, 0.5), (0.8, 0.2), (0.2, 0.5), (0.5, 0.4)\}$
$\widetilde{C}_3^4 = \{(0.8, 0.2), (0.6, 0.2), (0.7, 0.1), (0.2, 0.7), (0.2, 0.7)\}, \widetilde{C}_4^4 = \{(0.3, 0.5), (0.5, 0.5), (0.3, 0.7), (0.2, 0.5), (0.4, 0.4)\}$
$\widetilde{C}_5^4 = \{(0.8, 0.2), (0.6, 0.2), (0.3, 0.7), (0.2, 0.7), (0.2, 0.7)\}, \widetilde{C}_6^4 = \{(0.3, 0.5), (0.5, 0.5), (0.7, 0.2), (0.2, 0.7), (0.2, 0.7)\}$
$\widetilde{C}_7^4 = \{(0.2, 0.6), (0.3, 0.6), (0.6, 0.3), (0.1, 0.6), (0.1, 0.6)\}, \widetilde{C}_8^4 = \{(0.3, 0.5), (0.5, 0.5), (0.3, 0.7), (0.2, 0.7), (0.2, 0.7)\}$
$\widetilde{C}_9^4 = \{(0.2, 0.6), (0.3, 0.6), (0.3, 0.7), (0.1, 0.6), (0.1, 0.6)\}, \widetilde{C}_{10}^4 = \{(0.2, 0.6), (0.3, 0.6), (0.6, 0.3), (0.1, 0.7), (0.1, 0.7)\}$
$\widetilde{C}_{11}^4 = \{(0.2, 0.6), (0.3, 0.6), (0.3, 0.7), (0.1, 0.7), (0.1, 0.7)\}, \widetilde{C}_{\emptyset}^4 = \{(1, 0), (1, 0), (1, 0), (1, 0), (1, 0), (1, 0)\}$

Here, the IF concept's lattice design of the given four objects with spatio-temporal attributes with the Q_4 quarter of time granule is given in Figure 4.

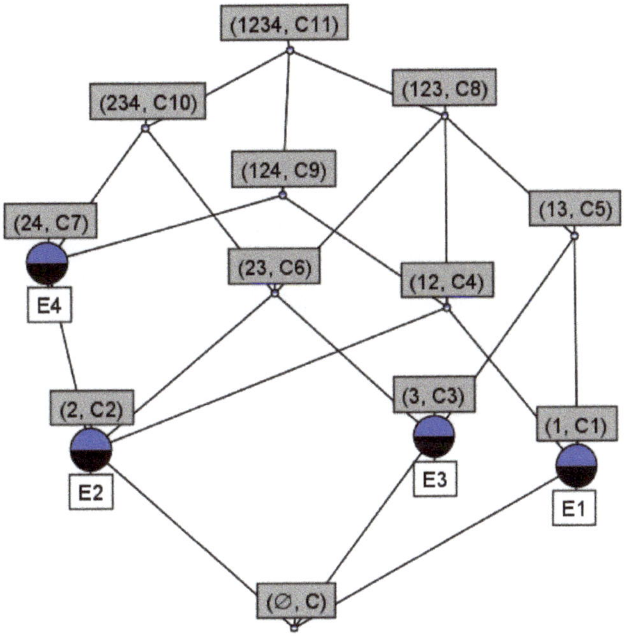

Figure 4. IF concept's lattice diagram of four objects with spatial and Q_4 quarter of time granule attributes.

Now, according to Equation (1), the IG of each lattice designed with the four events showing the objects along with each quarter of the time granulation is given below:

$Lattice_1$(designed with Q_1 quarter of time granulation) $IG : 0.53$
$Lattice_2$(designed with Q_2 quarter of time granulation) $IG : 0.58$
$Lattice_3$(designed with Q_3 quarter of time granulation) $IG : 0.60$
$Lattice_4$(designed with Q_4 quarter of time granulation) $IG : 0.52$

Here, $Lattice_3$, designed with the Q_3 quarter of time granulation, gives more IG than the other three lattices designed with the other three quarters of time granulation, respectively. A higher IG leads to more interesting results with a less focused view of the data. Now, the granulation measures COV and SP of $Lattice_3$ IF concepts can be measured through Equation (2) and Equation (3), respectively. According to Equations (2)–(4), the COV, SP, and Q value of each IF concept of $Lattice_3$ is given in Table 4.

Table 4. Granulation measures of each IF concept of $Lattice_3$.

	$COV(C) = \left[\left(\frac{D}{G} \times \frac{1}{N}\sum_{i=1}^{N} c\left(x_{\mu_j}\right)\right) + \frac{\pi_j}{2}\right]$	$SP(C) = \left[1 - \frac{len(d)}{range}\right] \times \left[\alpha - \frac{1}{n-1}\sum_{X \neq X^*} G(x)\right]$	$Q(C) = cov(C) \times (SP(C))^{\zeta}$
C_1	0.365	0.95	0.34675
C_2	0.38	0.89	0.3382
C_3	0.4	0.96	0.384
C_4	0.5	0.92	0.46
C_5	0.5	0.93	0.465
C_6	0.41	0.93	0.3813
C_7	0.44	0.92	0.4048
C_8	0.55	0.92	0.506
C_9	0.45	0.92	0.414
C_{10}	0.59	0.92	0.5428
C_{11}	0.585	0.94	0.5499
C_{12}	0.57	0.91	0.5187
C_{13}	0	0	0

Now, if the Q_3 quarter of time granulation is decomposed into more parts, then this decomposition of the Q_3 quarter may provide more interesting results. For this purpose, let $Q_{3,1}$, $Q_{3,2}$, and $Q_{3,3}$ contain the July, August, and September IF data, respectively. This is the second decomposition of the IF concept lattice designed through the Q_3 quarter of time granulation. Thus, the four events' IF data with spatio-temporal attributes of the Q_3 quarter's second decomposition are given in Table 5.

Table 5. Events with Four Spatial and Three (decomposed) $Q_{3,1}$, $Q_{3,2}$, and $Q_{3,3}$ Temporal Attributes Data.

	$Place_1$	$Place_2$	$Place_3$	$Place_4$	$Q_{3,1}$	$Q_{3,2}$	$Q_{3,3}$
E_1	(0.9, 0.1)	(0.6, 0.2)	(0.3, 0.7)	(0.8, 0.1)	(0.9, 0.0)	(0.0, 0.9)	(0, 0)
E_2	(0.3, 0.5)	(0.5, 0.5)	(0.8, 0.2)	(0.2, 0.5)	(1, 0)	(0, 1)	(0, 0)
E_3	(0.8, 0.2)	(0.6, 0.2)	(0.7, 0.1)	(0.2, 0.7)	(0.8, 0.1)	(0.1, 0.9)	(0, 0)
E_4	(0.2, 0.6)	(0.3, 0.6)	(0.6, 0.3)	(0.1, 0.6)	(0.9, 0.1)	(0.1, 0.8)	(0, 0)

The IG of each lattice, $Lattice_{3,1}$, $Lattice_{3,2}$, and $Lattice_{3,3}$, with second decomposition of $Q_{3,1}$, $Q_{3,2}$, and $Q_{3,3}$ quarters of time granulation, respectively, is given below:

$Lattice_{3,1}$ (designed with $Q_{3,1}$ quarter of time granulation) $IG: 0.63$

$Lattice_{3,2}$ (designed with $Q_{3,2}$ quarter of time granulation) $IG: 0.46$

$Lattice_{3,3}$ (designed with $Q_{3,3}$ quarter of time granulation) $IG: 0.44$

It shows that $Lattice_{3,1}$, made with the $Q_{3,1}$ quarter of time granulation, gives more IG than the other lattices of timed granulations. Moreover, the granulation measures of the each concept lattice (as made with $Lattice_3$), i.e., made with the $Q_{3,1}$ quarter of time granulation, are given as in Table 6.

Likewise, it can be observed that the granule $Lattice_2$, designed with the Q_2 quarter of time granulation with an IG of 0.58, is the second highest IG. So, the granulation measures COV, SP, and the Q value of the lattice, i.e., made with the Q_2 quarter of time granulation, are given as in Table 7.

Note, the value of "$\zeta = 1$" is used because of the primary decomposition of the granules. Here, primary decomposition means partitioning the data into months, because the first decided decomposition is set to one month. Moreover, partitioning one month into two timeslots would be the secondary decomposition; in that case, the value of "ζ" is 0.5. The applicability of the proposed approach is the knowledge discovery of periodical events' occurrences (co-occurrences), nonoccurrences, and uncertainty of occurrences/nonoccurrences in spatial and temporal aspects through IF datasets by applying FCA and GrC.

Table 6. Granulation measures of each IF concept of $Lattice_{3,1}$.

	$COV(C) = \left[\left(\frac{D}{G} \times \frac{1}{N}\sum_{i=1}^{N} c\left(x_{\mu_j}\right)\right) + \frac{\pi_j}{2}\right]$	$SP(C) = \left[1 - \frac{len(d)}{range}\right] \times \left[\alpha - \frac{1}{n-1}\sum_{X \neq X^*} G(x)\right]$	$Q(C) = cov(C) \times (SP(C))^{\zeta}$
C_1	0.365	0.9	0.3285
C_2	0.39	0.89375	0.3485625
C_3	0.455	0.91875	0.4180313
C_4	0.52	0.8875	0.4615
C_5	0.47	0.8875	0.417125
C_6	0.5	0.93125	0.465625
C_7	0.56	0.89375	0.5005
C_8	0.515	0.9	0.4635
C_9	0.57	0.86875	0.4951875
C_{10}	0.65	0.9125	0.593125
C_{11}	0.64	0.8875	0.568
C_{12}	0	0	0

Table 7. Granulation measures of each IF concept of $Lattice_2$.

	$COV(C) = \left[\left(\frac{D}{G} \times \frac{1}{N}\sum_{i=1}^{N} c\left(x_{\mu_j}\right)\right) + \frac{\pi_j}{2}\right]$	$SP(C) = \left[1 - \frac{len(d)}{range}\right] \times \left[\alpha - \frac{1}{n-1}\sum_{X \neq X^*} G(x)\right]$	$Q(C) = cov(C) \times (SP(C))^{\zeta}$
C_1	0.175	0.9	0.1575
C_2	0.13	0.89375	0.116188
C_3	0.12	0.93125	0.11175
C_4	0.21	0.9125	0.191625
C_5	0.2	0.9	0.18
C_6	0.18	0.91875	0.165375
C_7	0.19	0.94375	0.179313
C_8	0.21	0.95625	0.200813
C_9	0.24	0.91875	0.2205
C_{10}	0.195	0.93125	0.181594
C_{11}	0.2	0.975	0.195
C_{12}	0	0	0

7. Results and Discussion

The experiments were performed on a 64-bit system (Intel Core i3-4010U, 1.70 GHz, 4 GB RAM). Python (version 3.7) was used to construct the IF concepts' lattice structures in the experimental evaluation section. In the experimental evaluation of this research article, IF data are taken to process the proposed methodology. Additionally, this IF data contain four events, happening at four places in a year. For the first decomposition, one-year timeslot data are partitioned into four quarters of the time granulation of events happening at the given four places, where events show the objects and places, with time granulation data indicating the attributes. The purpose of this methodology is to analyze the spatio-temporal perspectives of the IF granule. More specifically, the idea is to find out whether the granulation of IF data provides more interesting results. In the experimental evaluation, the IG of the four lattices designed with the four events (objects) is analyzed first, which happens at four places in four different quarters of the year, showing the spatio-temporal attributes given as

$Lattice_1$(designed with Q_1 quarter of time granulation) $IG : 0.53$
$Lattice_2$(designed with Q_2 quarter of time granulation) $IG : 0.58$
$Lattice_3$(designed with Q_3 quarter of time granulation) $IG : 0.60$
$Lattice_4$(designed with Q_4 quarter of time granulation) $IG : 0.52$

Hence, the IG of $Lattice_3$ made with the Q_3 quarter of time granulation is higher than the IG of all three lattices, so $Lattice_3$ is chosen for further granulation measures. The COV, SP, and Q value of each of $Lattice_3$'s IF concept are calculated and given in Table 4. For the second decomposition, the Q_3 quarter is partitioned into three more timeslots, $Q_{3,1}$, $Q_{3,2}$, and $Q_{3,3}$, and the IG of lattices is made with the second partitioned timeslots, given as

$Lattice_{3,1}$ (designed with $Q_{3,1}$ quarter of time granulation) $IG : 0.63$
$Lattice_{3,2}$ (designed with $Q_{3,2}$ quarter of time granulation) $IG : 0.46$
$Lattice_{3,3}$ (designed with $Q_{3,3}$ quarter of time granulation) $IG : 0.44$

It can be observed that the IG of the lattice with the $Q_{3,1}$ quarter of time granulation is greater than all the other IGs of the second decomposition lattices; therefore, if the granulation measures of $Lattice_{3,1}$ with the $Q_{3,1}$ quarter of time granulation are checked in Table 6, it can be seen that most of the IF concepts of the second decomposed lattice have more COV and Q values than those of $Lattice_3$ with the Q_3 quarter of time granulation. Hence, the granularity of data in IF sets gives more interesting results.

8. Comparison with Previous SOTA (State of the Art) Approaches

8.1. Comparison with Previous Spatial and Temporal Approaches Using FCA and GrC

This approach and its results are compared with other SOTA methodologies based on the research methodology, the GrC perspective of spatial and temporal aspects and the data viewpoint with the FCA algorithm. In [1], the authors present and evaluate a method which uses an existing approach to discover periodic events in the data to combine time-based granulation and three-way decisions to support decision makers in understanding and reasoning on the learned granular structures conceptualizing spatial–temporal events. In [7], the methodology interprets, represents, and implements sequential three-way GrC with a framework of temporal–spatial multigranularity learning, which is described with the temporality of data and the spatiality of parameters. The method in [31], based on the GrC and FCA technique, proposes an approach which focuses on the temporal aspect of data to extracte knowledge concerning the periodic occurrences of events. In the context of three-way GrC, the authors in [46] introduce three extensional ideas, temporal, spatial, spatial–temporal-based trisecting–acting–outcome (TAO) frameworks for the construction of a multilevel composite granular structure.

In the literature, knowledge discovery through spatial and temporal aspects of data uses the classical FCA algorithm (using single-value attributes) and the GrC paradigm for the occurrences and co-occurrences of events. However, there can be three aspects of events: occurrences (and co-occurrences), nonoccurrences, and uncertainty of occurrences/nonoccurrences with respect to spatial and temporal aspects of data. In this proposed approach, IF datasets were used for events, such that event occurrences (and co-occurrences), nonoccurrences, and uncertainty of occurrences/nonoccurrences in spatial and temporal views can be indicated through the μ, γ, and π values, respectively. GrC was used to discover the periodicity in the data at various abstraction levels, while FCA was used to discover the granulation levels and process the granulation measures to understand IF concepts. References [1,31] use an FCA-based single-value attribute for the single aspect of event occurrences (and co-occurrences) with respect to the spatial and temporal aspects, while [7,46] use granular structures for the spatial and temporal aspects of data. The main advantages of the proposed approach over the existing approaches are discovering the periodicity of spatial–temporal events data given in IF sets through GrC and the FCA algorithm and predicting event occurrences, (and co-occurrences), nonoccurrences, and uncertainty of occurrences/nonoccurrences in spatial and temporal views of data through IF sets. The comparison of the proposed approach with other SOTA approaches is presented in Table 8.

8.2. Comparison with Finding IE/IG

IG is computed through IE (uncertainty) in data. In GrC, the approaches [31,35] calculate IE and IG using single-value attributes for the FCA while considering the one aspect of event occurrences (co-occurrences). However, the proposed approach based on the GrC paradigm uses IF datasets for the attributes of FCA that improves the results of IG. Additionally, unlike the existing approaches, the proposed approach provides three aspects of event occurrences (co-occurrences), nonoccurrence, and uncertainty of occurrence/nonoccurrence in the spatial and temporal views of data. The comparison of (improved results computed through) the proposed approach with other SOTA approaches [31,35] is presented in Table 9.

Here, the IG results obtained with the approaches of [31,35] are unchanged due to the different IF μ and γ values in all the attributes shared by the objects in each lattice.

Table 8. Comparison with other SOTA approaches.

Research Article	Research Methodology	GrC (Spatial or Temporal) Perspective	Data Viewpoint with FCA/IF Sets
[1]	A method to combine time-based granulation and three-way decisions to understand and reason on learned granular structures and discover periodic events.	Spatial and temporal aspects of data granularity	FCA-based single-value attribute
[7]	The method implements sequential three-way GrC by a spatial–temporal multigranularity learning framework, described with the temporality of data and spatiality of parameters.	Spatial and temporal aspects of data granularity	-
[31]	A method based on GrC and FCA to focus the temporal aspect and extract the knowledge concerning periodic occurrences of events in data.	Temporal aspect of data granularity.	FCA-based single-value attribute.
[46]	Temporal, spatial, and spatial–temporal-based trisecting–acting–outcome (TAO) frameworks for the construction of multilevel composite granular structures are introduced.	Spatial, temporal, and spatial–temporal aspects of data granularity	-
Proposed Approach	This approach analyzes and predict event occurrences, nonoccurrences, and uncertainty of occurrences/nonoccurrences through spatial and temporal aspects given in IF sets' data using GrC and FCA.	Temporal aspect of data granularity in IF datasets	IF set values using granular computing and the FCA algorithm

Table 9. Comparison with other research methodologies to find IG. Higher values are bolded.

Lattice No.	Results Obtained with Approaches Used [31,35]	Results Obtained with the Proposed Approach
$Lattice_1$	0.25	**0.53**
$Lattice_2$	0.25	**0.58**
$Lattice_3$	0.25	**0.60**
$Lattice_4$	0.25	**0.52**
$Lattice_{3,1}$	0.25	**0.63**
$Lattice_{3,2}$	0.25	**0.46**
$Lattice_{3,3}$	0.25	**0.44**

8.3. Comparison with Finding COV, SP, and Q Value

COV, SP, and Q value are important granulation measures to analyze the granule. In [31], granules are represented in the form of formal concepts and GrC and evaluated through these granulation measures; moreover, in [44,45], these granulation measures are proposed for the granules represented in fuzzy and IF sets. In existing approaches, granulation measures are used only in the perspectives of GrC with the FCA algorithm [31], or on fuzzy and IF sets [44,45]. However, the granulation measures in the proposed approach are used in the perspective of GrC, FCA, and IF sets. In the proposed approach, IF concepts are made and represented as granules, where the granulation measures are used to evaluate those granules. The comparison given in Tables 10 and 11 shows that the granulation measures used in the proposed approach give improved results.

Table 10. Comparison with other Research Methodologies to find the granulation measures (COV, SP, and Q value) of $Lattice_3$. Higher values are bolded.

	COV, SP and Q Value Obtained with Approaches Used in [44,45]			COV, SP and Q Value Obtained with Proposed Approach		
$Lattice_3$ IF Concepts	COV	SP	Q Value	COV	SP	Q Value
C_1	**0.66**	0.175	0.1155	0.365	**0.95**	**0.34675**
C_2	**0.52**	0.425	0.221	0.38	**0.89**	**0.3382**
C_3	**0.6**	0.15	0.09	0.4	**0.96**	**0.384**
C_4	0.4	0.325	0.13	**0.5**	**0.92**	**0.46**
C_5	0.4	0.25	0.1	**0.5**	**0.93**	**0.465**
C_6	**0.52**	0.275	0.143	0.41	**0.93**	**0.3813**
C_7	**0.48**	0.325	0.156	0.44	**0.92**	**0.4048**
C_8	0.4	0.325	0.13	**0.55**	**0.92**	**0.506**
C_9	0.4	0.3	0.12	**0.45**	**0.92**	**0.414**
C_{10}	0.32	0.325	0.104	**0.59**	**0.92**	**0.5428**
C_{11}	0.38	0.25	0.095	**0.585**	**0.94**	**0.5499**
C_{12}	0.32	0.35	0.112	**0.57**	**0.91**	**0.5187**
C_{13}	1	0	0	0	0	0

Table 11. Comparison with other Research Methodologies to find the granulation measures (COV, SP, and Q value) of $Lattice_{3,1}$. Higher values are bolded.

	COV, SP and Q Value Obtained with Approaches Used in [44,45]			COV, SP and Q Value Obtained with Proposed Approach		
$Lattice_{3,1}$ IF Concepts	COV	SP	Q Value	COV	SP	Q Value
C_1	**0.66**	0.4	0.264	0.365	**0.9**	**0.328**
C_2	**0.56**	0.425	0.238	0.39	**0.89375**	**0.348**
C_3	**0.62**	0.325	0.2015	0.455	**0.91875**	**0.418**
C_4	0.44	0.45	0.198	**0.52**	**0.8875**	**0.462**
C_5	**0.54**	0.45	0.243	0.47	**0.8875**	**0.417**
C_6	0.5	0.275	0.1375	0.5	**0.931**	**0.466**
C_7	0.42	0.425	0.179	**0.56**	**0.894**	**0.5005**
C_8	0.42	0.4	0.168	**0.515**	**0.9**	**0.464**
C_9	0.36	0.525	0.189	**0.57**	**0.86875**	**0.495**
C_{10}	0.4	0.35	0.14	**0.65**	**0.9125**	**0.593**
C_{11}	0.34	0.45	0.153	**0.64**	**0.8875**	**0.568**
C_{12}	1	0	0	0	0	0

The proposed approach is compared with other SOTA approaches by applying granulation measures on the IF datasets given in Section 6 (experimental evaluation). These IF datasets contain events as objects and spatial and temporal attributes, in which the temporal attribute is decomposed into four quarters, Q_1, Q_2, Q_3, and Q_4 of the annual periodicity of time granulation, and four granules are created in the first decomposition. Afterwards, the IG of each granule is computed to determine the granule with more IG. FCA is then used to construct lattices from each granule, and granulation measures are performed on the decided granule (with more IG). As shown in Table 9, the IG obtained with the proposed approach is greater than that obtained with other approaches [31,35]. In Table 9, the IG obtained with the other approaches is the same for all the lattices, because none of the objects have identical IF values. Furthermore, in Tables 10 and 11, most of the granulation measures (COV, SP, and Q value) of $Lattice_3$ and $Lattice_{3,1}$ obtained with the proposed approach are greater than the existing approaches [44,45]. Hence, it can be observed that the proposed approach provides improved results for IG, COV, and Q value obtained from the IF datasets and processed through GrC and the FCA algorithm.

9. Conclusions and Future Work

This research suggests a novel approach to determine occurrences (and co-occurrences), nonoccurrences, and uncertainty of occurrences/nonoccurrences of events based on GrC and IF datasets with spatio-temporal attributes. The FCA algorithm was used to analyze the granulation level and granulation measures. Furthermore, different measures are proposed to analyze granulation levels formed with the IF datasets. The originality of this proposed methodology is to discover the periodical occurrences (and co-occurrences), nonoccurrences, and uncertainty of occurrences/nonoccurrences in IF datasets with spatio-temporal attributes using FCA and granulation measures. Here, the limited IF datasets indicating the spatial and temporal aspects of data are considered for the experimentation and work of the proposed methodology. This can be implemented on a large number of IF datasets in the context of big data for the scalability of the proposed methodology. In the real world, this approach can be used to discover the significance in periodicities of data related to storm occurrences, digital forensics, and electronic and smart video surveillance by constructing a timeline to analyze and predict information. Moreover, the proposed approach does not provide an automatic or semiautomatic process to predict an event's occurrence in granular structures. The authors aim to address these additions in future works.

Author Contributions: I.A.: conceptualization, methodology, software, visualization, formal analysis, investigation, writing—original draft, and writing—review and editing. Y.L.: conceptualization, methodology, formal analysis, writing—review and editing, supervision, investigation, and funding acquisition. W.P.: writing—review and editing, suggestions, guidance, formal analysis, investigation, supervision, and validation. All authors have read and agreed to the published version of the manuscript.

Funding: Y. Li is supported by the National Science Foundation of China (Grants No. 12071271 and No. 11671244).

Institutional Review Board Statement: Not applicable.

Informed Consent Statement: Not applicable.

Data Availability Statement: Data are contained within the article.

Conflicts of Interest: The authors declare no conflict of interest.

References

1. Gaeta, A.; Loia, V.; Orciuoli, F.; Parente, M. Spatial and temporal reasoning with granular computing and three way formal concept analysis. *Granul. Comput.* **2021**, *6*, 797–813. [CrossRef]
2. Li, J.; Mei, C.; Xu, W.; Qian, Y. Concept learning via granular computing: A cognitive viewpoint. *Inf. Sci.* **2015**, *298*, 447–467. [CrossRef]
3. Li, J.; Mei, C.; Aswani, C. On rule acquisition in decision formal contexts. *Int. J. Mach. Learn. Cybern.* **2013**, *4*, 721–731. [CrossRef]
4. Xu, W.; Li, W. Granular Computing Approach to Two-Way Learning Based on Formal Concept Analysis in Fuzzy Datasets. *IEEE Trans. Cybern.* **2014**, *46*, 366–379. [CrossRef] [PubMed]
5. Wei, L.; Wan, Q. Granular Transformation and Irreducible Element Judgment Theory Based on Pictorial Diagrams. *IEEE Trans. Cybern.* **2016**, *46*, 380–387. [CrossRef]
6. Zhou, J.; Yang, S.; Wang, X.; Liu, W. Granule Description based on Compound Concepts. *arXiv* **2021**, arXiv:2111.00004.
7. Yang, X.; Zhang, Y.; Fujita, H.; Liu, D.; Li, T. Local temporal-spatial multi-granularity learning for sequential three-way granular computing. *Inf. Sci.* **2020**, *541*, 75–97. [CrossRef]
8. Xin, X.W.; Sun, J.B.; Xue, Z.A.; Song, J.H.; Peng, W.M. A novel intuitionistic fuzzy three-way decision model based on an intuitionistic fuzzy incomplete information system. *Int. J. Mach. Learn. Cybern.* **2022**, *13*, 907–927. [CrossRef]
9. Zhao, Y.; Li, T.; Luo, C. Spatial–temporal fuzzy information granules for time series forecasting. *Soft Comput.* **2021**, *25*, 1963–1981. [CrossRef]
10. Cui, J.; Zhao, J. Optimal route planning of traffic multi-source route based on granular computing. *J. Ambient Intell. Humaniz. Comput.* **2021**, 1–11. [CrossRef]
11. Dubois, D.; Prade, H. Bridging gaps between several forms of granular computing. *Granul. Comput.* **2016**, *1*, 115–126. [CrossRef]
12. Sang, B.; Long, B.; Pang, J.; Xu, W. The Method of Data Analysis in Intuitionistic Fuzzy Generalized Consistent Decision Formal Context. *Entropy* **2019**, *21*, 262. [CrossRef] [PubMed]
13. Bloch, I. Lattices of fuzzy sets and bipolar fuzzy sets, and mathematical morphology. *Inf. Sci.* **2015**, *181*, 2002–2015. [CrossRef]
14. Pang, J.; Zhang, X.; Xu, W. Attribute Reduction in Intuitionistic Fuzzy Concept Lattices. *Abs. App. Anal.* **2013**, 22–24. [CrossRef]
15. Zadeh, L.A. Fuzzy Sets. *Inf. Control* **1965**, *8*, 338–353. [CrossRef]
16. Atanassov, K.T. Intuitionistic fuzzy sets. *Fuzzy Sets Syst.* **1986**, *20*, 87–96. [CrossRef]

17. Atanassov, K.T. Intuitionistic Fuzzy Sets. *Stud. Fuzziness Soft Comput.* **1999**, *35*, 142–149.
18. Atanassov, K.T. *On Intuitionistic Fuzzy Sets Theory*, 1st ed.; Springer: Berlin/Heidelberg, Germany, 2012; Volume 283, pp. 142–149.
19. Szmidt, E.; Kacprzyk, J. Distances Between Intuitionistic Fuzzy Sets: Straightforward Approaches may not work. In Proceedings of the 2006 3rd International IEEE Conference Intelligent Systems, London, UK, 4–6 September 2006.
20. Szmidt, E. *Distances and Similarities in Intuitionistic Fuzzy Sets*, 1st ed.; Springer: Berlin/Heidelberg, Germany, 2014.
21. Zhu, Y.J.; Li, D.F. A new definition and formula of entropy for intuitionistic fuzzy sets. *J. Intell. Fuzzy Syst.* **2016**, *30*, 3057–3066. [CrossRef]
22. Wei, C.; Zhang, Y. Entropy Measures for Interval-Valued Intuitionistic Fuzzy Sets and Their Application in Group Decision-Making. *Math. Probl. Eng.* **2015**, *2015*, 563745. [CrossRef]
23. Chaira, T. Application of Fuzzy/Intuitionistic Fuzzy Set in Image Processing. *Fuzzy Set Its Ext.* **2019**, *9*, 237–257.
24. Faizi, S.; Sałabun, W.; Rashid, T.; Zafar, S.; Watróbski, J. Intuitionistic fuzzy sets in multi-criteria group decision making problems using the characteristic objects method. *Symmetry* **2020**, *12*, 1382. [CrossRef]
25. Bujnowski, P.; Szmidt, E.; Kacprzyk, J. Intuitionistic Fuzzy Decision Tree: A New Classifier. In Proceedings of the 7th IEEE International Conference Intelligent Systems IS'2014, Warsaw, Poland, 24–26 September 2014; Springer: Berlin/Heidelberg, Germany, 2015; pp. 779–790.
26. Zou, L.; Zhang, Z.; Long, J. An efficient algorithm for increasing the granularity levels of attributes in formal concept analysis. *Expert Syst. Appl.* **2016**, *46*, 224–235. [CrossRef]
27. Pedrycz, W. Granular Computing—The Emerging Paradigm. *J. Uncertain Syst.* **2007**, *1*, 38–61.
28. Lin, T.Y. Granular computing, Announcement of the BISC Special Interest Group on Granular Computing. *IEEE Int. Con. Gr. Comp.* **2005**, *1*, 85–90.
29. Smarandache, F. Neutrosophic Set—A Generalization of the Intuitionistic Fuzzy Set. *J. Def. Resour. Manag. (JoDRM)* **2010**, *1*, 107–116.
30. Pedrycz, W. *An Introduction to Computing with Fuzzy Sets*, 1st ed.; Springer: Berlin/Heidelberg, Germany, 2021.
31. Loia, V.; Orciuoli, F.; Pedrycz, W. Towards a granular computing approach based on Formal Concept Analysis for discovering periodicities in data. *Knowl.-Based Syst.* **2018**, *146*, 1–11. [CrossRef]
32. Tan, A.; Wu, W.Z.; Qian, Y.; Liang, J.; Chen, J.; Li, J. Intuitionistic Fuzzy Rough Set-Based Granular Structures and Attribute Subset Selection. *IEEE Trans. Fuzzy Syst.* **2019**, *27*, 527–539. [CrossRef]
33. Zhou, L. Formal concept analysis in intuitionistic fuzzy formal context. In Proceedings of the 2010 Seventh International Conference on Fuzzy Systems and Knowledge Discovery 2010, Yantai, China, 10–12 August 2010; Volume 5, pp. 2012–2015.
34. Bao, H.; Wu, W.Z.; Zheng, J.W.; Li, T.J. Entropy based optimal scale combination selection for generalized multi-scale information tables. *Int. J. Mach. Learn. Cybern.* **2021**, *12*, 1427–1437. [CrossRef]
35. Huang, C.; Li, J. Attribute significance, consistency measure and attribute reduction in formal concept analysis. *Neural Netw. World* **2016**, *26*, 607–623. [CrossRef]
36. Li, J.; He, Z.; Zhu, Q. An entropy-based weighted concept lattice for merging multi-source geo-ontologies. *Entropy* **2013**, *15*, 2303–2318. [CrossRef]
37. Szmidt, E.; Kacprzyk, J. Entropy for intuitionistic fuzzy sets. *Fuzzy Sets Syst.* **2001**, *118*, 467–477. [CrossRef]
38. Joshi, R.; Kumar, S. A New Parametric Intuitionistic Fuzzy Entropy and its Applications in Multiple Attribute Decision Making. *Int. J. Appl. Comput. Math.* **2018**, *4*, 52. [CrossRef]
39. Huang, B.; Li, H.X.; Feng, G.F.; Zhuang, Y.L. Distance-based Information Granularity and Hierarchical Structure for an Intuitionistic Fuzzy Granular Space. *Fuzzy Inf. Eng.* **2016**, *8*, 147–168. [CrossRef]
40. Zhang, S.; Guo, P.; Zhang, J.; Wang, X.; Pedrycz, W. A completeness analysis of frequent weighted concept lattices and their algebraic properties. *Data Knowl. Eng.* **2012**, *81*, 104–117. [CrossRef]
41. Pedrycz, W. Algorithmic Developments of Information Granules of Higher Type and Higher Order and Their Applications. *Fuzzy Log. Soft Comput. Appl.* **2016**, *3*, 27–41.
42. Kuznetsov, S.O.; Makhalova, T. On interestingness measures of formal concepts. *Inf. Sci.* **2018**, *442*, 202–219. [CrossRef]
43. Lloret-climent, M.; Pérez-gonzaga, S. Coverage and invariability in fuzzy systems. *Int. J. Gen. Syst.* **2013**, *43*, 96–104. [CrossRef]
44. Pedrycz, W. Concepts and Design Aspects of Granular Models of Type-1 and Type-2. *Int. J. Fuzzy Log. Intell. Syst.* **2015**, *15*, 87–95. [CrossRef]
45. Yager, R.R. Some aspects of intuitionistic fuzzy sets. *Fuzzy Optim. Decis. Mak.* **2009**, *8*, 67–90. [CrossRef]
46. Yang, X.; Li, T.; Liu, D.; Fujita, H. A temporal-spatial composite sequential approach of three-way granular computing. *Inf. Sci.* **2019**, *486*, 171–189. [CrossRef]

axioms

MDPI

Article

Application of the Methodology of Multi-Valued Logic Trees with Weighting Factors in the Optimization of a Proportional Valve

Adam Deptuła [1], Michał Stosiak [2], Rafał Cieślicki [2,*], Mykola Karpenko [3], Kamil Urbanowicz [4], Paulius Skačkauskas [3] and Anna Małgorzata Deptuła [1]

1 Faculty of Production Engineering and Logistics, Opole University of Technology, 76 Prószkowska St., 45-758 Opole, Poland
2 Faculty of Mechanical Engineering, Wrocław University of Science and Technology, 7/9 Łukasiewicza St., 50-371 Wrocław, Poland
3 Faculty of Transport Engineering, Vilnius Gediminas Technical University, Saulėtekio al. 11, LT-10223 Vilnius, Lithuania
4 Faculty of Mechanical Engineering and Mechatronics, West Pomeranian University of Technology, 70-310 Szczecin, Poland
* Correspondence: rafal.cieslicki@pwr.edu.pl

Abstract: Hydraulic valves are used to determine the set values of hydraulic quantities (flow rate, pressure, or pressure difference) in a hydraulic system or its part. This is achieved through the appropriate throttling of the stream flowing through the valve, which is automatically set by the operator (e.g., opening the throttle valve). The procedures for determining its static and dynamic properties were described using the example of modeling a two-stage proportional relief valve. Subsequently, the importance of the design and operational parameters was determined using multi-valued logic trees. Modeling began with the determination of equations describing the flow and movement of moving parts in a valve. Based on the equations, a numerical model was then created, e.g., in the Matlab/Simulink environment (R2020b). The static characteristics were obtained as the result of a model analysis of slow changes in the flow rate through the valve. Various coefficients of logical products have not been taken into account in the separable and common minimization processes of multi-valued logic equation systems in any available literature. The results of the model tests can be used to optimize several types of hydraulic valve constructions.

Keywords: multi-valued logic trees; hydraulic proportional valve; weighting factors; optimization

MSC: 03B50; 03B70; 03B80; 05C05

Citation: Deptuła, A.; Stosiak, M.; Cieślicki, R.; Karpenko, M.; Urbanowicz, K.; Skačkauskas, P.; Deptuła, A.M. Application of the Methodology of Multi-Valued Logic Trees with Weighting Factors in the Optimization of a Proportional Valve. *Axioms* **2023**, *12*, 8. https://doi.org/10.3390/axioms12010008

Academic Editor: Oscar Castillo

Received: 1 November 2022
Revised: 9 December 2022
Accepted: 13 December 2022
Published: 22 December 2022

1. Introduction

In recent years, intensive development in the field of hydraulic valves has been observed. This development is mainly related to the integration of electronics designed to control the valves. Modern hydraulic valves—especially those controlled via the proportional technique—are often equipped with various types of sensors, e.g., an inductive spool-position sensor inside the body of a proportional valve. The integration of classic hydraulics with electronics and sensors creates new, previously unattainable possibilities for using hydraulic proportional valves [1]. The course of the control signal of proportional valves is shown in the form of a block diagram in Figure 1.

An analog electrical signal with a voltage value typically not greater than 10 V is fed to an electronic amplifier. From the electronic amplifier, the electric control signal is fed through wires with a current that usually does not exceed 1.5 A per coil of a proportional electromagnet. Depending on the type of proportional electromagnet, a force or displacement of the proportional electromagnet armature is generated. If the valve uses a proportional solenoid with an adjustable stroke, a displacement of the electromagnet armature is generated proportionally to the value of the control current. This affects the proportional valve's control element (e.g., a spool-bushing pair or seat plug), causing its displacement (x). If the valve uses a proportional solenoid with a regulated force, the F force is generated proportionally to the value of the control current on the armature of the proportional solenoid. This force is transmitted to the valve control, which is usually a poppet in the proportional pressure valve. With a change in the displacement of the valve actuator or the force acting on it, the Q flow rate or the p pressure functionally vary depending on if a proportional valve is controlling the flow rate or pressure. These parameters control the operation of the hydraulic receiver where the current determines the n or v speed of the hydraulic receiver and the pressure determines the external M or F load.

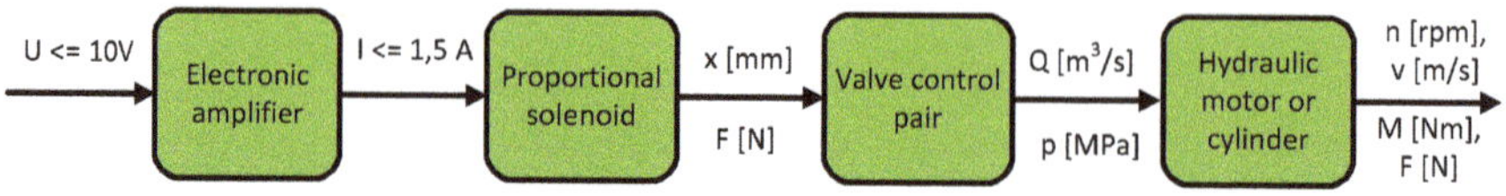

Figure 1. Schematic diagram of the control signal in the proportional control technique.

There are no significant differences in terms of the mechanical design between conventionally controlled valves and proportionally controlled valves. The main difference relies on the fact that, in proportional valves, instead of a spring, hand wheel, lever, or conventional solenoid, there are one or more proportional solenoids. There are two types of proportional electromagnets: force-adjustable and stroke-adjustable. Their use depends on the type and function of the proportional valve and is determined by its characteristics. The benefits of using proportional valves include combining several functions in one valve, a smooth control of flow and pressure parameters, the ability to program the valve and the receiver controlled by it, and the reduction of dynamic surpluses [2]. Proportional valves also have some disadvantages in comparison to conventional ones, including a higher price, stricter requirements regarding purity of the working liquid, and sensitivity to operating conditions (moisture, salinity of the environment, and external mechanical vibrations). Technically speaking, proportional valves were initially a bridge between conventionally (mechanically or electrically) controlled valves and servo valves. Presently, the latest proportional control valves have dynamic parameters equal to those of servo valves and sometimes even surpass them [3]. For example, it can be stated that the limit frequency of a two-stage servo valve is 240–270 Hz depending on the manufacturer, and the limit frequency of the latest-generation proportional valve with VCD (Voice Coil Drive) technology is 350 Hz. Several years ago, this frequency was 6–10 Hz for a single-stage proportional valve [4]. In many industries, particularly mechanical engineering, proportional relief valves with one—or more often, two—stages are widespread. An example of the use of proportional valves is their use in the hydraulic system for lifting and lowering loads with significant masses [5] such as agricultural machinery [6], CNC machine tools, hydraulic presses, wheel loaders, and ships.

Related Work

The research to determine the importance of hydraulic valves' design and/or operational parameters is still ongoing. For example, study [7] optimized the relief valve by minimizing partial multi-valued logic functions. Multi-valued logical equations which constituted design guidelines for the entire series of types of such valves were used. The analysis of the stability of hydraulic elements based on the systems of multi-valued logical equations and the method of multi-valued logical trees, taking into account weighting factors, allows for the consideration of the conditions of global stability. The most favorable result is the relationship specification, which binds the design and operational parameters limitations. In addition, the conditions that limit the parameters of the valve and the system are brought to a simple analytical and graphical relationship. Overall, it is limited to a relief valve system operated directly, general stability conditions, and a computerized time-course solution with different variable coefficients.

The modeling of hydraulic systems usually uses ordinary differential equations. From these equations a system of equations is created, initial conditions are assumed, and, after parameterization of the equations, the equations are solved to obtain time courses of the relevant parameters of the hydraulic system, e.g., pressure as a function of time or the velocity of the receiver as a function of time. These are models with focused parameters. One hydraulic system sometimes exhibits wave phenomena that lead to hydraulic resonance. This is referred to as a hydraulic long line. In such cases, partial differential equations are used for modeling and the method of characteristics (MOC) is used to solve them. This paper considers a system in which no wave phenomena occur and uses ordinary differential equations to describe the valve state. Decision-support systems are also applied to hydraulic and pneumatic systems [8–16]. The paper [8] mainly presents related methods, from classical clustering and classification topics to database methods (e.g., association), and from database methods (e.g., association rules, data cubes) to newer and more advanced topics (e.g., SVD/PCA, wavelets, support vector machines). The work of [9–12] focused on concepts for integrating decision-support systems of poorly structured data with a data warehouse based on relational or multidimensional structures. In [13], a framework was developed to evaluate different rainwater-discharge options for urban areas in arid regions. The modeling of rainfall runoff was carried out using the Hydrological-Engineering-Centre and Hydrological-Modelling-System (HEC-HMS). Hydraulic modeling was carried out using SewerGEM to evaluate the effectiveness of the various alternatives for a given design flood [14,15]. The authors of [14,15] presented further applications of multi-criteria decision support methods. In particular, in the work [15] of the Geospatial Information System (GIS), a multi-criteria decision-making system (MCDM) was applied to logic. The decision-making Trial and Evaluation Laboratory (DEMATEL) approach was used to create a network of relationships between criteria. The author of [17] described a model-driven decision-support system (software tool) implementing a model-based online leak-detection and localization methodology that is useful for a large class of water distribution networks.

The present work presents the use of multi-valued logical trees with multivalent weighting factors in the analysis of a two-stage proportional relief valve and a nozzle-aperture preliminary stage [18–20]. A significant amount of literature exists on the applications of decision trees in decision-making systems. However, there are only a small number of publications on their application in design methodology. Cognitive decision theories seek sufficient and effective solutions for so-called real-world problems and well-defined problems. There are a number of decision-support methods that are familiar to the authors and, in particular, have already been used by the authors to solve a number of problems in decision-support areas, e.g., in the use of special types of parametric dependency graphs [21,22]; inductive decision trees [23,24]; and in particular multi-valued logic trees [25]. Specifically, the recent paper has shown how methods based on multi-valued logic trees can be very beneficial when other methods are ineffective. However, multi-valued logic tree methods have plenty of advantages in design methodology and are still being developed. The advantage of the method of multi-valued logical trees is that the measurement data can be recorded by means of appropriate formal notations and it is even possible to combine complex quantitative and qualitative features with different degrees of detail according to the rules of the multi-valued morphological array. The canonical alternative normal form (KAPN) of a bivariate or multi-valued logical function describes all variants, i.e., true (realizable) solutions of a given problem obtained according to the rules of the morphological table, as the full array of combinations of values of logical variables describes all theoretical variants. As a result of minimization (after applying the Quine–McCluskey algorithm), one obtains from the realizable solutions the true sub-solutions as a shortened alternative normal form of the SAPN of the logical function. In this way, the real sub-solutions of the problem are appropriately grouped and therefore the computational time required to obtain the most important real sub-solutions is reduced.

2. The Tested Object

The tested object is a two-stage proportional relief valve with a preliminary nozzle-aperture stage (Figure 2) [23]. Figure 2 demonstrates a two-stage proportional relief valve. The main stage is pressure controlled, while the pilot is controlled by a proportional solenoid. Changing the pressure in the chamber above the main-stage spool is possible by throttling the fluid flowing out of the pilot. This throttling is altered by changing the position of the diaphragm driven by the proportional solenoid.

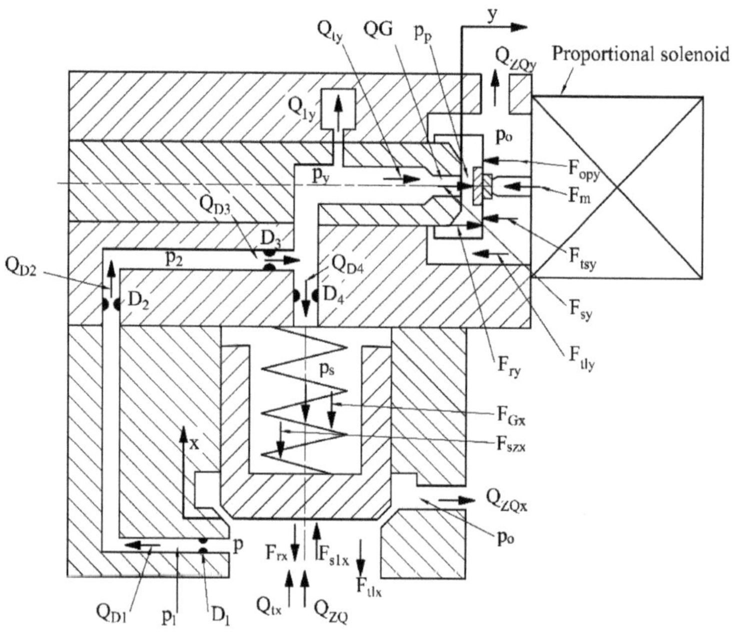

Figure 2. The tested two-stage proportional relief valve.

Figure 3 shows the drive system with a proportional valve and a receiver.

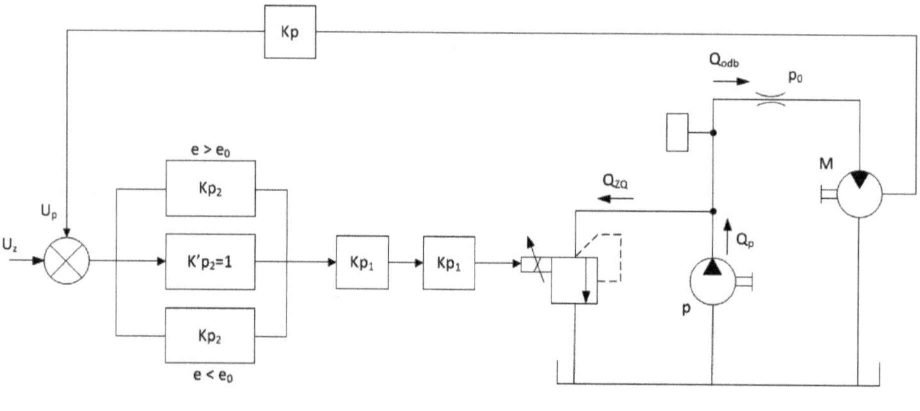

Figure 3. Diagram of the drive system.

The receiver in the analyzed system is a throttle valve whose performance characteristics are described as follows:

$$\begin{cases} p \leq 1\ MPa : Q_{odb} = 1.2446666 \cdot 10^{-10} p, \\ 1\ MPa \leq p \leq 6\ MPa : Q_{odb} = 0.3533333 \cdot 10^{-10} p + 0.8913333 \cdot 10^{-4}, \\ p \leq 6\ MPa : Q_{odb} = 0.2425893 \cdot 10^{-10} p + 14.55 \cdot 10^{-5}. \end{cases} \quad (1)$$

where Q_{odb} is the hydraulic actuator flow rate.

In order to describe the flow through a proportional valve it is necessary to consider the value of the loss factor as a function of the displacement of the moving element. The actual course is similar to the solution of a second-order differential equation with a variable throttling factor. This relationship is described in the following form [26]:

$$\begin{array}{l} k_{vx} = 0.82 \cdot [1 - \exp(-b \cdot 10^3 \cdot \frac{x}{2}) \cos(10^3 \sqrt{-\Delta})], \\ \Delta < 0 \end{array} \quad (2)$$

where:

$$\begin{array}{l} b = 5 + \frac{5 \cdot 10^7}{p}; \\ \Delta = b^2 - 100\pi^2, \\ \Delta > 0 \end{array} \quad (3)$$

and

$$k_{vx} = 0.82[1 - \exp(-b - \sqrt{-\Delta}) 10^3 \frac{x}{2}]. \quad (4)$$

The following course was used in the control stage ($\Delta y < 0$):

$$\begin{array}{c} k_{vy} = 0.75\left[1 - \exp\left(-b_y \cdot 10^3 \cdot \frac{y}{2}\right) \cos\left(10^3 y \sqrt{-\Delta y}\right)\right] \\ \Delta y > 0 \end{array} \quad (5)$$

where:

$$\begin{array}{l} b_y = 40 + \frac{1.5 \cdot 10^8}{p_y + 10^5}, \\ \Delta y = b_y^2 - 100\pi^2. \end{array} \quad (6)$$

The force generated by the electromagnetic transducer used in the valve is described as follows:

$$\begin{array}{l} F_m = 73.19631(i - 0.045), \\ di = \frac{1}{T_m}\left(\frac{U}{18} - i\right)dt, \end{array} \quad (7)$$

where $T_m = 15$ ms when i increases $\left(\frac{U}{18} - i > 0\right)$ and $T_m = 7.5$ ms when i decreases $\left(\frac{U}{18} - i < 0\right)$.

Mathematical Model of the Tested Valve

The mathematical model of the valve under consideration was built on the basis of ordinary differential equations of the second order. The first equation of the system of equations is the flow rate balance equation, which takes into account the compressibility of the working fluid (its capacitance).

The flow balance of the drive system can be written as [23]:

$$Q_p = Q_{zQ} + Q_{1x} + Q_{odb}. \quad (8)$$

The flow balance through the main valve stage is described as:

$$Q_{zQ} = Q_{zQx} + Q_{D1} + Q_{tx}. \quad (9)$$

The flow through the nozzle is described as:

$$Q_{D1} = Q_{D2} = Q_{D3}, \quad (10)$$

$$Q_{DG} = Q_{zQY} + Q_{tY}. \tag{11}$$

The flow balance through the control stage is described as:

$$Q_{D3} = Q_{1Y} + Q_{zQY} + Q_{tY}. \tag{12}$$

In addition, the flow rate is distinguished in the main stage as:

$$Q_{1x} = \frac{V_x}{B} \cdot \frac{dp}{dt} = \frac{4.33735 \cdot 10^{-3}}{1.4 \cdot 10^9} \frac{dp}{dt} = 3.098107 \cdot 10^{-12} \frac{dp}{dt}, \tag{13}$$

and at the control stage as:

$$Q_{1y} = \frac{V_y}{B} \cdot \frac{dp}{dt} = \frac{1.2 \cdot 10^{-6}}{1.4 \cdot 10^9} \frac{dp}{dt} = 0.857 \cdot 10^{-15} \frac{dpy}{dt}, \tag{14}$$

The flow rate through the valve is represented as:

$$\begin{aligned} &Q_z = \sqrt{\tfrac{2}{\rho}} \cdot k(k_v x) \sqrt{p - p_0}, \\ &with \\ &p_0 \ll p, \end{aligned} \tag{15}$$

- through the main stage:

$$Q_{zQx} = \sqrt{\frac{2}{892}} \cdot \pi \cdot 22 \cdot 10^{-3} \cdot \sin 30^\circ (k_{vx} \cdot x) \sqrt{p}, \tag{16}$$

$$Q_{zQx} = 1.6355097 \cdot 10^{-3} (k_{vx} \cdot x) \sqrt{p}, \tag{17}$$

- through the control stage:

$$Q_{zQy} = \sqrt{\frac{2}{892}} \cdot \pi \cdot 1.8 \cdot 10^{-3} (k_{vy} \cdot y) \sqrt{p}, \tag{18}$$

$$Q_{zQy} = 0.2676292 \cdot 10^{-3} (k_{vy} \cdot y) \sqrt{p}. \tag{19}$$

Ultimately, the flow rates are represented as:

- through the nozzle D_1:

$$Q_{D1} = a_1 (p - p_1) = 0.2370513 \cdot 10^{-10} (p - p_1). \tag{20}$$

- through the nozzle D_3:

$$Q_{D3} = a_3 (p_2 - p_y) = 0.2370486 \cdot 10^{-10} (p_2 - p_y). \tag{21}$$

An additional equation described is the equilibrium equation of the forces acting on the valve control element (according to d'Alembert's principle) on the main stage and the secondary stage. This equation takes into account the forces of inertia, spring stiffness, frictional force, and the hydrodynamic reaction force associated with the change in momentum of the fluid stream.

Forces in the valve:

Dynamic loads:

$$F_d = m \frac{d^2 x}{dt^2}, \tag{22}$$

In the main stage:

$$F_{dx} = \left[0.675 + \frac{1}{3}(0.008 + 0.00439)\right]\frac{d^2x}{dt^2} = 0.70631\frac{d^2x}{dt^2}, \tag{23}$$

where the following values indicate:

- 0.0675—the mass of the main stage slider;
- 0.008—spring mass;
- 0.00439—the mass of the associated liquid.

In the control stage:

$$F_{dy} = 0.03\frac{d^2y}{dt^2}. \tag{24}$$

Sticky friction:

$$F_{t1} = \frac{A_{st} \cdot \mu}{L_0} \cdot \frac{dx}{dt}, \tag{25}$$

- forces in the main stage:

$$F_{t1x} = \frac{\pi \cdot 22 \cdot 10^{-3} \cdot 10.5 \cdot 10^{-3} \cdot 0.06265}{5 \cdot 10^{-6}} = 9.0885102\frac{dx}{dt}, \tag{26}$$

- forces in the control stage:

$$F_{t1y} = \frac{32 \cdot 10^{-6} \cdot 0.06265}{12 \cdot 10^{-6}}\frac{dy}{dt} = 0.1670666\frac{dy}{dt}. \tag{27}$$

Forces of the hydrodynamic reaction are described as follows:

- of the main stage:

$$F_{rx} = 2k_x \cos\theta(k_{vx}x)p = 2 \cdot \pi \cdot 22 \cdot 10^{-5} \cdot \sin 30^\circ \cdot 1 \cdot \cos 35^\circ (k_{vx}x)p, \tag{28}$$

$$F_{rx} = 56.59033 \cdot 10^{-6} \cdot (k_{vx}x)p, \tag{29}$$

- of the nozzle-aperture pair:

$$F_{ry} = \frac{16A_y(k_{vy}y)^2}{d_{DG}^2}P_p, \tag{30}$$

$$F_{ry} = \frac{16 \cdot \pi/4(1.65 \cdot 10^{-3})}{(1.5 \cdot 10^{-3})^2}(k_{vy}y)^2 = 15.1976(k_{vy}y)^2 P_p. \tag{31}$$

The dynamic equations of the proportional valve forces are described at any point in the transient state after the introduction of the step function:

of the main stage:

$$F_{dx} = -F_{t1x} - F_{rx} - F_{szx} - F_{Gx} + F_{s1x} - F_{s2x}. \tag{32}$$

of the control stage:

$$F_{dy} = -F_{t1y} + F_{ry} + F_{sy} - F_{tsy} - F_{opy} - F_m. \tag{33}$$

The feedback loop equation is written as follows: when $U_z - U_p - e_0 < 0$,

$$\frac{du}{dt} = K_M\left[K_{p1}(U_z - U_p) + K_{p2}(U_z - U_p - e_0)\right], \tag{34}$$

when $U_z - U_p + e_0 < 0$,

$$\frac{du}{dt} = K_M \left[K_{p1}(U_z - U_p) + K_{p2}(U_z - U_p + e_0) \right], \tag{35}$$

if none of these conditions are met:

$$\begin{gathered} -e_0 < U_z - U_p < e_0, \\ \text{to} \\ \frac{du}{dt} = K_M K_{p1}(U_z - U_p). \end{gathered} \tag{36}$$

The output equations for the computer simulation of the operation of the hydraulic part are shown in Appendix A.

3. Methodology of Multi-Valued Logic Trees with Weight Coefficients as Discrete Optimization

The methodology presented is based on two algorithms:

1. The Quine–McCluskey method of minimizing partial multi-valued logical functions,
2. The Quine–McCluskey method of minimising partial multi-valued logical functions with multi-valued weighting factors.

3.1. Quine-Mc Cluskey Algorithm for the Minimization of Partial Multi-Valued Logical Functions

In the case of logic trees, the logical values of the variables are encoded on the branches of the tree. There can only be one Boolean variable per level of the tree, with the number of floors being equal to the number of independent variables of a given Boolean function. Representing a given Boolean function written in canonical alternative normal form (KAPN) on a logic tree involves encoding the individual canonical products on a tree path from the root to the end vertex. An individual path on the tree (from root to vertex) is a component of the singularity of the logical function, describing the realization of one possible solution. On the contrary, the set of paths is the set of all possible solutions. Figure 4 shows a logic tree in which a fixed Boolean function of three variables is encoded.

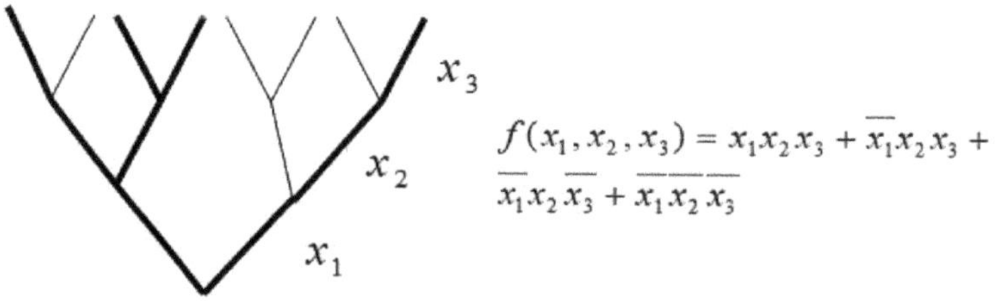

Figure 4. Boolean function of three variables encoded on a logic tree.

In the Quine–McCluskey algorithm, a truncated alternative normal form (SAPN) and eventually a minimum alternative normal form (MAPN) are obtained by simplifying the Boolean functions encoded in KAPN (Figure 5).

A minimized form of the output function (with a minimum number of literals) is subsequently obtained. However, given that so-called isolated branches exit, this is not the minimum decision form, meaning that there is no continuity between the root and the vertices. In the case of multi-valued logical functions—as in Boolean functions—the notions of incomplete gluing and elementary absorption, which are applied to the APN of a given logical function, play a fundamental role in the search for prime implicants.

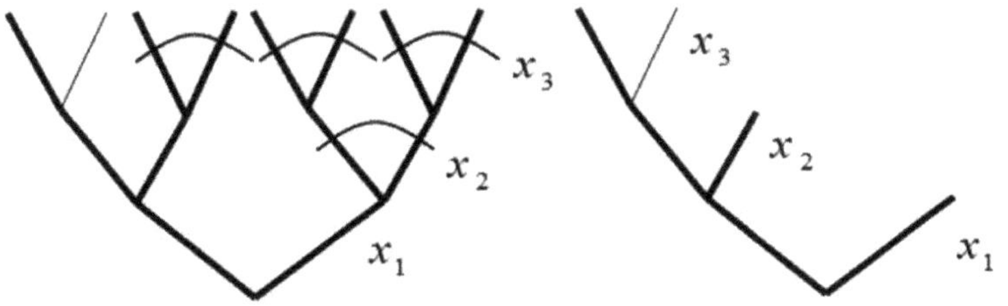

Figure 5. Logic tree and simplified logic tree.

A **gluing** operation is called a transformation:

$$Aj_o(x_r) + \ldots + Aj_{m_r-1}(x_r) = A. \quad (37)$$

where $r = 1, \ldots, n$ and A denotes an elementary partial product, of which, variables of the individual literals belong to the set $\{x_1, \ldots, x_{r-i}, x_{r+i}, \ldots, x_n\}$.

An **incomplete gluing** operation is called a transformation:

$$Aj_o(x_r) + \ldots + Aj_{m_r-1}(x_r) = A + Aj_o(x_r) + \ldots + Aj_{m_r-1}(x_r), \quad (38)$$

where $r = 1, \ldots, n$ and A denotes a partial product of which the variables of the individual literals belong to a set of $\{x_1, \ldots, x_{r-i}, x_{r+i}, \ldots, x_n\}$.

An elementary absorption operation is called a transformation:

$$Aj_u(x_r) + A = A, \quad (39)$$

where $0 \le u \le m_r - 1$, $1 \le r \le n$, and A denotes a partial product of which the variables of the individual literals belong to a set of $\{x_1, \ldots, x_{r-1}, x_{r+1}, \ldots, x_n\}$. If the above equation holds, then A absorbs $Aj_u(x_r)$. Signs (v) denote that a given partial product of the elementary, written using the digits of the system $(m_1, \ldots, m_n)$-positional, takes part in the gluing with those products that have a sign (v) in the same column. The notation marks of the gluing operation are entered separately in the columns and not in a single column as was the case in previous literature studies of bivalent cases. In the case of equal, multivalued variables $x_1, \ldots, x_n$ of a given logical function, the set of first implicants is obtained as a special case from different multi-valued variables.

Example 1. *Using the relationship:*

$$Aj_0(x_r) + \ldots + Aj_{m-1}(x_r) = A, \; Aj_u(x_r) + A = A, \quad (40)$$

where $A = A(x_1, \ldots, x_{r-1}, x_{r+1}, \ldots, x_n)$,

$$j_u(x_r) = \begin{cases} m-1 & , \; u = x_r \\ 0 & , \; u \neq x_r \end{cases} \quad 0 \le u \le m-1; \quad (41)$$

The successive steps of minimizing a multi-valued logical function can be represented as follows:

0	2	0
1	0	1
2	0	0

0	2	1
1	1	1
2	0	1
2	1	0

0	2	2
1	2	1
2	0	2
2	1	1

2	1	2
2	2	1

0	2	-
2	0	-
1	-	1

2	1	-
-	2	1
2	-	1

	020	200	101	021	201	210	111	022	121	202	211	212	221
02-	*			*				*					
20-		*			*					*			
1-1			*				*		*				
21-						*					*	*	
-21				*					*				*
2-1					*						*		*

Finally, two NAPNs and MAPNs of a given logic function are obtained, written using m-position system numbers: {(02-), (20-), (1-1), (21-), (-21)} and {(02-), (20-), (1-1), (21-), (2-1)}.

The rank of importance of successive decision variables is determined using complex alternative normal forms through the swapping of floors in logical decision trees. The swapping of logical tree floors in complex, multi-valued logical functions establishes the rank of importance of logical variables from the most important (at the root) to the least important (at the top). There is a generalization of a bivariate quality indicator to a multivariate one; $(C_k - k_i m_i) + (k_i + K_i)$, where C_k represents the number of branches of the k-th floor, k_i is the simplification factor on the k-th floor of the m_i-value variable, and K_i represents the number of branches $(k-1)$-th floors from which the non-simplifying branches of the k-th floor are formed. In this way, it is possible to obtain the minimum complexity alternative normal form (MZAPN) of a given logical function without isolated branches on the decision tree and with a concomitant minimum number of real (realizable) branches, which in particular can be considered to be elementary design guidelines. All transformations refer to the so-called Quine—McCluskey algorithm for minimising individual partial multi-valued logical functions.

Example 2. *A multi-valued logical function* $f(x_1, x_2, x_3)$, *where* x_1, x_2 *and* x_3 *are 0, 1 and 2, respectively; with a numerically recorded KAPN: 100, 010, 002, 020, 101, 110, 021, 102, 210, 111, 201, 120, 022, 112, 211, 121, 212, 221 and 122; and with one MZAPN after applying the Quine—McCluskey algorithm for minimising individual partial multi-valued logical functions has 13 literals:*

$$\begin{aligned} f(x_1,x_2,x_3) = {} & j_o(x_1)(j_o(x_2)j_2(x_3) + j_1(x_2)j_o(x_3) + j_2(x_2)) \\ & + j_1(x_1) + j_2(x_1)(j_o(x_2)j_1(x_3) + j_1(x_2) + j_2(x_2)j_1(x_3)). \end{aligned} \tag{42}$$

Figure 6 shows all possible ZKAPNs of a given multi-valued logical function.

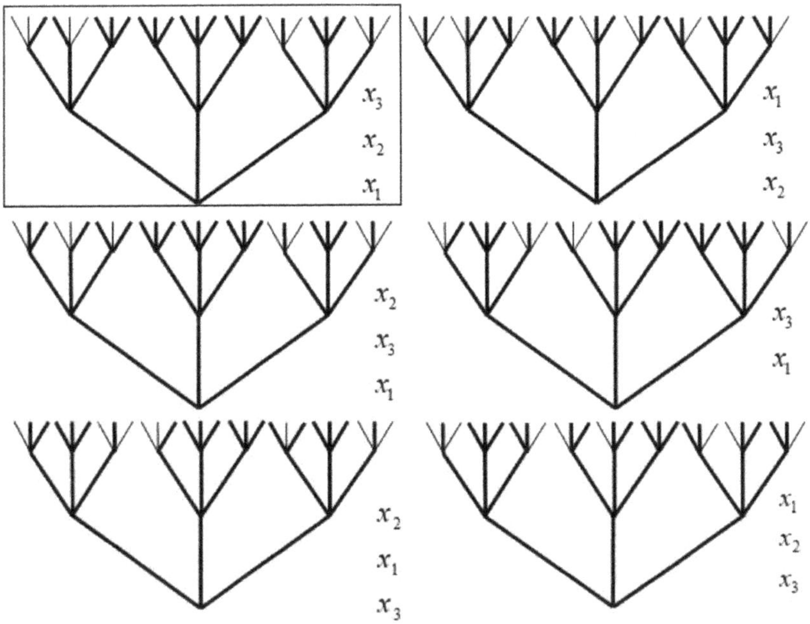

Figure 6. ZKAPN and MZAPN of the given logical function from Example 2.

1. The first stage of minimization due to x_3:

		V									
x_1	x_2	x_3									
1	0	0		V							
0	1	0						V			
0	0	2							V		
0	2	0	V								
1	0	1		V							
1	1	0			V						
0	2	1	V								
1	0	2		V							
2	1	0					V				
1	1	1			V						
2	0	1								V	
1	2	0				V					
0	2	2	V								
1	1	2			V						
2	1	1					V				
1	2	1				V					
2	1	2					V				
2	2	1									V
1	2	2				V					

2. The first stage of minimization due to x_1:

V x_1	x_2	x_3									
1	0	0			V						
0	1	0	V								
0	0	2				V					
0	2	0					V				
1	0	1						V			
1	1	0	V								
0	2	1		V							
1	0	2				V					
2	1	0	V								
1	1	1							V		
2	0	1						V			
1	2	0					V				
0	2	2								V	
1	1	2									V
2	1	1							V		
1	2	1		V							
2	1	2									V
2	2	1		V							
1	2	2								V	

3. The first stage of minimisation due to x_2:

x_1	**v** x_2	x_3									
1	0	0	V								
0	1	0					$\underline{V}$				
0	0	2						$\underline{V}$			
0	2	0					$\underline{V}$				
1	0	1		V							
1	1	0	V								
0	2	1							$\underline{V}$		
1	0	2			V						
2	1	0								$\underline{V}$	
1	1	1		V							
2	0	1				V					
1	2	0	V								
0	2	2						$\underline{V}$			
1	1	2			V						
2	1	1				V					
1	2	1		V							
2	1	2									$\underline{V}$
2	2	1				V					
1	2	2			V						

x_1: $19 - 2 \times 3 + 2 + 7 = 22$
x_2: $19 - 4 \times 3 + 4 + 5 = 16$
x_3: $19 - 5 \times 3 + 5 + 4 = 13$

Further minimisation steps for other variables:

		v					v				
	x_1	x_2					x_1	x_2			
	0	0		$\underline{V}$			0	0	$\underline{V}$		
-	1	0	V			-	1	0	$\underline{V}$		
	0	1		$\underline{V}$			0	1		$\underline{V}$	
-	0	2		$\underline{V}$		-	0	2			$\underline{V}$
-	1	1	V			-	1	1		$\underline{V}$	
	2	0			$\underline{V}$		2	0	$\underline{V}$		
-	2	1			$\underline{V}$	-	2	1		$\underline{V}$	
-	1	2	V			-	1	2			$\underline{V}$
	2	2			$\underline{V}$		2	2			$\underline{V}$

x_1: $9 - 0 \times 3 + 0 + 3 = 12$
x_2: $9 - 1 \times 3 + 1 + 2 = 9$

3.2. Generalization of the Quine–Mc Cluskey Algorithm for Minimization of Partial Multi-Valued Logical Functions for Multi-Valued Weighting Factors

In multi-valued logical functions with weighted products it is possible to apply the Quine–McCluskey algorithm for the minimization of multi-valued functions. As with the minimization of multi-valued logical functions without weighting coefficients, in the algorithm the elementary products are written as numbers in the corresponding positional systems. Additional elements and operations are introduced to account for the weighting coefficients.

In partial data of multi-valued logical functions $f_i(x_1, \ldots, x_n)$ n of variables $(m_1, \ldots, m_n)$, value-added gluing and pseudo-gluing operations should include weighting factors $(w_n, w_{n-1}, w_{n-2}, \ldots, w_1)$ assigned to the corresponding multi-valued logical products.

The Quine–McCluskey algorithm for minimizing multi-valued logical functions is built from n columns with $(w_1, \ldots, w_n)$ weighting factors.

Symbols indicating pseudo-gluing ($\underline{V}$) and gluing (v) sequentially relative to groups of indices differing by one are placed in the columns corresponding to the values of the weighting factors for the corresponding logical products.

Given multi-valued weighting coefficients, individual (parallel) pseudo-bonding operations sequentially against groups of indices, differing by at least one, and containing at most $(m_i - 1)$ elements can proceed in canonical products with different weighting coefficients.

The characters appear in different columns. In addition, they may be in columns with a corresponding coefficient $(w_n, w_{n-1}, w_{n-2}, \ldots, w_1)$. Therefore, the columns with $(w_1, \ldots, w_n)$ weighting coefficients introduce position numbers p_i, with $i = 1, \ldots, n$, which is useful for calculating the quality of the minimization in further stages.

Definitions of 'pure' and 'impure' gluing are introduced for gluing operations of individual partial multi-valued logical functions with weighted coefficients.

Definition 1. *The pure gluing operation is the gluing of multi-valued canonical elementary products according to the Quine–McCluskey algorithm with the same weighting factor w_i.*

A pure gluing operation is a transformation of:

$$w_i A j_0(x_r) + \ldots + w_i A j_{m_r - 1}(x_r) = w_i A, \tag{43}$$

where $r = 1, \ldots, n$ and A represents a partial product of which the variables of the individual literals belong to a set of $\{x_1, \ldots, x_{r-i}, x_{r+i}, \ldots, x_n\}$. In n m-value variables, the weighting factor before the partial canonical product takes values in the interval $w_1, \ldots, w_n$, with $w_j = w_{j-1} + w_{j-2} + \ldots + w_1$ and $j = 2, \ldots, n$.

Definition 2. *The gluing operation according to the Quine–McCluskey algorithm of multi-valued canonical elementary products with different values of weight coefficients $(w_1, \ldots, w_n)$ is impure gluing.*

The impure gluing operation for multi-valued canonical elementary products is performed with respect to the weighting factor with the smallest value, i.e., $min\{w_1, \ldots, w_n\}$.

An impure bonding operation is a transformation:

$$\begin{aligned} & w_o A j_o(x_r) + \ldots + w_{m_r-1} A j_{m_r-1}(x_r) \\ & = (\min\{w_o, \ldots, w_{m_r-1}\}) \cdot A + \sum_{s=i_o,\ldots,i_{m_r-2}} w_s \cdot A \cdot j_s(x_r) \end{aligned} \tag{44}$$

where $r = 1, \ldots, n$, $w_s > min\{w_1, \ldots, w_{m_r-1}\}$, and A denotes a partial product of which the variables of the individual literals belong to a set of $\{x_1, \ldots, x_{r-i}, x_{r+1}, \ldots, x_n\}$. In $n(m_1, \ldots, m_n)$-value variables, the weighting factor w_i before the partial canonical product takes values in the interval $w_1, \ldots, w_n$, with w_1 where $j = 2, \ldots, n$.

Definition 3. *An incomplete gluing operation is a transformation that retains the original records to be glued after the algorithm has been executed in the result.*

Given that there is an isomorphic interpretation of logical transformations, the Quine–McCluskey algorithm for minimizing individual partial multi-valued logical functions can be considered with the weighting factors mentioned, which is important for describing the rank validity of design guidelines.

Example 3 with weighting factors. *In a partial logical function*$f(x_1, x_2, x_3)$*, written numerically in KAPN: 010, 100, 002, 011, 110, 012 and 112, the Quine–McCluskey algorithm for minimizing logical functions with multi-valued weight coefficients yields one MZAPN which has 11 literals of* $f(x_1, x_2, x_3)$*, i.e.,*

$$\begin{aligned} & f(x_1, x_3, x_2) = j_0(x_1)(1j_0(x_3)j_1(x_2)) + 2j_1(x_3)2j_1(x_2) + 2j_2(x_3)) \\ & + j_1(x_1)(1j_2(x_3)j_1(x_2)) + 2j_0(x_3)j_1(x_2)) \end{aligned} \tag{45}$$

while other ZAPN$f(x_1, x_2, x_3)$*,*$f(x_2, x_1, x_3)$*,*$f(x_2, x_3, x_1)$*and*$f(x_3, x_1, x_2)$*of a given logical function have 12 and*$f(x_3, x_2, x_1)$*13 literals, respectively.*

$$\begin{aligned} & f(x_2, x_3, x_1) = j_0(x_2)(1j_0(x_3)j_1(x_1) + 2j_2(x_3)j_0(x_1)) \\ & + j_1(x_2)(2j_0(x_3)j_1(x_1) + 2j_1(x_3)j_0(x_1) + 2j_1(x_3)j_0(x_1)) \end{aligned} \tag{46}$$

$$\begin{aligned} & f(x_2, x_1, x_3) = j_0(x_2)(2j_0(x_1)j_2(x_3) + 1j_1(x_1)j_0(x_3)) \\ & + j_1(x_2)(2j_0(x_1)(j_1(x_3) + j_2(x_3)) + j_1(x_1)(2j_0(x_3) + 1j_2(x_3))) \end{aligned} \tag{47}$$

$$\begin{aligned} & f(x_1, x_2, x_3) = j_0(x_1)(2j_0(x_2)j_2(x_3) + 2j_1(x_2)(j_1(x_3) + j_2(x_3))) \\ & + j_1(x_1)(1j_0(x_2)j_0(x_3) + j_1(x_2)(2j_0(x_3) + 1j_2(x_3))) \end{aligned} \tag{48}$$

$$\begin{aligned} & f(x_3, x_1, x_2) = j_0(x_3)(1j_0(x_1)j_1(x_2) + 2j_1(x_1)j_1(x_2)) \\ & + 2j_1(x_3)j_0(x_1)j_1(x_2) + j_2(x_3)(2j_0(x_1) + 1j_1(x_1)j_1(x_2)) \end{aligned} \tag{49}$$

$$\begin{aligned} & f(x_3, x_2, x_1) = j_0(x_3)(1j_0(x_2)j_1(x_1) + 2j_1(x_2)j_1(x_1)) \\ & + 2j_1(x_3)j_1(x_2)j_0(x_1) + j_2(x_3)(2j_0(x_2)j_0(x_1) + 2j_1(x_2)j_0(x_1)). \end{aligned} \tag{50}$$

The following are the successive steps in the minimisation of logical functions due to given decision variables:

			v												
w_i	x_1	x_2	x_3	$w_i = 2$						$w_i = 1$					
1	0	1	0							V					
1	1	0	0									$\underline{V}$			
2	0	0	2				$\underline{V}$								
2	0	1	1	$\underline{V}$						V					
2	1	1	0		$\underline{V}$										
2	0	1	2	$\underline{V}$						V					
1	1	1	2								$\underline{V}$				
		p_i		1	2	3	4	5	6	1	2	3	4	5	6

		v													
w_i	x_1	x_2	x_3	$w_i = 2$						$w_i = 1$					
1	0	1	0									$\underline{V}$			
1	1	0	0							V					
2	0	0	2		V										
2	0	1	1				$\underline{V}$								
2	1	1	0	$\underline{V}$						V					
2	0	1	2		V										
1	1	1	2											$\underline{V}$	
		p_i		1	2	3	4	5	6	1	2	3	4	5	6

	v														
w_i	x_1	x_2	x_3	$w_i = 2$						$w_i = 1$					
1	0	1	0								V				
1	1	0	0									V			
2	0	0	2				V								
2	0	1	1					V							
2	1	1	0		V						V				
2	0	1	2	V						V					
1	1	1	2							V					
		p_i		1	2	3	4	5	6	1	2	3	4	5	6

			V												
	w_i	x_2	x_3	$w_i = 2$						$w_i = 1$					
2(012)	1-	1	2							$\underline{V}$					
2(110)	1-	1	0							$\underline{V}$					
	2	1	1	$\underline{V}$											
	2	0	2		$\underline{V}$										
	2	0	0		$\underline{V}$										
		p_i		1	2	3	4	5	6	1	2	3	4	5	6

		V													
	w_i	x_2	x_3	$w_i = 2$						$w_i = 1$					
2(012)	1-	1	2							$\underline{V}$					
2(110)	1-	1	0								$\underline{V}$				
	2	1	1			$\underline{V}$									
	2	0	2	$\underline{V}$											
	2	0	0		$\underline{V}$										
		p_i		1	2	3	4	5	6	1	2	3	4	5	6

			V												
	w_i	x_1	x_3	$w_i = 2$						$w_i = 1$					
	1	0	0							$\underline{V}$					
2(110)	1-	1	0								$\underline{V}$				
	2-	0	2	$\underline{V}$											
	2	0	1	$\underline{V}$											
	1	1	2								$\underline{V}$				
		p_i		1	2	3	4	5	6	1	2	3	4	5	6

		V													
	w_i	x_1	x_3	$w_i = 2$						$w_i = 1$					
	1	0	0							$\underline{V}$					
2(110)	1-	1	0							$\underline{V}$					
	2-	0	2			$\underline{V}$									
	2	0	1		$\underline{V}$										
	1	1	2									$\underline{V}$			
		p_i		1	2	3	4	5	6	1	2	3	4	5	6

Tree interpretation.

Figure 7 shows the MZAPN of the multi-valued logical function from Example 3.

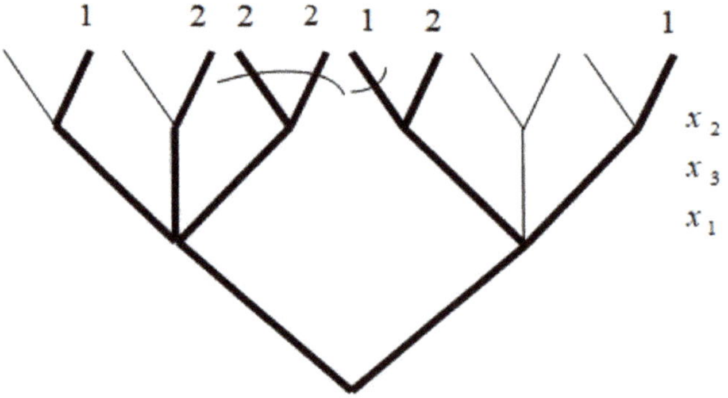

Figure 7. MZAPN logic tree of the multivalued logic function $f(x_1, x_3, x_2)$ from Example 3.

The proposed methodology can be described by the flow chart shown in Figure 8.

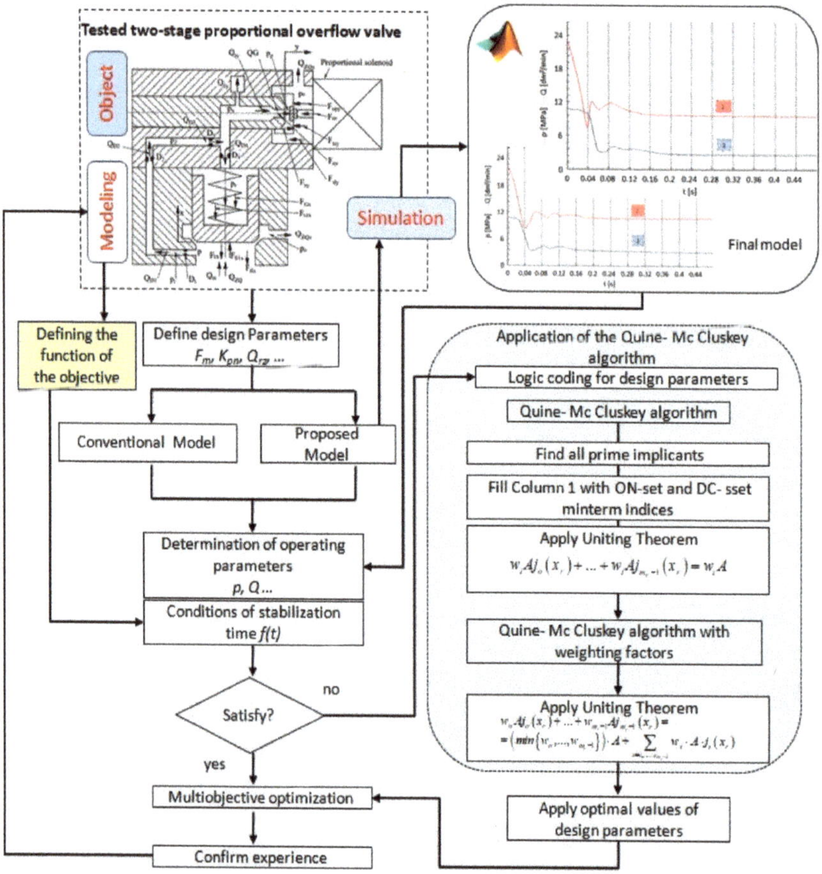

Figure 8. Flow chart of the proposed method (with example runs for the weighting factor $w_i = 2$).

The structuring of the described problem takes into account the methodology of multi-valued logical trees, allowing for the introduction of appropriate formal notations and even making it possible to combine complex quantitative and qualitative features with different degrees of detail according to the principles of a multidimensional morphological array. Therefore, there is no need to extend the generation process to sub-arrays when using a multidimensional morphological array as all information about the varieties of the main and detailed features and their numerous modifications can be immediately stored in this array and marked on the variant tree.

In addition, the morphological and decision tables can be encoded analytically and numerically according to the definitions and theorems of the logic of multi-valued decision processes. This enables a variant way of identifying and classifying information in computer science terms when seeking and modifying solutions in the design process.

In such a situation it is possible to introduce CAD, e.g., for the generation of all theoretical variants of the designed system, selection for realizability, search for realizable solutions and—most importantly—realizable sub-solutions, etc. In order to ensure the stable operation of the actual system, model tests are carried out on the basis of which of the relevant parameters are selected. The phenomena occurring during the flow of a medium are quite often not precisely defined, so it is necessary to identify an analytical model when carrying out such studies.

4. Application of the Methodology of Multi-Valued Logic Trees with Weighting Factors in the Optimization of a Proportional Valve

Tests have already been carried out for valves of the direct-acting UPZ type [4], which are designed to regulate the upstream pressure of steam and non-flammable, chemically inert gases and liquids regardless of the pressure at their outlet. Multivalent weighting factors were not considered in the tested valve class. For this reason, it was decided that an improved Quine–McCluskey algorithm with weighting factors for the hydraulic proportional valve would be used. Therefore, three 'novelties' are presented in this paper.

One of the optimal methods presented are multi-valued logic algorithms. For example, in [24] the authors presented a description of the dynamics of molecular states caused by a sequence of laser pulses using multi-valued logic. In turn, the authors of [25] used multi-valued logical schemes to calculate significance measures based on incompletely-defined data. This method is based on the definition of a mathematical model of an analyzed system in the form of a structure function that determines the correlation of the system reliability and the states of its components.

In [27], the authors described the historical and technical background of MVL, as well as the areas of present and future applications of quadrivalent logic. It was also intended to serve as a guide for non-specialists. The wide application of multi-valued logic in particular in these microelectronic circuits is presented in [28]. Additionally, there are many original works describing the practical application of multi-valued logic trees.

In addition, there are other works in which multi-valued decision trees and logic algorithms have been applied. For example, the authors of [29] presented the applications of machine learning and classification and regression trees (CART) in medicine. Specifically, they presented the concept of a gradient-boosting algorithm. The authors of [30] presented the application of a rotation forest with decision trees as a base classifier and a new ensemble model in the spatial modeling of groundwater potential. The use of fault-tree analysis to calculate system-failure probability bounds from qualitative data in an intuitive, fuzzy environment is presented in paper [31]. Meanwhile, in paper [32] the authors adopted component fault trees (CFTs) to support fault tree analysis, failure mode, and effect analysis as extensions of SysML models. Boolean decision support methods were presented in paper [33]. A very modern optimization method was proposed by the authors of [34]: the use of root trees. The root-tree algorithm was used for high-order sliding mode control using a super-twist algorithm based on the DTC scheme for DFIG.

The initial conditions of a differential equation can be determined by entering $\frac{dx_i}{dt} = 0$. The simulations were performed using the Matlab/Simulink package:

$$\begin{cases} -801.2102 \cdot 10^{-3}(k_{vx}x_1)x_3 - 147224.3x_1 - 1925.135 + 5.3792244 \cdot 10^{-3}\left[(1 - 10^3x_1)x_3 - x_6\right] = 0, \\ 0.2851216 \cdot 10^9(1 - 1.32 \cdot 10^{-9}x_3) - 0.5279061 \cdot 10^9(k_{vx}x_1)\sqrt{x_3} - 7.65(x_3 - x_6) - 0.3227777 \cdot 10^{12}Q_{odb} = 0, \\ 0.7123874 \cdot 10^{-4}x_7 + 418.87733(k_{vy}x_4)^2x_7 - 33.33333F_m = 0, \\ 0.276556 \cdot 10^5(x_3 - x_6) - 0.312234 \cdot 10^{12}(k_{vy}x_4)\sqrt{x_6} = 0, \\ x_7 = x_6 - 0.2025169 \cdot 10^6(k_{vy}x_4)\sqrt{x_6}. \end{cases} \tag{51}$$

Assuming that:

$$U_z = U_p = 1\ V. \tag{52}$$

It can be obtained that:

$$\begin{aligned} U_z &= U_p = 1\ V, \\ Q_{odb} &= 12/6 \cdot 10^{-4}\left[\frac{m^3}{s}\right]. \end{aligned} \tag{53}$$

The Importance of the Design and/or Operational Parameters of a Hydraulic Proportional Valve

In the optimization process, the changed parameters of the proportional valve while observing the Q flow rate and p pressure are represented by the regulator $K_{p1} \cdot K_{p2}$ gain (as a complex variable), the Q_{obd} receiver flow rate (depending on the impulse input of the U_z control voltage), and the F_m magnetic force.

The arithmetic values of the tested parameters were selected for the analysis. They were coded by the authors of this work with logical decision variables:

$$\begin{aligned} &(K_{p1} \cdot K_{p2}) = 30 \sim 0; \\ &(K_{p1} \cdot K_{p2}) = 40 \sim 1; \\ &(K_{p1} \cdot K_{p2}) = 50 \sim 2; \\ &(K_{p1} \cdot K_{p2}) = 60 \sim 3; \\ &F_m = 1.96[\text{N}] \sim 0; \\ &F_m = 2.96[\text{N}] \sim 1; \\ &F_m = 3.96[\text{N}] \sim 2; \\ &F_m = 4.96[\text{N}] \sim 3; \\ &Q_{rz} = 36 \to 24\left[\text{dm}^3/\text{min}\right] \sim 0; \\ &Q_{rz} = 24 \to 12\left[\text{dm}^3/\text{min}\right] \sim 1; \\ &Q_{rz} = 36 \to 12\left[\text{dm}^3/\text{min}\right] \sim 2; \end{aligned} \tag{54}$$

In the operation of the relief valve, the authors introduced restrictions on the Q and p design parameters in terms of the stabilization time t_w:t_w < 0.48 t_0. Subsequently, dynamic calculations of the valve were carried out, resulting in the t_w:t_w < 0.48 t_0 limitation. Following the dynamic calculations, 23 charts were selected. The code changes of the K_{p1}, K_{p2}, Q_{rz} and F_m design parameters are presented in Table 1.

Furthermore, in the code changes of the $K_{p1} \cdot K_{p2}$, Q_{rz} and F_m design parameters multi-valued w_i weighting factors are introduced, similar to the relief valve. The greater the weighting number, the faster the Q and p functions reach a stable state ($t_t > t_j$).

The following weighting factors were adopted in the $t_w < 0.48\ t_0$ limitation:

- $w_i = 3$, $t_w \leq 0.16\ t_0$;
- $w_i = 2$, $0.16\ t_0 < t_w \leq 0.32\ t_0$;
- $w_i = 1$, $0.32\ t_0 < t_w \leq 0.48\ t_0$.

Table 1 presents the code changes of the $K_{p1} \cdot K_{p2}$, Q_{rz} and F_m design parameters, taking into account the multi-valued weighting factors and the $t_w < 0.48\ t_0$ limitation.

Notably, the value of the weighting factor for changes in the code $K_{p1} \cdot K_{p2}$, Q_{rz} and F_m design parameters in Table 1 is minimal among the coefficients defined separately in the Q and p function. If one of the functions stabilizes faster than the other, then the canonical product for the same code changes of $K_{p1} \cdot K_{p2}$, Q_{rz} and F_m parameters should be assigned a smaller weighting factor.

Table 1. KAPN for the K_{p1}, K_{p2}, Q_{rz} and F_m parameter code data, taking into account the w_i weighting factors.

w_i	F_m	K_{p1}, K_{p2}	Q_{rz}
2	2	1	2
2	2	3	2
2	2	2	1
2	2	2	2
2	1	2	1
3	3	0	2
1	1	0	2
2	0	2	1
1	0	2	2
2	0	2	0
3	0	3	1
2	0	3	2
3	0	1	1
1	0	1	2
3	0	1	0
2	0	0	1
1	0	0	2
1	1	2	2
2	1	1	2
1	1	3	2
1	3	2	2
1	3	1	2
3	3	3	2

In the system of multi-valued logic functions with weighting factors, weighting factors are assigned separately for each of the functions.

Figures 9–13 show the time periods of the Q and p functions with the weighting factor intervals marked w_i:p (red color) and Q (blue color).

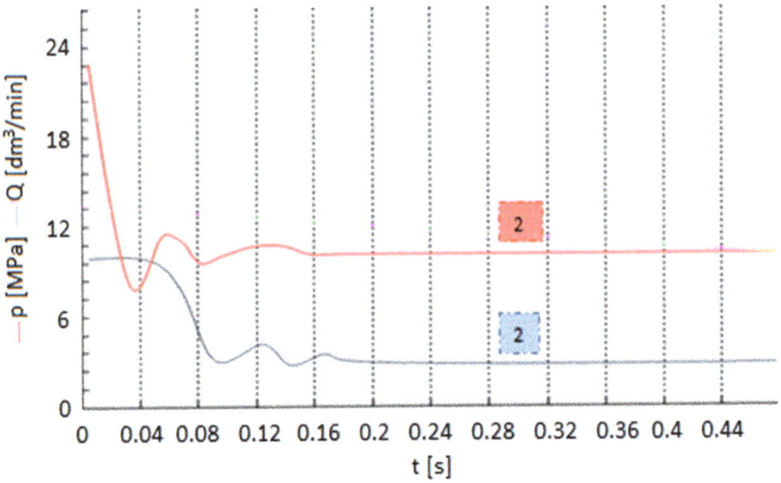

(a)

Figure 9. *Cont.*

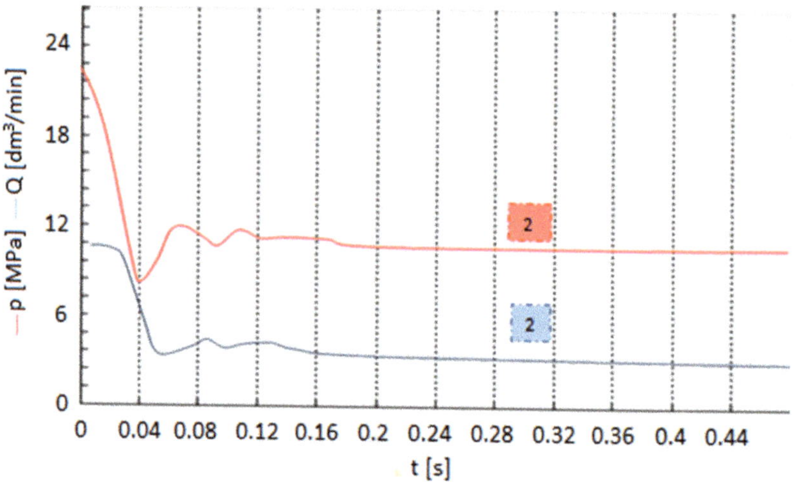

(**b**)

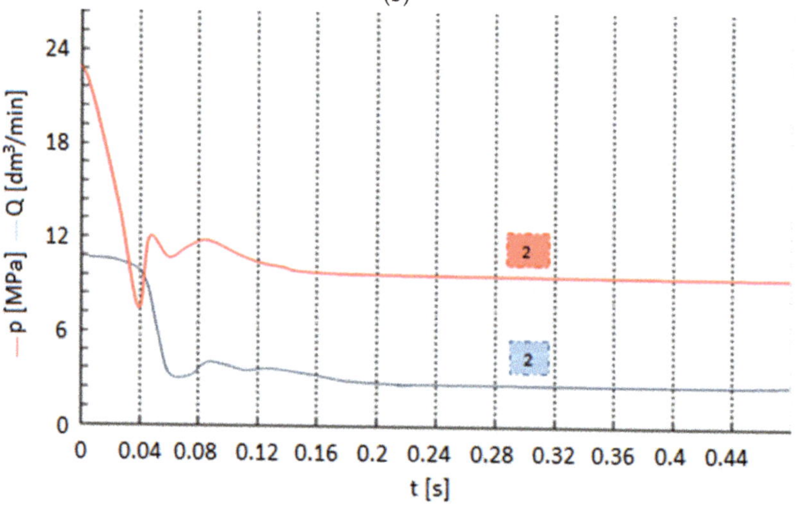

(**c**)

Figure 9. The Q and p time periods for code changes of the $K_{p1} \cdot K_{p2}$, Q_{rz} and F_m parameters where Q_{rz}: (**a**) 2(212), (**b**) 2(211) and (**c**) 2(210). Runs for a weighting factor value of $w_i = 2$.

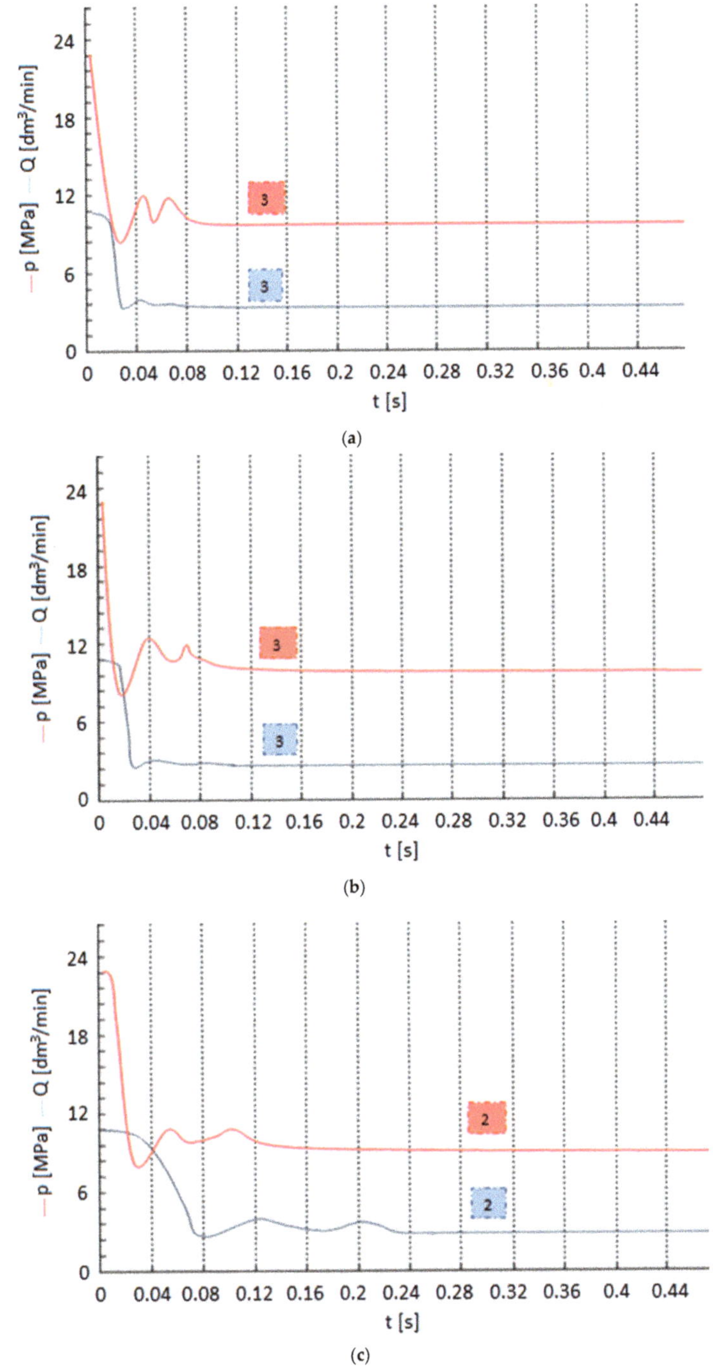

Figure 10. The Q and p time periods for code changes of the $K_{p1} \cdot K_{p2}$, Q_{rz} and F_m parameters where Q_{rz}: (**a**) 3(310), (**b**) 3(110) and (**c**) 2(010). Runs for a weighting factor value of w_i = 3—(**a**,**b**) and w_i = 2 for (**a**).

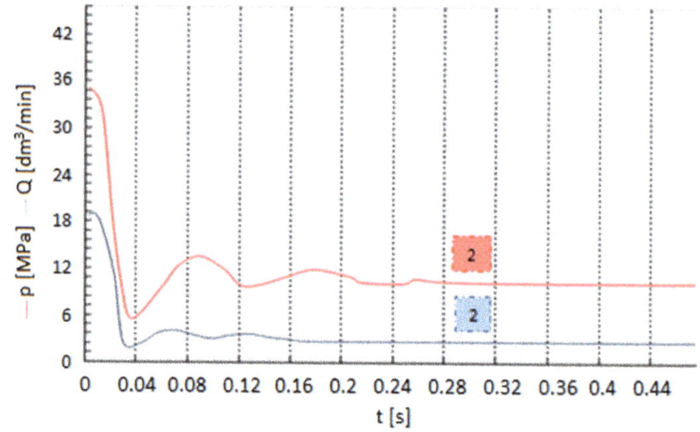

(**a**)

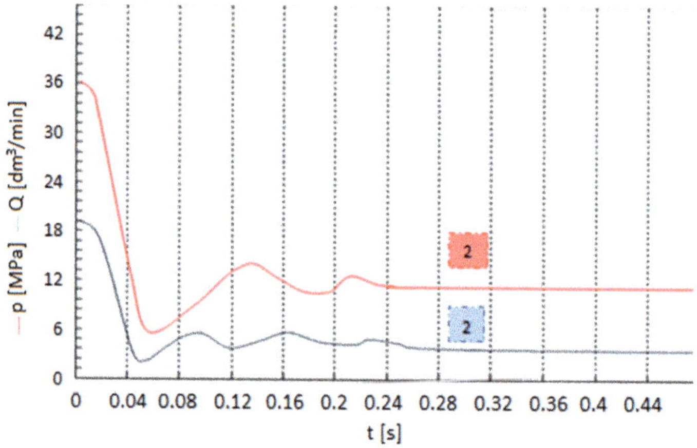

(**b**)

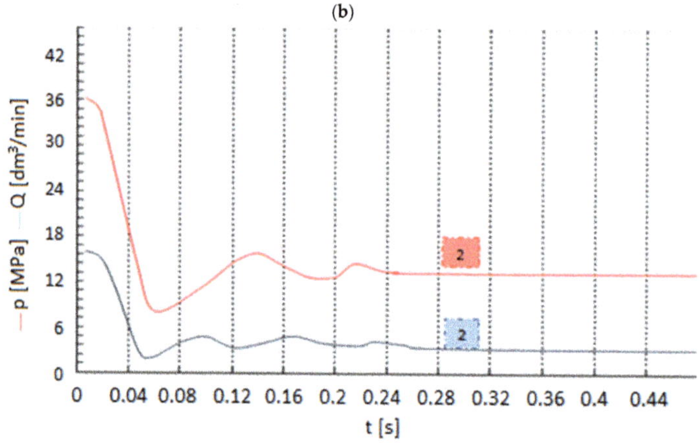

(**c**)

Figure 11. The Q and p time periods for code changes of the $K_{p1} \cdot K_{p2}$, Q_{rz}, F_m parameters, Q_{rz}: (**a**) 2(122), (**b**) 2(322), (**c**) 2(222). Runs for a weighting factor value of $w_i = 2$.

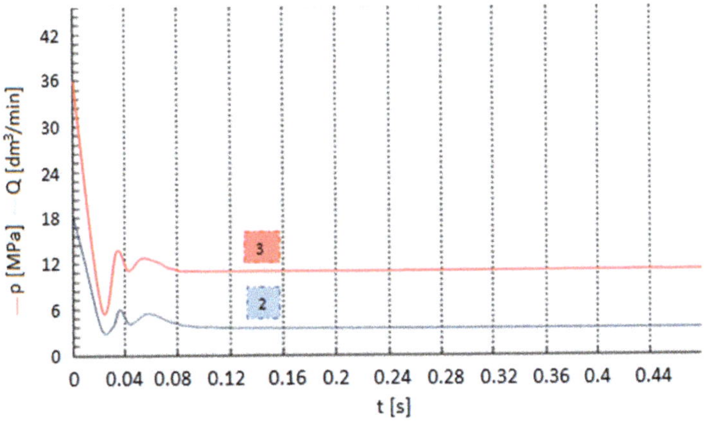

(a)

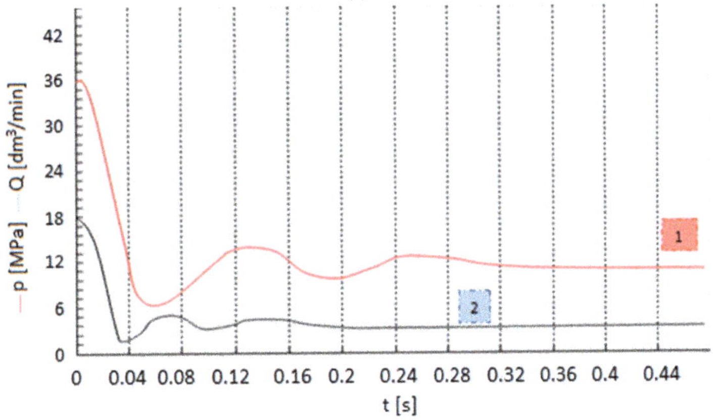

(b)

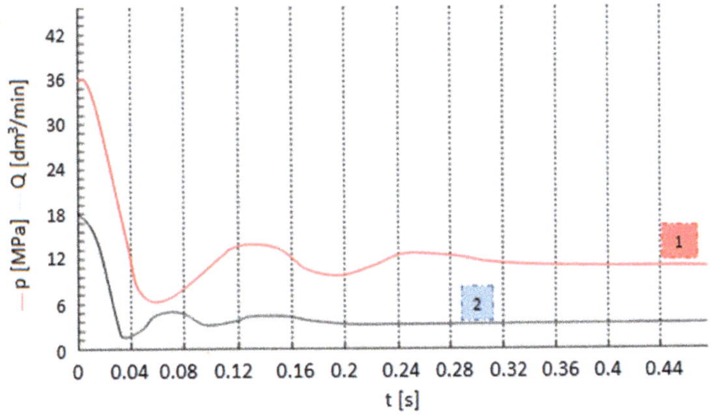

(c)

Figure 12. The Q and p time periods for code changes of the $K_{p1} \cdot K_{p2}$, Q_{rz} and F_m parameters where Q_{rz}: (**a**) 3(023), (**b**) 1(021) and (**c**) 1(220). Runs for a weighting factor value of $w_i = 3$ for (**a**) and $w_i = 1$ for (**b**,**c**).

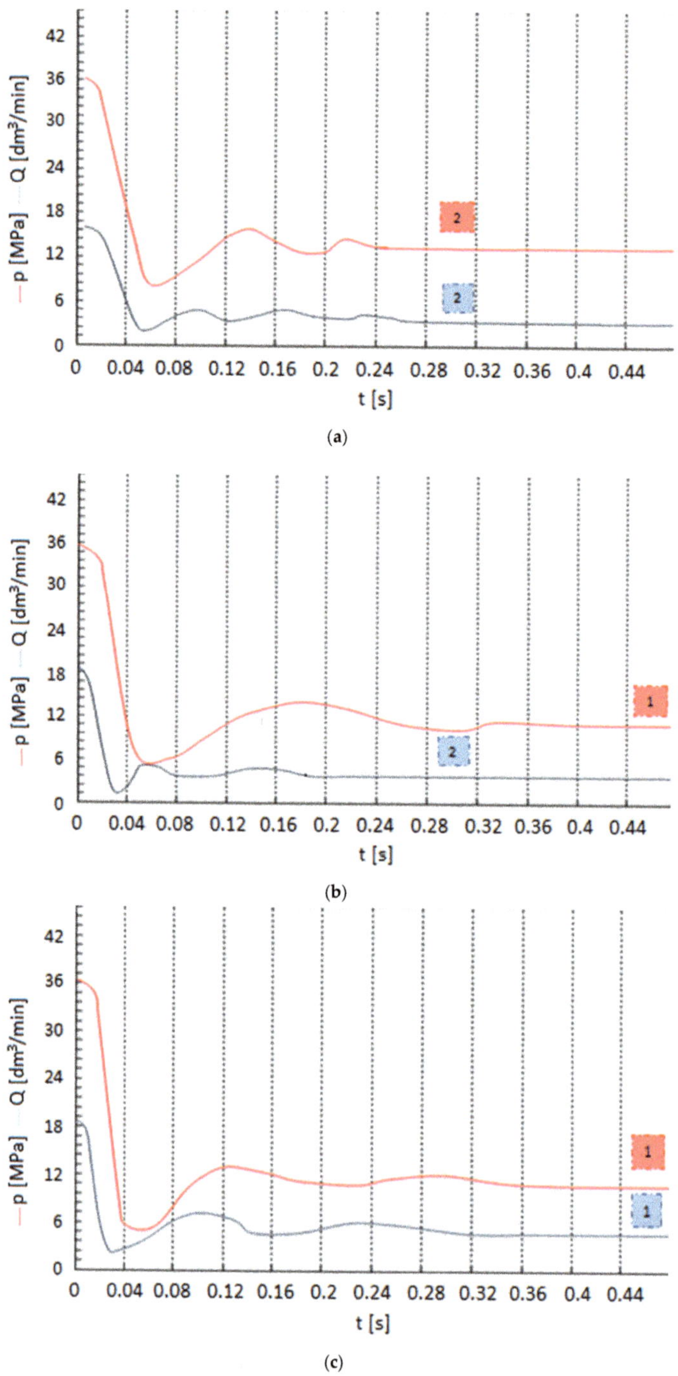

Figure 13. The Q and p time periods for code changes of the $K_{p1} \cdot K_{p2}$, Q_{rz} and F_m parameters where Q_{rz}: (**a**) 2(320), (**b**) 1(120) and (**c**) 1(020). Runs for a weighting factor value of $w_{\text{i}} = 2$ for (**a**) and $w_{\text{i}} = 1$ for (**b**,**c**).

The multi-valued logical trees with the weighting factors from Table 1 are shown in Figure 14.

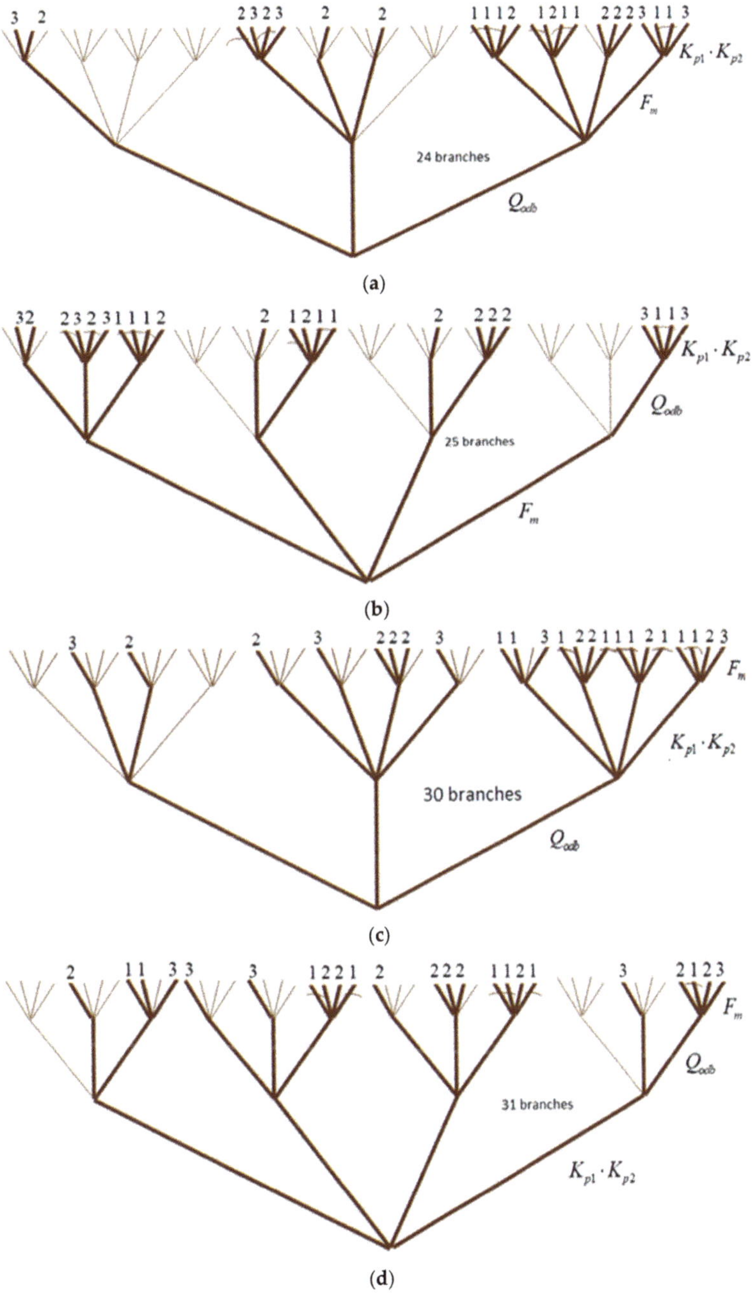

Figure 14. Multi-valued logical tree of the $K_{p1} \cdot K_{p2}$, Q_{rz} and F_m parameters with (**a**) 24 branches, (**b**) 25 branches, (**c**) 30 branches, and (**d**) 31 branches. 1, 2, 3—The values of the weighting factors w_i.

For the $t_w < 0.48\ t_0$ criterion of limitation, one optimal multi-valued logical tree is presented in Figure 14. For a hydraulic proportional valve, the most crucial parameter is the Q_{odb} flow rate of the receiver (depending on the U_z step function of the control voltage).

One of the issues presented in this paper is the application of Boolean equations in the optimization of machine systems. This paper generalizes the Quine–McCluskey algorithm for minimizing multi-valued logical functions with multi-valued weight coefficients. In addition, a procedure for the combinatorial solution of weighted multi-valued systems of logical equations describing design guidelines in terms of morphological analysis with the Rosser–Turguette axioms is discussed.

The application of the methodology of multi-valued logic trees with weighting coefficients for relief valves allows for the determination of alternative sets of design guidelines to find the most crucial design guidelines in any fixed design and/or operational parameters while ensuring that the constraints and extremes of the criterion are met. In particular, the novelty presented in this paper is:

- the development of a Quine–McCluskey algorithm for minimizing logical functions with weighted coefficients;
- the development of algorithms for multi-valued Boolean equations, allowing for the obtainment of the most important design guidelines in the process of optimization of machine systems; and
- carrying out calculations on a real object (relief valve) to confirm the developed algorithms.

5. Conclusions

This paper presents the use of multi-valued logical trees with weighting factors to determine the importance of the constructional and operational parameters of a two-stage proportional relief valve. As has been demonstrated by this research, relief valves do not keep up with a pressure increase in the system, react with a certain delay, and can vibrate under fixed operating conditions.

The above incorrect response of the valves usually occurs during the transition period. Hence, it is necessary to carry out model tests of valves in the transition state and to determine the importance of the operational parameters directly affecting their dynamics. Model tests aim to select essential parameters to ensure the stability of the real system. It is crucial to determine the importance of design and/or operational parameters during the model verification and subsequently select the appropriate optimization procedure.

This work discusses the procedure of a combinatorial solution for weight–multi-valued systems of logic equations describing the design guidelines in terms of morphological analysis with the preservation of Rosser–Turguette axioms. It has been shown that, in general, the minimization of logic functions with weight coefficients may be the same as without weight coefficients. However, a better reflection of the physical models of hydraulic relief systems was obtained through mathematical models. The literature shows that various coefficients of logical products have not been taken into account in the separable and common minimization of systems of multi-valued logic equations.

Three following '**novelties**' are presented in this paper:

1. The Quine–McCluskey algorithm was applied to completely new proportional valves previously not tested using such methods;
2. Multivariate weighting factors were taken into account, which allowed for the introduction of multi-valued weighting factors to determine the most important design guidelines. This made it possible to apply the method of multi-valued decision trees to solve the technological problems of the studied proportional valve series. It also made it possible to use systems of logical equations as a formal decision-making description of the study of the importance rank of changes in design and operating parameters as a method for optimizing relief valves and other hydraulic systems;
3. For the optimization process of hydraulic valve design, an approach using CFD computer simulation methods is encountered. However, any results obtained from

simulation solutions should be, at least to some extent, verified by reliable experimental studies.

Limits of the Methodology Used

Each of the KAPN products should be assigned corresponding discrete changes in parameter values. Therefore, it is not possible to fully apply the developed methods in continuous linear and non-linear optimisation. However, for construction/engineering purposes, the use of discrete analysis is preferable in the opinion of the authors (who have computational experience). If one were to change the numerical values of the input variables in a mathematical model, one would obtain changes in the values of the output variables. In order to obtain a different planned behaviour of a system (component), one can often make many changes to the numerical values of the input variables. Concerns related to change include: which values might be changed, how the change might be made (by increasing values, keeping them unchanged, or decreasing them), or in what order the variables might be changed, etc. Such conjecturing is akin to subjectively (according to a given designer) changing the numerical values in a mathematical model. This means that another designer, according to their own experience, may subjectively redesign the layout (element) quite differently for new work conditions that are identical to those of the previous designer.

The multi-valued weighting system of logical equations describing the design guidelines can be minimized separately or together with logical equivalence. Still, even in the bivalent (Boolean) case, the common minimization is not inferior to the separate minimization in terms of literal multiplicity. Increasing, reducing, or keeping the numerical values unchanged in the process of redesigning a system for other operating conditions can be coded using multi-valued logic while sets of design guidelines can be presented as sums of multi-valued logical products.

Model tests are particularly important in the design of new valves. These design parameters, which significantly affect the dynamics of valves, cannot be selected randomly (depending on the assumptions and experience of the designer). Their values should be closely related to the permissible peak overload of the controlled signal, operation speed, time constant, and eliminating vibration. Model tests will be more useful if the described valve is outlined more accurately in the transition state. Thus, building a correct analytical equation that presents a given valve in a dynamic course determines the sense of any theoretical considerations.

In further research, it will also be necessary to take into account the modified methodology of multi-valued logic trees as parametrically-playing out graphs, i.e., a heuristic simulation method for solving linear–dynamic decision models for relief valves. In the instance analyzed, a number of simplifications were additionally taken into account; for example, the impact of the closing element hitting the valve seat was not considered and the effect of the valve-wall compressibility was not taken into account. These factors will be considered in further papers. Additionally, a new control system using optimised proportional–directional control valves, throttling valves, and flow controllers will be proposed in further studies.

Author Contributions: Conceptualization, A.D., M.K. and K.U.; methodology, A.D. and K.U.; software, A.D. and P.S.; validation, A.D., M.K. and K.U.; formal analysis, A.D., R.C., M.S., M.K., K.U. and P.S.; investigation, A.D., M.S., M.K., K.U. and A.M.D.; resources, M.K. and A.M.D.; data curation, A.D., R.C., M.S., M.K., K.U. and P.S.; writing—original draft preparation, A.D., R.C., M.S., M.K., K.U. and P.S.; writing—review and editing, A.D., R.C., M.S., M.K., K.U. and A.M.D.; visualization, A.D., R.C., M.S., M.K. and K.U.; supervision, A.D. and M.K.; project administration, P.S.; funding acquisition, A.D., M.S., M.K. and K.U. All authors have read and agreed to the published version of the manuscript.

Funding: This research received no external funding.

Data Availability Statement: Not applicable.

Conflicts of Interest: The authors declare no conflict of interest.

Nomenclature

MZAPN	minimal complex alternative normal form;
ZKAPN	complex canonical alternative normal form;
$f(x_1, x_2, x_3)$	multi-valued logic function of three variables;
w_i	weighting factor for multi-valued logical products;
A	partial elementary product;
k_{vx}, k_{vy}	loss factors in the control stage of a hydraulic proportional valve;
F_m	electromagnetic force;
p	operating pressure;
Q_p	actual pump capacity;
Q_{D1}, Q_{D2}, Q_{D3}	flow rate through the D_1, D_2 and D_3 nozzles in a proportional valve;
Q_{odb}	receiver flow rate in a proportional valve;
K_{p1} K_{p2}	regulator boost in a proportional valve;
Q_t	theoretical pump capacity (for a fixed hydraulic system);
Q_{zp}	flow rate through a relief valve;
R_{p0}	the resultant internal leakage resistance in a system;
R_{pp}	the leakage resistance of a pump determined by means of volumetric efficiency;
R_{pz}	the leakage resistance of a relief valve determined by means of the slope of the valve static characteristic for pressures below the opening pressure;
R_r	the leakage resistance of a distributor;
R_s	the leakage resistance of a motor determined by means of volumetric efficiency.

Appendix A The Output Equations for the Computer Simulation of the Operation of the Hydraulic Part and the Model

The output equations to simulate the operation of a hydraulic part are presented in the following form:

$$\begin{cases} 1: \frac{dx_1}{dt} = x_2, \\ 2: \frac{dx_2}{dt} = -14846.301x_2 - 801.2102 \cdot 10^{-3}(k_{vx}x_1)x_3 - 147224.3x_1 \\ -1925.135 + 5.3792244 \cdot 10^{-3}\left[(1 - 10^3 x_1)x_3 - x_6\right], \\ 3: \frac{dx_3}{dt} = 0.2851216 \cdot 10^9(1 - 1.32 \cdot 10^{-9}x_3) \\ -0.5279061 \cdot 10^9(k_{vx}x_1)\sqrt{x_3} - 0.1226361 \cdot 10^9 x_2 - 7.65(x_3 - x_6) \\ -0.3227777 \cdot 10^{12} Q_{odb}, \\ 4: \frac{dx_4}{dt} = x_5, \\ 5: \frac{dx_5}{dt} = -5.5688865 \cdot 10^3 x_5 - 0.840264 \cdot 10^6 x_5^2 \mathrm{sign} x_5 \\ +0.7123874 \cdot 10^{-4}x_7 + 418.87733(k_{vy}x_4)^2 x_7 \\ -2.616 \mathrm{sign} x_5 - 33.33333F_m, \\ 6: \frac{dx_6}{dt} = 0.276556 \cdot 10^5(x_3 - x_6) - 0.312234 \cdot 10^{12}(k_{vy}x_4)\sqrt{x_6} \\ +0.4432633 \cdot 10^{12}x_3 - 2.060625 \cdot 10^9 x_5, \\ 7: x_7 = x_6 - 0.2025169 \cdot 10^6(k_{vy}x_4)\sqrt{x_6} - 1328.096x_5. \end{cases} \tag{A1}$$

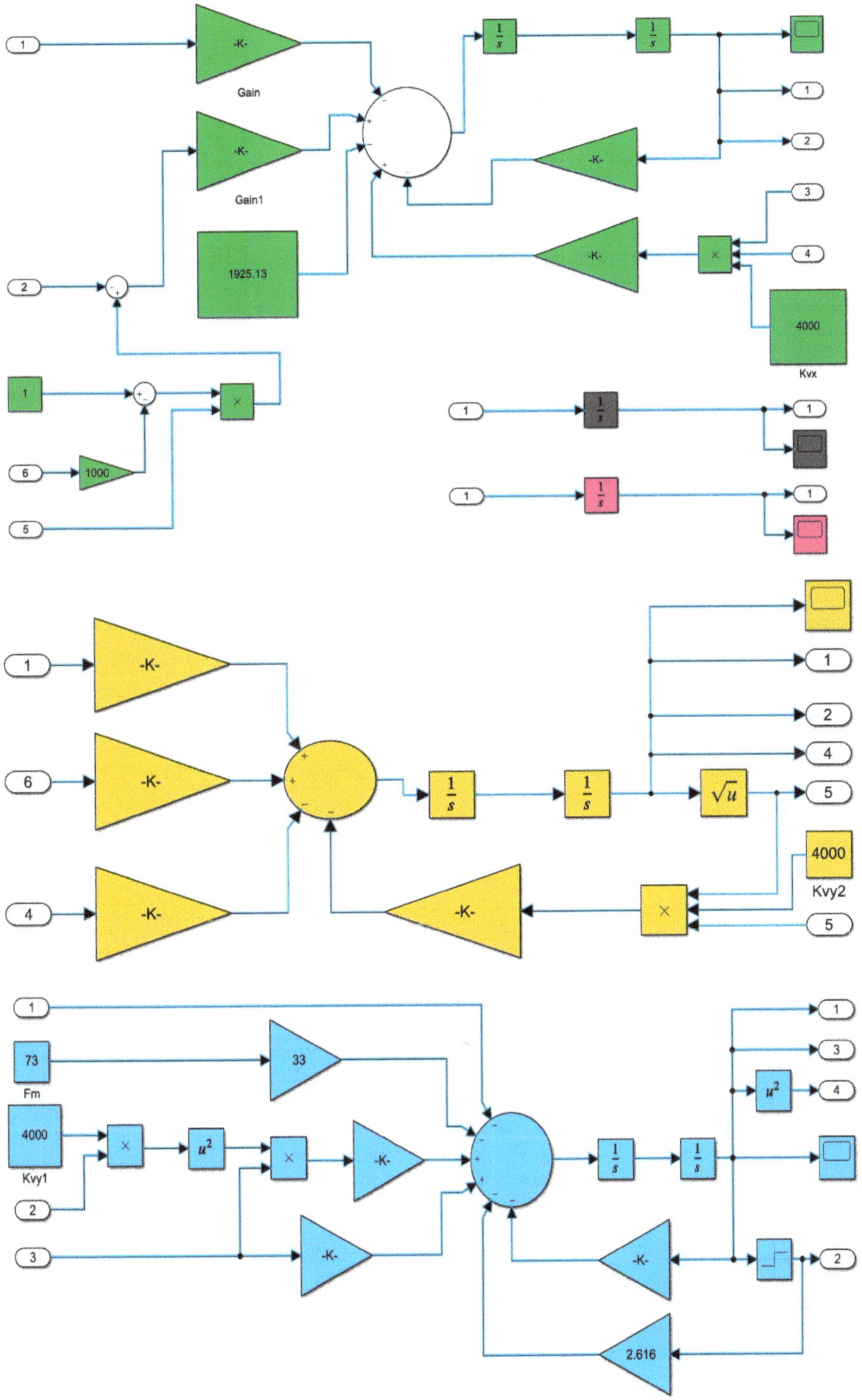

Figure A1. Model in Matlab. 1-6 describes inputs and outputs.

References

1. Bury, P.; Stosiak, M.; Urbanowicz, K.; Kodura, A.; Kubrak, M.; Malesińska, A. A Case Study of Open- and Closed-Loop Control of Hydrostatic Transmission with Proportional Valve Start-Up Process. *Energies* **2022**, *15*, 1860. [CrossRef]
2. Lin, T.; Chen, Q.; Ren, H.; Miao, C.; Chen, Q.; Fu, S. Influence of the Energy Regeneration Unit on Pressure Characteristics for a Proportional Relief Valve. *Proc. Inst. Mech. Eng. Part I J. Syst. Control. Eng.* **2017**, *231*, 189–198. [CrossRef]
3. Owczarek, P.; Rybarczyk, D.; Kubacki, A. Dynamic Model and Simulation of Electro-Hydraulic Proportional Valve. In *Automation 2017*; Szewczyk, R., Zieliński, C., Kaliczyńska, M., Eds.; Advances in Intelligent Systems and Computing; Springer International Publishing: Cham, Switzerland, 2017; Volume 550, pp. 99–107. ISBN 978-3-319-54041-2.
4. Han, M.; Liu, Y.; Liao, Y.; Wang, S. Investigation on the Modeling and Dynamic Characteristics of a Novel Hydraulic Proportional Valve Driven by a Voice Coil Motor. *SV-JME* **2021**, *67*, 223–234. [CrossRef]
5. Xie, H.; Liu, J.; Hu, L.; Yang, H.; Fu, X. Design of Pilot-Assisted Load Control Valve for Proportional Flow Control and Fast Opening Performance Based on Dynamics Modeling. *Sens. Actuators A Phys.* **2015**, *235*, 95–104. [CrossRef]
6. Kumar, S.; Tewari, V.K.; Bharti, C.K.; Ranjan, A. Modeling, Simulation and Experimental Validation of Flow Rate of Electro-Hydraulic Hitch Control Valve of Agricultural Tractor. *Flow Meas. Instrum.* **2021**, *82*, 102070. [CrossRef]
7. Deptuła, A. Application of Multi-Valued Weighting Logical Functions in the Analysis of a Degree of Importance of Construction Parameters on the Example of Hydraulic Valves. *Int. J. Appl. Mech. Eng.* **2014**, *19*, 539–548. [CrossRef]
8. Jayamalini, K.; Ponnavaikko, M. Research on Web Data Mining Concepts, Techniques and Applications. In Proceedings of the 2017 International Conference on Algorithms, Methodology, Models and Applications in Emerging Technologies (ICAMMAET), Chennai, India, 16–18 February 2017; pp. 1–5.
9. Bandaru, S.; Ng, A.H.C.; Deb, K. Data Mining Methods for Knowledge Discovery in Multi-Objective Optimization: Part A—Survey. *Expert Syst. Appl.* **2017**, *70*, 139–159. [CrossRef]
10. Mendes, R.; Vilela, J.P. Privacy-Preserving Data Mining: Methods, Metrics, and Applications. *IEEE Access* **2017**, *5*, 10562–10582. [CrossRef]
11. Liang, H.; Xian, A.; Mao, M.; Ni, P.; Wu, H. A Research on Remote Fracturing Monitoring and Decision-Making Method Supporting Smart City. *Sustain. Cities Soc.* **2020**, *62*, 102414. [CrossRef]
12. Alhumaid, M.; Ghumman, A.; Haider, H.; Al-Salamah, I.; Ghazaw, Y. Sustainability Evaluation Framework of Urban Stormwater Drainage Options for Arid Environments Using Hydraulic Modeling and Multicriteria Decision-Making. *Water* **2018**, *10*, 581. [CrossRef]
13. Kanani-Sadat, Y.; Arabsheibani, R.; Karimipour, F.; Nasseri, M. A New Approach to Flood Susceptibility Assessment in Data-Scarce and Ungauged Regions Based on GIS-Based Hybrid Multi Criteria Decision-Making Method. *J. Hydrol.* **2019**, *572*, 17–31. [CrossRef]
14. Zhang, X.; Yu, X.; Yu, K. Application of the Multi-Level Fuzzy Decision-Making Method in the Social Evaluation of Hydraulic Engineering Construction Project. In Proceedings of the Third International Workshop on Advanced Computational Intelligence, Suzhou, China, 25–27 August 2010; pp. 213–217.
15. Meseguer, J.; Mirats-Tur, J.M.; Cembrano, G.; Puig, V.; Quevedo, J.; Pérez, R.; Sanz, G.; Ibarra, D. A Decision Support System for On-Line Leakage Localization. *Environ. Model. Softw.* **2014**, *60*, 331–345. [CrossRef]
16. Patryka, M.A. *Algorytm Quine'a-Mc Cluskeya Minimalizacji Indywidualnych Cząstkowych Wielowartościowych Funkcji Logicznych*; Studia i Monografie; Politechnika Opolska: Opole, Poland, 1999.
17. Partyka, M.A. *Algorytm Quine'a-Mc Cluskeya Minimalizacji Indywidualnych Cząstkowych Wielowartościowych Funkcji Logicznych/Marian A. Partyka.*; Studia i Monografie/[Politechnika Opolska], z. 109; Wyd. 2 rozsz.; Politechnika Opolska: Opole, Poland, 1999.
18. Deptuła, A. *Zastosowanie Graficznych Struktur Decyzyjnych w Metodologii Projektowania i Zarządzania*; Studia i Monografie/Politechnika Opolska; Politechnika Opolska: Opole, Poland, 2020; Volume 3, ISBN 429-6063.
19. Deptuła, A.; Stosiak, M.; Karpenko, M.; Łapka, M. The Concept of Dependency Game Tree Graphs as a Black Box in the Analysis of Automatic Transmissions. *Transp. Telecommun. J.* **2022**, *23*, 207–219. [CrossRef]
20. Deptuła, A. Application of Game Graphs to Describe the Inverse Problem in the Designing of Mechatronic Vibrating Systems. In *Graph-Based Modelling in Engineering*; Zawiślak, S., Rysiński, J., Eds.; Mechanisms and Machine Science; Springer International Publishing: Cham, Switzerland, 2017; Volume 42, pp. 189–199. ISBN 978-3-319-39018-5.
21. Prażnowski, K.; Bieniek, A.; Mamala, J.; Deptuła, A. The Use of Multicriteria Inference Method to Identify and Classify Selected Combustion Engine Malfunctions Based on Vehicle Structure Vibrations. *Sensors* **2021**, *21*, 2470. [CrossRef]
22. Deptuła, A.; Augustynowicz, A.; Stosiak, M.; Towarnicki, K.; Karpenko, M. The Concept of Using an Expert System and Multi-Valued Logic Trees to Assess the Energy Consumption of an Electric Car in Selected Driving Cycles. *Energies* **2022**, *15*, 4631. [CrossRef]
23. Tomasiak, E. *Analiza Dynamiki Układu z Proporcjonalnym Zaworem Przelewowym*; Silesian University of Technology Publishing House: Gliwice, Poland, 1989; Volume 94.
24. Fresch, B.; Klymenko, M.V.; Levine, R.D.; Remacle, F. Multivalued Logic at the Nanoscale. In *Computational Matter*; Stepney, S., Rasmussen, S., Amos, M., Eds.; Natural Computing Series; Springer International Publishing: Cham, Switzerland, 2018; pp. 295–318. ISBN 978-3-319-65824-7.
25. Sedlacek, P.; Rabcan, J.; Kostolny, J. Importance Analysis of Multi-State System Based on Incompletely Specified Data by Multi-Valued Decision Diagrams. In Proceedings of the 2019 International Conference on Information and Digital Technologies (IDT, Zilina, Slovakia, 25–27 June 2019; pp. 409–416.
26. Yinshui, L.; Xiaojun, R.; Defa, W.; Donglin, L.; Xiaohui, L. Simulation and Analysis of a Seawater Hydraulic Relief Valve in Deep-Sea Environment. *Ocean Eng.* **2016**, *125*, 182–190. [CrossRef]

27. Smith The Prospects for Multivalued Logic: A Technology and Applications View. *IEEE Trans. Comput.* **1981**, *C-30*, 619–634. [CrossRef]
28. Fitting, M.; Orlowska, E. *Beyond Two: Theory and Applications of Multiple-Valued Logic*; Physica-Verlag: Heidelberg, Germany, 2003; ISBN 978-3-7908-1769-0.
29. Luna, J.M.; Gennatas, E.D.; Ungar, L.H.; Eaton, E.; Diffenderfer, E.S.; Jensen, S.T.; Simone, C.B.; Friedman, J.H.; Solberg, T.D.; Valdes, G. Building More Accurate Decision Trees with the Additive Tree. *Proc. Natl. Acad. Sci. USA* **2019**, *116*, 19887–19893. [CrossRef]
30. Naghibi, S.A.; Dolatkordestani, M.; Rezaei, A.; Amouzegari, P.; Heravi, M.T.; Kalantar, B.; Pradhan, B. Application of Rotation Forest with Decision Trees as Base Classifier and a Novel Ensemble Model in Spatial Modeling of Groundwater Potential. *Env. Monit Assess* **2019**, *191*, 248. [CrossRef]
31. Kaushik, M.; Kumar, M. An Application of Fault Tree Analysis for Computing the Bounds on System Failure Probability through Qualitative Data in Intuitionistic Fuzzy Environment. *Qual. Reliab. Eng.* **2022**, *38*, 2420–2444. [CrossRef]
32. Munk, P.; Nordmann, A. Model-Based Safety Assessment with SysML and Component Fault Trees: Application and Lessons Learned. *Softw. Syst. Model* **2020**, *19*, 889–910. [CrossRef]
33. Shukla, A.; Biere, A.; Pulina, L.; Seidl, M. A Survey on Applications of Quantified Boolean Formulas. In Proceedings of the 2019 IEEE 31st International Conference on Tools with Artificial Intelligence (ICTAI), Portland, OR, USA, 4–6 November 2019; pp. 78–84.
34. Benamor, A.; Benchouia, M.T.; Srairi, K.; Benbouzid, M.E.H. A Novel Rooted Tree Optimization Apply in the High Order Sliding Mode Control Using Super-Twisting Algorithm Based on DTC Scheme for DFIG. *Int. J. Electr. Power Energy Syst.* **2019**, *108*, 293–302. [CrossRef]

axioms

MDPI

Article

Linear Diophantine Fuzzy Rough Sets on Paired Universes with Multi Stage Decision Analysis

Saba Ayub [1], Muhammad Shabir [1], Muhammad Riaz [2], Faruk Karaaslan [3], Dragan Marinkovic [4,*] and Djordje Vranjes [5]

1 Department of Mathematics, Quaid-i-Azam University, Islamabad 45320, Pakistan
2 Department of Mathematics, University of the Punjab, Lahore 54590, Pakistan
3 Department of Mathematics, Çankırı Karatekin University, Çankırı 18100, Turkey
4 Department of Structural Analysis, Technical University of Berlin, 10623 Berlin, Germany
5 Academy of Technical and Art Applied Studies Belgrade, University of Belgrade, 11000 Belgrade, Serbia
* Correspondence: dragan.marinkovic@tu-berlin.de

Abstract: Rough set (RS) and fuzzy set (FS) theories were developed to account for ambiguity in the data processing. The most persuasive and modernist abstraction of an FS is the linear Diophantine FS (LD-FS). This paper introduces a resilient hybrid linear Diophantine fuzzy RS model (LDF-RS) on paired universes based on a linear Diophantine fuzzy relation (LDF-R). This is a typical method of fuzzy RS (F-RS) and bipolar FRS (BF-RS) on two universes that are more appropriate and customizable. By using an LDF-level cut relation, the notions of lower approximation (L-A) and upper approximation (U-A) are defined. While this is going on, certain fundamental structural aspects of LD-FAs are thoroughly investigated, with some instances to back them up. This cutting-edge LDF-RS technique is crucial from both a theoretical and practical perspective in the field of medical assessment.

Keywords: fuzzy set; linear Diophantine fuzzy sets; linear Diophantine fuzzy relations; level cut relations; rough approximations on two universes; decision analysis

Citation: Ayub, S.; Shabir, M.; Riaz, M.; Karaaslan, F.; Marinkovic, D.; Vranjes, D. Linear Diophantine Fuzzy Rough Sets on Paired Universes with Multi Stage Decision Analysis. *Axioms* **2022**, *11*, 686. https://doi.org/10.3390/axioms11120686

Academic Editor: Oscar Castillo

Received: 25 October 2022
Accepted: 26 November 2022
Published: 30 November 2022

1. Introduction

As one of the most effective methods for developing a set's embryonic concept, Zadeh [1] first proposed the idea of an FS in 1965. According to the attributes, FS permits grading a set's features in the range of $[0,1]$. Since the conception of the theory, FS has been developed in a variety of ways, including intuitionistic fuzzy set (IF-S) [2,3], bipolar FS (B-FS) [4], Pythagorean FS (P-FS) [5,6], q-rung orthopair FS (q-ROF-S) [7], and LD-FS [8].

In 2019, Riaz and Hashmi [8] unveiled LD-FS, one of the most exquisite and significant generalizations of FS. Using the control parameters, LD-FS eliminates the restrictions connected to the membership degree (MD) and non-membership degree (NMD) of the prevalent abstractions of IF-Ss, B-FSs, and q-ROF-S. LD-FS is the most practical mathematical model for decision making (DM), multi-attribute decision making (MADM), engineering, artificial intelligence (AI), and medicine, allowing the decision maker to freely choose the grades [8]. Today, LD-FS is the owner of a huge study (see [9–11]). Ayub et al. [12] advanced an impressive method of an LDF-R to broaden the concept of IF-R, in which they provide an in-depth analysis of its essential characteristics, algebraic structures, and application in decision analysis.

While binary relations play a significant role in several domains for the transmission of unique things. In 1971, Zadeh [13] proposed the fuzzification of binary relations and presented the idea of an F-R. Numerous significant applications of FSs and F-Rs may be found in MCDM, neural networks, databases, pattern recognition, AI, clustering, F-control, and uncertainty reasoning. A thorough analysis of FSs and F-Rs is offered in [14].

The necessity to expand F-R was similar to that of FS. In 1984, Atanassov [15] proposed the concept of IF-R. An IF-R, per Atanassov's definition [15], is a pair of F-Rs where the total of the coalition and alienation grades is less than or equal to 1. A soft set [16], being a parameterized collection of the universe objects, has robust applications in decision making. m-Polar neutrosophic topology provides a generalized topological structure for data analysis [17].

Pawlak [18,19] suggested an approach of RS to deal with uncertainty in intelligent systems as another abstraction of classical set theory. The L-A and U-A, which are used to define the M of objects in RS theory, are two sharp approximation (A) sets. The fundamental ideas of the RS theory, which reveals the hidden knowledge in information systems, are these approximations. AI, machine learning, conflict analysis, and data analysis are just a few fields where RS theory has been successfully applied.

Due to the equivalence relation (E-R) that underlies the RS theory, its application in practical situations is constrained. Numerous abstractions have been constructed to overcome the constraint of an E-R. For instance, RS based on a binary relation [20,21], a set-valued map [22], a tolerance relation [23], a similarity relation [24], a reflexive relation (R-R) and transitive relation (T-R) [25], a soft binary relation [26,27], a soft E-R [28], two E-Rs [29], a normal soft group [30], two soft binary relations, and two normal soft groups, demonstrates how an E-R may be adjusted with different granule interpretations. Zhan and Alcantud [31] proposed a new kind of soft rough covering by means of soft neighborhoods. Motivation of the proposed work is based on some existing methodologies such as attribute analysis [32], picture fuzzy aggregation [33], interval-valued picture fuzzy Maclaurin symmetric mean operator [34] complex interval-valued Pythagorean fuzzy aggregation [35], risk priority evaluation [36], roughness in soft-intersection groups [37], and roughness in modules of fractions [38]. Karamaşa et al. [39] proposed an extended SVN-AHP and MULTIMOORA method to for flight training organizations. Osintsev [40] suggested DEMATEL-ANP method for an evaluation of logistic flows in green supply chains.

1.1. Research Gap and Motivation

From all of the above-mentioned, the sequel summarizes the driving forces behind our research and the gaps that lie underneath it:

(1) With the conceptualizations of the rough FS (R-FS) and fuzzy RS (F-RS) models (see [41–44]), Dubios and Prade [45] started the unification of RS and FS. Several authors have researched this idea (see [46–48]).
(2) Incorporating two universes, Li and Wang [49] created the R-FSA imagination.
(3) Yang [50] provided some of the applications for the notion of the roughness of a crisp set of two universes.
(4) Yang et al. [51] presented the BF-RS's idea on dual universe along with some of its applications.
(5) Less research has been performed on the idea of roughness in dual universes, particularly in P-FS and q-ROF-S.
(6) Ayub et al. [52] carefully thought out a method of applying RS to LD-FS with the aid of LDF-R and its applications in DM.
(7) To the best of our knowledge, no research has been performed on the idea of LDF-S roughness using the level cut relation of an LDF-R.
(8) To close this knowledge gap in the investigation of the roughness of LD-FSs, we introduce an abstraction of LDF-Rs using the level cut relations of an LDF-R on two different universal sets.

1.2. Major Contributions

This study uses level-cut relations from an LDF-R of dual universes to examine the roughness of an LD-FS. The fore set and after set of the level cut relations are used to design the underlying operations of RSs, the L- and U-As. With the use of useful examples, certain fundamental conclusions about As are demonstrated. We also defined the terms "accuracy measure" (A-M) and "roughness measure" (R-M) for LDF-RS. Finally, an LDF-RSs application to medical diagnosis is made to demonstrate its viability in real life.

1.3. Organization of the Paper

The remainder of this article is organized as follows to facilitate the study: In Section 2, some hypothetical early conceptions of RS, LD-FS, and LDF-R are provided. Using an LDF-R and a thorough examination of the essential characteristics of approximations with examples, the concept of LDF-RS on two distinct universes is introduced in the third segment. Section 4 includes the A-M and R-M cues for the LDF-RS. The application of LDF-RSs is demonstrated with the help of an example in Section 5. Section 6 concludes the paper by summarizing the final remarks.

2. Preliminaries

This subsection consists of some essential knowledge of LD-FS, LDF-R and RS. Throughout this research, $\breve{\mathscr{U}}$, $\breve{\mathscr{U}}_1$ and $\breve{\mathscr{U}}_2$ will denote the initial universes, unless otherwise specified.

Definition 1 ([19]). *Let ρ be an $E-R$ on $\breve{\mathscr{U}}$. Then, the pair $(\breve{\mathscr{U}}, \rho)$ is known as an R approximation space (R-AS). For any subset $\mathcal{O}$ of $\breve{\mathscr{U}}$, the L-A $\underline{\mathcal{O}}_\rho$ and the U-A $\overline{\mathcal{O}}^\rho$ are defined as follows:*

$$\underline{\mathcal{O}}_\rho = \{v \in \breve{\mathscr{U}} : [v]_\rho \subseteq \mathcal{O}\} \text{ and } \overline{\mathcal{O}}^\rho = \{v \in \breve{\mathscr{U}} : [v]_\rho \cap \mathcal{O} \neq \emptyset\}$$

where $[v]_\rho$ signifies an E-class of $v \in \breve{\mathscr{U}}$ deduced by ρ. The boundary zone is indicated and described as follows:

$$BR(\mathcal{O}) = \overline{\mathcal{O}}^\rho - \underline{\mathcal{O}}_\rho$$

If $BR(\mathcal{O}) \neq \emptyset$, then $\mathcal{O}$ is known as an RS or otherwise a crisp set or a definable set. Based on these As, Pawlak characterized a crisp set $\mathcal{O} \subseteq \breve{\mathscr{U}}$ in the sequel:

- ⋆ *$\underline{\mathcal{O}}_\rho$ consists of the definite members and is known as the positive region (PR) of $\mathcal{O}$;*
- ⋆ *$\breve{\mathscr{U}} - \overline{\mathcal{O}}^\rho$ consists of the definite non-members and is known as the negative region (NR) of $\mathcal{O}$;*
- ⋆ *$BR(\mathcal{O})$ contains questionable members that may or may not be contained in $\mathcal{O}$ and is known as the boundary region (BR).*

Recently, Riaz and Hashmi [8] introduced an efficient approach to handling uncertainties that eradicate all the limitations related to affiliation and disassociation grades of the existing models (FS,B-FS,IF-S and P-FS).

Definition 2 ([8]). *An LD-FS on $\breve{\mathscr{U}}$ is an object defined as follows:*

$$\pounds_D = \{(v, < \Theta^M(v), \Theta^N(v) >, < \varpi^M(v), \varpi^M(v) >) : v \in \breve{\mathscr{U}}\}$$

where

$$\Theta^M, \Theta^N : \breve{\mathscr{U}} \to [0,1]$$

are M and NM functions and $\varpi^M(v), \varpi^N(v) \in [0,1]$ are the reference parameters of $\Theta^M(v), \Theta^N(v)$ respectively, such that $0 \leq \varpi^M(v)\Theta^M(v) + \varpi^N(v)\Theta^N(v) \leq 1$ satisfying $0 \leq \varpi^M(v) + \varpi^N(v) \leq 1$ for all $u \in \breve{\mathscr{U}}$. The hesitation part is defined as $\Lambda(v)\Pi(v) = 1 - (\varpi^M(v)\Theta^M(v) + \varpi^N(v)\Theta^N(v))$, where $\Pi(v)$ expresses the degree of indeterminacy, and $\Lambda(v)$ refers to the relevant reference parameter. We use the notion $LD-FS(\breve{\mathscr{U}})$ to represent the collection of all LD-FSs on $\breve{\mathscr{U}}$.

By using control parameters that correspond to the association and disassociation grades in Riaz and Hashmi's [8] motivation, Ayub et al. [12] have expanded the idea of IF-R [15] to LDF-R.

Definition 3 ([12]). *An expression of the following form is an LDF-R $\ddot{\rho}$ from $\breve{\mathscr{U}}_1$ to $\breve{\mathscr{U}}_2$:*

$$\ddot{\rho} = \{((v_1, v_2), < \Theta^M(v_1, v_2), \Theta^N(v_1, v_2) >, < \varpi^M(v_1, v_2), \varpi^N(v_1, v_2) >) : v_1 \in \breve{\mathscr{U}}_1, v_2 \in \breve{\mathscr{U}}_2\}$$

where the mappings

$$\Theta^M, \Theta^N : \breve{\mathscr{U}}_1 \times \breve{\mathscr{U}}_2 \to [0, 1]$$

indicate the M and NM F-Rs from $\breve{\mathscr{U}}_1$ *to* $\breve{\mathscr{U}}_2$*, respectively, and* $\varpi^M(v_1, v_2), \varpi^N(v_1, v_2) \in [0, 1]$ *are the relevant reference parameters to* $\Theta^M(v_1, v_2)$ *and* $\Theta^N(v_1, v_2)$*, respectively, fulfilling the requirement* $0 \leq \varpi^M(v_1, v_2)\Theta^M(v_1, v_2) + \varpi^N(v_1, v_2)\Theta^N(v_1, v_2) \leq 1$*, for all* $(v_1, v_2) \in \breve{\mathscr{U}}_1 \times \breve{\mathscr{U}}_2$ *with* $0 \leq \varpi^M(v_1, v_2) + \varpi^N(v_1, v_2) \leq 1$*. The hesitation part is defined as follows:*

$$\ddot{\gamma}(v_1, v_2)\ddot{\pi}(v_1, v_2) = 1 - (\varpi^M(v_1, v_2)\Theta^M(v_1, v_2) + \varpi^N(v_1, v_2)\Theta^N(v_1, v_2))$$

where $\ddot{\pi}(v_1, v_2)$ *is the hesitation index, and* $\ddot{\gamma}(v_1, v_2)$ *is the relevant reference parameter. For the sake of simplicity, we will use* $\ddot{\rho} = (< \Theta^M(v_1, v_2), \Theta^N(v_1, v_2) >, < \varpi^M(v_1, v_2), \varpi^N(v_1, v_2) >)$ *for an LDF-R from* $\breve{\mathscr{U}}_1$ *to* $\breve{\mathscr{U}}_2$*. The collection of all LDF-Rs from* $\breve{\mathscr{U}}_1$ *to* $\breve{\mathscr{U}}_2$ *will be designated by* $LDF - R(\breve{\mathscr{U}}_1 \times \breve{\mathscr{U}}_2)$*.*

With respect to finite universes $\breve{\mathscr{U}}_1$ and $\breve{\mathscr{U}}_2$, the matrix notation of an LDF-R is given in the sequel.

Definition 4 ([12])**.** *Let* $\ddot{\rho} = (< \Theta^M(u_i, v_j), \Theta^N(u_i, v_j) >, < \varpi^M(u_i, v_j), \varpi^N(u_i, v_j) >)$ *be an LDF-R from* $\breve{\mathscr{U}}_1$ *to* $\breve{\mathscr{U}}_2$*, where* $\breve{\mathscr{U}}_1 = \{u_1, u_2, ..., u_m\}$ *and* $\breve{\mathscr{U}}_2 = \{v_1, v_2, ..., v_n\}$*. Consider* $\Theta^M(u_i, v_j) = (\Theta^M_{ij})_{m\times n}$*,* $\Theta^N(u_i, v_j) = (\Theta^N_{ij})_{m\times n}$ *and* $\varpi^M(u_i, v_j) = (\varpi^M_{ij})_{m\times n}$*,* $\varpi^N(u_i, v_j) = (\varpi^N_{ij})_{m\times n}$*, with* $0 \leq \varpi^M_{ij} + \varpi^M_{ij} \leq 1$ *fulfilling* $0 \leq \varpi^M_{ij}\Theta^M_{ij} + \varpi^M_{ij}\Theta^N_{ij} \leq 1$ *for all* i, j*, where* $1 \leq i \leq m$ *and* $1 \leq j \leq n$*. Then, the following four matrices can be used to represent* $\ddot{\rho}$*:*

$$\Theta^M = (\Theta^M_{ij})_{m\times n} = \begin{pmatrix} \Theta^M_{11} & \Theta^M_{12} & \cdots & \Theta^M_{1n} \\ \Theta^M_{21} & \Theta^M_{22} & \cdots & \Theta^M_{2n} \\ . & . & \cdots & . \\ . & . & \cdots & . \\ . & . & \cdots & . \\ \Theta^M_{m1} & \Theta^M_{m2} & \cdots & \Theta^M_{mn} \end{pmatrix}, \Theta^N = (\Theta^N_{ij})_{m\times n} = \begin{pmatrix} \Theta^N_{11} & \Theta^N_{12} & \cdots & \Theta^N_{1n} \\ \Theta^N_{21} & \Theta^N_{22} & \cdots & \Theta^N_{2n} \\ . & . & \cdots & . \\ . & . & \cdots & . \\ . & . & \cdots & . \\ \Theta^N_{m1} & \Theta^N_{m2} & \cdots & \Theta^N_{mn} \end{pmatrix},$$

$$\varpi^M = (\varpi^M_{ij})_{m\times n} = \begin{pmatrix} \varpi^M_{11} & \varpi^M_{12} & \cdots & \varpi^M_{1n} \\ \varpi^M_{21} & \varpi^M_{22} & \cdots & \varpi^M_{2n} \\ . & . & \cdots & . \\ . & . & \cdots & . \\ . & . & \cdots & . \\ \varpi^M_{m1} & \varpi^M_{m2} & \cdots & \varpi^M_{mn} \end{pmatrix}, \varpi^N = (\varpi^N_{ij})_{m\times n} = \begin{pmatrix} \varpi^N_{11} & \varpi^N_{12} & \cdots & \varpi^N_{1n} \\ \varpi^N_{21} & \varpi^N_{22} & \cdots & \varpi^N_{2n} \\ . & . & \cdots & . \\ . & . & \cdots & . \\ . & . & \cdots & . \\ \varpi^N_{m1} & \varpi^N_{m2} & \cdots & \varpi^N_{mn} \end{pmatrix}$$

The following definitions describe some basic operations on LDF-Rs.

Definition 5 ([12])**.** *Let* $\ddot{\rho}_1 = (< \Theta^M_1(v_1, v_2), \Theta^N_1(v_1, v_2) >, < \varpi^M_1(v_1, v_2), \varpi^N_1(v_1, v_2) >)$ *and* $\ddot{\rho}_2 = (< \Theta^M_2(v_1, v_2), \Theta^N_2(v_1, v_2) >, < \varpi^M_2(v_1, v_2), \varpi^N_2(v_1, v_2) >)$ *be two LDF-Rs from* $\breve{\mathscr{U}}_1$ *to* $\breve{\mathscr{U}}_2$*. Then,*

(1) $\ddot{\rho}_1 \subseteq \ddot{\rho}_2$ *if and only if*

$$\Theta^M_1(v_1, v_2) \leq \Theta^M_2(v_1, v_2) \text{ and } \Theta^N_1(v_1, v_2) \geq \Theta^N_2(v_1, v_2),$$

$$\varpi^M_1(v_1, v_2) \leq \varpi^M_2(v_1, v_2) \text{ and } \varpi^N_1(v_1, v_2) \geq \varpi^N_2(v_1, v_2)$$

(2) $\ddot{\rho}_1 \cup \ddot{\rho}_2 = (< (\Theta^M_1 \cup \Theta^M_2)(v_1, v_2), (\Theta^N_1 \cap \Theta^N_2)(v_1, v_2) >, < \varpi^M_1(v_1, v_2) \vee \varpi^M_2(v_1, v_2),$ $\varpi^M_1(v_1, v_2) \wedge \varpi^N_2(v_1, v_2) >)$*, where*

$$(\Theta^M_1 \cup \Theta^M_2)(v_1, v_2) = \Theta^M_1(v_1, v_2) \vee \Theta^M_2(v_1, v_2) \text{ and}$$

$$(\Theta^N_1 \cap \Theta^N_2)(v_1, v_2) = \Theta^N_1(v_1, v_2) \wedge \Theta^N_2(v_1, v_2)$$

(3) $\ddot{\rho}_1 \cap \ddot{\rho}_2 = (< (\Theta_1^M \cap \Theta_2^M)(v_1, v_2), (\Theta_1^N \cup \Theta_2^N)(v_1, v_2) >, < \varpi_1^M(v_1, v_2) \wedge \varpi_2^M(v_1, v_2), \varpi_1^N(v_1, v_2) \vee \varpi_2^N(v_1, v_2) >)$, *where*

$$(\Theta_1^M \cap \Theta_2^M)(v_1, v_2) = \Theta_1^M(v_1, v_2) \wedge \Theta_2^M(v_1, v_2) \text{ and}$$

$$(\Theta_1^N \cup \Theta_2^N)(v_1, v_2) = \Theta_1^N(v_1, v_2) \vee \Theta_2^N(v_1, v_2)$$

(4) $\ddot{\rho}_1^c = (< \Theta_1^N(v_1, v_2), \Theta_1^M(v_1, v_2) >, < \varpi_1^N(v_1, v_2), \varpi_1^M(v_1, v_2) >)$.

for all $(v_1, v_2) \in \breve{\mathcal{U}}_1 \times \breve{\mathcal{U}}_2$.

Definition 6 ([12]). *Let* $\ddot{\rho}_1 = (< \Theta_1^M(v_1, v_2), \Theta_1^N(v_1, v_2) >, < \varpi_1^M(v_1, v_2), \varpi_1^N(v_1, v_2) >)$ *be an LDF-R over* $\breve{\mathcal{U}}_1 \times \breve{\mathcal{U}}_2$ *and* $\ddot{\rho}_2 = (< \Theta_2^M(v_1, v_2), \Theta_2^N(v_1, v_2) >, < \varpi_2^M(v_1, v_2), \varpi_2^N(v_1, v_2) >)$ *be an LDF-R over* $\breve{\mathcal{U}}_2 \times \breve{\mathcal{U}}_3$. *Then, their composition is denoted by* $\hat{\circ}$ *and is determined accordingly:*

$$\ddot{\rho}_1 \hat{\circ} \ddot{\rho}_2 = (< (\Theta_1^M \hat{\circ} \Theta_2^M)(v_1, v_3), (\Theta_1^N \hat{\circ} \Theta_2^N)(v_1, v_3) >, < (\varpi_1^M \hat{\circ} \varpi_2^M)(v_1, v_3), (\varpi_1^N \hat{\circ} \varpi_2^N)(v_1, v_3) >)$$

where

$$(\Theta_1^M \hat{\circ} \Theta_2^M)(v_1, v_3) = \vee_{x_2 \in \breve{\mathcal{U}}_2} (\Theta_1^M(v_1, v_2) \wedge \Theta_2^M(v_2, v_3))$$

$$(\Theta_1^N \hat{\circ} \Theta_2^N)(v_1, v_3) = \wedge_{x_2 \in \breve{\mathcal{U}}_2} (\Theta_1^N(v_1, v_2) \vee \Theta_2^N(v_2, v_3))$$

and

$$(\varpi_1^M \hat{\circ} \varpi_2^M)(v_1, v_3) = \vee_{u_2 \in \breve{\mathcal{U}}_2} (\varpi_1^M(v_1, v_2) \wedge \varpi_2^M(v_2, v_3))$$

$$(\varpi_1^N \hat{\circ} \varpi_2^N)(v_1, v_3) = \wedge_{u_2 \in \breve{\mathcal{U}}_2} (\varpi_1^N(v_1, v_2) \vee \varpi_2^N(v_2, v_3))$$

for all $(v_1, v_3) \in \breve{\mathcal{U}}_1 \times \breve{\mathcal{U}}_3$.

Definition 7 ([12]). *Let* $\ddot{\rho}$ *be an LDF-R on* $\breve{\mathcal{U}}$. *Then,* $\ddot{\rho}$ *is classified as:*

(1) *a reflexive LDF-R (R-LDF-R), if:*

$$\Theta^M(v, v) = 1, \Theta^N(v, v) = 0 \text{ and } \varpi^M(v, v) = 1, \varpi^N(v, v) = 0$$

for all $u \in \breve{\mathcal{U}}$.

(2) *a symmetric LDF-R (S-LDF-R), if*

$$\Theta^M(v_1, v_2) = \Theta^M(v_2, v_1), \Theta^N(v_1, v_2) = \Theta^N(v_2, v_1) \text{ and } \ddot{\alpha}(v_1, v_2) = \ddot{\alpha}(v_2, v_1), \ddot{\beta}(v_1, v_2) = \ddot{\beta}(v_2, v_1)$$

(3) *a transitive LDF-R (T-LDF-R), if*

$$\Theta^M \hat{\circ} \Theta^M \subseteq \Theta^M, \Theta^N \hat{\circ} \Theta^N \supseteq \Theta^N \text{ and } \varpi^M \hat{\circ} \varpi^M \subseteq \varpi^M, \varpi^N \hat{\circ} \varpi^N \supseteq \varpi^N$$

(4) *an equivalence LDF-R (E-LDF-R), if* $\ddot{\rho}$ *is a R-, S-, and T-LDF-R over* $\breve{\mathcal{U}}$.

If $|\breve{\mathcal{U}}| = n$, where $|.|$ indicates the quantity of items in $\breve{\mathcal{U}}$, $\ddot{\rho} = (< (\Theta_{ij}^M)_{n \times n}, (\Theta_{ij}^N)_{n \times n} >, < (\varpi_{ij}^M)_{n \times n}, (\varpi_{ij}^N)_{n \times n} >)$. Let $\Theta^M = (\Theta_{ij}^M)_{n \times n}$, $\Theta^N = (\Theta_{ij}^N)_{n \times n}$ and $\varpi^M = (\varpi_{ij}^M)_{n \times n}$, $\varpi^N = (\varpi_{ij}^N)_{n \times n}$. Then,

(1) $\ddot{\rho}$ is R, if $\Theta_{ii}^M = \varpi_{ii}^M = 1$, and $\Theta_{ii}^N = \varpi_{ii}^N = 0$, where $i, j = 1, 2, ..., n$.
(2) $\ddot{\rho}$ is S, if $(\Theta^M)^T = \Theta^M$, $(\Theta^N)^T = \Theta^N$ and $(\varpi^M)^T = \varpi^M$, $(ss\varpi^N)^T = \varpi^N$,
(3) $\ddot{\rho}$ is T, if $\Theta^M \hat{\circ} \Theta^M \subseteq \Theta^M$, $\Theta^N \hat{\circ} \Theta^N \supseteq \Theta^N$ and $\varpi^M \hat{\circ} \varpi^M \subseteq \varpi^M$, $\varpi^N \hat{\circ} \varpi^N \supseteq \varpi^N$.
(4) $\ddot{\rho}$ is E, if $\ddot{\rho}$ is R, S and T as well,

3. Some Properties of Linear Diophantine Fuzzy Relation

Ayub et al. [12] proposed the idea of LDF-R from $\breve{\mathcal{U}}_1$ to $\breve{\mathcal{U}}_2$. The purpose of this section is to introduce the idea of a level cut relation of an LDF-R. Additionally, we investigate a few of its crucial characteristics, including the R-, S-, and T-LDF-R in terms of its level cut relations.

Definition 8. *Let* $\ddot{\rho} = (<\Theta^M(v_1,v_2),\Theta^N(v_1,v_2)>,<\varpi^M(v_1,v_2),\varpi^N(v_1,v_2)>)$ *be an LDF-R from* $\breve{\mathscr{U}}_1$ *to* $\breve{\mathscr{U}}_2$*. Let* $\ddot{s},\ddot{t},\ddot{u},\ddot{v} \in [0,1]$ *be such that* $0 \leq \ddot{s}\ddot{u} + \ddot{t}\ddot{v} \leq 1$ *with* $0 \leq \ddot{u} + \ddot{v} \leq 1$*, and define the* $(<\ddot{s},\ddot{u}>,<\ddot{t},\ddot{v}>)$*−level cut relation of* $\ddot{\rho}$ *as follows:*

$$(\ddot{\rho})^{<\ddot{t},\ddot{v}>}_{<\ddot{s},\ddot{u}>} = \{(v_1,v_2) \in \breve{\mathscr{U}}_1 \times \breve{\mathscr{U}}_2 : \Theta^M(v_1,v_2) \geq \ddot{s}, \varpi^M(v_1,v_2) \geq \ddot{u} \text{ and } \Theta^N(v_1,v_2) \leq \ddot{t}, \varpi^N(v_1,v_2) \leq \ddot{v}\}$$

where

$$(\ddot{\rho})_{<\ddot{s},\ddot{u}>} = \{(v_1,v_2) \in \breve{\mathscr{U}}_1 \times \breve{\mathscr{U}}_2 : \Theta^M(v_1,v_2) \geq \ddot{s}, \varpi^M(v_1,v_2) \geq \ddot{u}\}$$

is said to be $<\ddot{s},\ddot{u}>$ *−level cut relation of* $\ddot{\rho}$*, and*

$$(\ddot{\rho})^{<\ddot{t},\ddot{v}>} = \{(v_1,v_2) \in \breve{\mathscr{U}}_1 \times \breve{\mathscr{U}}_2 : \Theta^N(v_1,v_2) \leq \ddot{t}, \varpi^N(v_1,v_2) \leq \ddot{v}\}$$

is called $<\ddot{t},\ddot{v}>$ *−level cut relation of* $\ddot{\rho}$*.*

Theorem 1. $\ddot{\rho}$ *is R-LDF-R if and only if* $(\ddot{\rho})^{<\ddot{t},\ddot{v}>}_{<\ddot{s},\ddot{u}>}$ *is R-R on* $\breve{\mathscr{U}}$*, for all* $\ddot{s},\ddot{u},\ddot{t},\ddot{v} \in [0,1]$*.*

Proof. Suppose that $\ddot{\rho}$ is R-LDF-R. By Definition 7 (1), $\Theta^M(v,v) = 1 \geq \ddot{s}, \Theta^N(v,v) = 0 \leq \ddot{t}$ and $\varpi^M(v,v) = 1 \geq \ddot{u}, \varpi^N(v,v) = 0 \leq \ddot{v}$, for all $\ddot{s},\ddot{t},\ddot{u},\ddot{v} \in [0,1]$ such that $0 \leq \ddot{s}\ddot{u} + \ddot{t}\ddot{v} \leq 1$ with $0 \leq \ddot{u} + \ddot{v} \leq 1$. Hence, $(x,x) \in (\ddot{\rho})^{<\ddot{t},\ddot{v}>}_{<\ddot{s},\ddot{u}>}$ for all $u \in \breve{\mathscr{U}}$.

Conversely, assume that $(\ddot{\rho})^{<\ddot{t},\ddot{v}>}_{<\ddot{s},\ddot{u}>}$ is R-R. If $\ddot{\rho}$ is not R-LDF-R, then for some $v \in \breve{\mathscr{U}}$ either $\Theta^M(v,v) \neq 1$, or $\Theta^N(v,v) \neq 0$ or $\varpi^M(v,v) \neq 1$ or $\varpi^N(v,v) \neq 0$, for some $\ddot{s},\ddot{t},\ddot{u},\ddot{v} \in [0,1]$. If $\Theta^M(v,v) \neq 1$. Taking $\ddot{s} = 1$, we have $(x,x) \notin (\ddot{\rho})^{<\ddot{t},\ddot{v}>}_{<\ddot{s},\ddot{u}>}$, which is a contradiction. The other three cases are similar. Hence, $(\ddot{\rho})^{<\ddot{t},\ddot{v}>}_{<\ddot{s},\ddot{u}>}$ is a R-R. □

Theorem 2. $\ddot{\rho}$ *is S-LDF-R if and only if* $(\ddot{\rho})^{<\ddot{t},\ddot{v}>}_{<\ddot{s},\ddot{u}>}$ *is S-R on* $\breve{\mathscr{U}}$*, for all* $\ddot{s},\ddot{u},\ddot{t},\ddot{v} \in [0,1]$*.*

Proof. Suppose that $\ddot{\rho}$ is S-LDF-R. Let $(v_1,v_2) \in (\ddot{\rho})^{<\ddot{t},\ddot{v}>}_{<\ddot{s},\ddot{u}>}$. By Definition 8, $\Theta^M(v_1,v_2) \geq \ddot{s}, \varpi^M(v_1,v_2) \geq \ddot{u}$ and $\Theta^N(v_1,v_2) \leq \ddot{t}, \varpi^N(v_1,v_2) \leq \ddot{v}$. Since $\ddot{\rho}$ is symmetric, so we have $\Theta^M(v_2,v_1) \geq \ddot{s}, \varpi^M(v_2,v_1) \geq \ddot{u}$ and $\Theta^N(v_2,v_1) \leq \ddot{t}, \varpi^N(v_2,v_1) \leq \ddot{v}$ (see Definition 7 (2)). Thus, $(v_2,v_1) \in (\ddot{\rho})^{<\ddot{t},\ddot{v}>}_{<\ddot{s},\ddot{u}>}$.

Conversely, assume that $(\ddot{\rho})^{<\ddot{t},\ddot{v}>}_{<\ddot{s},\ddot{u}>}$ is S-R on $\breve{\mathscr{U}}$. Letting $\Theta^M(v_1,v_2) = \ddot{s}, \varpi^M(v_1,v_2) = \ddot{u}$ and $\Theta^N(v_1,v_2) = \ddot{t}, \varpi^N(v_1,v_2) = \ddot{v}$, for some $\ddot{s},\ddot{t},\ddot{u},\ddot{v} \in [0,1]$ such that $0 \leq \ddot{s}\ddot{u} + \ddot{t}\ddot{v} \leq 1$ with $0 \leq \ddot{u} + \ddot{v} \leq 1$. It follows that $(v_1,v_2) \in (\ddot{\rho})^{<\ddot{t},\ddot{v}>}_{<\ddot{s},\ddot{u}>}$. By assumption on $(\ddot{\rho})^{<\ddot{t},\ddot{v}>}_{<\ddot{s},\ddot{u}>}$, we have $(v_2,v_1) \in (\ddot{\rho})^{<\ddot{t},\ddot{v}>}_{<\ddot{s},\ddot{u}>}$. Thus, $\Theta^M(v_2,v_1) \geq \ddot{s} = \Theta^M(v_2,v_1), \varpi^M(v_2,v_1) \geq \ddot{u} = \varpi^M(v_1,v_2)$ and $\Theta^N(v_2,v_1) \leq \ddot{t} = \Theta^N(v_1,v_2), \beta(v_2,v_1) \leq \ddot{v} = \varpi^N(v_1,v_2)$. By using similar arguments, other inequalities can be shown. Thus, $\ddot{\rho}$ is S-LDF-R on $\breve{\mathscr{U}}$. This completes the proof. □

Proposition 1. $\ddot{\rho}$ *is T-LDF-R if and only if*

$$\Theta^M(v_1,v_2) \wedge \Theta^M(v_2,v_3) \leq \Theta^M(v_1,v_3), \Theta^N(v_1,v_2) \wedge \Theta^N(v_2,v_3) \geq \Theta^N(v_1,v_3)$$

$$\text{and } \varpi^M(v_1,v_2) \wedge \varpi^M(v_2,v_3) \leq \varpi^M(v_1,v_3), \varpi^N(v_1,v_2) \wedge \varpi^N(v_2,v_3) \geq \varpi^N(v_1,v_3),$$

for all $v_1,v_2,v_3 \in \breve{\mathscr{U}}$*.*

Proof. Suppose that $\ddot{\rho}$ is T-LDF-R on $\breve{\mathscr{U}}$. By Definition 7 (3), $(\Theta^M \hat{\circ} \Theta^M)(v_1,v_3) \subseteq \Theta^M(v_1,v_3)$, $(\Theta^N \hat{\circ} \Theta^N)(v_1,v_3) \supseteq \Theta^N(v_1,v_3)$ and $(\varpi^M \hat{\circ} \varpi^M)(v_1,v_3) \subseteq \varpi^M(v_1,v_3), (\varpi^N \hat{\circ} \varpi^N)(v_1,v_3) \supseteq \varpi^N(v_1,v_3)$, for all $v_1,v_3 \in \breve{\mathscr{U}}$. Thus, $\Theta^M(v_1,v_2) \wedge \Theta^M(v_2,v_3) \leq \Theta^M(v_1,v_3), \Theta^N(v_1,v_2) \wedge \Theta^N(v_2,v_3) \geq \Theta^N(v_1,v_3)$ and $\varpi^M(v_1,v_2) \wedge \varpi^M(v_2,v_3) \leq \varpi^M(v_1,v_3)$, $\varpi^N(v_1,v_2) \wedge \varpi^N(v_2,

$v_3) \geq \varpi^N(v_1, v_3)$, for all $v_1, v_2, v_3 \in \breve{\mathscr{U}}$ (see Definition 6). The converse can be proven, similarly. □

Theorem 3. *$\ddot{\rho}$ is a T-LDF-R if and only if $(\ddot{\rho})^{<\ddot{t},\ddot{v}>}_{<\ddot{s},\ddot{u}>}$ is T-R on $\breve{\mathscr{U}}$, for all $\ddot{s}, \ddot{u}, \ddot{t}, \ddot{v} \in [0,1]$.*

Proof. Suppose that $\ddot{\rho}$ is T-LDF-R. Let $(v_1, v_2), (v_2, v_3) \in (\ddot{\rho})^{<\ddot{t},\ddot{v}>}_{<\ddot{s},\ddot{u}>}$. Then, $\Theta^M(v_1, v_2) \wedge \Theta^M(v_2, v_3) \geq \ddot{s}, \alpha(v_1, v_2) \wedge \alpha(v_2, v_3) \geq \ddot{u}$ and $\Theta^N(v_1, v_2) \vee \Theta^N(v_2, v_3) \leq \ddot{t}, \beta(v_1, v_2) \vee \beta(v_2, v_3) \leq \ddot{v}$ (see Definition 8). Using above Proposition 1, we obtain: $\Theta^M(v_1, v_3) \geq \ddot{s}, \varpi^M(v_1, v_3) \geq \ddot{u}, \Theta^N(v_1, v_3) \leq \ddot{t}, \varpi^N(v_1, v_3) \leq \ddot{v}$. Thus, $(v_1, v_3) \in (\ddot{\rho})^{<\ddot{t},\ddot{v}>}_{<\ddot{s},\ddot{u}>}$. □

Theorem 4. *$\ddot{\rho}$ is an E-LDF-R if and only if $(\ddot{\rho})^{<\ddot{t},\ddot{v}>}_{<\ddot{s},\ddot{u}>}$ is an E-R on $\breve{\mathscr{U}}$, for all $\ddot{s}, \ddot{t}, \ddot{u}, \ddot{v} \in [0,1]$.*

Proof. Theorems 1–3 have a direct impact on the proof. □

Now, to measure the 'resemblance', 'comparability' or 'closeness' of the objects in $\breve{\mathscr{U}}$, we define the following concept.

Definition 9. *$\ddot{\rho}$ is said to be a tolerance LDF-R (or compatible LDF-R), if it is R-LDF-R and S-LDF-R.*

To illustrate our above notions, we provide Example 2 below.

Example 1. *Let $\breve{\mathscr{U}} = \{v_1, v_2, v_3, v_4\}$. Construct an LDF-R $\ddot{\rho}$ on $\breve{\mathscr{U}}$ in matrix notation form as follows:*

$$\Theta^M = \begin{pmatrix} 1 & 0.725 & 0.862 & 0.921 \\ 0.725 & 1 & 0.815 & 0.132 \\ 0.862 & 0.815 & 1 & 0.325 \\ 0.921 & 0.132 & 0.325 & 1 \end{pmatrix}, \Theta^N = \begin{pmatrix} 0 & 0.218 & 0.125 & 0.215 \\ 0.218 & 0 & 0.651 & 0.334 \\ 0.125 & 0.651 & 0 & 0.728 \\ 0.215 & 0.334 & 0.728 & 0 \end{pmatrix},$$

$$\varpi^M = \begin{pmatrix} 1 & 0.71 & 0.81 & 0.89 \\ 0.71 & 1 & 0.75 & 0.11 \\ 0.81 & 0.75 & 1 & 0.21 \\ 0.89 & 0.11 & 0.21 & 1 \end{pmatrix}, \varpi^N = \begin{pmatrix} 0 & 0.16 & 0.10 & 0.11 \\ 0.16 & 0 & 0.25 & 0.34 \\ 0.10 & 0.25 & 0 & 0.64 \\ 0.11 & 0.34 & 0.64 & 0 \end{pmatrix}.$$

Using Definition 8 of $(<\ddot{s}, \ddot{u}>, <\ddot{t}, \ddot{v}>)$-level cut relation, we are able to obtain the following: For $\ddot{s} = \ddot{u} = 1, \ddot{t} = \ddot{v} = 0$,

$$(\ddot{\rho})^{<0,0>}_{<1,1>} = \{(v_1, v_1), (v_2, v_2), (v_3, v_3), (v_4, v_4)\}$$

For $\ddot{s} = 0.725$, $\ddot{u} = 0.71$ and $\ddot{t} = 0.218$, $\ddot{v} = 0.16$,

$$(\ddot{\rho})^{<0.218,0.16>}_{<0.725,0.71>} = \{(v_1, v_1), (v_1, v_2), (v_1, v_3), (v_2, v_1), (v_2, v_2), (v_3, v_1), (v_3, v_3), (v_4, v_1), (v_4, v_4)\}$$

For $\ddot{s} = 0.862$, $\ddot{u} = 0.81$ and $\ddot{t} = 0.125$, $\ddot{v} = 0.10$,

$$(\ddot{\rho})^{<0.125,0.10>}_{<0.862,0.81>} = \{(v_1, v_1), (v_1, v_3)(v_2, v_2), (v_3, v_1), (v_3, v_3), (v_4, v_4)\}$$

For $\ddot{s} = 0.921$, $\ddot{u} = 0.89$ and $\ddot{t} = 0.215$, $\ddot{v} = 0.11$,

$$(\ddot{\rho})^{<0.215,0.11>}_{<0.921,0.89>} = \{(v_1, v_1), (v_1, v_4), (v_2, v_2), (v_3, v_3), (v_4, v_1), (v_4, v_4)\}$$

For $\ddot{s} = 0.815$, $\ddot{u} = 0.75$ and $\ddot{t} = 0.651$, $\ddot{v} = 0.25$,

$$(\ddot{\rho})^{<0.651,0.25>}_{<0.815,0.75>} = \{(v_1, v_1), (v_1, v_3), (v_1, v_4), (v_2, v_2), (v_2, v_3), (v_3, v_1), (v_3, v_2), (v_3, v_3), (v_4, v_1), (v_4, v_4)\}$$

For $\ddot{s} = 0.132$, $\ddot{u} = 0.11$ and $\ddot{t} = 0.334$, $\ddot{v} = 0.34$,

$$(\ddot{\rho})^{<0.334,0.34>}_{<0.132,0.11>} = \{(v_1,v_1),(v_1,v_2),(v_1,v_3),(v_1,v_4),(v_2,v_1),(v_2,v_2),(v_2,v_4),(v_3,v_1),(v_3,v_3),(v_4,v_1),(v_4,v_2),(v_4,v_4)\}$$

For $\ddot{s} = 0.325$, $\ddot{u} = 0.21$ *and* $\ddot{t} = 0.728$, $\ddot{\upsilon} = 0.64$,

$$(\ddot{\rho})^{<0.728,0.64>}_{<0.325,0.21>} = (\breve{\mathscr{U}} \times \breve{\mathscr{U}}) \setminus \{(v_2,v_4),(v_4,v_2)\}$$

It is simple to observe that $(\ddot{\rho})^{<\ddot{t},\ddot{\upsilon}>}_{<\ddot{s},\ddot{u}>}$ *is an E-R on* $\breve{\mathscr{U}}$, *for each* $\ddot{s},\ddot{u},\ddot{t},\ddot{\upsilon}$. *Hence, by using Theorem 4,* $\ddot{\rho}$ *is an E-LDF-R on* $\breve{\mathscr{U}}$.

4. Linear Diophantine Fuzzy Rough Sets on Two Universes

In literature, R-As on two different universes using F-R are initiated by Sun and Ma [48]. Since the NM part is not discussed in F-R, Yang et al. [51] extended the concept of [48] to fuzzy bipolar relation (FB-R). In this segment, we generalize this concept to LDF-R and introduce a new concept of roughness called LDF-RS on two universes based on the after sets and fore sets of the level cut relation of an LDF-R (a crisp relation).

If $\ddot{\rho} \in LDF-R(\breve{\mathscr{U}}_1 \times \breve{\mathscr{U}}_2)$, then the triplet $\ddot{\mathbb{P}} = (\breve{\mathscr{U}}_1, \breve{\mathscr{U}}_2, \ddot{\rho})$ is called an LDF rough approximation space (LDF-RAS).

Definition 10. *Let* $\ddot{\mathbb{P}} = (\breve{\mathscr{U}}_1, \breve{\mathscr{U}}_2, \ddot{\rho})$ *be an LDF-RAS and* $\mathcal{Y} \subseteq \breve{\mathscr{U}}_2$. *Describe the L-A* $\underline{appr_{\ddot{\rho}^{<\ddot{t},\ddot{\upsilon}>}_{<\ddot{s},\ddot{u}>}}(\mathcal{Y})}$ *of* $\mathcal{Y}$ *and the U-A* $\overline{appr_{\ddot{\rho}^{<\ddot{t},\ddot{\upsilon}>}_{<\ddot{s},\ddot{u}>}}(\mathcal{Y})}$ *of* $\mathcal{Y}$ *as follows:*

$$\underline{appr_{\ddot{\rho}^{<\ddot{t},\ddot{\upsilon}>}_{<\ddot{s},\ddot{u}>}}}(\mathcal{Y}) = \{v_1 \in \breve{\mathscr{U}}_1 : \emptyset \neq v_1\ddot{\rho}^{<\ddot{t},\ddot{\upsilon}>}_{<\ddot{s},\ddot{u}>} \subseteq \mathcal{Y}\};$$

$$\overline{appr_{\ddot{\rho}^{<\ddot{t},\ddot{\upsilon}>}_{<\ddot{s},\ddot{u}>}}(\mathcal{Y})} = \{v_1 \in \breve{\mathscr{U}}_1 : \emptyset \neq v_1\ddot{\rho}^{<\ddot{t},\ddot{\upsilon}>}_{<\ddot{s},\ddot{u}>}, v_1\ddot{\rho}^{<\ddot{t},\ddot{\upsilon}>}_{<\ddot{s},\ddot{u}>} \cap \mathcal{Y} \neq \emptyset\}$$

Similarly, we can define the L-A $\underline{(\mathcal{X})appr_{\ddot{\rho}^{<\ddot{t},\ddot{\upsilon}>}_{<\ddot{s},\ddot{u}>}}}$ *and U-A* $\overline{(\mathcal{X})appr_{\ddot{\rho}^{<\ddot{t},\ddot{\upsilon}>}_{<\ddot{s},\ddot{u}>}}}$ *for any subset* $\mathcal{X} \subseteq \breve{\mathscr{U}}_1$ *as follows:*

$$\underline{(\mathcal{X})appr_{\ddot{\rho}^{<\ddot{t},\ddot{\upsilon}>}_{<\ddot{s},\ddot{u}>}}} = \{v_2 \in \breve{\mathscr{U}}_2 : \emptyset \neq \ddot{\rho}^{<\ddot{t},\ddot{\upsilon}>}_{<\ddot{s},\ddot{u}>}v_2 \subseteq \mathcal{X}\}$$

$$\overline{(\mathcal{X})appr_{\ddot{\rho}^{<\ddot{t},\ddot{\upsilon}>}_{<\ddot{s},\ddot{u}>}}} = \{v_2 \in \breve{\mathscr{U}}_2 : \emptyset \neq \ddot{\rho}^{<\ddot{t},\ddot{\upsilon}>}_{<\ddot{s},\ddot{u}>}v_2, \ddot{\rho}^{<\ddot{t},\ddot{\upsilon}>}_{<\ddot{s},\ddot{u}>}v_2 \cap \mathcal{X} \neq \emptyset\}$$

where $v_2\ddot{\rho}^{<\ddot{t},\ddot{\upsilon}>}_{<\ddot{s},\ddot{u}>} = \{v_2 \in \breve{\mathscr{U}}_2 : (v_1,v_2) \in \ddot{\rho}^{<\ddot{t},\ddot{\upsilon}>}_{<\ddot{s},\ddot{u}>}\}$ *and* $\ddot{\rho}^{<\ddot{t},\ddot{\upsilon}>}_{<\ddot{s},\ddot{u}>}v_2 = \{v_1 \in \breve{\mathscr{U}}_1 : (v_1,v_2) \in \ddot{\rho}^{<\ddot{t},\ddot{\upsilon}>}_{<\ddot{s},\ddot{u}>}\}$.

Remark 1.

(1) *If* $\breve{\mathscr{U}}_1 = \breve{\mathscr{U}}_2$, *then the L-A and U-A for any* $\mathcal{X} \subseteq \breve{\mathscr{U}}_1$ *can also be defined as in the above Definition 10.*

(2) *All the notions and results for any subset* $\mathcal{Y}$ *of* $\breve{\mathscr{U}}_2$ *from Definition 11 to Theorem 5 can be proved in similar manners for any subset* $\mathcal{X} \subseteq \breve{\mathscr{U}}_1$.

Definition 11. *Let* $\ddot{\mathbb{P}} = (\breve{\mathscr{U}}_1, \breve{\mathscr{U}}_2, \ddot{\rho})$ *be an LDF-RAS and* $\mathcal{Y} \subseteq \breve{\mathscr{U}}_2$. *Then, the following sets are defined as follows:*

(1) $LDF-POS_{\ddot{\mathbb{P}}}(\mathcal{Y}) = \underline{appr_{\ddot{\rho}^{<\ddot{t},\ddot{\upsilon}>}_{<\ddot{s},\ddot{u}>}}}(\mathcal{Y})$;

(2) $LDF-BND_{\ddot{\mathbb{P}}}(\mathcal{Y}) = \overline{appr_{\ddot{\rho}^{<\ddot{t},\ddot{\upsilon}>}_{<\ddot{s},\ddot{u}>}}(\mathcal{Y})} - \underline{appr_{\ddot{\rho}^{<\ddot{t},\ddot{\upsilon}>}_{<\ddot{s},\ddot{u}>}}}(\mathcal{Y})$;

(3) $LDF-NEG_{\ddot{\mathbb{P}}}(\mathcal{Y}) = \breve{\mathscr{U}}_2 - \overline{appr_{\ddot{\rho}^{<\ddot{t},\ddot{\upsilon}>}_{<\ddot{s},\ddot{u}>}}(\mathcal{Y})} = (\overline{appr_{\ddot{\rho}^{<\ddot{t},\ddot{\upsilon}>}_{<\ddot{s},\ddot{u}>}}(\mathcal{Y})})^c$.

are called the PR, BR and NR of $\mathcal{Y} \subseteq \breve{\mathscr{U}}_2$, *respectively.*

In the sequel of this manuscript, we mean $\ddot{\mathbb{P}} = (\breve{\mathcal{U}}_1, \breve{\mathcal{U}}_2, \ddot{\rho})$ as a LDF-RAS and $\ddot{s}, \ddot{u} \in (0,1], \ddot{t}, \ddot{v} \in [0,1)$.

Proposition 2. *Let $\mathcal{Y}_1, \mathcal{Y}_2 \subseteq \breve{\mathcal{U}}_2$. Then,*

(1) $\underline{appr}_{\ddot{\rho}^{<\ddot{t},\ddot{v}>}_{<\ddot{s},\ddot{u}>}}(\mathcal{Y}_1) \subseteq \overline{appr}_{\ddot{\rho}^{<\ddot{t},\ddot{v}>}_{<\ddot{s},\ddot{u}>}}(\mathcal{Y}_1)$;

(2) $\overline{appr}_{\ddot{\rho}^{<\ddot{t},\ddot{v}>}_{<\ddot{s},\ddot{u}>}}(\varnothing) = \varnothing = \underline{appr}_{\ddot{\rho}^{<\ddot{t},\ddot{v}>}_{<\ddot{s},\ddot{u}>}}(\varnothing)$;

(3) *If* $\mathcal{Y}_1 \subseteq \mathcal{Y}_2$, *then* $\underline{appr}_{\ddot{\rho}^{<\ddot{t},\ddot{v}>}_{<\ddot{s},\ddot{u}>}}(\mathcal{Y}_1) \subseteq \underline{appr}_{\ddot{\rho}^{<\ddot{t},\ddot{v}>}_{<\ddot{s},\ddot{u}>}}(\mathcal{Y}_2)$;

(4) $\mathcal{Y}_1 \subseteq \mathcal{Y}_2$, *then* $\overline{appr}_{\ddot{\rho}^{<\ddot{t},\ddot{v}>}_{<\ddot{s},\ddot{u}>}}(\mathcal{Y}_1) \subseteq \overline{appr}_{\ddot{\rho}^{<\ddot{t},\ddot{v}>}_{<\ddot{s},\ddot{u}>}}(\mathcal{Y}_2)$;

(5) $\underline{appr}_{\ddot{\rho}^{<\ddot{t},\ddot{v}>}_{<\ddot{s},\ddot{u}>}}(\mathcal{Y}_1 \cap \mathcal{Y}_2) = \underline{appr}_{\ddot{\rho}^{<\ddot{t},\ddot{v}>}_{<\ddot{s},\ddot{u}>}}(\mathcal{Y}_1) \cap \underline{appr}_{\ddot{\rho}^{<\ddot{t},\ddot{v}>}_{<\ddot{s},\ddot{u}>}}(\mathcal{Y}_2)$;

(6) $\overline{appr}_{\ddot{\rho}^{<\ddot{t},\ddot{v}>}_{<\ddot{s},\ddot{u}>}}(\mathcal{Y}_1 \cap \mathcal{Y}_2) \subseteq \overline{appr}_{\ddot{\rho}^{<\ddot{t},\ddot{v}>}_{<\ddot{s},\ddot{u}>}}(\mathcal{Y}_1) \cap \overline{appr}_{\ddot{\rho}^{<\ddot{t},\ddot{v}>}_{<\ddot{s},\ddot{u}>}}(\mathcal{Y}_2)$;

(7) $\underline{appr}_{\ddot{\rho}^{<\ddot{t},\ddot{v}>}_{<\ddot{s},\ddot{u}>}}(\mathcal{Y}_1 \cup \mathcal{Y}_2) \supseteq \underline{appr}_{\ddot{\rho}^{<\ddot{t},\ddot{v}>}_{<\ddot{s},\ddot{u}>}}(\mathcal{Y}_1) \cup \underline{appr}_{\ddot{\rho}^{<\ddot{t},\ddot{v}>}_{<\ddot{s},\ddot{u}>}}(\mathcal{Y}_2)$;

(8) $\overline{appr}_{\ddot{\rho}^{<\ddot{t},\ddot{v}>}_{<\ddot{s},\ddot{u}>}}(\mathcal{Y}_1 \cup \mathcal{Y}_2) = \overline{appr}_{\ddot{\rho}^{<\ddot{t},\ddot{v}>}_{<\ddot{s},\ddot{u}>}}(\mathcal{Y}_1) \cup \overline{appr}_{\ddot{\rho}^{<\ddot{t},\ddot{v}>}_{<\ddot{s},\ddot{u}>}}(\mathcal{Y}_2)$

Proof. All the assertions can be easily proved by using Definition 10. □

Note that: if $x\ddot{\rho}^{<\ddot{t},\ddot{v}>}_{<\ddot{s},\ddot{u}>} \neq \varnothing$, then the assertions (1) and (2) may not hold (see Example 2).

Example 2. *Let $\breve{\mathcal{U}}_1 = \{u_1, u_2, u_3\}$ and $\breve{\mathcal{U}}_2 = \{v_1, v_2, v_3\}$ be the universal sets. Then, we define an LDF-R $\ddot{\rho}$ from $\breve{\mathcal{U}}_1$ to $\breve{\mathcal{U}}_2$ in the matrix notations given as below:*

$$\Theta^M = \begin{pmatrix} 0.77 & 0.57 & 0.67 \\ 0.55 & 0.48 & 0.50 \\ 0.68 & 0.45 & 0.43 \end{pmatrix}, \Theta^N = \begin{pmatrix} 0.71 & 0.41 & 0.56 \\ 0.80 & 0.72 & 0.46 \\ 0.54 & 0.40 & 0.22 \end{pmatrix},$$
$$\varpi^M = \begin{pmatrix} 0.51 & 0.50 & 0.61 \\ 0.46 & 0.40 & 0.37 \\ 0.54 & 0.39 & 0.35 \end{pmatrix}, \varpi^N = \begin{pmatrix} 0.49 & 0.46 & 0.38 \\ 0.52 & 0.58 & 0.58 \\ 0.45 & 0.56 & 0.61 \end{pmatrix}.$$

Using Definition 8 of $(<\ddot{s}, \ddot{u}>, <\ddot{t}, \ddot{v}>)$-level cut relation, for $\ddot{s} = 0.77, \ddot{u} = 0.51, \ddot{t} = 0.71, \ddot{v} = 0.49$, we can obtain:

$$u_1\ddot{\rho}^{<0.71,0.49>}_{<0.77,0.51>} = \{v_1\}, u_2\ddot{\rho}^{<0.71,0.49>}_{<0.77,0.51>} = u_3\ddot{\rho}^{<0.71,0.49>}_{<0.77,0.51>} = \varnothing$$

Suppose $\mathcal{Y} = \{v_1, v_2\}$. Then by Definition 10,

$$\underline{(\mathcal{Y})appr}_{\ddot{\rho}^{<0.71,0.49>}_{<0.77,0.51>}} = \mathcal{U}_1, \overline{(\mathcal{Y})appr}_{\ddot{\rho}^{<0.71,0.49>}_{<0.77,0.51>}} = \{u_1\}$$

$$\underline{(\varnothing)appr}_{\ddot{\rho}^{<0.71,0.49>}_{<0.77,0.51>}} = \{u_2, u_3\}, \overline{(\varnothing)appr}_{\ddot{\rho}^{<0.71,0.49>}_{<0.77,0.51>}} = \varnothing$$

$$\underline{(\mathcal{U}_2)appr}_{\ddot{\rho}^{<0.71,0.49>}_{<0.77,0.51>}} = \mathcal{U}_1, \overline{(\mathcal{U}_2)appr}_{\ddot{\rho}^{<0.71,0.49>}_{<0.77,0.51>}} = \{u_1\}$$

Thus, we obtain that $\underline{(\varnothing)appr}_{\ddot{\rho}^{<0.71,0.49>}_{<0.77,0.51>}} \neq \varnothing$ and $\overline{(\mathcal{U}_2)appr}_{\ddot{\rho}^{<0.71,0.49>}_{<0.77,0.51>}} \neq \mathcal{U}_1$. However, if $u\ddot{\rho}^{<0.71,0.49>}_{<0.77,0.51>} \neq \varnothing$, then:

$$\underline{(\mathcal{U}_2)appr}_{\ddot{\rho}^{<0.71,0.49>}_{<0.77,0.51>}} = \overline{(\mathcal{U}_2)appr}_{\ddot{\rho}^{<0.71,0.49>}_{<0.77,0.51>}} = \{u_1\} \neq \mathcal{U}_1$$

(see Proposition 3).

Proposition 3. *Let $\ddot{\rho}$ be a R-LDF-R on $\breve{\mathcal{U}}_1$ and $\ddot{s}, \ddot{u} \in (0,1], \ddot{t}, \ddot{v} \in [0,1)$. For any subset $\mathcal{Y} \subseteq \breve{\mathcal{U}}_1$, the following properties hold:*

(1) $\underline{appr_{\ddot{p}^{<\ddot{t},\ddot{v}>}_{<\ddot{s},\ddot{u}>}}}(\mathcal{Y}) \subseteq \mathcal{Y} \subseteq \overline{appr_{\ddot{p}^{<\ddot{t},\ddot{v}>}_{<\ddot{s},\ddot{u}>}}}(\mathcal{Y})$;

(2) $\underline{appr_{\ddot{p}^{<\ddot{t},\ddot{v}>}_{<\ddot{s},\ddot{u}>}}}(\breve{\mathscr{U}}_1) = \breve{\mathscr{U}}_1 = \overline{appr_{\ddot{p}^{<\ddot{t},\ddot{v}>}_{<\ddot{s},\ddot{u}>}}}(\breve{\mathscr{U}}_1)$.

Proof. The proof is straightforward. □

Lemma 1. *Suppose that* $\ddot{s}_1, \ddot{s}_2, \ddot{u}_1, \ddot{u}_2 \in (0,1]$ *and* $\ddot{t}_1, \ddot{t}_2, \ddot{v}_1, \ddot{v}_2 \in [0,1)$ *such that* $\ddot{s}_1 \leq \ddot{s}_2$, $\ddot{u}_1 \leq \ddot{u}_2$ *and* $\ddot{t}_2 \leq \ddot{t}_1$, $\ddot{v}_2 \leq \ddot{v}_1$. *Then,*

$$\ddot{p}^{<\ddot{t}_2,\ddot{v}_2>}_{<\ddot{s}_2,\ddot{u}_2>} \subseteq \ddot{p}^{<\ddot{t}_1,\ddot{v}_1>}_{<\ddot{s}_1,\ddot{u}_1>}.$$

Proof. Let $(v_1, v_2) \in \ddot{p}^{<\ddot{t}_2,\ddot{v}_2>}_{<\ddot{s}_2,\ddot{u}_2>}$. Using Definition 8, $\Theta^M(v_1,v_2) \geq \ddot{s}_2$, $\varpi^M(v_1,v_2) \geq \ddot{u}_2$ and $\Theta^N(v_1,v_2) \leq \ddot{t}_2$, $\varpi^N(v_1,v_2) \leq \ddot{v}_2$. Since $\ddot{s}_1 \leq \ddot{s}_2$, $\ddot{u}_1 \leq \ddot{u}_2$ and $\ddot{t}_2 \leq \ddot{t}_1$, $\ddot{v}_2 \leq \ddot{v}_1$, so

$$\Theta^M(v_1,v_2) \geq \ddot{s}_2 \geq \ddot{s}_1, \varpi^M(v_1,v_2) \geq \ddot{u}_2 \geq \ddot{u}_1 \text{ and } \Theta^N(v_1,v_2) \leq \ddot{t}_2 \leq \ddot{t}_1, \varpi^N(v_1,v_2) \leq \ddot{v}_2 \leq \ddot{v}_1$$

Hence, $\Theta^M(v_1,v_2) \geq \ddot{s}_1$, $\varpi^M(v_1,v_2) \geq \ddot{u}_1$ and $\Theta^N(v_1,v_2) \leq \ddot{t}_1$, $\varpi^N(v_1,v_2) \leq \ddot{v}_1$. Thus $(v_1,v_2) \in \ddot{p}^{<\ddot{t}_1,\ddot{v}_1>}_{<\ddot{s}_1,\ddot{u}_1>}$. □

Proposition 4. *With the same assumptions as in the above Lemma 1, suppose that* $\mathcal{Y} \subseteq \breve{\mathscr{U}}_2$. *Then, the following assertions are true:*

(1) $\overline{appr_{\ddot{p}^{<\ddot{t}_2,\ddot{v}_2>}_{<\ddot{s}_2,\ddot{u}_2>}}}(\mathcal{Y}) \subseteq \overline{appr_{\ddot{p}^{<\ddot{t}_1,\ddot{v}_1>}_{<\ddot{s}_1,\ddot{u}_1>}}}(\mathcal{Y})$,

(2) $\underline{appr_{\ddot{p}^{<\ddot{t}_1,\ddot{v}_1>}_{<\ddot{s}_1,\ddot{u}_1>}}}(\mathcal{Y}) \subseteq \underline{appr_{\ddot{p}^{<\ddot{t}_2,\ddot{v}_2>}_{<\ddot{s}_2,\ddot{u}_2>}}}(\mathcal{Y})$.

Proof. (1) Let $v_1 \in \overline{appr_{\ddot{p}^{<\ddot{t}_2,\ddot{v}_2>}_{<\ddot{s}_2,\ddot{u}_2>}}}(\mathcal{Y})$. From Definition 10, $v_2 \in v_1\ddot{p}^{<\ddot{t}_2,\ddot{v}_2>}_{<\ddot{s}_2,\ddot{u}_2>} \cap \mathcal{Y}$ for some $v_2 \in \breve{\mathscr{U}}_1$. Since $v_1\ddot{p}^{<\ddot{t}_2,\ddot{v}_2>}_{<\ddot{s}_2,\ddot{u}_2>} \subseteq v_1\ddot{p}^{<\ddot{t}_1,\ddot{v}_1>}_{<\ddot{s}_1,\ddot{u}_1>}$, therefore $v_2 \in v_1\ddot{p}^{<\ddot{t}_1,\ddot{v}_1>}_{<\ddot{s}_1,\ddot{u}_1>} \cap \mathcal{Y}$ (using Lemma 1). Hence, $v_1 \in \overline{appr_{\ddot{p}^{<\ddot{t}_1,\ddot{v}_1>}_{<\ddot{s}_1,\ddot{u}_1>}}}(\mathcal{Y})$.

(2) Let $v_1 \in \underline{appr_{\ddot{p}^{<\ddot{t}_1,\ddot{v}_1>}_{<\ddot{s}_1,\ddot{u}_1>}}}(\mathcal{Y})$. By Definition 10, $v_1\ddot{p}^{<\ddot{t}_1,\ddot{v}_1>}_{<\ddot{s}_1,\ddot{u}_1>} \subseteq \mathcal{Y}$. From Lemma 1, $v_1\ddot{p}^{<\ddot{t}_2,\ddot{v}_2>}_{<\ddot{s}_2,\ddot{u}_2>} \subseteq \mathcal{Y}$. This proves that $v_1 \in \underline{appr_{\ddot{p}^{<\ddot{t}_2,\ddot{v}_2>}_{<\ddot{s}_2,\ddot{u}_2>}}}(\mathcal{Y})$. □

The inclusions in Proposition 4 may not hold, as is demonstrated in the sequel.

Example 3. *Let us revisit Example 2, assume* $\ddot{s}_1 = 0.55, \ddot{u}_1 = 0.46, \ddot{t}_1 = 0.80, \ddot{v}_1 = 0.52$ *and* $\ddot{s}_2 = 0.77, \ddot{u}_2 = 0.51, \ddot{t}_2 = 0.71, \ddot{v}_2 = 0.49$. *Then by Definition 8,*

$$u_1\ddot{p}^{<0.80,0.52>}_{<0.55,0.46>} = \breve{\mathscr{U}}_2, u_2\ddot{p}^{<0.80,0.52>}_{<0.55,0.46>} = u_3\ddot{p}^{<0.80,0.52>}_{<0.55,0.46>} = \{v_1\}$$

$$u_1\ddot{p}^{<0.71,0.49>}_{<0.77,0.51>} = \{v_1\}, u_2\ddot{p}^{<0.71,0.49>}_{<0.77,0.51>} = u_3\ddot{p}^{<0.71,0.49>}_{<0.77,0.51>} = \emptyset$$

Take $\mathcal{Y} = \{v_1\}$, *then by Definition 10, we have:*

$$\underline{appr_{\ddot{p}^{<0.71,0.49>}_{<0.77,0.51>}}}(\mathcal{Y}) = \overline{appr_{\ddot{p}^{<0.71,0.49>}_{<0.77,0.51>}}}(\mathcal{Y}) = \{u_1\}$$

$$\underline{appr_{\ddot{p}^{<0.80,0.52>}_{<0.55,0.46>}}}(\mathcal{Y}) = \{u_2, u_3\}, \overline{appr_{\ddot{p}^{<0.80,0.52>}_{<0.55,0.46>}}}(\mathcal{Y}) = \breve{\mathscr{U}}_1$$

Since $\ddot{s}_1 < \ddot{s}_2$, $\ddot{u}_1 < \ddot{u}_2$ *and* $\ddot{t}_1 > \ddot{t}_2$, $\ddot{v}_1 > \ddot{v}_2$, *but* $\overline{appr_{\ddot{p}^{<0.71,0.49>}_{<0.77,0.51>}}}(\mathcal{Y})$ *and* $\underline{appr_{\ddot{p}^{<0.80,0.52>}_{<0.55,0.46>}}}(\mathcal{Y}) \nsubseteq \underline{appr_{\ddot{p}^{<0.71,0.49>}_{<0.77,0.51>}}}(\mathcal{Y})$.

Lemma 2. *Let* $\ddot{\rho}_1, \ddot{\rho}_2 \in LDF - R(\breve{\mathscr{U}}_1 \times \breve{\mathscr{U}}_2)$ *be such that* $\ddot{\rho}_1 \subseteq \ddot{\rho}_2$. *Then,*

$$\ddot{\rho}_{1}{}^{<\ddot{t},\ddot{v}>}_{<\ddot{s},\ddot{u}>} \subseteq \ddot{\rho}_{2}{}^{<\ddot{t},\ddot{v}>}_{<\ddot{s},\ddot{u}>}$$

Proof. Let $(v_1, v_2) \in \ddot{\rho}_{1}{}^{<\ddot{t},\ddot{v}>}_{<\ddot{s},\ddot{u}>}$. By Definition 8, $\Theta_1^M(v_1, v_2) \geq \ddot{s}$, $\varpi_1^M(v_1, v_2) \geq \ddot{u}$ and $\Theta_1^N(v_1, v_2) \leq \ddot{t}$, $\varpi_1^N(v_1, v_2) \leq \ddot{v}$. Since $\ddot{\rho}_1 \subseteq \ddot{\rho}_2$, therefore $\ddot{s} \leq \Theta_1^M(v_1, v_2) \leq \Theta_2^M(v_1, v_2)$, $\ddot{u} \leq \varpi_1^M(v_1, v_2) \leq \varpi_2^M(v_1, v_2)$ and $\ddot{t} \geq \Theta_1^N(v_1, v_2) \geq \Theta_2^N(v_1, v_2)$, $\ddot{v} \geq \varpi_1^N(v_1, v_2) \geq \varpi_2^N(v_1, v_2)$. Hence, $\Theta_2^M(v_1, v_2) \geq \ddot{s}$, $\varpi_2^M(v_1, v_2) \geq \ddot{u}$ and $\Theta_2^N(v_1, v_2) \leq \ddot{t}$, $\varpi_2^N(v_1, v_2) \leq \ddot{v}$. Thus, $(v_1, v_2) \in \ddot{\rho}_{2}{}^{<\ddot{t},\ddot{v}>}_{<\ddot{s},\ddot{u}>}$. □

Proposition 5. *With the same notations as in Lemma 2, assume that* $\mathcal{Y} \subseteq \breve{\mathscr{U}}_2$. *Then,*

(1) $\underline{appr}_{\ddot{\rho}_{2}{}^{<\ddot{t},\ddot{v}>}_{<\ddot{s},\ddot{u}>}}(\mathcal{Y}) \subseteq \underline{appr}_{\ddot{\rho}_{1}{}^{<\ddot{t},\ddot{v}>}_{<\ddot{s},\ddot{u}>}}(\mathcal{Y})$,

(2) $\overline{appr}_{\ddot{\rho}_{1}{}^{<\ddot{t},\ddot{v}>}_{<\ddot{s},\ddot{u}>}}(\mathcal{Y}) \subseteq \overline{appr}_{\ddot{\rho}_{2}{}^{<\ddot{t},\ddot{v}>}_{<\ddot{s},\ddot{u}>}}(\mathcal{Y})$.

Proof. (1) Let $v \in \underline{appr}_{\ddot{\rho}_{2}{}^{<\ddot{t},\ddot{v}>}_{<\ddot{s},\ddot{u}>}}(\mathcal{Y})$. Then, $v\ddot{\rho}_{2}{}^{<\ddot{t},\ddot{v}>}_{<\ddot{s},\ddot{u}>} \subseteq \mathcal{Y}$. By Lemma 2, $v\ddot{\rho}_{1}{}^{<\ddot{t},\ddot{v}>}_{<\ddot{s},\ddot{u}>} \subseteq v\ddot{\rho}_{2}{}^{<\ddot{t},\ddot{v}>}_{<\ddot{s},\ddot{u}>} \subseteq \mathcal{Y}$. Hence, $x\ddot{\rho}_{1}{}^{<\ddot{t},\ddot{v}>}_{<\ddot{s},\ddot{u}>} \subseteq \mathcal{Y}$. This proves that $v \in \underline{appr}_{\ddot{\rho}_{1}{}^{<\ddot{t},\ddot{v}>}_{<\ddot{s},\ddot{u}>}}(\mathcal{Y})$. Similar to the proof of (1), proof of (2). □

5. Accuracy Measure and Roughness Measure for LDF-RSs on Two Universes

The concept of A-M and R-M was first invented by Pawlak in 1982 in order to define the imprecision of R-As. Our perception of the accuracy of the data relating to an E-R for a given classification is based on these numerical measures. In [51], Yang et al. gave the idea of A-M and R-M for BF-RSs on dual universes. In this passage, we extend this concept to LDF-RSs on two universes.

With respect to a Pawlak A-S $P = (\breve{\mathscr{U}}, \rho)$, where ρ is an E-R on $\breve{\mathscr{U}}$. Then the A-M and R-M of $\mathcal{O}$ of $\breve{\mathscr{U}}$ are defined as follows, respectively:

$$AM(\mathcal{O}) = \frac{\underline{\rho(\mathcal{O})}}{\overline{\rho(\mathcal{O})}} \text{ and } RM(\mathcal{O}) = 1 - AM(\mathcal{O}).$$

We define the subsequent ideas by using the same pattern.

Definition 12. *Let* $\ddot{\mathbb{P}} = (\breve{\mathscr{U}}_1, \breve{\mathscr{U}}_2, \ddot{\rho})$ *be an LDF-RAS and* $\mathcal{Y} \subseteq \breve{\mathscr{U}}_2$, *define the AM of* $\mathcal{Y}$ *with respect to* $\ddot{\rho}$ *as follows:*

$$\mathbb{AM}(\mathcal{Y}) = \frac{|\underline{appr}_{\ddot{\rho}^{<\ddot{t},\ddot{v}>}_{<\ddot{s},\ddot{u}>}}(\mathcal{Y})|}{|\overline{appr}_{\ddot{\rho}^{<\ddot{t},\ddot{v}>}_{<\ddot{s},\ddot{u}>}}(\mathcal{Y})|}$$

where $|.|$ *indicates the number of elements in the sets. After that, we define the RM of* $\mathcal{Y} \subseteq \breve{\mathscr{U}}_2$ *with respect to* $\ddot{\rho}$ *as follows:*

$$\mathbb{RM}(\mathcal{Y}) = 1 - \mathbb{AM}(\mathcal{Y})$$

Remark 2. *The following points can be deduced from definition 12 given above:*

(1) $\mathbb{AM}(\mathcal{Y}), \mathbb{RM}(\mathcal{Y}) \in [0, 1]$.

(2) *If* $\ddot{s} = \ddot{u} = 1$ *and* $\ddot{t} = \ddot{v} = 0$, *then* $\mathbb{AM}(\mathcal{Y}) = 1$ *and* $\mathbb{RM}(\mathcal{Y}) = 0$.

In the following, we construct an example for the clarification of the above Definition 12.

Example 4. *In Example 3, for* $\ddot{s}_1 = 0.55, \ddot{u}_1 = 0.46, \ddot{t}_1 = 0.80, \ddot{v}_1 = 0.52$ *and* $\mathcal{Y} = \{y_1\}$, *we have:*

$$\underline{appr}_{\ddot{\rho}^{<0.71,0.49>}_{<0.77,0.51>}}(\mathcal{Y}) = \overline{appr}_{\ddot{\rho}^{<0.71,0.49>}_{<0.77,0.51>}}(\mathcal{Y}) = \{x_1\}$$

Thus, by Definition 12, $\mathbb{MA}(\mathcal{Y}) = 1$ *and* $\mathbb{MR}(\mathcal{Y}) = 0$. *Hence, our information related to* $\ddot{\rho}$ *is accurate up to grade 1, which means that* $\ddot{\rho}$ *describes the objects of* $\mathcal{Y}$ *absolutely accurately. On the other hand, for* $\ddot{s}_2 = 0.77, \ddot{u}_2 = 0.51, \ddot{t}_2 = 0.71, \ddot{v}_2 = 0.49$ *and* $\mathcal{Y} = \{y_1\}$, *we have:*

$$\underline{appr_{\ddot{\rho}^{<0.80,0.52>}_{<0.55,0.46>}}}(\mathcal{Y}) = \{x_2, x_3\}, \overline{appr_{\ddot{\rho}^{<0.80,0.52>}_{<0.55,0.46>}}}(\mathcal{Y}) = \breve{\mathscr{U}}_1$$

Then, $\mathbb{MA}(\mathcal{Y}) = \frac{2}{3}$ *and* $\mathbb{MR}(\mathcal{Y}) = \frac{1}{3}$. *Hence, our information related to* $\ddot{\rho}$ *is accurate up to grade 0.6666, which means that* $\ddot{\rho}$ *describes the items of* $\breve{\mathscr{U}}_2$ *accurately up to grade 0.6666.*

In the following result, we describe a connection of the A-M $\mathbb{AM}(\mathcal{Y})$ and R-M $\mathbb{RM}(\mathcal{Y})$ about the union and intersection of $\mathcal{Y}_1$ and $\mathcal{Y}_2$ on the universe $\breve{\mathscr{U}}_2$.

Theorem 5. *Let* $\ddot{\mathbb{P}} = (\breve{\mathscr{U}}_1, \breve{\mathscr{U}}_2, \ddot{\rho})$ *be a LDF-RAS and* $\mathcal{Y}_1, \mathcal{Y}_2$ *are any non-empty subsets of* $\breve{\mathscr{U}}_2$. *Then, A-M and R-M of* $\mathcal{Y}_1$, $\mathcal{Y}_2$, $\mathcal{Y}_1 \cup \mathcal{Y}_2$ *and* $\mathcal{Y}_1 \cap \mathcal{Y}_2$ *the following relations;*

(1) $\mathbb{MR}(\mathcal{Y}_1 \cup \mathcal{Y}_2)|\overline{appr_{\ddot{\rho}^{<\ddot{t},\ddot{v}>}_{<\ddot{s},\ddot{u}>}}}(\mathcal{Y}_1) \cup \overline{appr_{\ddot{\rho}^{<\ddot{t},\ddot{v}>}_{<\ddot{s},\ddot{u}>}}}(\mathcal{Y}_2)| \leq \mathbb{MR}(\mathcal{Y}_1)|\overline{appr_{\ddot{\rho}^{<\ddot{t},\ddot{v}>}_{<\ddot{s},\ddot{u}>}}}(\mathcal{Y}_1)| + \mathbb{MR}(\mathcal{Y}_2)|\overline{appr_{\ddot{\rho}^{<\ddot{t},\ddot{v}>}_{<\ddot{s},\ddot{u}>}}}(\mathcal{Y}_2)| - \mathbb{MR}(\mathcal{Y}_1 \cap \mathcal{Y}_2)|\overline{appr_{\ddot{\rho}^{<\ddot{t},\ddot{v}>}_{<\ddot{s},\ddot{u}>}}}(\mathcal{Y}_1) \cap \overline{appr_{\ddot{\rho}^{<\ddot{t},\ddot{v}>}_{<\ddot{s},\ddot{u}>}}}(\mathcal{Y}_2)|$;

(2) $\mathbb{MA}(\mathcal{Y}_1 \cup \mathcal{Y}_2)|\overline{appr_{\ddot{\rho}^{<\ddot{t},\ddot{v}>}_{<\ddot{s},\ddot{u}>}}}(\mathcal{Y}_1) \cup \overline{appr_{\ddot{\rho}^{<\ddot{t},\ddot{v}>}_{<\ddot{s},\ddot{u}>}}}(\mathcal{Y}_2)| \geq \mathbb{MA}(\mathcal{Y}_1)|\overline{appr_{\ddot{\rho}^{<\ddot{t},\ddot{v}>}_{<\ddot{s},\ddot{u}>}}}(\mathcal{Y}_1)| + \mathbb{MA}(\mathcal{Y}_2)|\overline{appr_{\ddot{\rho}^{<\ddot{t},\ddot{v}>}_{<\ddot{s},\ddot{u}>}}}(\mathcal{Y}_2)| - \mathbb{MA}(\mathcal{Y}_1 \cap \mathcal{Y}_2)|\overline{appr_{\ddot{\rho}^{<\ddot{t},\ddot{v}>}_{<\ddot{s},\ddot{u}>}}}(\mathcal{Y}_1) \cap \overline{appr_{\ddot{\rho}^{<\ddot{t},\ddot{v}>}_{<\ddot{s},\ddot{u}>}}}(\mathcal{Y}_2)|$

Proof. The proof resembles that of Theorem 3.3 in [51]. □

6. An Application of LDF-RSs on Two Different Universes

In the literature, a number of scientists have developed various techniques for medical diagnosis. Sun and Ma [48] presented an application of the F-RS model on two distinct domains in clinical diagnosis systems. Since the information is insufficient in the case of F-RS, Yang et al. [51] expanded the idea of Sun and Ma [48] to BF-RS model on two distinct cosmologies. LD-FSs are more efficient in decision analysis than the prevailing concepts of FS, IF-S, B-FS and q-ROF-S. Therefore, we need to extend the existing technique of BF-RS to a more general and robust model, namely LDF-RS on two contrasting universes and utilize this notion in clinical diagnosis.

Suppose that $\breve{\mathscr{U}}_1$ refers to the collection of afflicted people and $\breve{\mathscr{U}}_2$ indicates the group of symptoms. Let $\ddot{\mathbb{P}} = (\breve{\mathscr{U}}_1, \breve{\mathscr{U}}_2, \ddot{\rho})$ be LDF-RAS. If $(v_1, v_2) \in \ddot{\rho}^{<\ddot{t},\ddot{v}>}_{<\ddot{s},\ddot{u}>}$, for all $v_1 \in \breve{\mathscr{U}}_1$ and $v_2 \in \breve{\mathscr{U}}_2$, then we say that the sufferer x has the symptom y and the percentage of the patient who exhibits symptom y is at least $\ddot{s}$ and the degree of its corresponding parameter is not less than $\ddot{u}$, the sufferer's degree of symptom y non-existence is not greater than $\ddot{t}$, and the degree of its corresponding parameter is not greater than $\ddot{v}$.

We are aware that a certain illness has a number of common symptoms. We denote a certain disease by $\mathcal{Y} = \{\mathfrak{y}_i \in \breve{\mathscr{U}}_2 : i \in I\}$ for any $\mathcal{Y} \subseteq \breve{\mathscr{U}}_2$ and make the following inferences using the PR, NR, and BR described in Definition 11:

Let $v \in \breve{\mathscr{U}}_1$ be a given certain sufferer. Then,

(1) If $v \in LDF - POS_{\ddot{\mathbb{P}}}(\mathcal{Y}) = \underline{appr_{\ddot{\rho}^{<\ddot{t},\ddot{v}>}_{<\ddot{s},\ddot{u}>}}}(\mathcal{Y})$ and $v\ddot{\rho}^{<\ddot{t},\ddot{v}>}_{<\ddot{s},\ddot{u}>} \neq \emptyset$, that is, he must have illness $\mathcal{Y}$, at which point the patient urgently requires treatment.

(2) If $v \in LDF - BND_{\ddot{\mathbb{P}}}(\mathcal{Y}) = \overline{appr_{\ddot{\rho}^{<\ddot{t},\ddot{v}>}_{<\ddot{s},\ddot{u}>}}}(\mathcal{Y}) - \underline{appr_{\ddot{\rho}^{<\ddot{t},\ddot{v}>}_{<\ddot{s},\ddot{u}>}}}(\mathcal{Y})$, consequently, he will be the doctor's second choice because he is not diagnosed based on these symptoms, even though he may have the disease $\mathcal{Y}$.

(3) If $v \in \mathcal{LDFNEG}_{\ddot{\mathbb{P}}}(\mathcal{Y})$, that is, $v \in (\overline{appr_{\ddot{\rho}^{<\ddot{t},\ddot{v}>}_{<\ddot{s},\ddot{u}>}}}(\mathcal{Y}))^c$, consequently, he does not have illness $\mathcal{Y}$ and does not require treatment.

Let us use a specific case to demonstrate this.

Example 5. *Let $\breve{\mathscr{U}}_1 = \{p_1, p_2, p_3, p_4\}$ be the group of certain victims and $\breve{\mathscr{U}}_2 = \{q_1, q_2, q_3\}$ be the set of some symptoms. Consider an LDF-R $\ddot{\rho}$ from $\breve{\mathscr{U}}_1$ to $\breve{\mathscr{U}}_2$. It describes the M and NM grades, together with the grades of their parameters, for each patient pi in relation to the symptom qj in the following matrices:*

$$\Theta^M = \begin{pmatrix} 0.80 & 0.54 & 0.68 \\ 0.71 & 0.45 & 0.40 \\ 0.57 & 0.36 & 0.75 \\ 0.85 & 0.81 & 0.62 \end{pmatrix}, \Theta^N = \begin{pmatrix} 0.35 & 0.46 & 0.38 \\ 0.36 & 0.72 & 0.43 \\ 0.46 & 0.56 & 0.47 \\ 0.21 & 0.32 & 0.25 \end{pmatrix},$$

$$\varpi^M = \begin{pmatrix} 0.71 & 0.50 & 0.62 \\ 0.62 & 0.38 & 0.30 \\ 0.46 & 0.26 & 0.60 \\ 0.80 & 0.78 & 0.59 \end{pmatrix}, \beta = \begin{pmatrix} 0.24 & 0.48 & 0.38 \\ 0.38 & 0.52 & 0.70 \\ 0.54 & 0.66 & 0.40 \\ 0.20 & 0.18 & 0.28 \end{pmatrix}.$$

Let $\mathcal{Y} = \{q_1, q_2\}$ symbolize a specific sickness, and there are two signs of this condition in clinic.

***Case-1**: For $\ddot{s} = 0.45$, $\ddot{u} = 0.38$ and $\ddot{t} = 0.72$, $\ddot{v} = 0.52$, we have:*

$$p_1\ddot{\rho}^{<0.72,0.52>}_{<0.45,0.38>} = p_4\ddot{\rho}^{<0.72,0.52>}_{<0.45,0.38>} = \breve{\mathscr{U}}_2, p_2\ddot{\rho}^{<0.72,0.52>}_{<0.45,0.38>} = \{q_1, q_2\}, p_3\ddot{\rho}^{<0.72,0.52>}_{<0.45,0.38>} = \{q_3\}$$

(see Definition 8). By simple computations, the L-A and U-A of $\mathcal{Y}$ are given below:

$$\underline{appr_{\ddot{\rho}^{<0.72,0.52>}_{<0.45,0.38>}}}(\mathcal{Y}) = \{p_2\}, \overline{appr_{\ddot{\rho}^{<0.72,0.52>}_{<0.45,0.38>}}}(\mathcal{Y}) = \{p_1, p_2, p_4\}$$

Using Definition 10, $LDF - POS_{\mathbb{p}}(\mathcal{Y}) = \{p_2\}$, $LDF - BND_{\mathbb{p}}(\mathcal{Y}) = \{p_1, p_4\}$ and $LDF - NEG_{\mathbb{p}}(\mathcal{Y}) = \{p_3\}$. Furthermore, by Definition 12, the A-M and R-M are calculated as:

$$\mathbb{MA}(\mathcal{Y}) = \frac{1}{3}, \mathbb{MR}(\mathcal{Y}) = \frac{2}{3}$$

Thus, we interpret the subsequent results:

(1) Patient p2 must be afflicted with illness $\mathcal{Y}$ and requires emergency medical attention.
(2) We cannot guarantee that patients p1 and p4 are suffering from illness $\mathcal{Y}$ based on these symptoms. The doctor will therefore choose the second option.
(3) The sickness $\mathcal{Y}$ does not affect patient p3.

***Case-2**: For $\ddot{s} = 0.57$, $\ddot{u} = 0.46$ and $\ddot{t} = 0.46$, $\ddot{v} = 0.54$, we have:*

$$p_1\ddot{\rho}^{<0.46,0.54>}_{<0.57,0.46>} = \{q_1, q_3\}, p_2\ddot{\rho}^{<0.46,0.54>}_{<0.57,0.46>} = \{q_1\} = p_3\ddot{\rho}^{<0.46,0.54>}_{<0.57,0.46>}, p_4\ddot{\rho}^{<0.46,0.54>}_{<0.57,0.46>} = \breve{\mathscr{U}}_2.$$

(using Definition 8). By simple calculations, the L- and U-As of $\mathcal{Y}$ are as follows:

$$\underline{appr_{\ddot{\rho}^{<0.46,0.54>}_{<0.57,0.46>}}}(\mathcal{Y}) = \{p_2, p_3\}, \overline{appr_{\ddot{\rho}^{<0.46,0.54>}_{<0.57,0.46>}}}(\mathcal{Y}) = \breve{\mathscr{U}}_2$$

Using Definition 10, $\mathcal{LDF}POS_{\mathbb{p}}(\mathcal{Y}) = \{p_2, p_3\}$, $\mathcal{LDF}BND_{\mathbb{p}}(\mathcal{Y}) = \{p_1, p_4\}$ and $\mathcal{LDF}NEG_{\mathbb{p}}(\mathcal{Y}) = \varnothing$. Further, using Definition 12, the A-M and R-M are computed as follows:

$$\mathbb{MA}(\mathcal{Y}) = \frac{1}{2}, \mathbb{MR}(\mathcal{Y}) = \frac{1}{2}$$

Thus, we conclude that:

(1) Patients p2 and p3 must endure illness $\mathcal{Y}$, and he requires prompt medical attention.
(2) Regarding patients p1 and p4, we cannot guarantee whether or not they are experiencing the symptoms of illness $\mathcal{Y}$. The doctor will therefore choose the second option.
(3) No one who suffers has a healthy diagnosis.

Remark 3.

(◇) *Based on the analysis discussed earlier, we may infer that decision precision rises with approximation precision, as in [51]. Thus, a precise decision can be made by a doctor using the proposed method of LDF-RSs.*

(◇) *Furthermore, our proposed technique of LDF-RSs allows reducing the likelihood of a surgical misconception.*

(◇) *Additionally, the LDF-RS model, and because of the application of control or reference factors found in LD-FSs, the applied approach may help decision-makers arrive at a precise and scientific conclusion in circumstances where they frequently encounter one another.*

Comparative Analysis

In this section, we contrast our findings with a few of Yang et al. [51], Sun and Ma [48] and Ayub et al.'s [52] previously used methods.

Example 6. *For [48], consider our previous example 5, where* $\breve{\mathscr{U}}_1 = \{p_1, p_2, p_3, p_4\}$ *and* $\breve{\mathscr{U}}_2 = \{q_1, q_2, q_3\}$. *The following describes the M grades for each patient pi in connection to the symptom qj and F-R* Θ^M *on* $\breve{\mathscr{U}}_1 \times \breve{\mathscr{U}}_2$:

$$\Theta^M = \begin{pmatrix} 0.80 & 0.54 & 0.68 \\ 0.71 & 0.45 & 0.40 \\ 0.57 & 0.36 & 0.75 \\ 0.85 & 0.81 & 0.62 \end{pmatrix},$$

Using Definition 3.3 of [48] for level cuts, we obtain the following for $\ddot{s} = 0.45$:

$$p_1\Theta^M_{0.45} = p_4\Theta^M_{0.45} = \breve{\mathscr{U}}_2, p_3\Theta^M_{0.45} = \{q_1, q_3\}, p_2\Theta^M_{0.45} = \{q_1, q_2\}$$

For $\mathcal{Y} = \{q_1, q_2\}$, *the L- and U-As are obtained by using Definition 3.3 of [48] below:*

$$\underline{appr_{\Theta^M_{0.45}}}(\mathcal{Y}) = \{p_2\}, \overline{appr_{\Theta^M_{0.45}}}(\mathcal{Y}) = \breve{\mathscr{U}}_2$$

Therefore, $P - R(\mathcal{Y}) = \{p_2\}$, $B - R(\mathcal{Y}) = \{p_1, p_3, p_4\}$ *and* $N - R(\mathcal{Y}) = \varnothing$. *As a result, the following conclusions may be made from this information:*

(1) *Patient p2 needs immediate medical care as he must deal with the sickness* $\mathcal{Y}$.

(2) *We are unable to confirm if patients p1, p3, and p4 are displaying the signs of sickness* $\mathcal{Y}$. *Therefore, the doctor will select choice number two.*

(3) *Nobody who is ill has a clear diagnosis.*

For $\ddot{s} = 0.57$, *we have:*

$$p_1\Theta^M_{0.57} = p_3\Theta^M_{0.57} = \{q_1, q_3\}, p_2\Theta^M_{0.57} = \{q_1\}, p_4\Theta^M_{0.57} = \breve{\mathscr{U}}_2$$

The L- and U-As for $\mathcal{Y}$ *are found by applying Definition 3.3 of [48] below:*

$$\underline{appr_{\Theta^M_{0.57}}}(\mathcal{Y}) = \{p_3\}, \overline{appr_{\Theta^M_{0.57}}}(\mathcal{Y}) = \breve{\mathscr{U}}_2$$

Therefore, $P - R(\mathcal{Y}) = \{p_3\}$, $B - R(\mathcal{Y}) = \{p_1, p_2, p_4\}$ *and* $N - R(\mathcal{Y}) = \varnothing$. *Thus, it follows that:*

(1) *Patient p3 is suffering from illness* $\mathcal{Y}$ *and needs immediate medical care.*

(2) *We are unable to confirm if patients p1, p2, and p4 are displaying the signs of sickness* $\mathcal{Y}$. *Therefore, the doctor will select choice number two.*

(3) *There is no healthy diagnosis for someone who is suffering.*

Example 7. *We use the same Example 5 with BF-R which is expressed in the Table 1 for [51]:*

Table 1. ρ_B.

$\mathcal{U}_1\backslash\mathcal{U}_2$	q_1	q_2	q_3
p_1	$<0.80, 0.20>$	$<0.54, 0.46>$	$<0.68, 0.30>$
p_2	$<0.71, 0.25>$	$<0.45, 0.45>$	$<0.40, 0.43>$
p_3	$<0.57, 0.40>$	$<0.36, 0.56>$	$<0.75, 0.25>$
p_4	$<0.85, 0.12>$	$<0.81, 0.15>$	$<0.62, 0.25>$

Using Definition 3.1 of [51], the $<\ddot{s},\ddot{t}>$ *−level cuts for* $\ddot{s}=0.45$ *and* $\ddot{t}=0.54$*, we have the sequel:*

$$p_1(\rho_B)^{<0.45,0.54>} = p_4(\rho_B)^{<0.45,0.54>} = \mathcal{U}_2, p_2(\rho_B)^{<0.45,0.54>} = \{q_1,q_2\}, p_3(\rho_B)^{<0.45,0.54>} = \{q_3\}$$

From Definition 3.2 of [51], the L-, and U-As of $\mathcal{Y}$ *are given below:*

$$\underline{appr_{(\rho_B)^{<0.45,0.54>}}}(\mathcal{Y}) = \{p_2\}, \overline{appr_{(\rho_B)^{<0.45,0.54>}}}(\mathcal{Y}) = \{p_1,p_2,p_4\}$$

Therefore, $P-R(\mathcal{Y})=\{p_2\}$, $B-R(\mathcal{Y})=\{p_1,p_4\}$ *and* $N-R(\mathcal{Y})=\{p_3\}$. *Thus, based on these findings, the following inferences can be made:*

(1) *Patient p2 must suffer from disease* $\mathcal{Y}$*, so he requires urgent medical attention.*
(2) *We are uncertain as to whether patients p1 and p4 are exhibiting the signs of sickness* $\mathcal{Y}$*. Therefore, the doctor will select choice number two.*
(3) *Patient* p_3 *was declared to be in good health and does not require any additional care.*

Now, for $\ddot{s}=0.57$ *and* $\ddot{t}=0.40$*, using Definition 3.1 of [51] for* $<\ddot{s},\ddot{t}>$ *−level cuts, we obtain the following:*

$$p_1(\rho_B)^{<0.45,0.54>} = p_3(\rho_B)^{<0.45,0.54>} = \{q_1,q_3\}, p_2(\rho_B)^{<0.45,0.54>} = \{q_1\}, p_4(\rho_B)^{<0.45,0.54>} = \mathcal{U}_2$$

By using Definition 3.2 of [51] and simple calculations, we obtain the L-A and U-A of $\mathcal{Y}$ *in the sequel:*

$$\underline{appr_{(\rho_B)^{<0.57,0.40>}}}(\mathcal{Y}) = \{p_2\}, \overline{appr_{(\rho_B)^{<0.57,0.40>}}}(\mathcal{Y}) = \mathcal{U}_2$$

Therefore, $P-R(\mathcal{Y})=\{p_2\}$, $B-R(\mathcal{Y})=\{p_1,p_3,p_4\}$ *and* $N-R(\mathcal{Y})=\varnothing$. *Based on these results, we conclude that:*

(1) *Patient p2 has to have illness* $\mathcal{Y}$*, so he needs to get medical help right away.*
(2) *We cannot guarantee that patients p1, p3, and p4 are displaying the signs of sickness* $\mathcal{Y}$ *or not. Therefore, the doctor will select choice number two.*
(3) *Nobody who is in pain has a good diagnosis.*

Example 8. *For [52], consider the same LDF-R as in Example 5. By using Definition 9 of [52], we obtain the L-, and U-As for* $\mathcal{Y}=\{q_1,q_2\}$ *and* $\ddot{s}=0.45$, $\ddot{u}=0.38$ *as follows:*

$$\underline{\ddot{\rho}(\mathcal{Y})}_{<0.45,0.38>} = \{p_2\}, \overline{\ddot{\rho}(\mathcal{Y})}^{<0.45,0.38>} = \mathcal{U}_1$$

For $\ddot{t}=0.72$ *and* $\ddot{v}=0.52$*, the L-A and U-A are as follows:*

$$\underline{\ddot{\rho}(\mathcal{Y})}_{<0.72,0.52>} = \{p_1,p_2,p_4\}, \overline{\ddot{\rho}(\mathcal{Y})}^{<0.72,0.52>} = \varnothing$$

Thus, $P-R(\mathcal{Y})=(\{p_2\},\varnothing)$, $B-R(\mathcal{Y})=(\{p_1,p_3,p_4\},\{p_1,p_2,p_4\})$ *and* $N-R(\mathcal{Y})=(\varnothing,\{p_3\})$. *These findings allow for the following inferences:*

(1) *Patient p2 must deal with the ailment* $\mathcal{Y}$*, necessitating immediate medical attention. Since there is no other patient in the area, we can declare with certainty that this patient does not have illness* $\mathcal{Y}$*.*
(2) *We cannot ensure that patients p1, p3, and p4 are exhibiting the symptoms of sickness* $\mathcal{Y}$*. Consequently, the doctor will pick option number two.*

(3) *Nobody who is in pain has a good diagnosis.*
Now, for $\ddot{s} = 0.57$, $\ddot{u} = 0.46$ *the L-, and U-As are as follows:*

$$\underline{\ddot{\rho}(\mathcal{Y})}_{<0.57,0.46>} = \{p_2\}, \overline{\ddot{\rho}(\mathcal{Y})}^{<0.45,0.38>} = \mathcal{U}_1$$

For $\ddot{t} = 0.46$ *and* $\ddot{v} = 0.54$, *the L-A and U-As of* $\mathcal{Y}$ *are as follows:*

$$\underline{\ddot{\rho}(\mathcal{Y})}_{<0.46,0.54>} = \mathcal{U}_1, \overline{\ddot{\rho}(\mathcal{Y})}^{<0.46,0.54>} = \varnothing$$

Thus, $P - R(\mathcal{Y}) = (\{p_2\}, \varnothing)$, $B - R(\mathcal{Y}) = (\{p_1, p_3, p_4\}, \mathcal{U}_1)$ *and* $N - R(\mathcal{Y}) = (\varnothing, \varnothing)$. *These lead us to conclude that:*

(1) *Patient p2 must deal with ailment* $\mathcal{Y}$, *necessitating immediate medical attention. Since there is no other patient in the area, we can declare with certainty that this patient does not have illness* $\mathcal{Y}$.
(2) *We cannot confirm whether patients p1, p3, and p4 are exhibiting the signs of sickness* $\mathcal{Y}$. *As a result, the doctor will go with option number two.*
(3) *No one with a diagnosis of illness is healthy.*

7. Conclusions

The concept of LD-FS is a very powerful and convenient tool to describe the uncertainties in many practical problems, which involves decisions. The decision makers can freely choose the degree of truthness and the degree of falsity by making the use of reference or control parameters. Thus, LD-FS enhanced the space of truthness degree and falsity degree and removed the limitations of these degrees as in the existing concepts of FS, IF-S, B-FS, P-FS and q-ROF-S. In this paper, the existing notions of the F-RS model and BF-RS model on two universes have been generalized into the LDF-RS model on two universes as a more convenient and a robust model. The basic notions of lower and upper LDF-RAS have been defined by employing the after sets and fore sets of the $(<\ddot{s}, \ddot{u}>, <\ddot{t}, \ddot{v}>)$-level cut relation of an LDF-Rs. Some important results related to the L- and U-As have been proved with illustrative examples. Furthermore, to illustrate the application of LDF-RSs, an example has been employed. Further research on the proposed ideas of this research paper applied to other practical applications is needed, which may lead to many fruitful outcomes.

Author Contributions: S.A., M.S., and M.R., contributed to the investigation, methodology, and writing—original draft preparation. F.K., D.M., and D.V., contributed to the supervision, investigation, and funding acquisition. S.A. contributed to the application, formal analysis, and data analysis. All authors have read and agreed to the published version of the manuscript.

Funding: Support has been received from the German Research Foundation and the TU Berlin.

Data Availability Statement: This manuscript contains hypothetical data and can be used by anyone by citing this article.

Acknowledgments: The authors wish to acknowledge the support received from the German Research Foundation and the TU Berlin.

Conflicts of Interest: The authors declare that they have no conflict of interest regarding the publication of the research article.

References

1. Zadeh, L.A. Fuzzy Sets. *Inf. Control* **1965**, *8*, 338–353. [CrossRef]
2. Atanssov, K.T. Intuintionistic Fuzzy Sets. *Fuzzy Sets Syst.* **1986**, *20*, 87–96. [CrossRef]
3. Atanssov, K.T. More on Intuintionistic Fuzzy Sets. *Fuzzy Sets Syst.* **1989**, *33*, 37–45. [CrossRef]

4. Zhang, W.R. Bipolar fuzzy sets and relations: A computational framework for cognitive modeling and multiagent decision analysis. In Proceedings of the Industrial Fuzzy Control and Intelligent Systems Conference, and The NASA Joint Technology Workshop on Neural Networks and Fuzzy Logic and Fuzzy Information Processing Society Biannual Conference, San Antonio, TX, USA, 18–21 December 1994; pp. 305–309.
5. Yager, R.P. Pythagorean fuzzy subsets. In Proceedings of the IFSA World Congress and NAFIPS Anual Meeting, Edmonton, AB, Canada, 24–28 June 2013; pp. 57–61.
6. Yager, R.P. Pythagorean membership grades in multi-criteria decision maiking. *IEEE Trans. Fuzzy Syst.* **2014**, *22*, 958–965. [CrossRef]
7. Yager, R.P. Generalized orthopair fuzzy sets. *IEEE Trans. Fuzzy Syst.* **2017**, *25*, 1222–1230. [CrossRef]
8. Riaz, M.; Hashmi, M.R. Linear Diophantine fuzzy set and its applications towards multi-attribute decision-making problems. *J. Intell. Fuzzy Syst.* **2019**, *37*, 5417–5439. [CrossRef]
9. Almagrabi, A.O.; Abdullah, S.; Shams, M. A new approach to q-linear Diophantine fuzzy emergency decision support system for COVID19. *J. Ambient. Intell. Humaniz. Comput.* **2022**, *13*, 1687–1713. [CrossRef]
10. Kamaci, H. Linear Diophantine fuzzy algebraic structures. *J. Ambient. Intell. Humaniz. Comput.* **2021**, *12*, 10353–10373. [CrossRef]
11. Riaz, M.; Hashmi, M.R.; Kulsoom, H.; Pamucar, D.; Chu, Y.M. Linear Diophantine fuzzy soft rough sets for the selection of sustainable material handling equipment. *Symmetry* **2020**, *12*, 1215. [CrossRef]
12. Ayub, S.; Shabir, M.; Riaz, M.; Aslam, M.; Chinram, R. Linear Diophantine Fuzzy relations and their algebraic properties with decision making. *Symmetry* **2021**, *13*, 945. [CrossRef]
13. Zadeh, L.A. Similarity Relations and Fuzzy Orderings. *Inf. Sci.* **1971**, *3*, 177–200. [CrossRef]
14. Wang, X.Z.; Ruan, D.; Kerre, E.E. Mathematics of fuzziness-Basic Issues. In *Studies in Fuzziness and Soft Computing*; Springer: Berlin/Heidelberg, Germany, 2009; Volume 245, pp. 1–227.
15. Atanassov, K.T. Intuitionistic Fuzzy Relations (IFRs). In *On Intuitionistic Fuzzy Sets Theory. Studies in Fuzziness and Soft Computing*; Springer: Berlin/Heidelberg, Germany, 2012; Volume 283, pp. 147–193. [CrossRef]
16. Molodtsov, D. Soft set theory-first results. *Comput. Math. Appl.* **1999**, *37*, 19–31. [CrossRef]
17. Hashmi, M.R.; Riaz, M.; Smarandache, F. m-polar neutrosophic topology with applications to multi-criteria decision-making in medical diagnosis and clustering analysis. *Int. J. Fuzzy Syst.* **2020**, *22*, 273–292. [CrossRef]
18. Pawlak, Z. Rough sets. *Int. J. Inf. Comp. Sci.* **1982**, *11*, 341–356. [CrossRef]
19. Pawlak, Z. *Rough Sets-Theoretical Aspects of Reasoning Anout Data*; Kluwer Academic Publishing: Dordrecht, The Netherlands, 1991.
20. Yao, Y.Y. Constructive and algebraic methods of the theory of rough sets. *Inf. Sci.* **1998**, *109*, 21–47. [CrossRef]
21. Zhu, W. Generalized rough sets based on relations. *Inf. Sci.* **2007**, *177*, 4997–5011. [CrossRef]
22. Davvaz, B. A short note on algebraic $T-$rough sets. *Inf. Sci.* **2008**, *178*, 3247–3252. [CrossRef]
23. Skowron, A.; Stepaniuk, J. Tolerance approximation spaces. *Fundam. Inform.* **1996**, *27*, 245–253. [CrossRef]
24. Slowinski, R.; Vanderpooten, D. Similarity relation as a basis for rough approximations. *ICS Res. Rep.* **1995**, *53*, 249–250.
25. Qin, K.; Yang, J.; Pei, Z. Generalized rough sets baased on reflexive and transitive relations. *Inf. Sci.* **2008**, *178*, 4138–4141. [CrossRef]
26. Kanwal, R.S.; Shabir, M. Roughness in semigroups by soft binary relations. *J. Intell. Fuzzy Syst.* **2018**, *35*, 1–14.
27. Li, Z.; Xie, N.; Gao, N. Rough approximations based on soft binary relations and knowledge bases. *Soft Comput.* **2017**, *21*, 839-852. [CrossRef]
28. Ali, M.I. A note on soft sets, rough soft sets, fuzzy soft sets. *Appl. Soft. Comput.* **2011**, *11*, 3329–3332.
29. Qian, Y.; Liang, J.; Yao, Y.; Dang, C. MGRS: A Multigranulation rough set. *Inf. Sci.* **2010**, *180*, 949–970. [CrossRef]
30. Ayub, S.; Shabir, M.; Mahmood, W. New types of soft rough sets in groups by normal soft groups. *Comput. Appl. Math.* **2020**, *39*, 67. [CrossRef]
31. Zhan, J.; Alcantud, J.C.R. A novel type of soft rough covering and its application to multicriteria group decision making. *Artif. Intell. Rev.* **2019**, *52*, 2381–2410. [CrossRef]
32. Feng, F.; Akram, M.; Davvaz, B.; Leoreanu-Fotea, V. Attribute analysis of information systems based on elementary soft implications. *Knowl.-Based Syst.* **2014**, *70*, 281–292. [CrossRef]
33. Riaz, M.; Farid, H.M.A. Picture fuzzy aggregation approach with application to third-party logistic provider selection process. *Rep. Mech. Eng.* **2022**, *3*, 318–327. [CrossRef]
34. Ashraf, A.; Ullah, K.; Hussain, A.; Bari, M. Interval-Valued Picture Fuzzy Maclaurin Symmetric Mean Operator with application in Multiple Attribute Decision-Making. *Rep. Mech. Eng.* **2022**, *3*, 301–317. [CrossRef]
35. Ali, Z.; Mahmood, T.; Ullah, K.; Khan, Q. Einstein Geometric Aggregation Operators using a Novel Complex Interval-valued Pythagorean Fuzzy Setting with Application in Green Supplier Chain Management. *Rep. Mech. Eng.* **2021**, *2*, 105–134. [CrossRef]
36. Zhou, B.; Chen, J.; Wu, Q.; Pamucar, D.; Wang, W.; Zhou, L. Risk priority evaluation of power transformer parts based on hybrid FMEA framework under hesitant fuzzy environment. *Facta Univ. Ser. Mech. Eng.* **2022**, *20*, 399–420. [CrossRef]
37. Ayub, S.; Mahmood, W.; Shabir, M.; Nabi, F.G. Applications of roughness in soft-intersection groups. *Comput. Appl. Math.* **2019**, *8*, 1–16. [CrossRef]
38. Chen, Z.; Ayub, S.; Mahmood, W.; Mahmood, A.; Jung, C.Y. A study of roughness in modules of fractions. *IEEE Access* **2019**, *7*, 93088–93099. [CrossRef]

39. Karamaşa, C.; Karabasevic, D.; Stanujkic, D.; Kookhdan, A.; Mishra, A.; Ertürk, M. An extended single-valued neutrosophic AHP and MULTIMOORA method to evaluate the optimal training aircraft for flight training organizations. *Facta Univ. Ser. Mech. Eng.* **2021**, *19*, 555–578. [CrossRef]
40. Osintsev, N.; Rakhmangulov, A.; Baginova, V. Evaluation of logistic flows in green supply chains based on the combined DEMATEL-ANP method. *Facta Univ. Ser. Mech. Eng.* **2021**, *19*, 473–498. [CrossRef]
41. Mahmood, W.; Nazeer, W.; Kang, S.K. The lower and upper approximations and homomorphisms between lower and upper approximations in quotient groups. *J. Intell. Fuzzy Syst.* **2017**, *33*, 2585–2594. [CrossRef]
42. Mahmood, W.; Ahmad, M.S.; Nazeer, W.; Kang, S.M. A comparision between lower and upper approximations in groups with respect to group homomorphisms. *J. Intell. Fuzzy Syst.* **2018**, *35*, 1–11.
43. Shabir, M.; Shaeen, T. A new methodolgy for fuzzification of rough sets based on $\alpha-$indiscernibility. *Fuzzy Sets Syst.* **2016**, *16*, 1–19. [CrossRef]
44. Tsang, E.C.; Chen, D.; Yeung, D.S.; Wang, X.Z.; Lee, J.W. Attributes reduction using fuzzy rough sets. *IEEE Trans. Fuzzy Syst.* **2008**, *16*, 1130–1141. [CrossRef]
45. Dubois, D.; Prade, H. Fuzzy rough sets and rough fuzzy sets. *Int. J. Gen. Syst.* **1990**, *17*, 191–209. [CrossRef]
46. Gul, R.; Shabir, M. Roughness of a set by $(\alpha, \beta)-$indiscernibility of Bipolar fuzzy relation. *Comput. Appl. Math.* **2020**, *39*, 1–22. [CrossRef]
47. Liu, G.L. Rough set theory based on two universal sets and its applications. *Knowl. Based Syst.* **2010**, *23*, 110–115. [CrossRef]
48. Sun, B.Z.; Ma, W.M. Fuzzy rough set model on two different universes and its applications. *Appl. Math. Model.* **2011**, *35*, 1798–1809. [CrossRef]
49. Li, T.J.; Zhang, W.X. Rough fuzzy approximations on two universes of discourse. *Inf. Sci.* **2008**, *178*, 892–906. [CrossRef]
50. Yang, H.L. A note on Rough set theory based on two universal sets and its applications. *Knowl.-Based Syst.* **2010**, *24*, 465–466. [CrossRef]
51. Yang, H.L.; Li, S.G.; Wang, S.; Wang, J. Bipolar fuzzy rough set model on two different universes and it applications. *Knowl.-Based Syst.* **2012**, *35*, 94–101. [CrossRef]
52. Ayub, S.; Shabir, M.; Riaz, M.; Mahmood, W.; Bozanic, D.; Marinkovic, D. Linear Diophantine Fuzzy Rough Sets: A New Rough Set Approach with Decision Making. *Symmetry* **2022**, *14*, 525. [CrossRef]

axioms

MDPI

Article

Proving, Refuting, Improving—Looking for a Theorem

Branislav Boričić

Faculty of Economics, University of Belgrade, Belgrade 11000, Serbia; boricic@ekof.bg.ac.rs

Abstract: Exploring the proofs and refutations of an abstract statement, conjecture with the aim to give a formal syntactic treatment of its proving–refuting process, we introduce the notion of extrapolation of a possibly unprovable statement having the form *if A, then B*, and propose a procedure that should result in the new statement *if A′, then B′*, which is similar to the starting one, but provable. We think that this procedure, based on the extrapolation method, can be considered a basic methodological tool applicable to prove–refute–improve any conjecture. This new notion, extrapolation, presents a dual counterpart of the well-known interpolation introduced in traditional logic sixty-five years ago.

Keywords: extrapolation; interpolation; proving; refuting; improving

MSC: 03B05; 03B80; 03A10

1. Introduction

Lakatos' monumental play 'Proofs and Refutations' (see [1]) can be considered a demonstration of applying the proof–refutation (or conjecture–refutation) method as a practical realization of the falsificationism concept advocated and supported at that time, among other authors, by [2]. At the same time, the concept of proving–refuting–improving, demonstrated in the same play, can be used as an effective interactive class model.

Refutation, as an isolated process, plays an extremely important role in the development of a pupil's critical thinking and has a crucial place in each study program syllabus. We deem that examples of finding and treating incorrectness in some reasoning and argumentation are at least of equal didactic importance as those with correct derivations and proofs. Such examples present and help incite critical thinking.

First, let us explain in brief what we mean under the term 'extrapolation'. As we know, interpolation deals with finding statements C and D, which are in between A and B, when $A \vdash B$; i.e., 'A implies B', is provable, meaning that all three sequents $A \vdash C$, $C \vdash D$ and $D \vdash B$ are provable. In this case, the sequent $C \vdash D$ presents an interpolant for $A \vdash B$. On the other side, if $A \vdash B$ is refutable, i.e., $A \nvdash B$, then we are looking for two statements C and D, such that $C \vdash A$, $B \vdash D$ and $C \vdash D$ are all provable; in this case, the sequent $C \vdash D$ will be an extrapolant for $A \nvdash B$.

In this paper, we extend the proving–refuting method by its immediate result—improving—and place it in a wider logical context relating it with the well-known concept of interpolation, with a new concept, extrapolation, as its dual. Both these notions, extrapolation and interpolation, are closely connected with many aspects of abductive reasoning [3]. The improving process, based deeply on the extrapolation method, is presented through several examples. Let me repeat here that once, a long time ago, my teacher Aleksandar Kron told me: 'Oh, how many times I fell asleep with a proof, and woke up with a counterexample'. This was the essence of the proving–refuting–improving process, during the daily journey of any scientist from a conjecture to the truth (see [4]). This process, consisting of proving and refuting attempts producing an improvement of the starting conjecture, is presented formally as an methodological procedure for discovering better statements. In fact, this can be considered a kind of Hegelian–Marxist dialectic scheme: thesis–antithesis–synthesis. However, the crucial cognition is that the essential step of this

Citation: Boričić, B. Proving, Refuting, Improving—Looking for a Theorem. *Axioms* **2022**, *11*, 559. https://doi.org/10.3390/axioms11100559

Academic Editors: Oscar Castillo and Radko Mesiar

Received: 1 August 2022
Accepted: 11 October 2022
Published: 15 October 2022

procedure is based on extrapolation, which is a dual to the well-known logical feature of reasoning—the interpolation property. We introduce the notion of extrapolation as a counterpart of interpolation. We do this in general form, independently of the basic logic. Namely, our definition depends neither on language—we do not use connectives—nor on logic—we suppose that our deduction relation is not necessarily linked to classical logic. Pure propositional logics open the problem of existence of a minimal extrapolant, which seems particularly interesting in case of infinitely valued systems.

2. Interpolation and Extrapolation—A General Idea

A typical form of a scientific statement is that 'B follows from A', denoted by $A \vdash B$, expressing a causal relationship between A and B. Refutation of such a statement consists of argumentation presenting at least one example (interpretation) where A is satisfied, but B is not.

The turnstyle symbol will be used in an informal way, not connected to any particular logical system, but assuming its rudimentary structural properties such as identity ($A \vdash A$), weakening ($A \vdash B$ implies $A, C \vdash B$), permutation ($A, B \vdash C$ implies $B, A \vdash C$), contraction ($A, A \vdash B$ implies $A \vdash B$) and transitivity ($A \vdash B$ and $B \vdash C$ imply $A \vdash C$).

Establishing a statement $A \vdash B$ as a conjecture means that we believe that $A \vdash B$ holds, but also that this is partly under question; does $A \vdash B$? In order to obtain a final conclusion regarding the truthfulness of our conjecture, we try to prove and to refute it. This process implies finding examples supporting $A \vdash B$ and counterexamples refuting $A \vdash B$, as well as looking for similar statements $A' \vdash B'$ that are, by their nature, weaker than $A \vdash B$ in cases when $A \vdash B$ is refutable, and stronger than $A \vdash B$ in cases when $A \vdash B$ is provable.

Let us consider the two apparently simplest cases of causal connection: (i) $A \vdash B$ is not proven and (ii) $A \vdash B$ is proven, where A and B are two arbitrary sentences. In the second case (ii), we can assert that there are two propositions C and D such that the following statements are provable: $A \vdash C, C \vdash D$ and $D \vdash B$. If C and D are logically equivalent, then we recognize here a form of the well-known Craig interpolation theorem (see [5]), pointing out that the form presented here can be considered as its slight generalization. In a similar way, we will deal with the first case (i) and suppose that there are two propositions C and D such that the following statements are provable: $C \vdash A$, $B \vdash D$ and $C \vdash D$, obtaining a form that is somehow dual to interpolation (ii) and which could be treated as a kind of extrapolation.

We point out that the term 'duality' is used here in a quite different meaning than in classical two-valued logic. For each statement of the form $A \vdash B$, provable or unprovable, we consider a provable statement $C \vdash D$. If $A \vdash C$ and $D \vdash B$ are provable, then $C \vdash D$ is called an interpolant, while when $C \vdash A$ and $B \vdash D$ are provable, then $C \vdash D$ is called an extrapolant. Consequently, C and D as parts of an interpolant are in consequent of A and antecedent of B, respectively, but as parts of an extrapolant, they have 'dually' just the opposite roles; C is in antecedent of A and D is in consequent of B.

More accurately, if we suppose that $A \vdash B$ is any statement, provable or not, then (i) $C \vdash D$ is its *extrapolant* if all statements $C \vdash A$, $B \vdash D$ and $C \vdash D$ are provable; (ii) $C \vdash D$ is its *interpolant* if all statements $A \vdash C$, $D \vdash B$ and $C \vdash D$ are provable. We omit here more formal details such as variable sharing and the context of a particular logical system for the deduction relation.

Note that in the case that an interpolant exists, the original statement $A \vdash B$ is provable. However, in the case that an extrapolant exists, we can conclude nothing regarding the provability of $A \vdash B$. The most interesting cases in the sequel of this paper will be exactly those (i) when $A \nvdash B$, i.e., $A \vdash B$ is unprovable. The challenges before us here are how to find some 'good' extrapolants for $A \nvdash B$ and (ii) when $A \vdash B$ is provable, how to find its 'good' interpolants. This is because in both these cases, the statement $C \vdash D$ should present an improvement of $A \vdash B$, which will be explained below.

The term 'interpolation' is justified by the simple fact that we insert a new statement $C \vdash D$ in between A and B, with an obvious possibility to infer $A \vdash B$ from $A \vdash C$,

$C \vdash D$ and $D \vdash B$. Similarly, the extrapolation process involves looking for a statement C 'before' A, because $C \vdash A$, and a statement D 'after' B, because $B \vdash D$. Both requirements, interpolation and extrapolation, have some trivial solutions. If $A \vdash B$ is proven, then both forms $A \vdash A$ and $B \vdash B$ present possible interpolants. Furthermore, for any $A \vdash B$, all statements $\bot \vdash \top$, $\bot \vdash A$ and $B \vdash \top$ present its extrapolants, where we use the symbols $\top$ and $\bot$, respectively, to denote truth and absurdity constants. Later, after sharpening both notions, extrapolation and interpolation, following the spirit of Craig's interpolation theorem and practical applications of extrapolation, we will see that trivial solutions have no importance (as usual).

Example 1 (Lakatos' Proofs and Refutations). *In his famous work, by giving a picturesque presentation of the proving–refuting process, Lakatos (see [1]) begins with an incorrect and refutable formulation of Euler's Polyhedral Theorem. The dialog between a teacher and his pupils starts with the teacher's provocation: "In our last lesson we arrived at a conjecture concerning polyhedra, namely, that for all polyhedra $V - E + F = 2$, where V is the number of vertices, E the number of edges and F the number of faces. We tested it by various methods. But we have not yet proven it. Has anybody found a proof?" After that, through a few iterations, the teacher, together with his pupils, by using a proving–refuting–improving method, obtains and proves the correct form of Euler's Polyhedral Theorem: for all convex polyhedra, $V - E + F = 2$.*

Example 2 (Elementary Geometry). *Let $\mathbf{RTr(a,b,c)}$ denote any right triangle with sides a, b, c, where c is its hypothenuse, and $\mathbf{Tr(a,b,c)}$ denotes any triangle with sides a, b, c. Some of the known elementary geometric facts can be formulated by means of a deduction relation as follows:*

Triangle Inequality: $\mathbf{Tr(a,b,c)} \vdash \mathbf{a+b>c}$.

Pythagorean Theorem: $\mathbf{RTr(a,b,c)} \vdash \mathbf{a^2+b^2=c^2}$ *and* $a^2+b^2=c^2 \vdash \mathbf{RTr(a,b,c)}$.

We also have two obvious facts: $\mathbf{RTr(a,b,c)} \vdash \mathbf{Tr(a,b,c)}$*; i.e., each right triangle is a triangle and, in elementary algebra,* $a^2+b^2=c^2 \vdash a+b>c$ *for any positive reals a, b, c (see [6]). In order to illustrate the extrapolation phenomenon in this context, we consider the following negative statement:*

$$\mathbf{Tr(a,b,c)} \nvdash \mathbf{a^2+b^2=c^2}$$

By the extrapolation approach, bearing in mind that $\mathbf{RTr(a,b,c)} \vdash \mathbf{Tr(a,b,c)}$ *and* $a^2+b^2=c^2 \vdash a+b>c$*, we can infer the following statements:* $\mathbf{RTr(a,b,c)} \vdash \mathbf{a^2+b^2=c^2}$, $\mathbf{Tr(a,b,c)} \vdash \mathbf{a+b>c}$ *and* $\mathbf{RTr(a,b,c)} \vdash \mathbf{a+b>c}$*, as possible extrapolants. Deeming the proving–refuting–improving process one of the most important methods of knowledge growth, the author of this text, with a group of his brilliant students (Aleksanra Djoković, Bojana Tujković, Ivana Čekrdžić, Aleksandar Elezović, Doroteja Djordjević and Milan Perić), during the spring semester 2014, set up a musical performance under the title 'Proofs and refutations: devoted to the glorious triangle', at the Faculty of Economics, University of Belgrade. That performance was deeply inspired by [1] but, for the sake of better understanding the basic message, instead of Euler's Polyhedral Theorem, considered in the original Lakatos' play, we dealt with proofs and refutations of the Pythagorean Theorem.*

Example 3 (Propositional Calculus). *Here, we present some more subtle examples of interpolants and extrapolants. Let $\wedge$ and $\vee$ denote the conjunction and disjunction connectives, respectively. (i) The form $p \vee q \vdash p \wedge q$ is unprovable, i.e., $p \vee q \nvdash p \wedge q$, and it can be improved by the following forms: $p \vdash p$, $q \vdash q$, $p \vdash p \vee q$, $q \vdash p \vee q$ and $p \wedge q \vdash p \vee q$; this is not a complete list of its extrapolants. (ii) The form $p \wedge q \vdash p \vee q$ is provable and it can be improved by the following interpolants: $p \wedge q \vdash p$, $p \vdash p \vee q$, $p \vdash p$ and $q \vdash q$; this is not a complete list of its interpolants. Let us note that the examples of extrapolants and interpolants considered here are compatible not only with classical, but also with many non-classical propositional logics.*

Example 4 (Set-Theoretic Interpretation). *Due to the immediate link between the set-theoretic inclusion relation and the classical implication connective, the interpolation and extrapolation have a rough illustrative and a quite simple set-theoretic interpretation. Namely, if for two sets A and B*

we have $A \subseteq B$, then the sets C and D, such that $A \subseteq C \subseteq D \subseteq B$, can be considered as the basic constituents of an interpolant $C \subseteq D$ for $A \subseteq B$. On the other side, if $A \not\subseteq B$, then the sets C and D, such that $C \subseteq A$, $B \subseteq D$ and $C \subseteq D$, define an extrapolant $C \subseteq D$ for $A \not\subseteq B$.

Example 5 (Impossibility Tradition). *In spite of their great methodological and logical importance (see [7,8]), impossibility theorems raise a natural question: how they can be transformed into the corresponding relevant possibility results? Each such transformation is based on some proving–refuting–improving process that starts with the improving, i.e., with an extrapolation step. Let us discuss two simple cases of impossibility theorems.*

*Incommensurability of the diagonal and the side of a square: if a is the side of a square and d is its diagonal, then $a = 1 \vdash d \notin \mathbf{N}$, i.e., $a = 1 \nvdash d \in \mathbf{N}$, where **N** is the set of natural numbers. By replacing (weakening) $d \in \mathbf{N}$ with $d \in \mathbf{Q}$, bearing in mind that $d \in \mathbf{N} \vdash \mathbf{d} \in \mathbf{Q}$ where **Q** is the set of rational numbers, we also obtain by extrapolation an invalid statement $a = 1 \vdash d \in \mathbf{Q}$. The next iteration is finding an appropriate extrapolant for the statement $a = 1 \nvdash d \in \mathbf{Q}$. Obviously, by replacing $d \in \mathbf{Q}$ with $d \in \mathbf{R}$, bearing in mind that $d \in \mathbf{Q} \vdash \mathbf{d} \in \mathbf{R}$ where **R** is the set of reals, we obtain a valid positive statement $a = 1 \vdash d \in \mathbf{R}$, i.e., a possibility result.*

*Unsolvability of the equation $x^2 + a = 0$, $a \in \mathbf{R}$, in the field of reals: $a \in \mathbf{R} \wedge \mathbf{x}^2 + \mathbf{a} = \mathbf{0} \nvdash \mathbf{x} \in \mathbf{R}$ leads to two simple positive possibilities. By antecedent weakening, from $a \leq 0 \vdash a \in \mathbf{R}$, we obtain $a \leq 0 \wedge x^2 + a = 0 \vdash x \in \mathbf{R}$, or, by consequent weakening, from $x \in \mathbf{R} \vdash \mathbf{x} \in \mathbf{C}$ where **C** is the set of complex numbers, we have $a \in \mathbf{R} \wedge \mathbf{x}^2 + \mathbf{a} = \mathbf{0} \vdash \mathbf{x} \in \mathbf{C}$, i.e., solvability of that equation in the field of complex numbers.*

In a similar way, but with more complex argumentation and context, Arrow's Impossibility Theorem (see [7–9]), the most popular and important result in Social Choice Theory during the last century, has generated a number of possibility results. Variations of the corresponding possibility theorems (see [10]), obtained by weakening the antecedent or consequent of Arrow's original theorem, can be considered as effective examples of applying the proving–refuting–improving process as well.

Here, we will explain why we do believe that both interpolants and extrapolants present improvements of our initial statement $A \vdash B$. (i) If $A \vdash B$ is not provable, then its extrapolant $C \vdash D$, which is provable, obtained from an unprovable statement, presents its improvement, bearing in mind that from the initial statement $A \vdash B$ of low quality (unprovable), we obtain its extrapolant $C \vdash D$, a statement of higher quality (provable). (ii) If $A \vdash B$ is provable, then its interpolant $C \vdash D$, which is provable together with $A \vdash C$ and $C \vdash B$, can be used as a sufficient condition to infer the initial statement $A \vdash B$, and from this point of view it can be considered as its essence—its improvement—enabling us to prove and better understand the meaning of the initial statement $A \vdash B$.

3. Extrapolation—More Formally

Let us discuss a more subtle aspect of extrapolation including some views of relevance logic. A deduction of B from hypothesis A is acceptable relevance logic if this deduction employs every element of A. Another syntactic relevance principle, known as *variable sharing condition*, is that if A entails B, then $\mathrm{At}A \cap \mathrm{At}B \neq \emptyset$, where $\mathrm{At}A$ denotes the set of all atomic formulae, i.e., propositional letters, occurring in A (see [11]). Variable sharing is not sufficient, but it is a necessary condition for relevance.

Now, we can formulate more ambitious expectations, including some kind of variable sharing principle.

Interpolation property: If $\mathrm{At}A \cap \mathrm{At}B \neq \emptyset$ and $A \vdash B$, then there exist C and D such that $\mathrm{AtC} \cup \mathrm{At}D \subseteq \mathrm{At}A \cap \mathrm{At}B$, $A \vdash C$, $D \vdash B$ and $C \vdash D$.

Extrapolation property: If $\mathrm{At}A \cap \mathrm{At}B \neq \emptyset$ and $A \nvdash B$, then there exist C and D such that $\mathrm{AtC} \cup \mathrm{At}D \subseteq \mathrm{At}A \cap \mathrm{At}B$, $C \vdash A$, $B \vdash D$ and $C \vdash D$.

The interpolation property is defined in accordance with Craig's well-known approach (see [5]). The extrapolation property tends to find relevant, non-trivial and, in some sense, minimal statements C and D establishing an extrapolant.

Let us note here that Craig's original definition deals with only one formula C, such that $A \vdash C$ and $C \vdash B$, as an interpolant for $A \vdash B$. In this spirit, it would be possible to redefine our notion of extrapolant C for $A \not\vdash B$ so that $C \vdash A$ and $B \vdash C$. It is not difficult to see that this approach with one formula playing the role of interpolant (or extrapolant) is logically equivalent to our definition employing two formulae in both cases.

The logical, methodological, philosophical and, even algebraic aspects of interpolation have been analyzed, discussed and explained in detail as a necessary part of most textbooks in logic (see [12,13]). Here, we will attempt to elucidate the logical sense of extrapolation. Bearing in mind the following derivation:

$$\dfrac{\dfrac{C \vdash A \qquad \dfrac{A \vdash B}{C, A \vdash B, D}\,\text{weakening} \times 2 \qquad B \vdash D}{C, C \vdash D, D}\,\text{cut} \times 2}{C \vdash D}\,\text{contraction} \times 2$$

the extrapolation can be considered to be a weakening of the antecedent and the consequent of $A \vdash B$, respectively, by special statements C and D, such that $C \vdash A$ and $B \vdash D$ (Instead of $\{A, B\} \vdash \{C, D\}$, we will write simply $A, B \vdash C, D$, which, according to the traditional classical logic proof-theoretic interpretation, can be understood as $A \wedge B \vdash C \vee D$). The procedure will be satisfiable when, from an unprovable statement, we obtain a provable one, i.e., when, in fact, from $A \not\vdash B$, we obtain $C \vdash D$, where C and D are in the corresponding causal connections with A and B, respectively. In practice, when we search for an adequate statement, instead of reasoning starting with the explicit application of weakening rules, as above, the pure derivation with the cut rules

$$\dfrac{C \vdash A \qquad A \vdash B \qquad B \vdash D}{C \vdash D}\,\text{cut} \times 2$$

hides the presence of weakening. On the other side, we have to emphasize that it would be wrong to understand the extrapolation just as a simple weakening, because it is a very restricted and specific weakening in order to find the relevant extrapolant.

Extrapolation is formally, in the context of classical logic, equivalent to the left and the right side weakening rules, bearing in mind the following derivations

$$\dfrac{C, A \vdash A \quad A \vdash B}{C, A \vdash B} \text{ and } \dfrac{A \vdash B \quad B \vdash B, D}{A \vdash B, D}$$

Nevertheless, the extrapolation, as defined, seems more restrictive and suggests some kind of 'relevant' weakening. Namely, the above two derivations are classically, and even intuitionistically, admissible, but not from the point of view of relevance logic. This is the reason why the extrapolation can be essentially considered as a process partly supported by relevant logic principles, bearing in mind that variable sharing conditions for C with A and B with D are satisfied, but not necessary for C with D.

In case of an unprovable statement $A \vdash B$, when we look for some of its improvements $C \vdash D$, in order to avoid trivial solutions and to find the best one, if possible, we define the notion of minimal sentences:

Minimal extrapolants: Suppose $A \vdash B$ is not proven and $C \vdash D$ is its extrapolant. C will be called *a minimal sentence* for A, B and D, in this order, if for each C', such that $C \vdash C'$ is provable and $C' \vdash C$ is unprovable, one of the statements $C' \vdash A$ or $C' \vdash D$ is unprovable. In a dual way, D will be called *a minimal sentence* for A, B and C, in this order, if for each D', such that $D \vdash D'$ is unprovable and $D' \vdash D$ is provable, one of the statements $B \vdash D'$ or $C \vdash D'$ is unprovable. In cases when both hold, C is a minimal sentence for A, B and D, and D is a minimal sentence for A, B and C; then, the statement $C \vdash D$ is called *a minimal extrapolant* for $A \vdash B$.

The central question now is the following one: does a minimal extrapolant exist (and when)? It depends on the logical context, clearly. For instance, in m-valued propositional logics, due to the existence of finitely many nonequivalent formulae over any finite set of atomic formulae (propositional letters), we always have the possibility to choose the minimal sentences. The next question is: does the minimal nontrivial extrapolant exist (and when)? Moreover, how could a nontrivial statement be characterized?

Example 6. *Obviously, for any two sentences A and B, such that* $A \nvdash B$ *and* $p \in \mathrm{At}A \cap \mathrm{At}B$*, the statement* $p \wedge \neg p \vdash p \rightarrow p$ *presents an extrapolant. This is a trivial example.*

Example 7. *Let us consider again some extrapolants* $p \wedge q \vdash p \vee q$*,* $p \vdash p \vee q$*,* $p \wedge q \vdash p$ *and* $p \vdash p$ *of the statement* $p \vee q \vdash p \wedge q$*. In the case of extrapolant* $p \wedge q \vdash p \vee q$*, the statement* $p \wedge q$ *is not minimal for* $p \vee q$*,* $p \wedge q$ *and* $p \vee q$ *because there is a statement, p such that* $p \wedge q \vdash p$*, and both* $p \vdash p \vee q$ *and* $p \wedge q \vdash p$ *are provable. On the other hand, the statement p is a minimal one for* $p \vee q$*,* $p \wedge q$ *and* $p \vee q$*, and this is a way to find a new and 'better' extrapolant* $p \vdash p \vee q$*. In the case of this extrapolant* $p \vdash p \vee q$*, although p is a minimal for* $p \vee q$*,* $p \wedge q$ *and* $p \vee q$*, the proposition* $p \vee q$ *is not minimal for* $p \vee q$*,* $p \wedge q$ *and p because, for the statement p, we have that* $p \vdash p \vee q$ *and both* $p \vdash p \vee q$ *and* $p \vdash p$ *are provable, while p is a minimal statement for* $p \vee q$*,* $p \wedge q$ *and p. Let us note also that the examples considered here have a general character and are compatible with both classical and intuitionistic propositional logics.*

Example 8. *In set-theoretic interpretation, when* $A \nsubseteq B$*, the parts of minimal extrapolants will be the sets in between* $C = A \cap B$ *and* $D = A \cup B$ *with respect to the inclusion relation. In general,* $C = A \cap B \subseteq B = D$ *will be a minimal extrapolant for* $C = A \cap B (\subseteq A)$*,* $A (\nsubseteq B)$ *and* $B \subseteq D = B$*, and* $C = A (\subseteq D = A \cup B)$ *will be a minimal extrapolant for* $A = C (\subseteq A)$*,* $A (\nsubseteq B)$ *and* $B (\subseteq D = A \cup B)$*.*

4. More Examples

The importance of propositional language is founded, inter alia, on its simplicity. Propositional context is usually suitable for explaining and understanding the differences between various philosophical concepts for the foundations of mathematics. For instance, the spirit of essential variations between Platonism, intuitionism and relevance is already visible on the level of classical, intuitionistic and relevant propositional logics. On the other side, the founding of any serious mathematical theory needs much more than a propositional language. Here, we will try to present the idea of extrapolation in the context of the first-order predicate language.

The general symbolic form of an Impossibility Theorem stating that 'there does not exist an object x such that A implies B', is

$$\neg \exists x (A \rightarrow B)$$

The first-order sentence $\neg \exists x (A(x) \rightarrow B(x))$ can be presented in a classically equivalent way as $\neg(\forall x A(x) \rightarrow \exists x B(x))$, or a bit more informally as "$\forall x A(x)$ does not imply $\exists x B(x)$", i.e., $\forall x A(x) \nvdash \exists x B(x)$. Here, we want to describe an application of extrapolation method on

$$\forall x A(x) \nvdash \exists x B(x)$$

Namely, we are looking for sentences C and D such that $C \vdash \forall x A(x)$, $\exists x B(x) \vdash D$ and $C \vdash D$, where the last statement presents an extrapolant and, simultaneously, a transformation of an 'impossibility' result into a 'possibility' one.

On the level of general first-order languages examples, we analyze an 'impossibility case'.

Example 9. *Let us consider the following statement:* $\forall x (A \vee B) \nvdash \exists x (A \wedge B)$*, having exactly the form of an impossibility theorem. If we try to weaken the antecedent* $\forall x (A \vee B)$ *by (1)* $\forall x A \vee \forall x B$ *or by (2)* $\forall x A$*, and the consequent* $\exists x (A \wedge B)$ *by (3)* $\exists x A \wedge \exists x B$ *or by (4)* $\exists x A$*, we do not obtain extrapolants by combining (1) with (3), (1) with (4) or (2) with (3); only the combination (2) with (4) gives an extrapolant, because* $\forall x A \vdash \forall x (A \vee B)$*,* $\exists x (A \wedge B) \vdash \exists x A$*, and* $\forall x A \vdash \exists x A$*.*

We also consider some relationships between binary relations properties.

Example 10. *The logic of preferences is usually based on axioms concerning some properties of a binary relation P, called a preference relation. For instance, the list of axioms contains irreflexivity (Ir),* $\forall x \neg P(y,x)$*, asymmetry (As),* $\forall x \forall y (P(x,y) \rightarrow \neg P(y,x))$*, transitivity (Tr),* $\forall x \forall y \forall z (P(x,y) \wedge P(y,z) \rightarrow P(x,z))$ *and connectivity (Cn),* $\forall x \forall y \forall z (P(x,y) \rightarrow P(x,z) \vee P(z,y))$*. It is an easy exercise to show that* $\mathrm{Cn} \nvdash \mathrm{Tr}$*, but, bearing in mind that* $\mathrm{As} \wedge \mathrm{Cn} \vdash \mathrm{Cn}$*,* $\mathrm{As} \wedge \mathrm{Cn} \vdash \mathrm{Tr}$ *and* $\mathrm{Tr} \vdash \mathrm{Tr}$*, we conclude that* $\mathrm{As} \wedge \mathrm{Cn} \vdash \mathrm{Tr}$ *presents an extrapolant and an improvement of the initial statement. In a similar way, we can find that the same statement,* $\mathrm{As} \wedge \mathrm{Cn} \vdash \mathrm{Tr}$ *is an extrapolant for both* $\mathrm{Ir} \wedge \mathrm{Cn} \nvdash \mathrm{Tr}$ *and* $\mathrm{As} \wedge \mathrm{Tr} \nvdash \mathrm{Cn}$*.*

5. A Proving–Refuting–Improving Procedure

Each theorem, or more generally, each scientific statement, can be expressed in the following form: *if* Γ*, then* Δ. Γ presents a set of hypotheses (given context or a theory) and Δ is a consequence (conclusion). This is the reason why the basic form we use in this part of the paper is $\Gamma \vdash \Delta$, an informal deduction relation (entailment) $\vdash$ between two finite sets of sentences Γ (antecedent) and Δ (consequent), with the intended meaning that it is possible to infer a conclusion Δ, interpreted as a disjunction of all elements of Δ, from the hypotheses set Γ, interpreted as a conjunction of all elements of Γ. The Greek capitals $\Gamma, \Delta, \ldots$, with or without subscripts or superscripts, will be used as metavariables over finite sets of sentences denoted by Latin capitals $A, B, C, D, \ldots$ We also use $\Gamma \models \Delta$ with the usual model theoretic, meaning that if all elements of Γ are true, then at least one element of Δ is true. This will be the context enabling us to express that $\Gamma \vdash \Delta$, or $A \vdash B$, is provable or unprovable, and that $\Gamma \models \Delta$, or $A \models B$, is refutable or irrefutable.

The idea of a proving–refuting–improving procedure has been hinted at by [4]. Here, we will develop it further. In both cases when $\Gamma \vdash \Delta$ is provable or unprovable, i.e., when $\Gamma \models \Delta$ is valid or refutable, we define the following four sets: Γ-antecedent, Γ-consequent, Δ-antecedent and Δ-consequent, respectively, as $\Gamma_{\mathrm{ant}} = \{A_1^a, \ldots, A_m^a\}$, $\Gamma_{\mathrm{con}} = \{A_1^c, \ldots, A_m^c\}$, $\Delta_{\mathrm{ant}} = \{B_1^a, \ldots, B_n^a\}$ and $\Delta_{\mathrm{con}} = \{B_1^c, \ldots, B_n^c\}$, corresponding to the sets $\Gamma = \{A_1, \ldots, A_m\}$ and $\Delta = \{B_1, \ldots, B_n\}$, such that, for each i $(1 \leq i \leq m)$, $A_i^a \vdash A_i$ and $A_i \vdash A_i^c$ are provable, and for each j $(1 \leq j \leq n)$, $B_j^a \vdash B_j$ and $B_j \vdash B_j^c$ are provable.

The main problem here is to define concrete content of sets $\Gamma_{\mathrm{ant}}, \Gamma_{\mathrm{con}}, \Delta_{\mathrm{ant}}$ and Δ_{con} in this general case, because the condition that $A_i^a \vdash A_i$ is provable has infinitely many solutions for A_i^a. On the other hand, each particular problem in some specific part of mathematics gives the researcher a freedom to use his intuition during the process of 'looking for a better theorem'.

The two elementary steps in our proving–refuting–improving procedure as follows:

Step (i): if $\Gamma \vdash \Delta$ is not proven or $\Gamma \models \Delta$ is refuted, we are looking for some $A_i^a \in \Gamma_{\mathrm{ant}}$ or some $B_j^c \in \Delta_{\mathrm{con}}$ for which the provability of $\Gamma' \vdash \Delta'$ can be reconsidered, where $\Gamma' \cup \Delta'$ is obtained from $\Gamma \cup \Delta$ by substituting at least one occurrence of A_i by A_i^a in Γ or at least one occurrence of B_j by B_j^c in Δ;

Step (ii): if $\Gamma \vdash \Delta$ is proven, or $\Gamma \models \Delta$ is not refuted, we are looking for some $A_i^c \in \Gamma_{\mathrm{con}}$ or $B_j^a \in \Delta_{\mathrm{ant}}$ for which the provability of $\Gamma' \vdash \Delta'$ can be reconsidered, where $\Gamma' \cup \Delta'$ is obtained from $\Gamma \cup \Delta$ by substituting at least one occurrence of A_i by A_i^c in Γ or at least one occurrence of B_j by B_j^a in Δ.

In both cases (i) and (ii), the result will be a statement $\Gamma' \vdash \Delta'$. If $\Gamma' \vdash \Delta'$ is provable, then the procedure can be stopped and $\Gamma' \vdash \Delta'$ will present a generalized extrapolant or interpolant for $\Gamma \vdash \Delta$ in cases (i) and (ii), respectively. Otherwise, if we cannot decide if $\Gamma' \vdash \Delta'$ is provable or if $\Gamma' \vdash \Delta'$ is refutable, then we proceed with step (i) on $\Gamma' \vdash \Delta'$.

Finally, in the sequel, we apply the same procedure on $\Gamma' \vdash \Delta'$; i.e., firstly, we try to prove $\Gamma' \vdash \Delta'$ or to falsify $\Gamma' \models \Delta'$. If $\Gamma' \vdash \Delta'$ is not proven or $\Gamma' \models \Delta'$ is falsifiable, then we apply the procedure (i) on $\Gamma' \vdash \Delta'$ in order to obtain a new statement $\Gamma'' \vdash \Delta''$. If $\Gamma' \vdash \Delta'$ is provable or $\Gamma' \models \Delta'$ is not refuted, then we apply the procedure (ii) on $\Gamma' \vdash \Delta'$

in order to obtain a new statement $\Gamma'' \vdash \Delta''$. This process is called the *proving–refuting–improving procedure.*

Let us point out that a similar form of a generalized interpolant appears in S. Maehara's approach to interpolation in the context of sequent calculi (see [13]).

Note that the sentence '$\Gamma \vdash \Delta$ is not proven' does not exclude the case that $\Gamma \vdash \Delta$ can be provable, and sentence '$\Gamma \models \Delta$ is not refuted' does not exclude the case that $\Gamma \models \Delta$ can be refutable. Namely, if some fact is not proven, maybe, in the future, it could be proven, and if some fact has not been refuted up to now, it could be refuted later.

The above procedure, part (i), proving–refuting–improving, was based on methodological ideas promoted by Popper–Lakatos' proof–refutation (also known as conjecture–refutation) falsificationism (see [1,2]). Furthermore, the transformation of $\Gamma \vdash \Delta$ into $\Gamma' \vdash \Delta'$, generally, can be considered a kind of Hegelian–Marxist dialectic scheme: thesis–antithesis–synthesis, which is obviously parallel with our scheme consisting of (i) and (ii), defining the process of proving–refuting–improving.

The statement $\Gamma' \vdash \Delta'$ presents an improvement of $\Gamma \vdash \Delta$ in case (i), in a sense that from an unprovable statement $\Gamma \vdash \Delta$, we obtain a statement $\Gamma' \vdash \Delta'$, which may be provable; but if $\Gamma \vdash \Delta$ is provable, then $\Gamma' \vdash \Delta'$ is provable as well. On the other hand, the statement $\Gamma' \vdash \Delta'$ presents an improvement of $\Gamma \vdash \Delta$ in case (ii), in the sense that from a provable statement $\Gamma \vdash \Delta$, we obtain a provable statement $\Gamma' \vdash \Delta'$ from which $\Gamma \vdash \Delta$ can be derived; i.e., $\Gamma' \vdash \Delta'$ is more general than $\Gamma \vdash \Delta$. These are the reasons to treat $\Gamma' \vdash \Delta'$ as an improvement of $\Gamma \vdash \Delta$ in both cases. This also means that any possible application of our procedure to a provable statement cannot produce an unprovable statement.

If reconsideration of $\Gamma \vdash \Delta$ provides a statement $\Gamma' \vdash \Delta'$, consisting of some new elements of $\Gamma_{\text{ant}} \cup \Gamma_{\text{con}} \cup \Delta_{\text{ant}} \cup \Delta_{\text{con}}$, then, obviously, $\Gamma' \vdash \Delta'$ presents an improvement of $\Gamma \vdash \Delta$. More accurately, we can justify our procedure by some kind of soundness statement:

Theorem 1.

(i) If the statement $\Gamma' \vdash \Delta'$ is obtained from $\Gamma \vdash \Delta$ by applying step (i), then $\Gamma' \vdash \Delta'$ can be inferred from $\Gamma \vdash \Delta$;

(ii) If the statement $\Gamma' \vdash \Delta'$ is obtained from $\Gamma \vdash \Delta$ by applying step (ii), then $\Gamma \vdash \Delta$ can be inferred from $\Gamma' \vdash \Delta'$.

Proof. By induction on $n + m$—the number of statements belonging to $\Gamma \cup \Delta$: in case (i), from both, $\Gamma \vdash \Delta$ and $A_i^a \vdash A_i$, and $\Gamma \vdash \Delta$ and $B_j \vdash B_j^c$, by the hypothetical syllogism rule, we can infer $\Gamma' \vdash \Delta'$. In case (ii), from both pairs, $\Gamma' \vdash \Delta'$ and $A_i \vdash A_i^c$, and from $\Gamma' \vdash \Delta'$ and $B_j^a \vdash B_j$, by the hypothetical syllogism rule, we can infer $\Gamma \vdash \Delta$. □

Let us note that in the particular case when A_i^a is true or when B_j^c is a false statement, applying step (i) of our procedure produces the effects of enthymematic reasoning (see [14]).

A rare and unexpected case, which is not covered by (i) and (ii), is when the statement $\Gamma \vdash \Delta$ is undecidable, i.e., the case when it is possible to show that $\Gamma \vdash \Delta$ is neither provable nor refutable. Such examples are connected with highly formalized concepts and will not be our focus.

This procedure can be considered a sequence of consecutive attempts to falsify a statement and then to save it as a supplementary conjecture or to give it a new semantic interpretation. In this way, a progressive improvement of the initial claim is enabled.

In order to visualize the transformation process of $\Gamma \vdash \Delta$ into $\Gamma' \vdash \Delta'$ with the help of Γ_{ant}, Γ_{con}, Δ_{ant} and Δ_{con}, we give a 2*D*-presentation of relationships between elements of Γ and Δ, with or without subscripts or superscripts:

$$\begin{array}{ccccccc}
A_1^a & & A_m^a & & B_1^a & & B_n^a \\
\top & & \top & & \top & & \top \\
A_1, & \ldots, & A_m & ?\vdash & B_1, & \ldots, & B_m \\
\top & & \top & & \top & & \top \\
A_1^c & & A_m^c & & B_1^c & & B_n^c
\end{array}$$

where, for instance, the first column

$$\begin{array}{c}
A_1^a \\
\top \\
A_1 \\
\top \\
A_1^c
\end{array}$$

of this $2D$-presentation means that both $A_1^a \vdash A_1$ and $A_1 \vdash A_1^c$ are provable. Consequently, by some replacements of A_i with A_i^a or with A_i^c, $(1 \le i \le m)$, and some replacements of B_j with B_j^a or with B_j^c, $(1 \le j \le n)$, we obtain this new form $\Gamma' \vdash \Delta'$. The symbol '$? \vdash$', appearing above, stands for '$\nvdash$' or '$\vdash$'.

6. Concluding Remarks

An unproven statement of hypothetical character, a conjecture, is usually treated in one of the following two ways: we try to prove it, or we try to refute it. Then, for a proven statement, we try to find its interpolants, in order to simplify its proof and to better understand the nature of its proof, but for a refuted, i.e., unprovable, statement, we look for its extrapolants, trying to find a similar and relevant but provable statement.

Briefly, if we start with a statement of the form $A \vdash B$, then we have, syntactically, two possibilities to obtain from $A \vdash B$ a better statement: if $A \vdash B$ is unproven, we will look for its extrapolant presenting a provable statement relevant for $A \vdash B$, but if $A \vdash B$ is proven, then we will find its interpolant relevant for $A \vdash B$, better explaining the nature of $A \vdash B$. Namely, the basic principle respected in the process of transforming $A \vdash B$ into a 'better statement' $A' \vdash B'$ is that all side statements occurring in derivations, such as $C \vdash A$ and $B \vdash D$, are provable, except the principal statement $A \vdash B$, which can be, but does not have to be, provable, and that each step in the considered derivation is made strictly in accordance with the sound logical inference rules.

In working versions of this paper, we used the term 'algorithm' for the proving–refuting–improving process, but later we accepted the term 'procedure' as the appropriate one. Namely, it is not clear if the step transforming $\Gamma \nvdash \Delta$ into $\Gamma' \vdash \Delta'$ is well defined, in the sense that we do not know if the problem of provability of both $\Gamma \vdash \Delta$ and $\Gamma' \vdash \Delta'$ is decidable.

Finally, let us note that while the phenomenon of interpolation is usually treated as a property of an axiomatic theory or a logical system, because even some natural propositional logics do not possess it (see [15]), extrapolation, although observed as a dual to interpolation, presents essentially a method of transforming an unprovable statement $A \vdash B$ into a 'similar', but provable one: $A' \vdash B'$.

We also point out that if there is a grain of suspicion that a counterexample to our conjecture exists, it will be of great didactic importance in developing and stirring the critical reasoning of students and researchers. This has to find a central place in all study programs as a basic goal of education, together with stimulating creative thinking.

Funding: This research received no external funding.

Acknowledgments: The author thanks the anonymous reviewers for making valuable suggestions and helpful comments.

Conflicts of Interest: The authors declare no conflict of interest.

References

1. Lakatos, I. Proofs and Refutations. *Br. J. Philos. Sci.* **1963**, *14*, 1–25. 120–139. 221–245. 296–342. [CrossRef]
2. Popper, K.R. *Conjectures and Refutations: The Growth of Scientific Knowledge*; Basic Books: New York, NY, USA, 1962.
3. Gabbay, D.M.; Woods, J. *The Reach of Abduction*; Elsevier: Amsterdam, The Netherlands, 2005.
4. Boričić, B. Model, proving and refuting. In *Quantitative Models in Economics*; Koćović, J., Eds.; Faculty of Economics, University of Belgrade: Belgrade, Serbia, 2018; pp. 3–19.
5. Craig, W. Three uses of the Herbrand–Gentzen theorem in relating model theory and proof theory. *J. Symb. Log.* **1957**, *22*, 269–285. [CrossRef]
6. Birkhoff, G.D.; Beatley, R. *Basic Geometry*; AMS Chelsea Publishing: Providence, RI, USA, 1959.
7. Boričić, B. Logical and historical determination of impossibility theorems by Arrow and Sen. *Econ. Ann.* **2007**, *52*, 7–20. [CrossRef]
8. Boričić, B. Dictatorship, liberalism and the Pareto rule: possible and impossible. *Econ. Ann.* **2009**, *54*, 45–54. [CrossRef]
9. Arrow, K. *Social Choice and Individual Values*; John Wiley: New York, NY, USA, 1963.
10. Sen, A. Quasi–Transitivity, Rational Choice and Collective Decisions. *Rev. Econ. Stud.* **1969**, *36*, 381–393. [CrossRef]
11. Anderson, A.R.; Belnap, N.D., Jr. *Entailment: The Logic of Relevance and Necessity*; Princeton University Press: Princeton, NJ, USA, 1975; Volume I.
12. Chang, C.C.; Keisler, H.J. *Model Theory*; North-Holland Publishing: Amsterdam, The Netherlands, 1973.
13. Takeuti, G. *Proof Theory*; North-Holland Publishing: Amsterdam, The Netherlands, 1975.
14. Anderson, A.R.; Belnap, N.D., Jr. Enthymemes. *J. Philos.* **1961**, *58*, 713–723. [CrossRef]
15. Maksimova, L.L. Interpolation properties of superintuitionistic logics. *Stud. Log.* **1979**, *38*, 419–428. [CrossRef]

axioms

Article

Spatial Fuzzy C-Means Clustering Analysis of U.S. Presidential Election and COVID-19 Related Factors in the Rustbelt States in 2020

Shianghau Wu

Department of International Business, Chung Yuan Christian University, Taoyuan City 320314, Taiwan; antonwoo888@hotmail.com

Abstract: The rustbelt states play a key role in determining the vote turnout in the U.S. elections. The current study attempts to utilize the spatial fuzzy C-means method to analyze the U.S. presidential election in the rustbelt states in 2020. We intend to explore that the U.S. presidential election had related factors, including COVID-19-related factors, such as the mask-wearing percentage and the COVID-19 death tolls in each county of the rust belt states. Contrary to the related literature, the study uses education level, number of house units, unemployment rate, household income, COVID-19-related factors and the share of Republican's votes in the presidential election. The results indicate that spatial generalized fuzzy C-means analysis has better clustering results than the C-means clustering method. Moreover, the COVID-19 death toll in each county did not affect the Republican's vote share in the rustbelt states, while the mask-wearing behavior in some regions had a negative impact on the Republican's vote share.

Keywords: spatial fuzzy C-means; COVID-19; rustbelt states

MSC: 03B52; 03C45

Citation: Wu, S. Spatial Fuzzy C-Means Clustering Analysis of U.S. Presidential Election and COVID-19 Related Factors in the Rustbelt States in 2020. *Axioms* **2022**, *11*, 401. https://doi.org/10.3390/axioms11080401

Academic Editor: Oscar Castillo

Received: 29 June 2022
Accepted: 10 August 2022
Published: 15 August 2022

1. Introduction

The U.S. presidential election in 2020 was influenced by the COVID-19 pandemic, including increasing infections, death tolls, and lockdowns. The previous literature indicated that political polarization was aggravated due to intense fear during the disaster [1,2]. People tended to search for assuage by insisting on their conservative political viewpoints and supporting the ruling party, while other scholars believed that some voters would punish the political elite for worse management during the natural or man-made disaster. Since COVID-19-related policies were created in a very short period of time, without full deliberation, it was possible to arouse public discontent [3]. People were more supportive of their governments during the early stage of the COVID-19 pandemic [4]. However, the evaluations of the policies about the pandemic were influenced by two polarized mindsets. Some voters chose to punish the politicians for the conditions caused by the pandemic, which were out of their control, while some voters were attentive to the political elites' reactions and determined their feelings accordingly [5].

The previous literature about the U.S. presidential election in 2020 focused on the effects of COVID-19 on the U.S. presidential election results. Hart (2021) stated that the COVID-19 pandemic seemed to have decreased the support for Trump among the Democrats, while it increased for independent voters [6]. Baccini et al. [7] pointed out that COVID-19-related factors negatively affected Donald Trump's re-election, and the effect was stronger in urban areas. They also observed that COVID-19 had a positive effect on the voters' mobilization for Joe Biden. The rustbelt states are traditionally "swing states" in the U.S. presidential elections, including Illinois, Wisconsin, Indiana, Michigan, Ohio, West Virginia, Pennsylvania, and New York. Geographical and racial divergences increased in the counties of rustbelt states in the past five years [8]. The geographical factors enable these divergences to become more visible, and people tend to live in more politically polarized conditions [9]. The voting results of rustbelt states have a pivotal influence on the whole country. However, there are fewer instances in the literature about the voting results' analysis of the rustbelt states. Gimpel [10] pointed out that some counties in rustbelt states changed their support to the Democrats in the presential election in 2020. The influencing factors of the voting results need to be examined. In order to analyze the topic more thoroughly, we attempt to analyze the COVID-19 pandemic effects along with the regional factors' influence, the related economic variables, and the Republican's support rate in the 2020 U.S. presidential election.

The structure of this research is as follows: the Research Method Section presents our research design and related descriptive statistics of the variables. The Discussion Section presents the results of the research model. The research findings are listed in the Conclusions Section.

2. Methodology

2.1. Research Method

The current study used the spatial fuzzy C-means clustering method to analyze the influencing factors of COVID-19 on the U.S. presidential election. In order to explore the impacts of COVID-19 and other factors, such as social and geographical factors, as the mentioned in the Introduction, the study also used educational level, number of house units, unemployment rate, and household income variables to create the clustering. The previous literature utilized daily experience sampling (ESM) to analyze the impact of COVID-19 on employee uncertainty [11]. Di Nardo et al. (2019) utilized the literature review method to provide useful information about COVID-19 infection on neonates and children [12]. Regarding the fuzzy clustering approach, Indelicato et al. (2022) used the method with the fuzzy TOPSIS model to analyze the determinants of immigrants in Cuenca, Ecuador [13]. Compared to the COVID-19-related research about its effects on U.S. elections, the study considered spatial factors and attempted to describe the regional differences under the influence of these variables.

2.2. Data Description

The study explored the influencing factors of the pandemic on the 2020 U.S presidential election. The study used the Republican's voting share (X_1) in the U.S. presidential election in 2020 as one of the variables related to the U.S. presidential election. The data were obtained from the web repository (https://github.com/tonmcg/US_County_Level_Election_Results_08-20 (accessed on 6 August 2022)); it collected the 2020 election results at the county level, which were scraped from the results published by Fox News, Politico, and the New York Times.

In order to measure mask-wearing behavior in the rustbelt states (X_2), the study used the dataset collected by the survey firm, Dynata. Dynata surveyed 250 thousand respondents in the U.S. between 2 and 14 July 2020. The survey asked the respondents whether or not they wore face masks often in public. The responses included "always", "frequently", "sometimes", "rarely", and "never", according to the descending frequency.

The variables (X_3, X_4, X_5, X_6) were obtained from the dataset of the U.S. Census Bureau. These variables were released on a flow basis throughout each year.

The study also used the death toll (X_7) before the U.S. presidential election as a COVID-19-related variable. Other variables included education level and household economic condition. The descriptive statistics of all the variables are listed in Tables 1 and 2:

Table 1. All variables used for clustering.

Variable	Meaning
X_1	Republican's share of votes in U.S. presidential election
X_2	The share of respondents who thought they wore face masks often
X_3	The number of housing units
X_4	The number of residents who were high-school graduates or above
X_5	Unemployment rate
X_6	Household income
X_7	Death toll of COVID-19 cases

Table 2. Descriptive statistics of all variables.

Statistic	N	Mean	St.Dev	Min.	Max.
X_1	669	0.662	0.127	0.120	0.900
X_2	669	0.536	0.139	0.190	0.880
X_3	669	52,630.64	135,268.2	1107	2,204,019
X_4	669	34,032.23	84,810.53	616	1,314,995
X_5	669	4.591	1.273	2.400	13.00
X_6	669	52,867.07	12,235.31	26,278	115,301
X_7	669	71.175	306.17	0	5517

2.3. C-Means Clustering

Initially, the study used the classical C-means method to create the fuzzy unsupervised classification. The fuzziness degree (m) was set at 1.5 in order to obtain the satisfied results. The classical C-means method includes the following two equations. The first equation is the updated values of membership in each iteration of u_{ik} [14]:

$$u_{ik} = \frac{\left(||x_k - v_i||^2\right)^{\frac{-1}{m-1}}}{\sum_{j=1}^{c}\left(||x_k - v_j||^2\right)^{\frac{-1}{m-1}}} \quad (1)$$

The center of the cluster is as follows:

$$v_i = \frac{\sum_{k=1}^{N} u_{ik}^m (x_k)}{\sum_{k=1}^{N} u_{ik}^m} \quad (2)$$

In Equations (1) and (2), x_k represents the observation of k's value, v_i is the value of the center of the cluster i, c is the cluster number, and m is the index of fuzziness.

2.4. Fuzzy C-Means Clustering

Fuzzy C-means clustering is an algorithm that permits a data point to pertain to two or more clusters. Let $X = \{x_1, x_2, \ldots, x_n\}$ represent an image with n pixels, where x_i is the gray value of the ith pixel. The objective function of the standard FCM algorithm is as follows:

$$J = \sum_{k=1}^{K} \sum_{i=1}^{n} u_{ki}^m ||x_i - v_k||^2 \quad (3)$$

In Equation (3), the center of the kth cluster is v_k $(1 \le k \le K)$, and u_{ki} $(1 \le k \le K, 1 \le i \le n)$ is the membership degree function value of the ith pixel, which pertains to the kth cluster. u_{ki} also needs to meet the requirements of the following constraints:

$$\sum_{k=1}^{K} u_{ki} = 1, \quad u_{ki} \in [0,1], \quad 0 \le \sum_{i=1}^{n} u_{ki} \le n \quad (4)$$

In Equation (3), the distance between x_i and v_k is used in the Euclidean form, and parameter m (m > 1) is a weighting parameter that relates to the level of fuzziness and the resulting partition. The minimization of the objective function in Equation (3) can obtain the updated equations of the membership degree function u_{ki} and the cluster center v_k as follows:

$$u_{ki} = \frac{1}{\sum_{i=1}^{k} \left(\frac{||x_i - v_k||^2}{||x_i - v_l||^2}\right)^{\frac{1}{m-1}}} \quad (5)$$

$$v_k = \frac{\sum_{i=1}^{n} u_{ki}^m x_i}{\sum_{i=1}^{n} u_{ki}^m} \quad (6)$$

The goal of these functions is to obtain suitable clusters for the data points.

2.5. Spatial Fuzzy C-Means Clustering

Fuzzy C-means clustering (FCM) has shortcomings due to its sensitivity to noise. Some algorithms were developed to overcome this shortcoming by utilizing the spatial information obtained from the neighborhood window around each pixel. Mean spatial information and median spatial information are two prevalent types of local information. The mean spatial information of the ith pixel is denoted as follows [15]:

$$\delta_i = \frac{1}{|S_i|} \sum_{p \epsilon S_i} x_p \quad (7)$$

In Equation (7), S_i is the set of neighboring pixels in a window centered at the ith pixel, and $|S_i|$ represents its cardinality. The median spatial information can be represented as:

$$\varepsilon_i = median\ \{x_p\},\ p \epsilon S_i \quad (8)$$

Most of the FCM algorithms utilize the above-mentioned local spatial information in the objective function; however, FCM algorithms with local spatial information can obtain a better image segmentation performance with a low noise level. The local spatial information obtained from the near pixels of a pixel is not efficient due to possible contamination. In fact, there are many pixels with a similar neighborhood configuration in an image. It is more beneficial to utilize pixels with a similar neighborhood configurations to the given pixel to obtain the spatial information than only using the neighboring pixels of the given pixel. Such types of spatial information can be taken as non-local spatial information. The non-local spatial information for the ith pixel $\overline{x_i}$ is calculated by the following equation [16]:

$$\overline{x}_i = \sum_{j \in w_i^r} w_{ij} x_j \quad (9)$$

In Equation (9), ω_i^r represents the r × r search window centered at the ith pixel. The non-local spatial information of the ith pixel is computed by using the pixels in the window. The weight between the ith and jth pixels can be denoted as w_{ij} $\left(j \in w_i^r\right)$, $0 \leq w_{ij} \leq 1$ and $\sum_{j \in w_i^r} w_{ij} = 1$. The weight w_{ij} is defined as follows:

$$w_{ij} = \frac{1}{Z_i} exp(-||x(N_i) - x(N_j)||_{2,\sigma}^2 / h^2) \quad (10)$$

In Equation (10), h means the filtering degree parameter and directs the decreasing weight function w_{ij}, and $Z_i = \sum_{j \in w_i^r} exp(-||x(N_i) - x(N_j)||_{2,\sigma}^2 / h^2)$ is the normalizing constant. The weight w_{ij} depends on the similarity between the ith and jth pixels. The similarity is computed by the Gaussian weighted Euclidean distance $||x(N_i) - x(N_j)||_{2,\sigma}^2$. The positive term σ is the Euclidean distance, which means the standard deviation of the Gaussian kernel. $x(N_i)$ is the gray level vector with an s × s square neighborhood N_i centered at ith pixel.

Fuzzy clustering algorithm with spatial information uses the spatial information for individual pixels to determine the spatial constant term, and then obtains the spatial constraint to the objective function of FCM.

3. Results

3.1. Fuzzy C-Means and Generalized Fuzzy C-Means Clustering

The study used the classical K-means to determine the number of clusters. According to Figure 1, the four clusters can explain almost 40% of the original data variance.

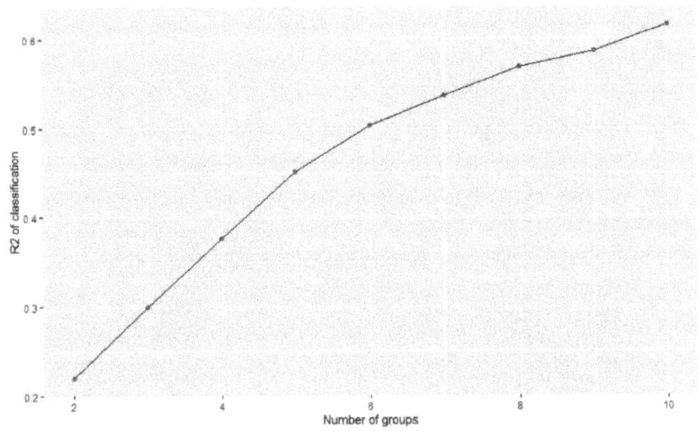

Figure 1. Impact of the number of groups on the explained variance.

Then, the study used the "fclust" package of R language to analyze the quality of the classification [17]. The study also utilized the "geocmeans" package of the R language to compute the generalized version of the c-means algorithm [18]. The algorithm can accelerate convergence and obtain less fuzzy results by adjusting the membership matrix at each iteration. It needs an extra beta parameter controlling the effectiveness of the modification. The modification only influences the formula updating the membership matrix.

$$u_{ki} = \frac{\left(\left|\left|x_k - v_j\right|\right|^2 - \beta_k\right)^{\frac{-1}{m-1}}}{\sum_{i=1}^{c}\left(\left|\left|x_k - v_j\right|\right|^2 - \beta_k\right)^{\frac{-1}{m-1}}} \tag{11}$$

In Equation (11), $\beta_k = min(||x_k - v||^2)$ and $0 \leq \beta \leq 1$. In order to choose an adequate value for this parameter, the study sought all the possible values between 0 and 1 with a step of 0.05. The results of the related index were obtained according to the ascending β values in Table 3.

Table 3. Some indices with ascending β values.

Beta	Silhouette Index	Xie and Beni Index	Explained Inertia
0	0.287	2.476	0.161
0.05	0.29	2.282	0.171
0.1	0.294	2.113	0.181
0.15	0.298	1.964	0.191
0.2	0.3	1.83	0.201
0.25	0.303	1.706	0.212
0.3	0.307	1.584	0.223
0.35	0.313	1.47	0.235
0.4	0.315	1.374	0.247
0.45	0.315	1.292	0.26
0.5	0.292	1.478	0.265

Table 3. Cont.

Beta	Silhouette Index	Xie and Beni Index	Explained Inertia
0.55	0.289	1.41	0.277
0.6	0.286	1.349	0.289
0.65	0.283	1.295	0.301
0.7	0.281	1.249	0.313
0.75	0.277	1.211	0.325
0.8	0.273	1.182	0.337
0.85	0.268	1.163	0.349
0.9	0.259	1.157	0.361
0.95	0.249	1.172	0.371
1	0.235	1.296	0.374

According to Table 1, the study chose beta = 0.8, maintained a satisfied silhouette index, increased the Xie and Beni index, and explained inertia. The results of GFCM (generalized version of fuzzy C-means clustering) and FCM are listed in Table 4.

Table 4. Comparison of the indices between GFCM and FCM.

	GFCM	FCM
Silhouette index	0.273	0.287
Partition entropy	0.323	0.951
Partition coeff	0.837	0.486
XieBeni index	1.182	2.476
Fukuyama Sugeno index	1096.84	1706.23
Explained inertia	0.337	0.161

The results indicate that the GFCM provides a less fuzzy solution (with higher explained inertia and lower partition entropy), but keeps a good silhouette index and a lower Xie and Beni index. The study created two membership matrices maps and the most likely group for each observation. The study used the function map clusters from geocmeans in R language. We set a threshold of 0.45. If an observation only obtained values below this probability in a membership matrix, it was marked as "undecided" (represented by transparency on the map).

In Figure 2, the left-hand-side graph was the fuzzy C-means clustering result. The right-hand-side graph was the generalized fuzzy C-means clustering result. We can observe that the right-hand-side graph had fewer undecided parts.

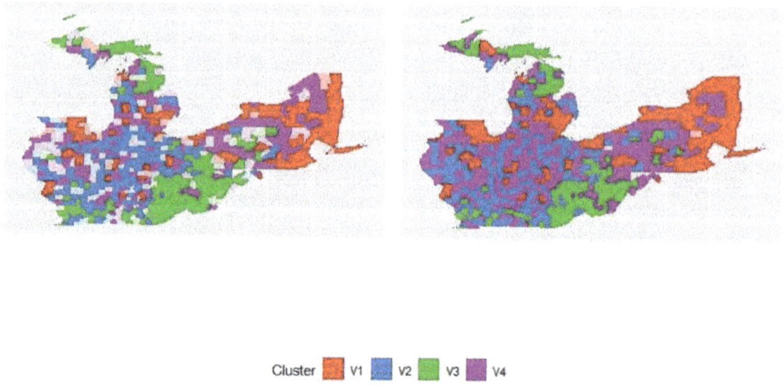

Figure 2. FCM and GFCM clusters.

3.2. Spatial C-Means and Generalized C-Means

The study used the SFCM function of R language to execute spatial c-means clustering. The first step was to determine a spatial weight matrix indicating the observations that were neighbors and the strength of their relationship. The study attempted to use a basic queen neighbor matrix (built with the spdep package of R language). The matrix should be row-standardized to ensure that the interpretation of all the parameters remains clear.

The two following equations indicate how the functions renewing the condition of the membership matrix and the centers of the clusters are modified.

$$u_{ik} = \frac{(||x_k - v_i||^2 + \alpha||\overline{x_k} - v_i||^2)^{\frac{-1}{m-1}}}{\sum_{j=1}^{c}(||x_k - v_i||^2 + \alpha||\overline{x_k} - v_i||^2)^{\frac{-1}{m-1}}} \tag{12}$$

$$v_i = \frac{\sum_{k=1}^{N} u_{ik}^m (x_k + \alpha\overline{x_k})}{(1+\alpha)\sum_{k=1}^{N} u_{ik}^m} \tag{13}$$

In Equations (12) and (13), $\overline{x}$ is the lagged version of x, and $\alpha \geq 0$.

The SFCM (spatial fuzzy C-means) can be taken as a spatially smoothed version of the classical c-means, and alpha controls the degree of spatial smoothness. This smoothing can be taken as an attempt to reduce the spatial overfitting of the classical c-means.

The study chose the best alpha value in order to reduce spatial inconsistency as much as possible and to maintain a good classification quality. The relationship between the spatial inconsistency and alpha value is shown in Figure 3.

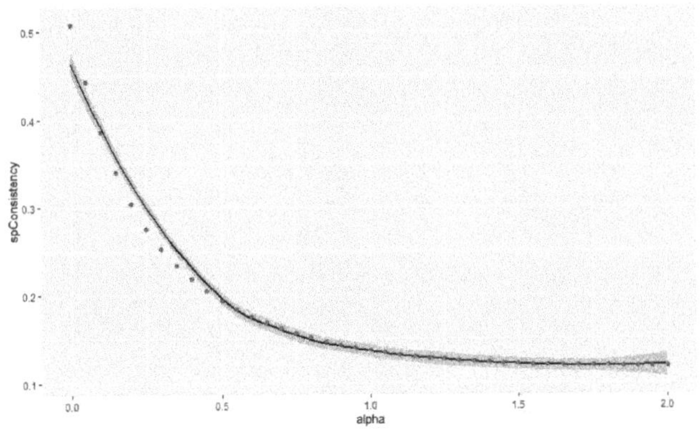

Figure 3. Link between alpha value and spatial inconsistency.

In Figure 3, the increasing alpha value results in the decrease in the spatial inconsistency.

In Figure 4, the explained inertia decreased when the alpha value increased and again followed an inverse function. The classification searched for a compromise between the original and lagged values. However, the loss was only 3% between alpha = 0 and alpha = 2.

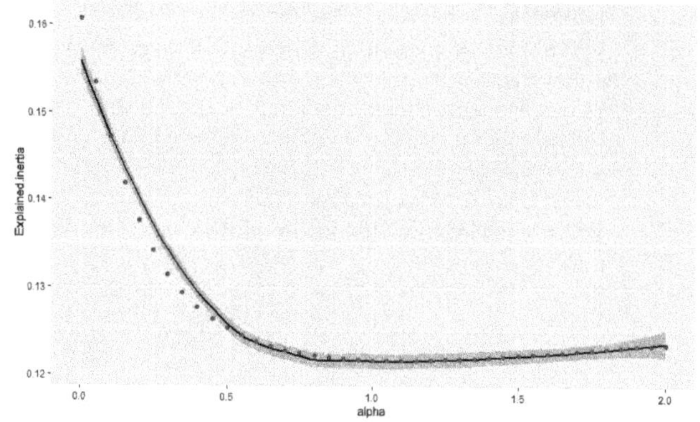

Figure 4. The relationship between the alpha value and explained inertia.

According to Figures 5 and 6, as a larger silhouette index means a better classification, and a smaller Xie and Beni index represents a better classification, the study intended to retain the alpha = 0.25 value to provide a good balance between spatial consistency and classification quality.

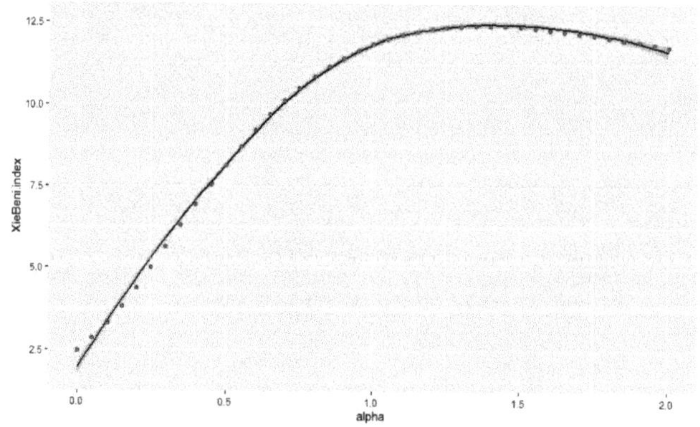

Figure 5. Link between alpha and Xie and Beni index.

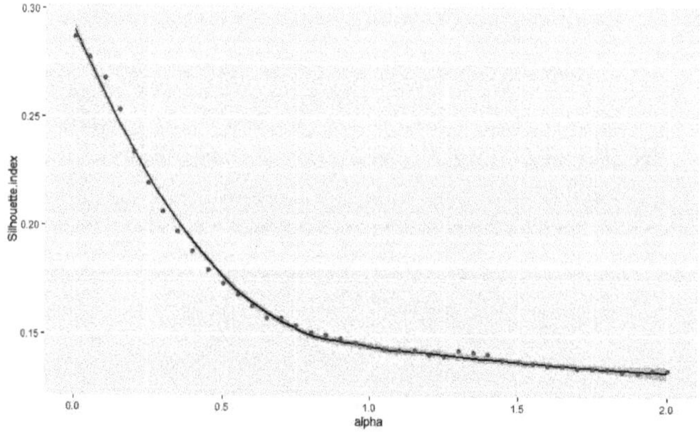

Figure 6. Link between alpha value and silhouette index.

3.3. *Spatial Generalized Fuzzy C-Means (SGFCM)*

In order to facilitate the clustering process of the SGFCM method, we needed to determine the alpha and beta values of the following equation regarding the center of the clusters.

$$u_{ik} = \frac{\left(||x_k - v_i||^2 - \beta_k + \alpha||\overline{x_k} - v_i||^2\right)^{\frac{-1}{m-1}}}{\sum_{j=1}^{c}\left(||x_k - v_i||^2 - \beta_k + \alpha||\overline{x_k} - v_i||^2\right)^{\frac{-1}{m-1}}} \quad (14)$$

The study attempted to use the multiprocessing approach to select the suitable alpha and beta values. The impact of alpha and beta values on the various indices is shown as follows:

Figures 7 and 8 indicate that some specific combinations of alpha and beta values generate good results in the range of 0.3 < alpha < 0.7 and 0.4 < beta < 0.6. Figure 9 shows that the selection of beta has no impact on spatial consistency.

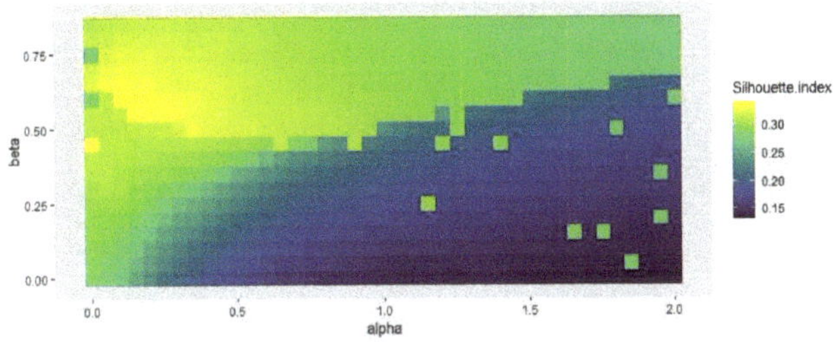

Figure 7. Influence of beta and alpha values on silhouette index.

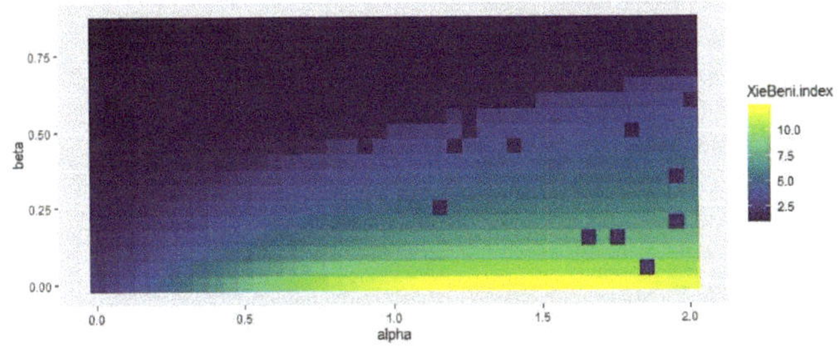

Figure 8. Influence of beta and alpha values on Xie and Beni index.

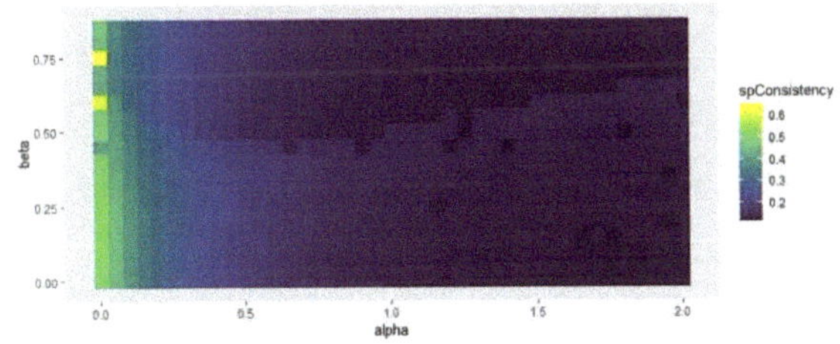

Figure 9. Influence of beta and alpha values on spatial inconsistency.

Regarding Figures 7–9, the study selected beta = 0.5 and alpha = 0.25, which obtained better results for all the indices considered. Based on the alpha and beta values, the study acquired the results of the SFCM and SGFCM results (see Table 5).

Table 5. Comparison of the indices between SFCM and SGFCM.

	SFCM	SGFCM
Silhouette index	0.219	0.319
Partition entropy	1.043	0.682
Partition coeff	0.431	0.633
XieBeni index	5.008	1.394
Fukuyama Sugeno index	1824.58	1290.69
Explained inertia	0.134	0.248
sp consistency	0.276	0.262

The results of the SGFCM are better concerning the semantic and spatial aspects due to the lower partition entropy, Xie Beni index, and Fukuyama Sugeno index, and higher values of other indices.

The SFCM and SGFCM clustering maps are listed as follows.

According to Figure 10, the right-hand-side graph is the SGFCM clustering map. The left-hand-side graph is the SFCM clustering map. We can observe that the undecided units are less on the SGFCM clustering map.

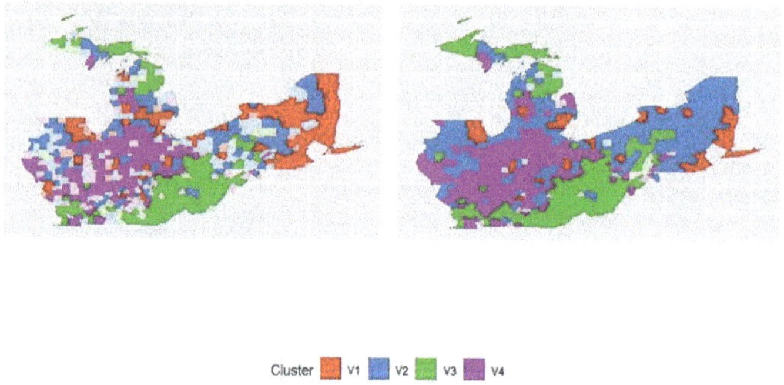

Figure 10. Most likely cluster and undecided units of SFCM and SGFCM.

3.4. Comparison of the Four Algorithms

The study attempted to perform a thorough spatial analysis and compare the spatial consistency of the four classifications (FCM, GFCM, SFCM, SGFCM) (see Table 6).

Table 6. Moran I index for the columns of the membership matrices among the four algorithms.

	FCM	GFCM	SFCM	SGFCM
Cluster 1	0.642	0.602	0.769	0.696
Cluster 2	0.349	0.187	0.501	0.66
Cluster 3	0.691	0.595	0.809	0.823
Cluster 4	0.205	0.14	0.674	0.73

The Moran I value according to the membership matrices were higher for SFCM and SGFCM, representing strongaer spatial structures in the classifications.

The study also checked that the values of spatial inconsistency for SGFCM were significantly lower than those of SFCM. The study used the previously mentioned 250 values obtained by permutations; we could calculate a pseudo p-value = 0.032 > 1/250 = 0.004. This means that the SGFCM algorithm did not have a predominant advantage over the SFCM algorithm. However, the SGFCM clustering map indicated that the undecided points were fewer than that of the SFCM.

We can observe that the undecided parts were fewer as compared with Figures 2 and 10.

4. Discussion

The study attempted to utilize the spatial fuzzy C-means clustering method to analyze the relationship among COVID-19-related factors and the vote share of Republicans in the U.S. presidential election in the rustbelt states in 2020. The study found that spatial generalized fuzzy C-means clustering (SGFCM) produced better results compared to the other three algorithms according to Table 3. The study also found the SGFCM clustering graph in Figure 10 presented better results because the uncertain parts (areas that did not belong to any cluster) were fewer compared to the other clustering results shown in Figure 2.

The descriptive statistics of the four clusters (Tables A1–A4) are listed in the Appendix A. According to the four tables, we can conclude the four clusters are as follows:

(1) First cluster: the cluster had lower X_1 (mean < 0.5), higher X_2, higher X_4, lower X_5, and higher X_6 values. Other variables did not seem obvious. We can conclude that people in this region were not inclined to support the Republican candidate, often wore masks, had more high-school graduates or above, had a lower unemployment rate, and a higher income. The first cluster included a little part of southeastern Pennsylvania, New York state and other scatter parts of the rustbelt states.

(2) Second cluster: The cluster had higher X_1 (mean > 0.5), higher X_2, lower X_4, lower X_5, and higher X_6 values. Other variables did not seem obvious. We can conclude that people in this region were inclined to support the Republican candidate, often wore masks, had less high-school graduates, a lower unemployment rate, and higher income. The second cluster included the larger part of New York state, most part of Michigan and northern Illinois.

(3) Third cluster: The cluster had higher X_1 (mean > 0.5), lower X_2, lower X_4, higher X_5, lower X_6, and higher X_7 values. This means that people in this region tended to support the Republican candidate, wore masks less frequently, had less high-school graduates or above, a higher unemployment rate, lower income, and higher COVID-19 death toll. The cluster included some parts of Kentucky, West Virginia and Ohio and other scatter parts of the rustbelt states.

(4) Fourth cluster: The cluster had higher X_1 (mean > 0.5), lower X_2, lower X_4, lower X_5, higher X_6, and higher X_7 values. This means that people in this region tended to support the Republican candidate, wore masks less frequently, had less high-school graduates or above, a lower unemployment rate, higher income, and higher COVID-19 death toll. The cluster included the larger part of Indiana, Ohio and part of Illinois.

The results seem to slightly contrast with the previous literature. Warshaw et al. (2020) found that COVID-19 fatalities decreased the support for Donald Trump in the 2020 presidential election [19]. However, our results show that the third and fourth clusters in the rustbelt states have higher COVID-19 death tolls with higher Republican vote shares and residents less inclined to wear face masks. Meanwhile, the second cluster had higher Republican vote shares and the residents there often wore face masks, while the COVID-19 death toll seemed unimportant. We can conclude that the COVID-19 death toll in each county did not affect the Republican vote shares in the rustbelt states, while the mask-wearing behavior in some regions had a negative impact on the Republican vote shares.

According to Figure 11, we can observe that cluster 2 accounts for the largest area in the rustbelt states. Cluster 1 accounts for the smallest area. The clustering results indicate that the U.S. presidential election-related factors and COVID-19-related factors are closely related to the clustering results. It enables the researchers in the related field to conduct further studies.

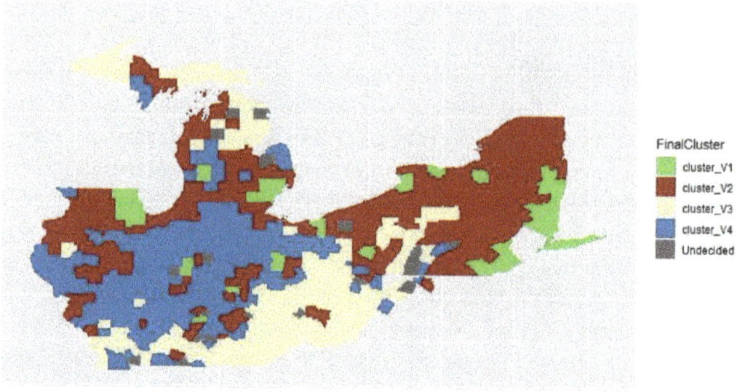

Figure 11. Final cluster of SGFCM.

5. Conclusions

The present study intended to use the spatial fuzzy C-means clustering to analyze the related factors of COVID-19 and the U.S. presidential election in the rustbelt states in 2020. The study found that the spatial generalized fuzzy C-means (SGFCM) method produced better clustering results. The SGFCM method divided the rustbelt states into four areas. The results imply that the COVID-19 death toll in each county did not affect the Republican vote shares in the rustbelt states, while the mask-wearing behavior in some regions had a negative impact on the Republican vote shares. It is worth conducting further research.

Funding: This research was supported by the Preliminary Research Resource Funding from Chung Yuan Christian University.

Institutional Review Board Statement: Not Applicable.

Informed Consent Statement: Not Applicable.

Data Availability Statement: The COVID-19-related data for the U.S. can be downloaded from https://github.com/nytimes/COVID-19-data (accessed on 6 August 2022). The U.S. presidential election results in each county can be downloaded from https://github.com/tonmcg/US_County_Level_Election_Results_08-20/blob/f9b5f335ad1c66a7eba681539db49eec0c22787b/2020_US_County_Level_Presidential_Results.csv (accessed on 6 August 2022). The education level and household economic condition can be downloaded from https://www.census.gov/ (accessed on 6 August 2022).

Acknowledgments: The author would like to show their gratitude for the preliminary research fund received by Chung Yuan Christian University.

Conflicts of Interest: The author declares no conflict of interest.

Appendix A

Table A1. Descriptive statistics for cluster 1.

	X_1	X_2	X_3	X_4	X_5	X_6	X_7
Q5	0.222	0.514	28	9872.6	2.9	46,288.2	7
Q10	0.27	0.549	67	16,480.8	3.2	49,515	19
Q25	0.37	0.641	198	41,764	3.4	58,222	45
Q50	0.446	0.742	379	132,127	3.8	66,270	81
Q75	0.533	0.788	501	211,597	4.2	86,108	103
Q90	0.614	0.82	596	347,971.4	4.9	94,521	153
Q95	0.678	0.842	632	522,061	5.4	100,887	165
Mean	0.448	0.71	342.689	168,655.4	3.901	70,973.15	80.35
Std	0.134	0.107	187.555	199,205.9	0.793	17,662.76	48.11

Table A2. Descriptive statistics for cluster 2.

	X_1	X_2	X_3	X_4	X_5	X_6	X_7
Q5	0.417	0.449	49.4	4579.6	3.1	43,118	9
Q10	0.463	0.487	89	5836.6	3.3	46,262	15
Q25	0.539	0.54	198	11,116	3.8	49,767	37
Q50	0.605	0.612	368	20,204	4.4	53,901	77
Q75	0.674	0.723	510	41,229	4.9	60,121	115
Q90	0.729	0.79	608	68,550	5.5	66,521	155
Q95	0.762	0.827	633.6	109,462	5.7	73,006.8	174.2
Mean	0.599	0.627	356.193	35,019.47	4.415	55,596.35	79.845
Std	0.105	0.119	186.098	62,713.13	0.899	9592.194	52.128

Table A3. Descriptive statistics for cluster 3.

	X_1	X_2	X_3	X_4	X_5	X_6	X_7
Q5	0.576	0.341	29.4	2415	3.84	30,950	7
Q10	0.624	0.368	56	3297	4.2	33,218	13
Q25	0.693	0.409	155	5072	4.9	38,171	43
Q50	0.747	0.475	341	8354	5.6	43,457	81
Q75	0.787	0.54	518	13,670	6.4	48,182	129
Q90	0.83	0.611	604	25,221	7.4	51,812.2	169
Q95	0.856	0.641	631.6	34,390.8	8.3	55,443.8	195
Mean	0.734	0.481	334.757	14,615.75	5.743	43,457.84	88.095
Std	0.088	0.097	199.112	47,465.07	1.377	8146.738	57.705

Table A4. Descriptive statistics for cluster 4.

	X_1	X_2	X_3	X_4	X_5	X_6	X_7
Q5	0.555	0.285	35	3184.2	2.7	41,799.2	9
Q10	0.602	0.33	60	4188.8	2.98	44,913	21
Q25	0.673	0.392	146	6912	3.3	48,342	49
Q50	0.728	0.462	289	11,761	4	52,798	97
Q75	0.76	0.529	473	18,689	4.5	57,705	145
Q90	0.789	0.584	585	33,791.4	5.1	63,827.4	175.4
Q95	0.809	0.627	629.6	45,496	5.46	67,758	193
Mean	0.707	0.459	308.856	18,494.64	4.009	53,761.27	98.385
Std	0.084	0.106	190.401	46,181.82	0.91	8948.192	58.712

References

1. Greenberg, J.; Pyszczynski, T.; Solomon, S.; Rosenblatt, A.; Veeder, M.; Kirkland, S.; Lyon, D. Evidence for terror management theory II: The effects of mortality salience on reactions to those who threaten or bolster the cultural worldview. *J. Pers. Soc. Psychol.* **1990**, *58*, 308. [CrossRef]
2. Kosloff, S.; Greenberg, J.; Weise, D.; Solomon, S. The effects of mortality salience on political preferences: The roles of charisma and political orientation. *J. Exp. Soc. Psychol.* **2010**, *46*, 139–145. [CrossRef]
3. Altiparmakis, A.; Bojar, A.; Brouard, S.; Foucault, M.; Kriesi, H.; Nadeau, R. Pandemic politics: Policy evaluations of government responses to COVID-19. *West Eur. Polit.* **2021**, *44*, 1159–1179. [CrossRef]
4. Bol, D.; Giani, M.; Blais, A.; Loewen, P. The effect of COVID-19 lockdowns on political support: Some good news for democracy? *Eur. J. Polit. Res.* **2020**, *60*, 497–505. [CrossRef]
5. Gasper, J.T.; Reeves, A. Make it rain? Retrospection and the attentive electorate in the context of natural disasters. *Am. J. Pol. Sci.* **2011**, *55*, 340–355. [CrossRef]
6. Hart, J. Did the COVID-19 pandemic help or hurt Donald Trump's political fortunes? *PLoS ONE* **2021**, *16*, e0247664. [CrossRef] [PubMed]
7. Baccini, L.; Brodeur, A.; Weymouth, S. The COVID-19 pandemic and the 2020 US presidential election. *J. Popul. Econ.* **2021**, *34*, 739–767. [CrossRef] [PubMed]
8. Panos, A. Reading about geography and race in the rural rustbelt: Mobilizing dis/affiliation as a practice of whiteness. *Linguist. Educ.* **2021**, *65*, 100955. [CrossRef]

9. Gugushvili, A.; Koltai, J.; Stuckler, D.; Mckee, M. Populism, and pandemics. *Int. J. Public Health* **2020**, *65*, 721–722. [CrossRef] [PubMed]
10. Gimpel, J.G. The 2020 election campaign was over quickly. *Polit. Geogr.* **2021**, 102430. [CrossRef]
11. Yoon, S.; McClean, S.T.; Chawla, N.; Kim, J.K.; Koopman, J.; Rosen, C.C.; Trougakos, J.P.; McCarthy, J.M. Working through an "infodemic": The impact of COVID-19 news consumption on employee uncertainty and work behaviors. *J. Appl. Psychol.* **2021**, *106*, 501–517. [CrossRef] [PubMed]
12. Di Nardo, M.; van Leeuwen, G.; Loreti, A.; Barbieri, M.A.; Guner, Y.; Locatelli, F.; Ranieri, V.M. A literature review of 2019 novel coronavirus (SARS-CoV2) infection in neonates and children. *Pediatr. Res.* **2021**, *89*, 1101–1108. [CrossRef] [PubMed]
13. Martin, J.C.; Bustamante-Sánchez, N.S.; Indelicato, A. Analyzing the Main Determinants for Being an Immigrant in Cuenca (Ecuador) Based on a Fuzzy Clustering Approach. *Axioms* **2022**, *11*, 74. [CrossRef]
14. Cai, W.; Chen, S.; Zhang, D. Fast and robust fuzzy c-means clustering algorithms incorporating local information for image segmentation. *Pattern Recognit.* **2007**, *40*, 825–838. [CrossRef]
15. Zhao, F.; Jiao, L.; Liu, H. Kernel generalized fuzzy c-means clustering with spatial information for image segmentation. *Digit. Signal Process. A Rev. J.* **2013**, *23*, 184–199. [CrossRef]
16. Zhao, F.; Liu, H.; Fan, J. A multiobjective spatial fuzzy clustering algorithm for image segmentation. *Appl. Soft Comput. J.* **2015**, *30*, 48–57. [CrossRef]
17. Ferraro, M.B.; Giordani, P.; Serafini, A. Fclust: An R Package for Fuzzy Clustering. *R J.* **2019**, *11*, 1–18. [CrossRef]
18. Gelb, J.; Apparicio, P. Apport de la classification floue c-means spatiale en géographie: Essai de taxinomie socio-résidentielle et environnementale à Lyon. *Cybergeo* **2021**, 1–26. [CrossRef]
19. Warshaw, C.; Vavreck, L.; Baxter-King, R. Fatalities from COVID-19 are reducing Americans' support for Republicans at every level of federal office. *Sci. Adv.* **2020**, *6*, eabd8564. [CrossRef] [PubMed]

axioms

MDPI

Article

Does Set Theory Really Ground Arithmetic Truth?

Alfredo Roque Freire

Center for Research and Development in Mathematics and Applications (CIDMA), Department of Mathematics, University of Aveiro, 3810-193 Aveiro, Portugal; alfredo.roque.freire@ua.pt

Abstract: We consider the foundational relation between arithmetic and set theory. Our goal is to criticize the construction of standard arithmetic models as providing grounds for arithmetic truth. Our method is to emphasize the incomplete picture of both theories and to treat models as their syntactical counterparts. Insisting on the incomplete picture will allow us to argue in favor of the revisability of the standard-model interpretation. We start briefly characterizing the expansion of arithmetic 'truth' provided by the interpretation in a set theory. Interpreted versions of an arithmetic theory into set theories generally have more theorems than the original. This theorem expansion is not complete however. Using this, the set theoretic multiversalist concludes that there are multiple legitimate standard models of arithmetic. We suggest a different multiversalist conclusion: while there is a single arithmetic structure, its interpretation in each universe may vary or even not be possible. We continue by defining the coordination problem. We consider two independent communities of mathematicians responsible for deciding over new axioms for ZF and PA. How likely are they to be coordinated regarding PA's interpretation in ZF? We prove that it is possible to have extensions of PA not interpretable in a given set theory ST. We further show that the number of extensions of arithmetic is uncountable, while interpretable extensions in ST are countable. We finally argue that this fact suggests that coordination can only work if it is assumed from the start.

Keywords: foundations of mathematics; arithmetic; set theory

Citation: Freire, A.R. Does Set Theory Really Ground Arithmetic Truth? *Axioms* **2022**, *11*, 351. https://doi.org/10.3390/axioms11070351

Academic Editors: Oscar Castillo and Radko Mesiar

Received: 19 May 2022
Accepted: 13 July 2022
Published: 21 July 2022

1. Overview

In this article, we study the idea of reducing arithmetic to set theory as a strategy for grounding arithmetic truth. The method of reduction we have in mind is interpretation. We say that a theory T_1 is interpreted in a theory T_2, when there is a uniform mapping of theorems of T_1 in theorems of T_2. This mapping should preserve the boolean structure and bound quantifiers of T_1 in a definable class of T_2. We will next indicate how model constructions can be understood as the establishment of interpretations between theories.

In what follows, we assume that mathematical structures exist independently of our ability to completely describe them. It is common practice, however, to refer to models as fully formed entities for which one can assert whether any formula is valid. This is generally done with Gödel-Tarski method within a set-theoretic metatheory. The fact that one can decide whether any formula φ is satisfied by a model M is simply given by the axiom of excluded middle in the metatheory. Although this strategy may help us to understand model-theoretic properties, it will not necessarily help us to concretely determine which are the valid formulas. For example, considering the standard model N of arithmetic built in a ZF metatheory, we indeed know that $\psi =$ "twin prime conjecture" is satisfied or not by the model. But that "N satisfies ψ" can still be unprovable from the point of view of ZF.

This is the reason why we will consider models via their syntactical representation through interpretations. Understanding models in this way will allow us to distinguish more precisely the undecidable instances of the form "N satisfies ψ" in the chosen metatheory. Structures should not be treated as syntactical constructions nevertheless. One may refer to a set-theoretic structure V as a platonic collection of objects; and due to our limited knowledge, the notion of satisfaction in V is vaguely defined. We can, however, define a precise notion of knowledge about satisfaction by fixing a set theoretic theory ST:

$$\text{We know that } V \models \varphi \text{ if, and only if, } ST \vdash \varphi \quad (1)$$

Now, each model definable in a given base model $V \models ST$ can be said be to the result of bounding the elements of V to a given interpretation I (this will be define precisely in the Section 2 with respect to arithmetic). By doing so, we can keep in mind our limited knowledge of models. Since, if $\mathcal{M}$ is definable in V (i.e., $\mathcal{M} = I^V$) and we do not know any other information about V other than that it satisfies ST, then

$$\text{We know } \mathcal{M} \models \varphi \text{ if, and only if, } ST \vdash \varphi^I \quad (2)$$

Furthermore, we investigate the grounding relation represented by interpreting PA in ZF. Notably, if one considers the standard interpretation of PA in ZF to be correct, then it expands what one known to be arithmetically true—i.e., many independent formulas in PA become theorems as we see them in ZF through the interpretation. But even though we expect that interpretations of PA in ZF expand knowledge of arithmetic truth, ZF does not completely decide on arithmetical formulas. Indeed, for every interpretation I of arithmetic in a recursive extension S of ZF, there is an arithmetical formula that S does not decide under this interpretation. At any stage in the development of ZF (a recursive extension), the concept of arithmetical truth will still be open. Some arithmetic formulas will be undecidable under the interpretation in any recursively extended set theory. Hence, it is possible to build two structures satisfying the set theory that disagree about the truth value of an arithmetic formula.

Taking a multiversalist view of set theory, Hamkins and others (see [1–3]) use a similar basis to advance a pluralist view of arithmetic. In [1], for example, Hamkins and Yang show that there are models of ZF that agree about what the standard model of arithmetic is and yet disagree about what is valid in the standard model. This (and other results) suggests that there are alternative models of arithmetic. In this article we use a different approach. Assuming we have good reasons to say that there is a unique arithmetic intended structure while maintaining a multiversalist view of set theory (this view is suggested by Koellner in [4]), we argue that the standard interpretation should be taken as revisable. Furthermore, it may happen that the structure of arithmetic is not definable in some set-theoretic universes.

It is due to this phenomena that we consider what we call the coordination problem: consider that there are two groups of mathematicians responsible for deciding over new axioms. The first will decide over axioms for arithmetic and the second for a set theory. How should we consider the relation between the two groups? Note that if we consider that the arithmetic group should conform to any development provided by the set theory group, it becomes hard to see in what sense the interpretation of arithmetic into set theory has any foundational role. This framework is indistinguishable from simply taking arithmetic to live in set theory.

If, however, the interpretation of arithmetic in set theory has a meaningful foundational role, it is important to consider the possibility of the coordination between the two theories to break. Is it possible that an extension of arithmetic not to be interpretable in any extension of a set theory? We show in Theorem 2 that for any extension A of PA and any extension S of ZF, there is an extension A^+ that is not interpretable in S. But, how likely is it to be the case? We will further show in Theorem 3 that there are uncountable consistent extensions of a recursive A, while only a countable number of interpretations of arithmetic in any set theory. For this reason, the addition of axioms to set theory and arithmetic by the two groups would preserve the interpretability relation only if coordination is assumed. We further conclude that this perfect coordination would empty the reductivist foundational role of set theory to arithmetic. Finally, we briefly explore an alternative foundational role that would avoid this problem.

2. The Standard Model of Arithmetic

The strategy of offering set-theoretical models to describe objects of a theory comes from the work of Tarski, Mostowsky, and Robinson in the 1940s [5]. Ever since this date, mathematicians and philosophers often resort to this strategy. It is generally accepted that once we start talking about models, we put aside the formal aspects of the mathematical subject and start talking about its objects and truths. Nevertheless, because of Gödel's incompleteness theorem and Löwenhein-Skolem theorem, there is no formal way to fix the model of any recursive extension of Peano arithmetic. It is impossible to say that the only model that satisfies our descriptions of arithmetic is the intended model, no matter how extensively we describe it. Still, using a set-theoretical apparatus, we can describe the intended model as $N = \langle \omega, +, ., 0, s \rangle$ (called standard model). We can then show that a set theory like ZF is expressive enough to define a truth predicate for this interpretation.

The literature on this subject generally presents two approaches for fixing the standard model: (i) one should offer extra-logical (or second-order) reasons for choosing N from the myriad possible models for arithmetic; (ii) one should abandon the model-theoretical construction and find other ways to ground arithmetic truth. A renewed version of (ii) can be seen in Gabbay's defense of a new kind of formalism [6]; Moreover, others may abandon a privileged emphasis on N, because we must focus on mathematical practice (Ferreirós [7]) or because we must commit ourselves to a realistic multiverse (Hamkins [8]). Still, differences of opinion are more common as to how and why we should follow project (i). Those like Williamson [9] argue for metaphysical reasons for setting N, others like Maddy [10], Quine [11] or Putnam [12] advocate ways to naturalize the reasons for N. Finally, a recent approach by Rodrigo Freire grounds N in mathematical practice using a normative basis in place of the Platonist commitment to N [13].

The question of the adequacy of N is often overlooked. Though one may find a vast literature on non-standard models of arithmetic, these are generally regarded as 'deviant' or not intended. They are indeed existing structures that satisfy an arithmetic theory, but they are not the one true model of arithmetic. The assumption behind this is that if something is a model of arithmetic, then it is N. We may not know why this is the intended model or even deny that such a model exists, but the conformity to N is hardly questioned. However, presenting N as an object without further consideration is a category mistake. Notably, a similar category mistake would be to say that 'there have been two sun revolutions since so and so'. The phrase 'two sun revolutions' is used as quantity of time, even though it describes a movement in reference to the Sun. Hence, the statement would be a category mistake unless, for instance, an implicit reference to Earth and not Mars is assumed. Precisely stated, N is an interpretation of PA in the language of membership. It represents therefore a construction of objects for arithmetic in terms of objects of a given set theory. Hence, it is only when we fix the objects for a set theory that the objects expressed in the construction N gain life.

For any given model of set theory $V \vDash ZF$, an arithmetic interpretation I can be understood as a procedure for obtaining a model $\mathcal{N}$ for PA. The model $\mathcal{N} = \langle Obj, +^{\mathcal{N}}, .^{\mathcal{N}}, 0^{\mathcal{N}}, s^{\mathcal{N}} \rangle$ is a set in the vaguely defined V with the appropriate meaning for the arithmetic symbols $+$ (sum), . (multiplication), 0 (constant zero) and s (successor function). The model $\mathcal{N}$ is built from the interpretation $I = \langle U, f_+, f_., f_s, zero \rangle$. The elements of I are formulas in the language of ZF: U is a formula with one free variable, f_+ and $f_.$ are formulas with three free variables, f_s is a formula with two free variables and $zero$ is a formula with one free variable. It is then necessary to prove in V that the formulas in $f_+(x,y,z)$, $f_.(x,y,z)$, $f_s(x,z)$ indeed represent functions with respect to the variable z and that $zero(x)$ is satisfied by a unique element in V. With these ingredients, we explicitly build in V the model $\mathcal{N}$:

1. $Obj = \{x \in V \mid V \vDash U(x)\}$.
2. $0^{\mathcal{N}} = a$ such that $V \vDash zero(a)$.
3. $+^{\mathcal{N}} = \{\langle x,y,z \rangle \mid x,y,z \in Obj$ and $V \vDash f_+(x,y,z)\}$.
4. $.^{\mathcal{N}} = \{\langle x,y,z \rangle \mid x,y,z \in Obj$ and $V \vDash f_.(x,y,z)\}$.

5. $s^{\mathcal{N}} = \{\langle x, y\rangle \mid x, y \in Obj \text{ and } V \models f_s(x, y)\}$.

We may refer to the model obtained from V using I as I^V. In this context, the standard interpretation $N = \langle U, f_+, f_., f_s, Zero\rangle$ is the case where $U(x)$ expresses in set theory 'x is an finite ordinal', $f_+(x, y, z)$ expresses 'z is the ordinal sum of x and y', $f_.(x, y, z)$ expresses 'z is the ordinal product of x and y', $f_s(x, z)$ expresses 'z is the ordinal successor of x' and $Zero(x)$ expresses 'x is the empty set'. We can then obtain that, independently on the choice of the base model $V \models ZF$, the model $N^V \models PA$.

Syntactically, we may use I to produce a uniform strategy for mapping formulas in the language of arithmetic $L(PA)$ to formulas in the language of set theory $L(ZF)$. As we assumed that $f_+(x, y, z)$ is a function in V, we may use, for simplicity, a function-like language defining $F_+(x, y)$ in ZF as "the z such that $f(x, y, z)$". Similarly, we define $F_.$, F_s and $Zero$. For every arithmetic formula φ, we define the partially interpreted formula φ^{I^*} by:

1. replacing in every atomic subformula of φ occurrence of the form $x + y$, $x.y$, $s(x)$, for $F_+(x, y))$, $F_.(x, y)$, $F_s(x)$ respectively;
2. replacing every occurrence of $\forall x(\psi)$ for $\forall x(U(x) \rightarrow \psi)$;
3. replacing every occurrence of $\exists x(\psi)$ for $\exists x(U(x) \wedge \psi)$;

If φ has free variables $x_1, x_2, \ldots, x_n$, the interpreted formula φ^I is defined as $(U(x_1) \wedge U(x_2) \wedge \ldots \wedge U(x_n)) \rightarrow \varphi^{I^*}$. With this, we can now say that ZF interprets PA with the standard interpretation N since every $\varphi \in PA$ is such that $ZF \vdash \varphi^N$.

Our idea is to insist on the incomplete picture of the set-theoretical representation of arithmetic. All we know about the vaguely defined V is that it is based on an incomplete theory ZF. Therefore, the picture of arithmetic obtained from reducing PA to V by N is also incomplete. In this context, it is worth paying attention to precisely what is decidedly valid in the standard construction with the syntactic notion $ZF \vdash \varphi^N$. If one only commits to the validity of the axioms of a set theory ST, the undecidable formulas in ST of the form φ^I are precisely the arithmetic formulas that one does not know if they are valid or not.

So to what are we committing in the case where we say that N is the standard model of arithmetic? As we will discuss in the next section, it depends on what is the chosen model V. It is in fact showing that the standard model has many representations (even isomorphic, though with different truth predicates), that Hamkins and Yang in [1] proposes a pluralist view of arithmetic. Notably, however, they still fix the standard interpretation–evaluating this interpretation in different structures of set theory. It seems like the single construction for the intended model of arithmetic is based on the idea condensed in the sentence: 'no matter which model of set theory one is assuming, the model of arithmetic would be given by N'. Indeed, the picture provided by the literature is that of ***revisable** truth for set theory and arithmetic*–but **unrevisable** reduction of arithmetic in set theory. In the next sections, we argue that to take the standard model to have a foundational role, one should assume the interpretation to be revisable. For now, we consider the characterization of arithmetic in set theory in more details.

Foundational Characterization of PA in ZF

Being I an interpretation of arithmetic in a set theory S, we call the set $A_I^S = \{\varphi \in L(PA) \mid S \vdash \varphi^I\}$ the expansion of arithmetic truth under the interpretation. Indeed some undecidable formulas φ of PA are 'true' in the standard model ($ZF \vdash \varphi^N$). This is the case for the Gödel formula, Goodstein's theorem and many others arithmetic results. We will thus consider more broadly the question of expansion of arithmetic truth from interpretations in set theories.

Given that I is an interpretation of an arithmetic theory A in a set theory S and $Th(A) = \{\varphi \mid A \vdash \varphi\}$, we expect to have $Th(A) \subsetneq A_I^S \subsetneq Arithmetic\ truth$, as we see in Figure 1:

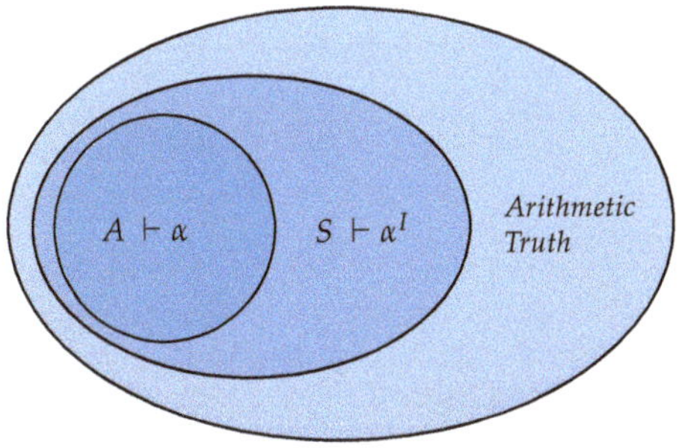

Figure 1. Expansion of validity under interpretation.

The reason for the expansion $Th(A) \subsetneq A_I^S$ is that, in the usual case, one expects to build a set-size model of arithmetic. Consequently, a consistency predicate for A should be expressed and proved in S. Consider the base case of PA and ZF with the standard interpretation N. Assuming a model V for ZF, we can build a model N^V satisfying PA. We then know that there are many valid formulas in N^V that are not provable in PA. The most immediate example is the consistency predicate $Con(PA)$; in fact, we know that the predicate is valid in N^V or, in other words, that $ZF \vdash (Con(PA))^I$.

Of course, from a given recursive extension S of ZF, one may simply choose the recursive arithmetic theory corresponding to the theorems in ST about the standard interpretation (i.e., A_N^S). But this is to *put the cart before the horse,* being open to the evaluation of extra valid formulas with respect to the current axiomatization of arithmetic (e.g., $\varphi \in A_N^S$ but such that φ is not proved in the current axiomatization of arithmetic) is a fundamental aspect in this study. In addition, there are important recent results that show fundamental mismatches between arithmetic and set theory. In fact, no subtheory of any extension of ZF is bi-interpretable with any extension of PA. This is a simple consequence of a theorem by Enayat and independently discovered by Hamkins and me: two different extensions of ZF can never be bi-interpretable [14–16] (the direct proof is done in the dissertation ([17] pp. 150–152). Together with the bi-interpretation of finite set theory and Peano arithmetic, the result follows. Hence, in order to obtain a set theory equivalent to PA we must add an axiom that contradicts ZF. Similarly, no compatible (with ZF) collection of set-theoretic concepts can perfectly mirror an axiomatization of arithmetic that extends PA.

We also note that the characterization of the foundation relation by theorem expansion relates to the mathematical practice. With the discovery of the Gödel's incompleteness theorem in [18], some resistance to the result was argued in the sense that the obtained undecidable statement had little mathematical meaning. Later on, Goodstein [19] proved that there are fast growing functions (called Goodstein sequences) that cannot be proved to be total in PA. The existence of these sequences is directly connected to the traditional Hydra problem, and thus it bears a clear mathematical meaning (see Caicedo's "Goodstein's function" [20]). Thus the question of foundation arises as to whether the interpretation of PA in set theory answers a significant arithmetical problem that was not possibly addressed by the axiomatization. And this is indeed the case as we consider Goodstein sequences.

Notably, important results in number theory have recently become so loaded with complicated techniques that mathematicians have begun to question whether the proofs extrapolated Peano's axioms. This is the case of Fermat's last theorem and the weak Goldbach conjecture, proved respectively by Andrew Wiles [21,22] and by Harald Helfgott [23]. This type of question is akin to the program of reverse mathematics and has drawn the attention of mathematicians like Harvey Friedman. However, the validity of those theorems, whether they depend or not on more axioms than PA, is hardly questioned. The choice is not commonly to add axioms to PA, but to investigate arithmetic truths in a theory that expands the extension of theorems. One is not however simply doing 'finite ordinal set theory' when dealing more loosely with arithmetic's axiomatization, as these 'stronger than PA' assumption should correspond to number theorists' intuitions about natural numbers.

We have discussed that interpretations of arithmetic in set theories generally expand what may be taken to be arithmetical truth ($Th(A) \subsetneq A_I^S$). Yet this expansion is not necessarily complete (A_I^S = arithmetic truth). A confusion in this regard is due to the idea that model constructions in set theories offer venues for defining truth for interpreted theories. Each interpretation I represents the appropriate model construction such that the grounding set theoretic model V can provide the notion of satisfaction $I^V \models \varphi$ for any formula. Eventually, we would have that for any formula γ, either $V^I \models \gamma$ or $V^I \models \neg\gamma$. However, as we have already discussed, a more syntactical approach makes it clear that this is simply the expression of the *excluded middle*. Indeed, "either $V^I \models \gamma$ or $V^I \models \neg\gamma$" should be syntactically represented by

$$ZF \vdash \gamma^I \vee \neg\gamma^I \tag{3}$$

Instead, what is really wanted is a notion like

$$ZF \vdash \gamma^I \text{ or } ZF \vdash \neg\gamma^I \tag{4}$$

As we suppose a base model V for ZF, we are at hand with an interpretation for ZF itself or with a loosely defined model. In this case, the notion of truth in a model is represented by "either $I^V \models \gamma$ or $I^V \models \neg\gamma$". However, if our supposition of a model V is not informed by any specific information other than $V \models ZF$, the interpretation works simply as the identity. Therefore, we return to the problem of establishing a notion as in (4).

However, Equation (4) is not achievable for any recursive extension of ZF. For a given interpretation I of arithmetic in a recursive extension S of ZF, there will be formulas of $L(PA)$ that are undecidable about arithmetic in S, that is, formulas φ in $L(PA)$ such that $S \nvdash \varphi^I$ and $S \nvdash (\neg\varphi)^I$. One may think that this is a direct consequence of Gödel's incompleteness for PA, as S could be seen as a recursive extension of PA. But this is false. As mentioned before, no subtheory of an extension of ZF is bi-interpretable with any extension of PA. Indeed, PA is bi-interpretable with the theory ZF_{fin} composed of ZF without axiom of infinity and with the addition of negation of infinity and transitive closure (see [24]). However, no extension of ZF_{fin} can be S, since S asserts the existence of infinite sets. In view of this, we prove the very simple theorem:

Theorem 1. *For a given interpretation I of PA in a recursive extension S of ZF, there will be formulas of $L(PA)$ such that $S \nvdash \varphi^I$ and $S \nvdash (\neg\varphi)^I$.*

Proof. To prove this, we should reinternalize the provability predicate under the interpretation. Let as consider $A = \{\varphi \mid S \vdash \varphi^I\}$. Notably, $PA \subseteq A$ and thus A can produce arithmetization for arithmetic formulas and for set-theoretic formulas. Let $\ulcorner\varphi\urcorner$ be the Gödel number of any formula φ in A or in S and $\ulcorner\langle\varphi_1, \varphi_2, \ldots, \varphi_n\rangle\urcorner$ the Gödel number of any sequence of formulas $\langle\varphi_1, \varphi_2, \ldots, \varphi_n\rangle$ in A or in S (as done in ([25] pp. 122–126)).

Since S is recursive, "$\ulcorner\langle\varphi_1, \varphi_2, \ldots, \varphi_n\rangle\urcorner$ is a proof in S" is recursive. From the representation theorem (see [25] pp. 126–128), there is a predicate $Pr_S(x, y)$ such that

$$A \vdash Pr_S(\ulcorner\langle\varphi_1, \varphi_2, \ldots, \varphi_n\rangle\urcorner, \ulcorner\psi\urcorner) \iff \langle\varphi_1, \varphi_2, \ldots, \varphi_n\rangle \text{ is a proof in S and } \psi \text{ is } \varphi_n \tag{5}$$

Moreover, the statement "ψ is the φ^I of some φ" is recursive. Then, from the representation theorem, there is a predicate $Fml_I(x)$ such that

$$A \vdash Fml_I(\ulcorner\psi\urcorner) \iff \psi \text{ is the } \varphi^I \text{ of some } \varphi \tag{6}$$

Defining $Th_S^A(y)$ as $\exists x(Pr_S(x, y) \wedge Fml_I(y))$, we can then use the diagonal lemma for the formula $\neg Th_S^A(y)$, obtaining a formula G such that

$$A \vdash G \leftrightarrow \neg Th_S(\ulcorner G\urcorner) \tag{7}$$

If $S \vdash G^I$, then $A \vdash Fml_I(\ulcorner G \urcorner)$ and $A \vdash Th_S(\ulcorner G \urcorner)$ from (5) and (6). From (7), we have $A \vdash \neg Th_S(\ulcorner G \urcorner)$, contradiction. To obtain a contradiction from $S \vdash \neg G^I$, we should reformulate the proof using the Rosser trick, although it will also work the same way as in ([25] pp. 131–132). Then the formula G obtained in the diagonalization for the equivalent Rosser-Gödel predicate is the undecidable arithmetic formula in S. □

This theorem can be understood as a **very small** expansion of Gödel's incompleteness theorem as we consider decidability under relations between theories. Moreover, it relates to results available in *Satisfaction is not absolute* [1]. In this article, Hamkins and Yang considered the idea that there may be arithmetical formulas ρ that two models of ZF disagree–even as these same models agree on what is the standard model for arithmetic. Though very important in the context of this paper, the result lacks a construction for the ρ formula. This formula is obtained as the existential for a number representing a formula. In fact, exhibiting ρ is not possible, since it would imply the inconsistency of ZF.

Put another way, we have shown a similar phenomenon in which disagreement can be exhibited. To make it possible, we considered a foundational view that accommodates our incomplete understanding of set theory and arithmetic. Thus, agreement on arithmetic is to be understood as having similar sets of known arithmetical truths $\{\varphi \mid S \vdash \varphi^N\}$, S being some stage (or alternative stage) in the development of ZF. In this sense, there is a formula ρ that would be true in some possible development of S and false in some other possible development of S. As a reviewer pointed out, Ali Enayat [26] has recently studied this phenomenon in a similar light. He points out that $N^{ZF} \subsetneq N^{ZFI}$, where I indicates the existence of an inaccessible cardinal. Interestingly, he also creates a natural way of describing the S's expansion of arithmetic. If $\theta_0, \theta_1, \ldots, \theta_i, \ldots$ is an enumeration of formulas of S and $S_n = \{\theta_i \mid i < n\}$, the resulting arithmetic obtained from S is PA together with statements $\varphi \to Con(S_n \cup \{\varphi^N\})$. Enayat later shows a series of results on how and to what extent set theory models can disagree over the standard model of arithmetic. The limit of his method for the purposes of the present article is that his main concern is a model-theoretical characterization of 'nonstandard' models (with respect to some background V) that are obtained in some S using the standard interpretation.

There are indeed various important open statements of finite set theory. The recent book "Extremal problems for finite sets" ([26] pp. 211–215) deals with some of those systematically: Erdős matching conjecture, Chvátal conjecture, Frankl's union-closed conjecture and so on. If some of these turn out to be undecidable in ZF (or ZFC), they will correspond to undecidable statements of arithmetic under the standard interpretation. The question we would like to propose is this: assuming that the standard interpretation of PA in ZF produces true arithmetic statements, should we simply say that if some set theorists decide to include some of those conjectures as axioms, then should number theorists accept the corresponding statements as arithmetic truths?

In particular, there has been an important debate regarding the multiversalist picture of set theory. Many set theorists today consider that there are indeed equally legitimate non-isomorphic set theoretic models. The motivations for this are various (see [8]). But do those motivations apply to arithmetic? With set theory, there is a fundamental limitation generally accepted even by many conservative set theorists: whenever we deal with a model of set theory, we should always set a limit to an ordinal level in the cumulative hierarchy. Therefore, there is at least a multiverse of set-theoretic models with respect to ordinal levels. Nothing similar to this is found in arithmetic intuitions. Natural numbers are precisely those one can effectively count and there is little to no reason to take a pluralist view with respect to arithmetic. Notice, however, that by accepting the multiversalist view of set theory together with the view that the one true reduction of arithmetic to set theory is the standard interpretation, we are consequently subscribing to a pluralist view of arithmetic. And this is precisely the conclusion drawn by Hamkins. Now, if there is only one model of arithmetic and many legitimate set theoretic models, it becomes fundamentally important to consider that the interpretation of arithmetic in set theory is revisable and that the model of arithmetic may not even characterizable in some set theoretic models. It is in view of this consideration that we should now investigate what we call *the coordination problem*.

3. The Coordination Problem

Let us consider the following fictional scenario for the development of set theory and arithmetic. There are two groups of mathematicians who would decide about new axioms for set theory and arithmetic. The first G_s is responsible for one (among possibly many) set-theoretic universe, and the second G_a for the arithmetic structure. Let us further assume that G_a agrees with the standard expansion of arithmetic in ZF (A_N^{ZF} is considered valid for G_a). How should we frame the relation between the two groups?

Consider that G_s have decided in favor of new axiom α to set theory ZF. In particular, this would expand the set of arithmetic truths in $A_N^{ZF+\alpha}$. Should G_a consider this new set to be true? This being the general attitude towards arithmetic means that the standard reduction determines new truths for arithmetic. In what sense does the standard interpretation provide a foundation for new arithmetical truths? If we think that the standard interpretation does this, it seems like we have simply assumed that arithmetic lives in set theory, without any further considerations. After all, this framework bounds the expansion of arithmetic truth to the expansion of set-theoretic truth. Therefore, G_a would not have any authority over new arithmetic axioms after all.

In order to make room for this setting, one should consider that we have a better understanding on how arithmetic is reduced to set theory than we have for each of the theories. And, for this to work in general, we should consider the reduction of arithmetic in set theory **unrevisable**.

Very often we consider ourselves to have a good understanding on relations between things that we may not have a good understanding. This is the case for translating a sentence like "Napoleon was an emperor". We may have a lot of doubts about the ontological status of the words used in this sentence and still be confident about how to translate it into Chinese.

Indeed, we may be more confident about the way we reduce arithmetic to set theory than about the truth in these theories. Yet this is not sufficient to assume the unrevisability of the reduction relation. After some investigation over the concept of emperor, one has realized that the standard translation of emperor in Chinese does not really represents what English speakers refer with 'emperor'. For instance, emperor is usually translated as 'Huangdi' in Chinese, even though this word associate the monarch with his divinity. In English, although often associated with divinity, the word emperor can be used without divine association. So a more intricate description as 'Napoleon was the non-divine man who ruled over the French empire' would be better (even if it is not practical).

If there are grounds for taking N to be a privileged interpretation, those would be based on partial representations of arithmetic and set theory. Therefore, the idea that N correctly works as a connection between the theories may be simply because we have not advanced the theories enough. This would be a similar case if a Chinese working in the translation of a western modern history book has been translating 'Emperor' as 'Huangdi'. It seems perfectly fine if he believed this to be a general translation, given that the only time he applied the translation was for the 'Emperor of the Holy Roman Empire'. But as he starts translating the Napoleonic period, the broader picture would force him to reconsider the generality of the translation.

A different picture would be the case where the Chinese translator invented a language where w means 'blue chair'. Finding someone else using w to refer to a red chair, he could correctly accuse the person to be using the word incorrectly. So this would be similar to the case where we consider arithmetic to be a definition inside set theory. But this being the case would imply that there is no foundational gain in studying the relation between the theories.

Whereas set theory has a foundational role for arithmetic, we may now consider that the standard interpretation is a good yet revisable set-theoretic inspection over arithmetic.

It is precisely because we assume the interpretation to be revisable that a foundational relation can be argued. As truth expands in both theories, we evaluate conflicts and revise, if necessary, the interpretation to accommodate changes. A summary of the steps in the coordination of G_a and G_s can be:

1. Every addition of axioms to one theory should provoke an inspection over the adequacy of the current interpretation of arithmetic in set theory.
2. If a conflict arises in the development of the theories, the two groups should meet to adjust the interpretation to prevent the conflict.
3. The adequacy of an interpretation should have reasons for itself apart from accommodating the interpretation.

As we see in Step 2, the two communities should sit together and reevaluate the state of the reduction, if necessary. Hopefully, these conferences would hardly occur. But we should allow some independence to each group. Otherwise, their development, especially on arithmetic, would turn out to be assumed by definition in the development of the other.

We have added some life to the grounding relation by allowing it to fail. However, there is still a deeper problem. The following scenario is still possible:

(i) Each instance of development allows one to fix the interpretation between the theories.
(ii) And at least one of the extensions of any state of arithmetic is not possibly interpreted in set theory.

Allowing both of these possibilities weakens the edifice of the grounding relation. Each moment in the development of the theories is an incomplete stage in which we cannot anticipate the impossibility of reductions occurring further in the development of the theories. From (i), any addition to the theories allows one to find (or keep) an interpretation of arithmetic. However, from (ii), finding those interpretations does not add to the idea that arithmetic is indeed reducible to a given set theory. This scenario is possible, as we will see in the next theorem.

Theorem 2. *Let S be a consistent extension of ZF and A a consistent recursive extension of PA, then there is a consistent extension A^* of A that is not interpretable in S.*

Proof. We extend the theory A by generating a sequence of theories that are not interpretable in S by a particular interpretation I. Being these theories compatible with each other, the union of them will not be interpretable in S.

Let $A_0 = A$ and $\{I_1, I_2, \ldots\}$ be an enumeration of all interpretations from PA language to ZF language. We generate a sequence of theories $A_0 \subseteq A_1 \subseteq \ldots \subseteq A_n \subseteq \ldots$ by adding **one** formula in each step. It should be noticed that the proof here is not constructive, meaning we are not using a recursive method to determine the new formula added to A_i to obtain A_{i+1}. Nonetheless, since every theory A_i will be the addition of i formulas to the recursively axiomatized A_0, then A_i is also recursively axiomatized. In this case, for every i, there is a formula G_i obtained by the Rosser-Gödel diagonalization argument. With this in mind, we define the A_i's as follows (abbreviation: $T \leq_J T'$ represents "T is interpreted in T' by J"):

Let $\varphi_0, \varphi_1, \ldots, \varphi_k, \ldots$ be an enumeration of arithmetic formulas.

1. If $A_i \leq_{I_i} S$ and there is a least k such that $A_i \nvdash \varphi_k$ and $S \vdash \varphi_k^{I_i}$, then

$$A_{i+1} = A_i \cup \{\neg\varphi_k\}$$

2. Otherwise,

$$A_{i+1} = A_i \cup G_i$$

Let $A^* = \bigcup_{i \in \omega} A_i$. We note that A^* is a consistent extension of A because in each step we add an unprovable formula.

Suppose A^* is interpretable by I in S, then $I = I_k$ for some natural number k. Notably, if a theory T is interpreted in a theory T', then any subtheory of T is interpreted in T' by the same interpretation. Thus the entire sequence of theories $\{A_1, A_2, \ldots\}$ is interpreted in S by I_k. In particular, we have $A_k \leq_{I_k} S$ and $A_{k+1} = A_i + \neg\varphi_q$ or $A_{k+1} = A_k + G_k$ as in the definition. If $A_{k+1} = A_i + \neg\varphi_q$, then option 1 in the definition was used and we have $S \vdash \varphi_q^{I_k}$. However, since S also interprets A_{k+1} with I_k, we have the contradiction $S \vdash \neg\varphi_q^{I_k}$. If $A_{k+1} = A_k + G_k$, then option 1 is not applied and we have either (i) $A_k \not\leq_{I_k} S$ or (ii) that, for all n, $A_i \vdash \varphi_n$ if, and only if, $S \vdash \varphi_n^{I_k}$. Note that (i) contradicts $A_k \leq_{I_k} S$. Moreover, since $A_i \nvdash G_i$, it follows from (ii) that $S \nvdash G_k^{I_k}$–which, in turn, implies the contradiction $A_{k+1} \not\leq_{I_k} S$. Therefore, A^* is not interpretable in S. □

Let $A = A_N^{ZF}$, Ak be the Ackermann interpretation of membership in arithmetic language and consider that a formula φ is equivalent to $(con(ZF))^{Ak}$ in A. Suppose also that the group G_a considers φ to be valid. Notably, this formula would represent a relation between natural numbers such that the standard interpretation stops being a correct interpretation of arithmetic. Similar constructions can be used to generate a myriad of examples. However, each of these examples can be subject to a 'contrary to intuition' kind of criticism. In the case presented, one may suggest that $(con(ZF))^{Ak}$ means that we are adding an axiom representing the consistency of ZF in the arithmetic without doing the same in the set theory. Simply adding the axiom $con(ZF)$ to our set theory would make the standard interpretation work again nicely. Nevertheless, we note that the phenomenon presented in the theorem is not exactly to add isolated axioms, but to add an enumeration of axioms to the arithmetic. Our suggestion is therefore that a bundle addition of axioms may force the theories to loose coordination. We also note that we do not impose the set theory S to be recursive. For this reason, one may simply consider that S is a complete extension of ZF. In this case, no addition to the set theory would possibly allow the theories to recover the interpretability relation.

We argued that it is possible for ZF and PA to part ways along the path of development. Although disturbing, this may simply account for the meaningfulness of the question about the reduction between the two theories. We have considered that we should conceive it to fail (even fatally, as in this case) in order not to take for granted that the reduction works. Note further that this pays tribute to the idea that by interpreting arithmetic in set theory we should inform something that was not simply given, i.e., that arithmetic lives in the realm of set theory. Nonetheless, we should now show the simple (and not a novelty) result that the number consistent extensions of PA is uncountable. Meanwhile, the number of interpretations is trivially countable. This means that we are in a situation similar to that of choosing a random number in the Real line expecting to find a natural number. Our claim is that, for this reason, the coordination between the systems can work only if the coordination is assumed from the beginning and as a principle.

Theorem 3. *Let A be a consistent recursive extension of PA, then there is a uncountable number of consistent extensions of A.*

Proof. From the incompletness theorem, there is a formula G that is undecidable in PA. Thus, both $PA + G$ and $PA + \neg G$ are consistent. Notably, this is still true for the addition of any finite number of new axioms $\alpha_1, \alpha_2, \ldots, \alpha_n$. There is a formula $G_{\langle i\rangle}$ that is undecidable in $A_{\langle i\rangle} = PA + \{\alpha_1, \alpha_2, \ldots, \alpha_n\}$ since $A_{\langle i\rangle}$ is a recursive extension. Let us then index PA extensions with binary codes (i.e. sequences of 0's and 1's) in the following way:

1. $A_{\langle 0\rangle} = PA$.
2. If $G_{\langle i\rangle}$ is the undecidable obtained with Rosser-Gödel technique $A_{\langle i\rangle}$, then $A_{\langle i1\rangle}$ is $A_{\langle i\rangle} + G_{\langle i\rangle}$ and $A_{\langle i0\rangle}$ is $A_{\langle i\rangle} + \neg G_{\langle i\rangle}$. (where $i1$ and $i0$ are the binary extension of the code i with the digits 1 and 0)
3. Let $FinBin$ be the set of all finite binary codes, the set $\Sigma = \{A_{\langle x\rangle} \mid x \in FinBin\}$ is a subset of finite extensions of PA.

Note that each member of Σ is an extension of PA with the addition of a finite number of formulas. Now we build infinite extensions of PA from Σ. Let $M : FinBin \to \Sigma$ be the map between binary codes and extensions in Σ. We say that $C : \omega \to FinBin$ is a chain in $FinBin$ when $\forall x, y \in \omega(x \leq y \to (C(y)$ extends the code of $C(x)))$. Also, if $x \in FinBin$, we write

$$x(n) = \begin{cases} \text{n'th digit of } x, & \text{if there is the n'th digit} \\ 0, & \text{otherwise} \end{cases}$$

If C is a chain in $FinBin$, then $dig_C = \langle (C(0))(0), (C(1))(1), \ldots, (C(n))(n), \ldots \rangle$ is an infinite binary code associated with the extension Ex_C obtained by

$$\bigcup \{C(i) \mid i \in \omega\}$$

We define Π as the set

$$\{\langle dig_C, Ex_C \rangle \mid C \text{ is a chain in } FinBin\}$$

Note that Π is a function from the set of all binary infinite codes to extensions of PA. Since infinite binary codes are uncountable, we need only to show that Π is injective and that the image of Π is composed of consistent extensions of PA.

Suppose that some Ex_C is not consistent; then there is a finite proof of the inconsistency of Ex_C. Hence, there is $n \in \omega$ such that $Ex_C^n = \bigcup \{C(i) \mid i \in n\} = C(n)$ is inconsistent. But this is false, since each $C(i+1)$ obtained by adding an unprovable formula to $C(i)$ and $C(0) = PA$ is assumed consistent.

Suppose that $\Pi(dig_{C_1}) = \Pi(dig_{C_2})$ and that $dig_{C_1} \neq dig_{C_2}$. Then there is the least i such that $dig_{C_1}(i+1) \neq dig_{C_2}(i+1)$. This means, without loss of generality, that $C_1(i+1) = C_1(i) + G_{C_1(i)}$, $C_2(i+1) = C_2(i) + \neg G_{C_2(i)}$ and $C_1(i) = C_2(i)$. Therefore, $\Pi(dig_{C_1})$ contains the formulas $G_{C_1(i)}$ and $\neg G_{C_1(i)}$. This is absurd, as we just showed that the image of Π is composed of consistent extensions of PA. □

We note that the same can be obtained, even if the starting point includes all theorems of the set theory S under the interpretation. Indeed, we can include the theorems under a given interpretation at any point without interfering with the result.

Although extensions like A^+ are in general not interpretable in S, the process of generating these theories is internalizable in S. Therefore, we may say that S proves the consistency statement for all these extensions. This is not enough to claim a proper foundational relation. The model construction emerging from this type of consistency proof is simply given by the existence of a model as in the Henkin canonical construction. Thus, the foundational model one can generate provides little more information than saying that the theory is consistent (see [27]). Therefore, we should not consider those cases as a path to avoid the problem discussed in this section.

As developed in this section, we should not consider that the addition of new axioms to the systems is, in principle, coordinated. Instead, the reducibility of arithmetical truth should be a result of the expressiveness of set theory. However, assuming that the choices of the two groups G_a and G_s would result in a interpretable arithmetic is similar to expect that a random choice of a real number to be a natural number (which has probability zero). It follows that coordination between the groups of mathematicians can only occur in principle. Hence, the reduction of arithmetic truth to set theory is not attainable unless assumed and the foundational relation should be based on other grounds.

To further elaborate on this conclusion, let us consider a metaphor. Picture the situation in which we have the unstable equilibrium of a sphere on a hill with a very small slope. We would like to say that the appearance of equilibrium represents our intuitions about the reduction between the theories being correct. Indeed, we have put the sphere in a position that appears to be an equilibrium. As the slope of the hill is very small, our perception of equilibrium works really well. However, even if it takes a long time, it will become evident that the interpretation of PA in ZF is not in equilibrium. We are, nonetheless, in a better position if we accept the multiversalist view of set theory. Under this assumption, we should thus say that there are indeed some universes perfectly coordinated with arithmetic under the standard interpretation, and there are some universes perfectly coordinated with arithmetic under other interpretations. However, these universes are only a small portion among a much larger multitude of possible universes of set theory.

The ideas developed in the present article, especially in Theorem 3, bring attention to the fact that we are talking about an unstable hill. No matter how the sphere appears to be at rest, we know that eventually it will gain traction and fall. The project of using N for grounding arithmetic truth is equivalent to finding the equilibrium peak of the hill. It seems to be a good project as we focus on the movement of the sphere–but an analysis of the geography of the hill is already sufficient to conclude this hill to be unstable. We should not base our foundational investigations on the guarantee that we have the correct interpretation in a fixed set theory. Instead, we should use the interpretations as it informs about arithmetic concepts and as it considers bundles of arithmetic formulas in the very expressive environment of set theory.

Our position is not that the standard interpretation N cannot play a foundational role. Alternatively, the very possibility of investigating expansions of arithmetic propositions provided by analyzing N (or other interpretations) is all the ground we need. In place of using foundational relations to establish 'arithmetic truth', we propose using the N interpretation to understand how bundles of arithmetical propositions relates to each other. In this case, we use the technical apparatus and the expressiveness of theories like ZF to analyze arithmetical concepts rather than fixing its truth.

4. Final Remarks

Rather than manipulating models of PA, we considered interpretations of PA in ZF. Our goal was to accommodate the incomplete picture of the set-theoretical metatheory into our analysis of the foundations of arithmetic. The standard interpretation expands what we may consider true in arithmetic: many undecidable formulas in PA become theorems when examined under the interpretation in ZF. This is a general phenomenon. For every well founded interpretation of recursive extensions of PA in extensions of ZF, the interpreted version of arithmetic has more theorems than the original. This shows that studying arithmetic inside set theory can be significant. As one considers these interpretations, one explores **expansion of arithmetic truth** and how the addition of bundles of axioms plays out.

We continued by introducing the coordination problem. We considered two independent communities of mathematicians responsible for deciding over new axioms of ZF and PA. Using this setting, we studied the possibility of coordinating PA with PA's interpretation in ZF. Nonetheless, we showed that it is possible to have extensions of PA that are not interpretable in a given set theory S. Moreover, we consider a given recursive extension A of PA and an extension S of ZF. Here, we prove that there are uncountable extensions of A while countable interpretations of arithmetic in S. This last result implies that the coordination between the two communities of mathematicians should be coordinated from the start. However, we argued that this would empty the foundational role of set theory over arithmetic.

We have, therefore, set a framework to criticize the notion of grounding truth between theories such as arithmetic and set theory, specially with respect to the idea of fixing an interpretation between the systems. Indeed, the multiversalist propagates their pluralism from set theory to arithmetic by relying on the standard interpretation. We reject this conclusion, arguing that it is the interpretation that should be revised. By allowing the interpretation of arithmetic into set theory to change, we make compatible the set theoretic pluralism with the view that there is a single arithmetic structure.

However, this is not to be understood as a general criticism of the idea of using set theory to investigate foundational matters regarding arithmetic. Instead, we have solely shown that it may be flawed to assume that a single set theory can really provide grounds for arithmetic truth or a definitive description of the universe of numbers. Our suggestion is therefore to consider a foundational relation that aims primarily at conceptual clarification of the concepts involved in the studied theory. An expressively rich environment such as set theory is armed with tools to study arithmetical relations in wider settings than it would be possible without leaving its deductive apparatus.

Funding: This research was supported by FCT through CIDMA and projects UIDB/04106/2020 and UIDP/04106/2020.

Data Availability Statement: Not applicable.

Conflicts of Interest: The authors declare no conflict of interest.

References

1. Hamkins, J.D.; Yang, R. Satisfaction is not absolute. *Rev. Symb. Log.* 2014, 1–34, *accepted*. Available online: http://jdh.hamkins.org/satisfaction-is-not-absolute/ (accessed on 18 May 2022).
2. Hamkins, J.D. The modal logic of arithmetic potentialism and the universal algorithm. *Mathematics* **2018**, 1–35, *under review*. Available online: http://jdh.hamkins.org/arithmetic-potentialism-and-the-universal-algorithm/ (accessed on 18 May 2022).
3. Hamkins, J.D.; Linnebo, O. The modal logic of set-theoretic potentialism and the potentialist maximality principles. *Rev. Symb. Log.* **2022**, *15*, 1–35. [CrossRef]
4. Koellner, P. Hamkins on the multiverse. In *Exploring the Frontiers of Incompleteness*; Harvard University: Cambridge, MA, USA, 2013.
5. Tarski, A.; Mostowski, A.; Robinson, R.M. *Undecidable Theories*; Elsevier: Amsterdam, The Netherlands, 1953; Volume 13.
6. Gabbay, M. A formalist philosophy of mathematics part I: Arithmetic. *Stud. Log.* **2010**, *96*, 219–238. [CrossRef]
7. Ferreirós, J. *Mathematical Knowledge and the Interplay of Practices*; Princeton University Press: Princeton, NJ, USA, 2015.
8. Hamkins, J.D. The set-theoretic multiverse. *Rev. Symb. Log.* **2012**, *5*, 416–449. [CrossRef]
9. Williamson, T. Absolute provability and safe knowledge of axioms. In *Gödel's Disjunction: The Scope and Limits of Mathematical Knowledge*; Phillip Books: New York, NY, USA, 2016; pp. 243–252.
10. Maddy, P. A second philosophy of arithmetic. *Rev. Symb. Log.* **2014**, *7*, 222–249. [CrossRef]
11. Quine, W.V. Ontological reduction and the world of numbers. *J. Philos.* **1964**, *61*, 209–216. [CrossRef]
12. Putnam, H. Mathematics without foundations. *J. Philos.* **1967**, *64*, 5–22. [CrossRef]
13. Freire, R.A. Interpretation and Truth in Set Theory. In *Contradictions, from Consistency to Inconsistency*; Springer: Cham, Switzerland, 2015.
14. Enayat, A. Variations on a Visserian Theme. In *Liber Amicorum Alberti: A tribute to Albert Visser*; College Publications: London, UK, 2016; pp. 99–110.
15. Freire, A.R.; Hamkins, J.D. Bi-interpretation in weak set theories. *J. Symb. Log.* **2021**, *86*, 609–634. [CrossRef]
16. Hamkins, J.D. Different set theories are never bi-interpretable. In *Mathematics and Philosophy of the Infinite*; Routledge: London, UK, 2018.
17. Freire, A.R. Estudo Comparado do Comprometimento Ontológico das Teorias de Classes e Conjuntos. Ph.D. Thesis, Universidad Estudal de Campinas, Campinas, Brazil, 2019.
18. Gödel, K. Über formal unentscheidbare Sätze der Principia Mathematica und verwandter Systeme I. *Monatshef. Math. Phys.* **1931**, *38*, 173–198. [CrossRef]
19. Goodstein, R.L. On the restricted ordinal theorem. *J. Symb. Log.* **1944**, *9*, 33–41. [CrossRef]
20. Caicedo, A.E. Goodstein's function. *Rev. Colomb. Matem.* **2007**, *41*, 381–391.
21. Wiles, A. Modular elliptic curves and Fermat's last theorem. *Ann. Math.* **1995**, *141*, 443–551. [CrossRef]
22. McLarty, C. What does it take to prove Fermat's Last Theorem? Grothendieck and the logic of number theory. *Bull. Symb. Log.* **2010**, *16*, 359–377. [CrossRef]
23. Helfgott, H.A. The ternary Goldbach conjecture is true. *arXiv* **2013**, arXiv:1312.7748.
24. Kaye, R.; Wong, T.L. On interpretations of arithmetic and set theory. *Notre Dame Form. Log.* **2007**, *48*, 497–510. [CrossRef]
25. Shoenfield, J.R. *Mathematical Logic*; Addison-Wesley Reading: London, UK, 1967; Volume 21.
26. Enayat, A. Standard models of arithmetic. In *Idées Fixes*; Kaså, M., Ed.; University of Gothenburg Publications: Gothenburg, Sweden, 2014; pp. 55–64.
27. Freire, A.R. Translating non Interpretable Theories. *S. Am. J. Log.* **2020**, *10*, 1–21.

axioms

MDPI

Article

A Story of Computational Science: Colonel Titus' Problem from the 17th Century

Trond Steihaug

Department of Informatics, University of Bergen, N-5020 Bergen, Norway; trond.steihaug@ii.uib.no

Abstract: Experimentation and the evaluation of algorithms have a long history in algebra. In this paper we follow a single test example over more than 250 years. In 1685, John Wallis published *A treatise of algebra, both historical and practical*, containing a solution of Colonel Titus' problem that was proposed to him around 1650. The Colonel Titus problem consists of three algebraic quadratic equations in three unknowns, which Wallis transformed into the problem of finding the roots of a fourth-order (quartic) polynomial. When Joseph Raphson published his method in 1690, he demonstrated the method on 32 algebraic equations and one of the examples was this quartic equation. Edmund Halley later used the same polynomial as an example for his new methods in 1694. Although Wallis used the method of Vietè, which is a digit–by–digit method, the more efficient methods of Halley and Raphson are clearly demonstrated in the works by Raphson and Halley. For more than 250 years the quartic equation has been used as an example in a wide range of solution methods for nonlinear equations. This paper provides an overview of the Colonel Titus problem and the equation first derived by Wallis. The quartic equation has four positive roots and the equation has been found to be very useful for analyzing the number of roots and finding intervals for the individual roots, in the Cardan–Ferrari direct approach for solving quartic equations, and in Sturm's method of determining the number of real roots of an algebraic equation. The quartic equation, together with two other algebraic equations, have likely been the first set of test examples used to compare different iteration methods of solving algebraic equations.

Keywords: Vietè's method; Newton–Raphson method; regula falsi method; testing of algorithms

MSC: 65-03; 68-03; 01A50; 01A55; 01A60

Citation: Steihaug, T. A Story of Computational Science: Colonel Titus' Problem from the 17th Century. *Axioms* **2022**, *11*, 287. https://doi.org/10.3390/axioms11060287

Academic Editor: Oscar Castillo

Received: 21 April 2022
Accepted: 22 May 2022
Published: 14 June 2022

1. Introduction

A problem brought to John Pell (1611–1685) in 1649, and discussed at the time with Silius Titus (1623–1704), was the following—to find numbers a, b, and c satisfying the equations

$$a^2 + bc = 16, \quad b^2 + ac = 17, \text{ and } c^2 + ab = 22. \tag{1}$$

A solution with positive integers is easily seen to be $a = 2$, $b = 3$, and $c = 4$, but Pell decided to challenge himself by changing the final equation:

$$a^2 + bc = 16, \quad b^2 + ac = 17, \text{ and } c^2 + ab = 18. \tag{2}$$

In 1662, Pell left notes on their progress for Titus and by the following year he and John Wallis had successfully solved it, calculating values of a, b, and c to 15 decimal places each [1]. The solution was printed in 1685 [2], derived from the general problem

$$a^2 + bc = l, \quad b^2 + ac = m, \text{ and } c^2 + ab = n.$$

Colonel Titus' problem is likely the earliest instance of a problem involving three simultaneous quadratic equations ([3], p. 34) and is one of the first algebraic problems leading to a quartic equation, an equation that is not derived from a problem in geometry or trigonometry.

A variant of the Colonel Titus problem is Question 113 in *Ladies' Diary* from 1725 shown in Figure 1

$$a^2 + bc = 920, \quad b^2 + ac = 980, \text{ and } c^2 + ab = 1000, \tag{3}$$

and was solved by John Turner in 1726. Turner only specifies the quartic equation to be solved and a solution a, b, c, of (3). Question 113 is also found in algebra textbooks in 1820 ([4], p. 405) and in 1840 ([5], p. 563).

The publications of collected questions in *Ladies' Diary* in 1774, 1775 [6,7], and 1817 [8] sparked new interest in Colonel Titus' problem.

A fourth variant of the problem was published in Question 209 in *The Scientific Receptacle* in 1796 and shown in Figure 2:

$$a^2 + bc = 1\,806\,520, \quad b^2 + ac = 2\,225\,275, \text{ and } c^2 + ab = 5\,567\,720. \tag{4}$$

John Ryley solved the problem and introduced a new way to solve it by expressing a and b as a fraction of c [9].

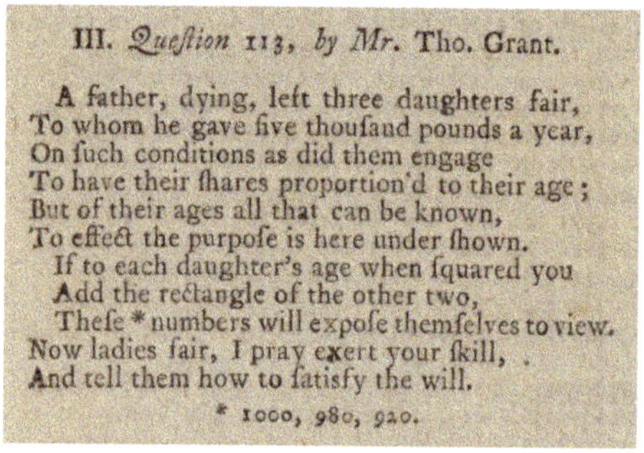
III. *Queſtion* 113, *by Mr.* Tho. Grant.

A father, dying, left three daughters fair,
To whom he gave five thouſand pounds a year,
On ſuch conditions as did them engage
To have their ſhares proportion'd to their age;
But of their ages all that can be known,
To effect the purpoſe is here under ſhown.
If to each daughter's age when ſquared you
Add the rectangle of the other two,
Theſe * numbers will expoſe themſelves to view.
Now ladies fair, I pray exert your ſkill,
And tell them how to ſatisfy the will.

* 1000, 980, 920.

Figure 1. Question 113, proposed by Thomas Grant in *Ladies Diary* from 1725, taken from Charles Hutton 1775 [7], p. 266. In the collection by Leybourn from 1817, the question is slightly rephrased [8], p. 145.

Wallis ([2], pp. 225–256) eliminates the variables b and c in (2) and reduces the three equations to a fourth-order algebraic equation

$$x^4 - 80x^3 + 1998x^2 - 14{,}937x + 5000 = 0 \tag{5}$$

where $x = 2a^2$. In the following we will use the term "Pell–Wallis equation" to refer to (5). To determine a root x^*, Wallis uses Viète's method and a is found through $a = \sqrt{x^*/2}$. To compute b, Wallis derives a cubic equation which follows from multiplying the first quadratic equation by a and the second by b and eliminates abc to obtain the cubic equation

$$17b - b^3 = 16a - a^3, \text{ where } a = \sqrt{\frac{1}{2}x^*}.$$

Having found a and b, the unknown c is found from the first quadratic $a^2 + bc = 16$.

One of the most classical problems in mathematics is the solution of systems of polynomial equations in several unknowns [10]. They arise in robotics, coding theory, optimization, mathematical biology, computer vision, game theory, statistics, machine learning, control theory, and numerous other areas [10]. Systems of quadratic polynomial equations appear in nearly every crypto-system [11] and in robotics [12].

For more than 250 years, the equation $x^4 - 80x^3 + 1998x^2 - 14937x + 5000 = 0$ has played an important role in the development of new methods, analyses of algebraic equations, and comparisons of methods for solving nonlinear equations.

In Section 2 we discuss four different approaches in solving Colones Titus' problem that have appeared in the literature and in Section 3 we discuss different techniques and methods using the Pell–Wallis Equation (5). For a modern treatment of numerical methods for roots of polynomials, see [13,14] and references therein. For solving systems of polynomial equations, see [10,11] and references therein.

2. Colonel Titus' Problem

Using the notation in Wallis algebra book from 1685 [2], Ch. LX–LXI, the general Colonel Titus problem is as follows. For given positive real numbers l, m, and n, find a, b, and c such that

$$a^2 + bc = l, \tag{6}$$
$$b^2 + ac = m, \text{ and} \tag{7}$$
$$c^2 + ab = n. \tag{8}$$

We review several solution techniques, mainly using what could be described as high-school algebra [15]. An elegant solution is given in *Solutions of the principal questions of Dr. Hutton's course of mathematics* by Thomas Stephens Davies, and we follow his solution technique.

From (6) and (7) we have

$$c = \frac{l - a^2}{b} \text{ and } c = \frac{m - b^2}{a}.$$

Equating the two expressions for c, we have a cubic equation in b

$$b^3 - mb + a(l - a^2) = 0.$$

From (8) and the two expression for c above, we have

$$n - ab = c^2 = \frac{l - a^2}{b}\frac{m - b^2}{a}$$

which is a quadratic equation in b

$$(l - 2a^2)b^2 + nab + (a^2 - l)m = 0.$$

Multiply the quadratic equation by b and the cubic equation by $l - 2a^2$ and subtract the two expressions to eliminate the cubic term. We now have two quadratic equations in b

$$(l - 2a^2)b^2 + nab + (a^2 - l)m = 0 \text{ and } nb^2 - mab + (a^2 - l)(l - 2a^2) = 0.$$

To eliminate b^2, multiply the first quadratic equation by n and the second by $l - 2a^2$ and subtract the two resulting quadratic equations. The result is a linear equation in b. Solve for b:

$$b = \frac{(l - a^2)(mn - (l - 2a^2)^2)}{a(n^2 + m(l - 2a^2))}.$$

Substitute the value for b in

$$nb - ma = \frac{(l - a^2)(mn^2 - m^2a^2 - n(l - a^2)(l - 2a^2))}{a(n^2 + m(l - 2a))}$$

and

$$\frac{1}{b}(a^2-l)(l-2a^2)=\frac{n(l-a^2)(l-2a^2)^2a(n^2+m(l-aa^2))}{(l-a^2)(mn-(l-2a^2)^2)}.$$

Equate the two expressions in $nb-ma=(l-a^2)(l-2a^2)/b$ and simplify

$$8a^8-20la^6+(18l^2-2mn)a^4+(5lmn-7l^3-m^3-n^3)a^2+(l^2-mn)^2=0.$$

Multiply the equation by 2 and let $x=2a^2$ and we have the equation

$$x^4-5lx^3+(9l^2-mn)x^2+(5lmn-7l^3-m^3-n^3)x+2(l^2-mn)^2=0. \quad (9)$$

For each real root, x^* of (9) a, b, and c, can be computed in the following way; a in $2a^2 = x^*$, b in $n\,b^2-ma\,b=(l-a^2)^2-a^2(l-a)$, and c in $a^2+bc=l$. For $l=16, m=17$, and $n=18$ we have the equation

$$x^4-80x^3+1998x^2-14937x+5000=0$$

which is (5).

Different techniques for solving Colonel Titus' problem have been suggested in the literature by philomaths and mathematicians, school teachers of mathematics, and professors of mathematics. The different solution techniques can mainly be divided in two groups; the first group is based on elimination and the second group on first reformulating the problem and then performing an elimination.

The first solution to Colonel Titus' problem was published by J. Wallis [2] and this was an elimination of the unknowns that results in the quartic Equation (5). To find the four positive roots of (5) Wallis used a digit-by-digit computation method. The solution of Colonel Titus' problem by Wallis was republished by Francis Maseres (1731–1824) in 1800, including numerous details ([16], pp. 187–239). However, Maseres did not use a digit-by-digit method to find the roots, but rather the Newton–Raphson method. Similar solutions using explicit elimination are found in [5,17–19], all leading to the same quartic Equation (5). J. Kirkby [20] in 1735 and A. Cayley [21] in 1860 used a general elimination theory, leading to the same quartic equation.

The method of introducing two new variables expressing the unknowns as a fraction of one of the other variable was studied by J. Ryley [9] in 1796, and made popular by William Frend [22] in 1800. Variations of this technique are found in [23–25]. Ivory expressed two of the unknowns as a difference of the third [26,27]. All these reformulations lead to quartic equations that are different from the quartic Equation (5). These quartic equations never reached the same popularity as (5).

Using iterative methods to solve the three equations simultaneously was suggested in the *Diarian Repository* [6] in 1774 and by Whitley [28] in 1824.

2.1. *Ladies' Diary 1725 Question 113*

We find a variation of Colonel Titus' problem in the journal *Ladies' Diary* from 1725 in Question 113 shown in Figure 1 where $l=920$, $m=980$, and $m=1000$.

In *Ladies' Diary* in 1726 John Turner (active in *Ladies' Diary* from 1726 to 1750 ([17], p. 423)) gives a solution of the problem and states the equation (using the notation in Wallis)

$$8a^8-20la^6+(18l^2-2mn)a^4+(5lmn-7l^3-m^3-n^3)a^2+l^4-2l^2mn+m^2n^2=0.$$

Let $x=2u^2$ and multiplying the equation by two gives (9). Turner gives the solution of Question 113 in *Ladies' Diary* to be 19.5991, 22.7788, and 23.5276. There are three minor typographical errors in the solution by Turner ([29], p. 7):

$$8a^8-18la^6+(18l^2{+}2mn)a^4+(5lmn-7l^3-m^3-n^3{-}mn)a^2+l^4-2l^2mn+m^2n^2=0.$$

These three typographical errors are repeated in *Diarian Miscellany* [7] and *Diarian Repository* [6] and one error is pointed out in the Errata of [8].

For $l = 920, m = 980$, and $n = 1000$, the Equation (9) has four positive roots approximately equal to 1937.6, 1881.6, 768.0, and 12.7, and the only root that gives reasonable ages is 768.0, and the ages are approximately $a = 19.5965, b = 22.7799$, and $c = 23.5286$.

2.2. A Renewed Interest in Colonel Titus' Problem

In *Diarian Repository* by S. Clark [6], pp. 190–191 (Archibald [30] states that Samuel Clark was the editor of this repository) from 1774; *Diarian Miscellany* by C. Hutton from 1775 [7], pp. 266 and 271; and later in Leybourn's four volume collection of questions in *Ladies' Diary* from 1817 [8], pp. 145–146, we find Question 113 and the three Equations (6)–(8). The three repositories [6–8] all reproduce John Turner's equation and solution (ages) but also give additional information or alternative solution techniques.

Leybourn also presents an additional solution of Colones Titus' problem provided by Mark Noble (a mathematician at Royal Military College (Sandhurst)) in the appendix in the fourth volume [17], pp. 255–259. The contribution is signed N and in the preface of Leybourn's first volume ([8], Preface page X) it is signed "this is Mark Noble".This is an elimination technique and it leads to the same quartic equation as in Wallis. Noble derives one cubic and one quadratic equation similar to the equations derived by Kirkby. Although Kirkby invokes a general elimination result from Newton ([31], p. 74), Noble carries out the elimination explicitly and obtains the Equation (9). Noble gives the roots of the polynomials and the different values of a, b, and c.

2.3. The Scientific Receptacle 1796 Question 209

The Scientific Receptacle published in 1796 the question shown in Figure 2 ([9], p. 77). The problem is find positive numbers (using the notation in Wallis) a, b, and c so that

$$a^2 + bc = 1{,}806{,}520, \quad b^2 + ac = 2{,}225{,}275, \text{ and } c^2 + ab = 5{,}567{,}720$$

with a solution published in a later issue in the same volume ([9], p. 95).

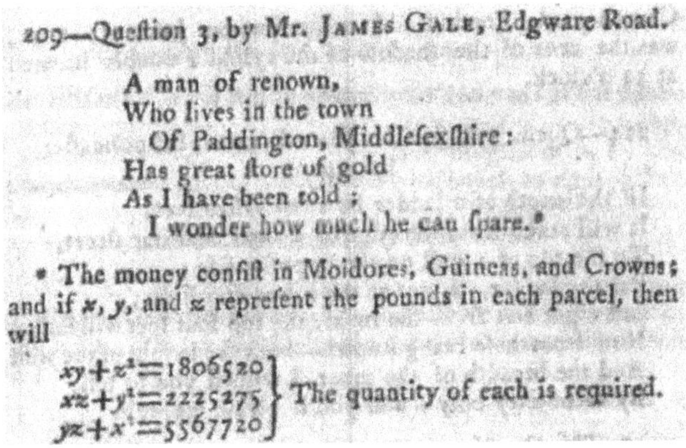
209—Queſtion 3, by Mr. JAMES GALE, Edgware Road.

A man of renown,
Who lives in the town
Of Paddington, Middleſexſhire:
Has great ſtore of gold
As I have been told;
I wonder how much he can ſpare.*

* The money conſiſt in Moidores, Guineas, and Crowns; and if x, y, and z repreſent the pounds in each parcel, then will

$$\left.\begin{array}{l} xy+z^2=1806520 \\ xz+y^2=2225275 \\ yz+x^2=5567720 \end{array}\right\} \text{The quantity of each is required.}$$

Figure 2. Question 209 in *The Scientific Receptacle* from 1796 proposed by James Gale.

John Ryley (1747–1815) published the solution of the problem in 1796 [9]. Ryley considered the three Equations (6)–(8) and introduced two new variables x and y so that

$$b = x\,c \text{ and } a = y\,c. \tag{10}$$

and derived the equation

$$(n^2 - lm)x^4 + (m^2 + ln)x^3 - 4mnx^2 + (n^2 + lm)x + m^2 - ln = 0. \tag{11}$$

From a root of (11), all other quantities can be determined. However, Ryley does not compute any root of (11) or values of a, b, and c for the given l, m, and n.

2.4. First Reformulation and then Elimination

J. Ryley was the first to express two of the unknowns as a fraction of the third. W. Frend (1757–1841) ([22], pp. 240–246) in 1800 provided a different derivation and introduced x and y so that

$$b = x\,a \text{ and } c = y\,a, \tag{12}$$

and derived the equation

$$(mn - l^2)x^4 - (ln + m^2)x^3 + 4lmx^2 - (l^2 + mn)x - m^2 + ln = 0. \tag{13}$$

A minor improvement of Frend's solution, avoiding a square root, was given by John Hellins (c. 1749–1827) in the introduction of the same volume in which Frend's solution was found [16], pp. lxxi–lxxii. By interchanging the variables, Equation (13) can be derived from (11).

For $l = 16, m = 17$, and $n = 18$ we obtain the equation

$$50x^4 - 577x^3 + 1088x^2 - 562x - 1 = 0.$$

The equation has four real solutions (or roots), of which one is negative. Maseres [16] (pp. 246–275) finds the three positive roots to be approximately 1.027179787, 1.17565, and 9.3388519 using Newton–Raphson iteration. Maseres regards the root 1.027179787 as "impossible" since y is negative. For a given root, y and the unknowns a, b, and c are easily found.

Maseres ends the tract with a comment that Mr. Frend's solution has the advantage that it saves the trouble of those very tedious and perplexing algebraic multiplications and divisions necessary in Dr. Wallis's solution [16], p. 275. A similar solution to Frend's was given by Tebay [25] in 1845. A third variation is to express a and b in terms of c [23].

James Ivory (1765–1842) [26] wrote that the solution provided by Wallis to the problem (2) was *remarkably operose and inellegant* and a solution of the same problem by Frend [22] is preferable to Wallis's solution. Ivory expressed two of the unknowns as a difference of the third and the analysis was printed in 1804 in [26], but with no numerical solution. Ivory restricts his analysis to the specific choice $l = 16$, $m = 17$, and $n = 18$. Ivory's analysis was mailed to Baron Maseres [27] p. 360 and Maseres added many details and a numerical solution based on the Newton–Raphson method [32].

Whitley [24], p. 121 wrote in 1824 that Mr. Ivory's solution was an elegant specimen of analysis and Davis [18], p. 274 in 1840 called it an exceedingly elegant investigation. Cockle [3] speculated that the analysis can be carried over to the case where $m = (n + l)/2$. It can be shown that the derivation by Ivory can be extended to the general case of l, m, and n. Maseres [32], pp. 371–395 computed the two positive roots of the quartic equation derived by Ivory and these correspond to the positive a, b, and c values provided by Wallis.

2.5. Simultaneous Solution of the Three Unknowns

In the *Repository Solution* section in the *Diarian Repository* [6], pp. 190–191 an iterative approach was suggested. First, find an approximate solution (in this case 23, 22.5, and 21.1); then, find a correction (x, y, and z) that solves the (linear) equations where the second order terms are eliminated. ... *then via the solution of the resulting equations, x, y, and z will be determined to a sufficient degree of exactness; if not, the operation must be again repeated with the last found values...* [6], pp. 190–191. This is Newton's method but no actual computations of a, b, and c are shown, except for finding the starting point for the iteration.

J. H. Swales, the editor of the *Liverpool Apollonius* asked its readers in 1823 to find a simpler solution than those given by Ivory [26], p. 156 and Frend [22], p. 240. Three traditional solutions were submitted by J. Whitley, Settle, and S. Ryley and a completely new approach using a fixed-point iteration method by Whitley was published in the next volume. In 1853, T. T. Wilkinson, in his series of articles on the *History of Mathematical Periodicals* wrote in relation to the *Liverpool Apollonius* (In *Mechanics Magazine*, Volume 58, 1853 p. 307) that the iterative method used by Whitley was one of the neatest and most effective methods of solving Colonel Titus' problem. The same appraisal was provided in 1865 in the *Educational Times* (*Educational Times p. 270, 1865 on Question 113 from the* Ladies' Diary).

The method proposed by Whitley [28], pp. 127–128 in 1824 is the fixed-point iteration

$$\begin{pmatrix} a_{k+1} \\ b_{k+1} \\ c_{k+1} \end{pmatrix} = \begin{pmatrix} \sqrt{l - b_k c_k} \\ \sqrt{m - a_k c_k} \\ \sqrt{n - a_k b_k} \end{pmatrix} \quad k \geq 0$$

with the starting point given by $a_0 = b_0 = c_0 = 3$, where $l = 16, m = 17$, and $n = 18$. Table 1 compares the fixed-point iteration to Newton's method for $F(a,b,c) \equiv (a^2 + bc - 16, b^2 + ac - 17, c^2 + ab - 18) = (0,0,0)$ with the starting point $(a_0, b_0, c_0) = (3,3,3)$.

Table 1. Fixed-point iterations of Whitley and Newton's method.

	Whitley		
k	a_k	b_k	c_k
1	2.6458	3.0104	3.1678
2	2.5423	2.9910	3.2242
3	2.5211	2.9785	3.2390
4	2.5205	2.9726	3.2415
5	2.5227	2.9703	3.2414
	Newton		
k	a_k	b_k	c_k
1	2.5833	2.9167	3.2500
2	2.5263	2.9698	3.2395
3	2.5255	2.9692	3.2406
4	2.5255	2.9692	3.2406

Arthur Cayley (1821–1895) considered Colonel Titus' problem and suggested that if $a = \frac{x}{z}$ and $b = \frac{y}{z}$ the equations become

$$\begin{aligned} x^2 + cyz - lz^2 &= 0 \\ y^2 + czx - mz^2 &= 0 \\ (c^2 - n)z^2 + xy &= 0 \end{aligned}$$

which are three homogeneous equations of second order in three unknowns [21]. However, Cayley did not solve the homogeneous equations. Schumacher solved this problem [33] in 1911.

2.6. Erroneous Solution

The achievements of Adrien Quentin Buée (1748–1825), also called Abbé Buée, are important in relation to the conceptual development of the negative numbers and for the graphical representation of the complex numbers. In [34], he considers Colonel Titus' problem and makes an attempt to solve it using geometry and complex numbers. He claims that the solution must be $a = 3.25x$, $b = 4.25x$, and $c = 5.25x$, where x is the area of a circle in the geometric construction. However, he does not find any correct solution to the problem.

3. The Pell–Wallis Equation

In the late 17th and early 18th centuries, there were numerous collections of algebraic equations [35]. Most practical algebraic equations were derived from geometric or trigonometric problems. An algebra book by John Ward from 1695 contains ten geometric problems with corresponding algebraic equations [36] and *The Young Mathematician's guide* from 1707 contains more than 20 practical problems from geometry and trigonometry, leading to algebraic equations [37]. However, The Pell–Wallis equation is derived from a different type of problem. The equation has been in use for 270 years, from the first time it appeared in print in 1685 to the most recent reference to the equation in a paper from 1955.

3.1. *Digit-by-Digit Methods*

The root finding method used by Wallis in 1685 was a digit-by-digit computation method [2]. The method used by Wallis was based on Vietè's method but it deviated from Vietè's method in the divisor used to compute the next digit [38]. In this method, the roots are computed with a very high degree of accuracy. With Horner's technique to compute shifted polynomials, the digit-by-digit approach became more efficient using Holdred's and Horner's divisor [38]. The Pell–Wallis equation is used as an example in Holdred [39], pp. 55–56 and Nicholson [40], pp. 74–76, 80–82 in 1820 and [41], p. 19; de Morgan [42], pp. 50–51 in 1839; Perkins [43], pp. 356–358 and Young [44], pp. 213–221 in 1842; Lobatto [45], pp. 114–166 in 1845; Schnuse [46], pp. 212–216 in 1850; and Onley [47], pp. 240–245 in 1878—all using digit-by-digit computation.

3.2. *Bracketing Methods*

In Vietè's method, the first digit of a root must be specified. This will normally lead to the determination of the intervals of the roots. Intervals of the real roots may also provide a starting point for linear interpolation. Cardano's golden rule and regula falsi are methods in which a root is bracketed. Application of the Newton–Raphson method and the Halley method, which are iterative methods, requires a starting point sufficiently close to a root/solution and this point is often determined to be in an interval including the root.

The Pell–Wallis equation has been used as an example in [48], p. 335, Kirkby [20] Part IV, pp. 32–34 in 1735; Frend [49], pp. 109–111 and [50] pp. 298–299 in 1799 and 1800. A more systematic approach was employed with the application of Sturm's theorem in [51] from 1839 and Young [52], pp. 159–161 in 1841. This method was also used by Siebel in 1880 and 1887 [53], pp. 406–407 [54], pp. 337–338 in an ad hoc way.

3.3. *Linear Interpolation*

The first use of the Pell–Wallis equation and interpolation occurred in 1732. Graaf [55], pp. 33–35 considered (5) and scaled the variable $x \leftarrow x/10$ in the interval of 0 to 3.6 and plotted the graph $(x, f(x))$, where $f(x)$ is the left-hand side of (5). Based on the graph, an interval where a solution exists was identified, and then linear interpolation. This is a variation of regula falsi [56] and Cardano's regula aurea [57], Chapter 30 methods, since both end points of the interval are changed in de Graaf's approach.

The method of John Davidson, a teacher in mathematics in Burntisland, involves a bracketing approach and linear interpolation [58], p. 114, [59], p. 38, as shown in his textbooks from 1814 and 1852. This is Cardano's golden rule [57], Chapter 30.

3.4. *The Newton–Raphson Method*

Wallis published his algebra book in 1685 [2] and it contained the first printed version of Newton's method. When Raphson presented his method in 1690 it was regarded as a different method. It was not until the mid-18th century that it became clear that the two methods generated the same sequence of iterations [35]. From a computational point of view, the methods are very different. Raphson demonstrated his method on 32 examples and the Pell–Wallis equation was given as example 21 [60] Problem XXI. Kirby [20], Part IV, pp. 35, 44–45 in 1735 used the Newton–Raphson method to find one of the roots of the Pell–Wallis equation.

In Volume III of *Scriptores logarithmici* from 1796, Francis Maseres used the Newton–Raphson method. First an approximation 0.3507 to the smallest root is found by using a series expansion and then two iterations are performed [61], pp. 718–725. Maseres writes "*...and this I take to be the very best method that can be employed to find the value of x to this degree of exactness*".

Lockhart [62] in 1839 argues that the numbers of digits required to compute an approximate solution using the Newton–Raphson method is not worse than Horner's digit-by-digit method, as presented by De Morgan [42] in 1839.

3.5. Halley's Method

Edmund Halley (1656–1742), in a paper from 1694, derived two methods, the rational and irrational method [63]. Halley pointed out that the Pell–Wallis Equation (5) was solved by Wallis using the method of Vieté and solved by Raphson using the Newton–Raphson method. Halley applied both methods to the Pell–Wallis equation. For the irrational method, two possible corrections can be used before the new iteration.

In 1710, Christian Wolff (1679–1754) provided a different derivation of Halley's irrational method and redid the computation method developed by Halley using the irrational method and the correction to find the largest root of (5) [64], pp. 192–194.

Philip Ronyane (1683–1755) applied Halley's rational and irrational methods. With the irrational method he use the two corrections used by Halley and gave a derivation of the corrections, whereas Halley has just stated them [65], pp. 242–244.

One of the earliest professors in mathematics in an American college was Isaac Greenwood (1702–1745) and two notebooks from his students—Samuel Langdon (1723–1797), who graduated from Harvard in 1740, and James Diman (1707–1788), who graduated in 1730—have been kept [66], ([67], pp. 3–17). A topic in the Diman notebook from 1730 is "Dr. Halley's theorems for solving equations of all sorts" and here we find (reproduced in [66], p. 64) three iterations with Halley's rational method on (5).

3.6. Ferrari–Cardano Approach

The linear shift $x - 20$ in the Pell–Wallis equation makes the term x^3 vanish and the depressed quartic equation is

$$x^4 - 402x^2 + 983x + 25{,}460 = 0. \tag{14}$$

Taking two slightly different approaches, Francis Maseres first finds the depressed quartic (14) and then, with reference to Ferrari, finds the resolvent cubic

$$v^3 - 201v^2 - 25460v - \frac{967{,}897}{8} = 0, \tag{15}$$

and, with reference to Descartes [68], p. 142, the resolvent cubic (in e^2) is

$$e^6 - 804u^4 + 59764e^2 - 966{,}289 = 0. \tag{16}$$

The four roots of the Pell–Wallis equation can then found [68], pp. 134–182. Maseres points out that the use of linear interpolation and one iteration with Newton–Raphson will require fewer arithmetic operations than the use of Ferrari-Cardano approach [68] p. 178.

William Rutherford (1798–1871) found the depressed quartic (14) and then derived the resolvent cubic equation (in u^2)

$$u^6 - \frac{402}{2}u^4 + \frac{59{,}764}{16}u^2 - \frac{966{,}289}{64} = 0. \tag{17}$$

From the resolvent cubic (17), using Horner's method, Rutherford found one root and the four roots of the Pell–Wallis equation [69], pp. 17–18.

Orson Pratt (1811–1881) [70], pp. 130–131 used the depressed quartic (14) and derived the resolvent depressed cubic

$$y^3 - 1{,}401{,}372y - 633{,}074{,}427 = 0.$$

A root of the depressed cubic is found using a digit-by-digit approach with a modified divisor in Vietè's method, to eleven decimal places, and then the roots of the Pell–Wallis equation are given.

Christian Heinrich Schnuse (1800–1878) considered the Pell–Wallis equation and derived the depressed quartic (14) and the resolvent cubic (17). Using a digit-by-digit approach, he found the same root of (17) as Rutherford in 1849 [46], pp. 358–359.

3.7. *Gräffe's Method*

D. Miguel Merino (1831–1905) translated and revised a work by Johann Franz Encke (1791–1865) [71] on the numerical solution of equations. Using Gräffe's method and one final Newton–Raphson iteration, the four roots are found [71], pp. 42–44. In Gräffe's method a sequence of polynomials is generated and the method is a "root-squaring" process and approximations to the roots can be computed from the coefficients of of the generated polynomials. The method works well for the Pell–Wallis equation since the roots are real, positive, and separated. The method is suitable for computation by hand, whereas computer implementations usually exhibit overflow after only a few steps. After a few steps, the estimates of the roots are good and suitable for a correction by means of Newton–Raphson iterations. The two smallest roots are correct with four decimal digits after four steps in Gräffe's method. Given that the two smallest roots have been accurately computed, the remaining two roots can be computed [72], pp. 74–75. Encke in 1839, Merino in 1879, and Rey Pastor [72] (1888–1962) in 1924 found it more convenient to work with the log of the coefficients of the polynomials.

3.8. *Miscellaneous Methods and Comments*

- Wells pointed out in 1698 that the Pell–Wallis equation was solved by Raphson, Halley, and Wallis using the Newton–Raphson method, Halley's methods, and Vietè's method [73], pp. 213–214.
- In 1716 [74], pp. 138–139, Struyck translated Halley's papers from 1694 into Dutch (French translation in 1912 [75], pp. 148–149).
- In the 4th edition of the *Theory of Equations* [76], pp. 269–270 from 1899, Burnside and Panton derived the resolvent cubic (16). They also showed that the roots are real [76], p. 194 and if two of the roots are known, the two remaining roots can easily be found [76], p. 267.
- With reference to [72] (pp. 74–75) for the Pell–Wallis equation Carlos Calvo Carbonell [77] derived the depressed quartic (14) and scaled the variable $\sqrt{402}x$ and obtained the equation

$$x^4 - x^2 + \frac{983}{\sqrt{402^3}}x + \frac{25{,}460}{402^2} = 0. \tag{18}$$

  By graphical inspection, the roots of (18) are located in intervals of length 0.01.For a point in the interval, a first correction method is a Newton-Raphson iteration, then a correction based on the next term in the Taylor expansion. The four roots are computed using two or three corrections.
- Silvestre François Lacroix (1765–1843) [78], p. 261 discussed the Pell–Wallis equation as a problem of scaling the coefficients and found that the two roots are between 0 and 10 and 10 and 20.

- Preston Albert Lambert (1862–1925), in 1903, used the Pell–Wallis equation to find the depressed fourth-order polynomial (14) and applied Maclaurin expansion to find an approximate solution [79], p. 92.
- Leonard Eugene Dickson (1874–1954), in his book on *Elementary theory of Equations* from 1914, used the Pell-Wallis equation as a problem. He first found two approximate roots r and s and then the next two roots r_1 and r_2 by solving using expressions for $r_1 + r_2$ and $r_1 - r_2$ as functions of r and s [80], p. 121.
- We find numerous examples of the use of the Pell–Wallis equation as an exercise or problem in the second half of the 19th century: [81], p. 218, [82], p. 116, [83], p. 350, [84], p. 14, [85] p. 358, [86], pp. 352–353, [87], p. 170, and [88], p. 307.

3.9. An Early Comparison of Four Algorithms on Three Examples

One of the first comparisons of the use of several algorithms on different problems is found in [16]. The methods used were Newton–Raphson, Halley's two methods, and regula falsi or linear interpolation. The latter method is called the *the differential method* in [16] or *the method of double position*. Maseres [16] p. 109 provides a reference to *A Course of Mathematics in Two Volumes, Composed for the Use of the Royal Military Academy* by Charles Hutton for the equivalence between the differential method and the method of double position.

The three equations tested were $x^3 - 17x^2 + 54x - 350 = 0$, $x^4 - 3x^2 + 75x - 10{,}000 = 0$, and the Pell–Wallis equation $-x^4 + 80x^3 - 1998x^2 + 14{,}937x - 5000 = 0$. These three examples are from Halley [63].

4. Concluding Remarks

We have shown that the three quadratic equations in three unknowns forming Colonel Titus' problem can be reduced to a single quartic equation using standard high school algebra. The different derivations of a quartic equation have been suggested by philomaths and mathematicians, school teachers of mathematics, and professors of mathematics over a period ranging from the mid-17th to the early 20th century. We find systems of quadratic equations in modern crypto-systems or robotics. Today, solutions can easily be obtained through the use of computer algebra systems implemented in Maple, Mathematica, or Wolfram. The modern theory related to solution methods, such as the use of a Gröbner basis, has not yet been explored in relation to Colonel Titus' problem.

We have seen that the quartic equation, the Pell–Wallis Equation (5), derived from Colonel Titus' problem, has been used for more than 250 years as a test example to develop methods to solve algebraic equations, techniques to determine the number of roots, or intervals of the roots, as well as in numerous textbooks. As a well-known equation, it has been included in the early numerical comparisons of root finding methods.

The references in this paper do not form a complete list of the use of this equation and Colonel Titus' problem.

Funding: This research received no external funding.

Institutional Review Board Statement: Not applicable.

Informed Consent Statement: Not applicable.

Data Availability Statement: Not applicable.

Conflicts of Interest: The author declares no conflict of interest.

References

1. Stedall, J.A. Tracing mathematical networks in seventeenth-century England. In *The Oxford Handbook of the History of Mathematics*; Robson, E., Stedall, J., Eds.; Oxford University Press: Oxford, UK, 2009; pp. 133–151.
2. Wallis, J. *A Treatise of Algebra, Both Historical and Practical*; Richard Davis: London, UK, 1685. [CrossRef]
3. Cockle, J. Horæ algebraicæ, XI Quadratic equations. *Mech. Mag.* **1849**, 50, 33–36.
4. Bonnycastle, J. *Treatise on Algebra, in Practice and Theory, with Notes and Illustrations*, 2nd ed.; J. Nunn: London, UK, 1820; Volume 1.

5. Williams, J.D. *An Elementary Treatise on Algebra, in Theory and Practice*; Hilliard, Gray & Co: Boston, MA, USA, 1840.
6. Anonymous. *The Diarian Repository; or, Mathematical Register: Containing a Complete Collection of All the Mathematical Questions Which Have Been Published in the Ladies Diary, from the Commencement of that Work in 1704, to the Year 1760; Together with Their Solutions Fully Investigated, According to the Latest Improvements. The Whole Designed as an Easy and Familiar Praxis for Young Students in Mathematical and Philosophical Learning by A Society of Mathematicians*; G. Robinson: London, UK, 1774.
7. Hutton, C. *The Diarian Miscellany: Consisting of All the Useful and Entertaining Parts, Both Mathematical and Poetical, Extracted from the Ladies' Diary, from the Beginning of that Work in the Year 1704, Down to the End of the Year 1773. With Many Additional Solutions and Improvements*; Vol. I, G. Robinson and R. Baldwin: London, UK, 1775.
8. Leybourn, T. *The Mathematical Questions, Proposed in the Ladies' Diary*; Vol. I, J. Mawman: London, UK, 1817.
9. Whiting, T. *The Scientific Receptacle*; Printed by W. Kemmish: London, UK, 1796.
10. Sturmfels, B. *Solving Systems of Polynomial Equations*; American Mathematical Society: Providence, RI, USA, 2002.
11. Ding, J.; Petzoldt, A.; Schmidt, D.S. Solving Polynomial Systems. In *Multivariate Public Key Cryptosystems*; Springer: New York, NY, USA, 2020; pp. 185–248. [CrossRef]
12. Cox, D.A.; Little, J.; O'Shea, D. Robotics and Automatic Geometric Theorem Proving. In *Ideals, Varieties, and Algorithms: An Introduction to Computational Algebraic Geometry and Commutative Algebra*; Springer International Publishing: Cham, Switzerland, 2015; pp. 291–343. [CrossRef]
13. McNamee, J.M. *Numerical Methods for Roots of Polynomials—Part I*; Elsevier Science: Amsterdam, The Netherlands, 2007.
14. McNamee, J.M.; Pan, V.Y. *Numerical Methods for Roots of Polynomials—Part II*; Elsevier Science: Amsterdam, The Netherlands, 2013.
15. Abhyankar, S.S. Historical ramblings in algebraic geometry and related algebra. *Am. Math. Mon.* **1976**, *83*, 409–448. [CrossRef]
16. Maseres, F. (Ed.) *Tracts on the Resolution of Affected Algebraic Equations by Dr. Halley's, Mr. Raphson's and Sir Isaac Newton's Methods of Approximation*; Printed by J.Davis and sold by J. White: London, UK, 1800.
17. Leybourn, T. *The Mathematical Questions, Proposed in the Ladies' Diary*; Vol. IV, J. Mawman: London, UK, 1817.
18. Davies, T.S. *Solutions of the Principal Questions of Dr. Hutton's Course of Mathematics*; Printed for Longman, Orme, & Co: London, UK, 1840.
19. Peacock, A. Brief solution of a celebrated algebraic problem. *Mech. Mag.* **1843**, *39*, 295–297.
20. Kirkby, J. *Arithmetical Institutions Containing a Compleat System of Arithmetic, Natural, Logarithmical, and Algebraical in All Their Branches*; B.Motte and C.Bathurst: London, UK, 1735.
21. Cayley, A. On a system of algebraic equations. *Philos. Mag. J. Sci.* **1860**, *20*, 341–342. [CrossRef]
22. Frend, W. Another solution of Colonel Titus's problem. In *Tracts on the Resolution of Affected Algebraic Equations*; Maseres, F., Ed.; Printed by J.Davis and sold by J. White: London, UK, 1800; pp. 240–275.
23. Settle, W. Second solution to Problem IV. *The Liverpool Apollonius, or the geometrical and philosophical repository* **1824**, *1*, 121.
24. Whitley, J. Colonel Titus' problem, Problem IV. *The Liverpool Apollonius, or the geometrical and philosophical repository* **1824**, *1*, 120–121.
25. Tebay, S. Question 22. *Preston Chronicle, No.1705, 3 May 1845* **1845**, p. 3.
26. Ivory, J. Article XVI. Solution to Colonel Titus's arithmetical problem. In *The Mathematical Repository*; Leybourn, T., Ed.; W. Glendinning: London, UK, 1804; Volume III, pp. 156–159.
27. Ivory, J. A new solution of Colonel Titus's arithmetical problem. In *Scriptores Logarithmici; Or a Collection of Several Curious Tracts*; Maseres, F., Ed.; Printed by R.Wilks and sold by J. White: London, UK, 1807; Volume VI, pp. 360–370. [CrossRef]
28. Whitley, J. A new and commodius method of solving Colonel Titus, and others of a similar kind. *The Liverpool Apollonius, or the geometrical and philosophical repository* **1824**, *1*, 127–128.
29. Beighton, H. (Ed.) *The Ladies' Diary Or Woman's Almanack, for the Year of Our Lord 1726*; Printed by A. Wilde, for the Company of Stationers: London, UK, 1726.
30. Archibald, R.C. Notes on Some Minor English Mathematical Serials. *Math. Gaz.* **1929**, *14*, 379–400. [CrossRef]
31. Newton, I. *Arithmetica Universalis; Sive de Compositione et Resolutione Arithmetica Liber*; Printed by Benj. Tooke: London, UK, 1707; Edited by William Whiston.
32. Maseres, F. The resolution of the biquadratic equation $34z + 5z^2 - 34z^3 - z^4 = 8$. In *Scriptores Logarithmici; Or a Collection of Several Curious Tracts*; Maseres, F., Ed.; Printed by R.Wilks and sold by J. White: London, UK, 1807; Volume VI, pp. 370–395. [CrossRef]
33. Schumacher, J. Das Colonel Titus's Problem. *Archiv der Mathematik und Physik* **1911**, *Series 3*, 141–154.
34. Buée, A. Solution of a problem of Col. Silas Titus. *Ann. Philos.* **1815**, *V*, 53–61.
35. Steihaug, T. Computational science in the eighteenth century. Test cases for the methods of Newton, Raphson, and Halley: 1685 to 1745. *Numer. Algorithms* **2020**, *83*, 1259–1275. [CrossRef]
36. Ward, J. *A Compendium of Algebra*; Author & by him sold: London, UK, 1695.
37. Ward, J. *The Young Mathematician's Guide. Being a Plain and Easie Introduction to the Mathematicks*; John Taylor: London, UK, 1707.
38. Steihaug, T. Computational Science in the 17th Century. Numerical Solution of Algebraic Equations: Digit–by–Digit Computation. In *Numerical Analysis and Optimization, NAO-V, Muscat, Oman, January 2020*; Al-Baali, M., Purnama, A., Grandinetti, L., Eds.; Springer Nature: Berlin, Germany, 2021; chapter 12, pp. 249–269. [CrossRef]

39. Holdred, T. *A New Method of Solving Equations with Ease and Expedition; by which the True Value of the Unknown Quantity is Found without Previous Reduction. With a Supplement, Containing Two Other Methods of Solving Equations, Derived from the Same Principle*; Printed by Richard Watts: London, UK, 1820.
40. Nicholson, P. *Essay on Involution and Evolution Particularly Applied to the Operation of Extracting the Roots of Equations and Numbers; According to a Process Entirely Arithmetical. A New Edition*; Davis and Dickson: London, UK, 1820.
41. Nicholson, P. *Analytical and Arithmetical Essays*; Davis and Dickson: London, UK, 1821.
42. De Morgan, A. Notices of the progress of the problem of evolution. *The Companion to the Almanac* **1839**, pp. 34–52.
43. Perkins, G.R. *A Treatise on Algebra: Embracing, Besides the Elementary Principles, All the Higher Parts Usually Taught in Colleges: Containing Moreover, the New Method of Cubic and Higher Equations, as well as the Development and Application of the More Recently Discovered Theorem of Sturm*; O.Hutchinson: Utica, NY, USA, 1842.
44. Young, J.R. *The Analysis and Solution of Cubic and Biquadratic Equations*; Souter and Law: London, UK, 1842.
45. Lobatto, R. (Ed.) *Lessen over de Hoogere Algebra*; Gebroeders Van Cleef: Amsterdam, The Netherlands, 1845.
46. Schnuse, C.H. *Die Theorie und Auflösung der höhern algebraischen und der transcendenten Gleichungen*; Eduard Leibrock: Braunschweig, Germany, 1850. [CrossRef]
47. Olney, E. *A University Algebra*; Sheldon & Co: New York, NY, USA, 1878.
48. Reyneau, C.R. *Analyse démontrée, ou la Méthode de résoudre les problèmes des mathématiques, Tome I*; Paris, chez Jacque Quillau, 1708.
49. Frend, W. *The Principles of Algebra or the True Theory of Equations Etablished on the Principles of Mathematical Demonstration. Part the second*; G.G. and J. Robinson: London, UK, 1799.
50. Frend, W. Article XXXV. Method of discovering the number of negative and impossible roots, in any equation. In *The Mathematical Repository*; Leybourn, T., Ed.; W. Glendinning: London, UK, 1801; Volume II, pp. 297–300.
51. Lockhart, J. *Extension of the Celebrated Theorem of C. Sturm, whereby the Roots of Numeral Equations may be Separated from Each Other, with Copious Examples*; D.A.Talboys: Oxford, UK, 1839.
52. Young, J.R. *Mathematical Dissertations for the Use of Students in the Modern Analysis*; John Souter: London, UK, 1841.
53. Siebel, A. Untersuchungen über algebraische gleichungen. *Archiv der Mathematik und Physik* **1880**, *56*, 394–419.
54. Siebel, A. Exacte Trennung der reellen Wurzeln numerischer algebraischen und transcendenten Gleichungen. *Archiv der Mathematik und Physik* **1887**, *Series 2*, 279–349.
55. de Graaf, I. *Analysis Aequationum Algebraïcarum, of Algemeene Ontbinding der Bepaalde Stelkonstige Vergelykingen van drie, vier, vyf, ses en meer Afmetingen*; Loots: Amsterdam, The Netherlands, 1732.
56. Papakonstantinou, J.M.; Tapia, R.A. Origin and Evolution of the Secant Method in One Dimension. *Am. Math. Mon.* **2013**, *120*, 500–518. [CrossRef]
57. Cardano, G. *Artis Magnae, Sive de Regulis Algebraicis*; Nuremberg, Germany, 1545. Ioh Petreius. English translation by T. Richard Witmer, The Rules of Algebra (Ars Magna), Cambridge, MA: MIT Press, 1968; reprinted as G. Cardano, Ars Magna or The Rules of Algebra, Garden City, NY: Dover Publications, 1993.
58. Davidson, J. *Supplement to the Practical Calculator*; Andrew Balfour: Edinburgh, UK, 1814.
59. Davidson, J. *Key to Davidson's System of Practical Mathematics: Containing Solutions to All the Exercises in that Work*; Bell & Bradfute: Edinburgh, UK, 1852.
60. Raphson, J. *Analysis Æquationum Universalis, seu ad Æquationes Algebraicas Resolvendas Methodus Generalis, et Expedita, Ex nova Infinitarum serierum Doctrina, Deducta ac Demonstrata*; Sold by Abel Swalle: London, UK, 1690.
61. Maseres, F. *Scriptores Logarithmici; Or a Collection of Several Curious Tracts*; Vol. III, J. Davis: London, UK, 1796.
62. Lockhart, J. *Resolution of Two Equations. Being a Homage to the Memory of the Founders and Benefactors of the University of Oxford, at the Commemoration Held on the 12th of June, 1839*; D.A.Talboys: Oxford, UK, 1839.
63. Halley, E. Methodus Nova Accurata et Facilis Inveniendi Radices Æquationum Quarumcumque Generaliter, Sine Prævia Reductione. *Philos. Trans. (1683–1775)* **1694**, *18*, 136–148. [CrossRef]
64. Wolff, C. *Der Anfangs-Gründe Aller Mathematischen Wiessenschaften. Letzter Theil. Welcher so wol die gemeine Algebra, als die Differential- und Integral-Rechnung, und einen Anhang Von den vornehmsten Mathematischen-Schriefften In sich begreifet*; Renger: Halle Magdeburgischen, Germany, 1710.
65. Ronayne, P. *A Treatise of Algebra in Two Books: The First Treating of the Arithmetical and the Second of the Geometrical Part*; Printed for W. Innys: London, UK, 1717.
66. Simons, L.G. Algebra at Harvard College in 1730. *Am. Math. Mon.* **1925**, *32*, 63–70. [CrossRef]
67. Simons, L.G. *Introduction of Algebra into Ameriçan Schools in the Eighteenth Century*; Department of the interior, Bureau of education Bulletin No.18: Washington, DC, USA, 1924.
68. Maseres, F. *Tracts on the Resolution of Cubick & Biquadratick Equations*; Wilks and Taylor: London, UK, 1803.
69. Rutherford, W. *The Complete Solution of Numerical Equations: In Which, by One Uniform Process, the Imaginary as Well as the Real Roots are Easily Determined*; G. Bell: London, UK, 1849.
70. Pratt, O. *New and Easy Method of Solution of the Cubic and Biquadratic Equations*; Longmans, Green, Reader, and Dyer: London, UK, 1866.
71. Encke, J.F. *Resolucion general de las escuaciones numéricas por el método de Gräffe. Translated and revised by D. Miguel Merino of* Allgemeine Auflösung der numerischen Gleichungen; E. Aguado: Madrid, Spain, 1879.
72. Rey Pastor, J. *Lecciones de álgebra*, 2nd ed.; Notes from a course in 1915–1916: Madrid, Spain, 1924.

73. Wells, E. *Elementa Arithmeticae Numerosae Et Speciosae*; Printed by Johan Croke: Oxford, UK, 1698.
74. Struyck, N. *Uytreekening der kansen in het speelen, door de arithematica en algebra, beneevens een verhandeling voor looteryen en interest*; Salomon Schouten: Amsterdam, The Nederlands, 1716.
75. Struyck, N. *Les oeuvres de Nicolas Struyck, 1687–1769. qui se rapportent au calcul des chances, à la statistique générale, à la statistique des décès et aux rentes viagères tirées des oeuvres complètes. Traduites du hollandais par J.A. Vollgraff*; Algemeene maatschappij van levensverzekering en lijfrente: Amsterdam, The Netherlands, 1912.
76. Burnside, W.S.; Panton, A.W. *The Theory of Equations: With an Introduction to the Theory of Binary Algebraic Forms, Vol 1*; Dublin University Press series, Hodges, Figgis, & Co: Dublin, Ireland, 1899.
77. Calvo Carbonell, C. Estudios sobre la resolución numérica de ecuaciones de 3.°, 4.°, y 5.° grado. *Gaceta Matemática* **1955**, *5–6*, 109–124.
78. Lacroix, S.F. *Élemens d'algèbre*; Crapelet-Duprat: Paris, France, 1799.
79. Lambert, P. New applications of Maclaurin's series in the solution of equations and in the expansion of functions. *Proc. Am. Philos. Soc.* **1903**, *42*, 85–95.
80. Dickson, L.E. *Elementary theory of equations*; John Wiley & sons: New York, USA, 1914.
81. Bonnycastle, J. *The Elements of Algebra with Many Useful and Important Additions, Adapted to the System of Instruction Pursued in the Universities and Military Colleges, by William Galbraith and William Rutherford*; Maclachlan, Stedwart & Com: Edinburgh, UK, 1848.
82. Chambers, W.; Chambers, R. *Exercises and Problems in Algebra with Answers and Hints to the Solutions*; W. and R. Chambers: London, UK, 1855.
83. Day, J. *An Introduction to Algebra: Being the First Part of A Course of Mathematics, Adapted to the Method of Instruction in the American Colleges*; Durrie & Peck: New Haven, CT, USA, 1857.
84. Pimentel, M.H. *Verzameling van vraagstukken en toepassingen over de hoogere algebra*; 'S Gravenhage: The Hague, The Netherlands, 1858.
85. Heis, E. *Sammlung von Beispielen und Aufgaben aus der allgemeinen Arithmetik und Algebra*; M. DuMont: Koeln, Germany, 1868.
86. Matthiessen, L. *Schlüssel zur Sammlung von Beispielen und Aufgaben aus der allgemeinen Arithmetik und Algebra*, 2nd ed.; Vol. 2, M. DuMont-Schauberg: Koeln, Germany, 1878.
87. Burnside, W.S.; Panton, A.W. *The Theory of Equations: With an Introduction to the Theory of Binary Algebraic Forms*; Dublin University Press series, Hodges, Figgis & Company: Dublin, Ireland, 1881.
88. Taylor, J.M. *A College Algebra*, 6th ed.; Allyn & Bacon: Boston, MA, USA; Chicago, IL, USA, 1889.

axioms

Article

Interval Type-3 Fuzzy Control for Automated Tuning of Image Quality in Televisions

Oscar Castillo [1,*], Juan R. Castro [2] and Patricia Melin [1]

[1] Division of Graduate Studies, Tijuana Institute of Technology, Tijuana 22414, Mexico; pmelin@tectijuana.mx
[2] School of Engineering, UABC University, Tijuana 22500, Mexico; jrcastror@uabc.edu.mx
* Correspondence: ocastillo@tectijuana.mx

Abstract: In this article, an intelligent system utilizing type-3 fuzzy logic for automated image quality tuning in televisions is presented. The tuning problem can be formulated as controlling the television imaging system to achieve the requirements of production quality. Previously, the tuning process has been carried out by experts, by manually adjusting the television imaging system on production lines to meet the quality control standards. In this approach, interval type-3 fuzzy logic is utilized with the goal of automating the tuning of televisions manufactured on production lines. An interval type-3 fuzzy approach for image tuning is proposed, so that the best image quality is obtained and, in this way, meet quality requirements. A system based on type-3 fuzzy control is implemented with good simulation results. The validation of the type-3 fuzzy approach is made by comparing the results with human experts on the process of electrical tuning of televisions. The key contribution is the utilization of type-3 fuzzy in the image tuning application, which has not been reported previously in the literature.

Keywords: interval type-3 fuzzy theory; fuzzy control; manufacturing

MSC: 03B52; 03E72; 62P30

Citation: Castillo, O.; Castro, J.R.; Melin, P. Interval Type-3 Fuzzy Control for Automated Tuning of Image Quality in Televisions. *Axioms* **2022**, *11*, 276. https://doi.org/10.3390/axioms11060276

Academic Editor: Alexander Šostak

Received: 21 April 2022
Accepted: 6 June 2022
Published: 9 June 2022

1. Introduction

In this article, the application of interval type-3 fuzzy theory [1–6] for automating the tuning process is presented. The tuning process involves a process of dynamically adjusting the image quality to achieve the best possible image in the end. A set of fuzzy rules that encapsulates the knowledge of experts in performing the tuning process has been designed. Based on these fuzzy rules we propose the automation of television tuning. Interval type-3 fuzzy enables the handling of the decision-making uncertainty for this problem in a better way than other available alternatives described in the literature, such as type-1 [7–9], interval type-2, and general type-2 fuzzy logic [10–18]. Of course, there are successful applications of type-1 fuzzy control in the recent literature, such as the excellent works presented in [19–21], but the main goal of this article was exploring the utilization of type-3 in this particular application and its comparison with type-2 and type-1.

The key issue that we are dealing with in this work is achieving a way to reproduce images in the best fashion in televisions. In the production of televisions, we usually find a section on the manufacturing line with the responsibility of adjusting the imaging system. Traditionally, an expert adjusts the imaging system using a remote controller, based on voltage and current values. Here, we are dealing with a system based on type-3 fuzzy for controlling the image tuning of televisions. The interval type-3 system has a rule base formed from expert knowledge about the tuning of televisions. The main reason behind the utilization of interval type-3 fuzzy logic is to model better the uncertainty in the decision-making process [6,22]. We need to consider the voltage, current intensity, time, and quality as fuzzy variables in the fuzzy rules [23] and define the membership functions (MFs) for these variables that reflect real data and the knowledge of experts.

Several important related works have demonstrated the efficiency of interval type-3 fuzzy logic systems (IT3FLSs) when compared to type-1 fuzzy logic systems (T1FLSs), interval type-2 fuzzy logic systems (IT2FLSs), and generalized type-2 fuzzy logic systems (GT2FLSs); and some of these works are highlighted in the following: in [24] a subsethood for type-n fuzzy sets is presented by Rickard et al.; in [25] a related approach to the design of interval type-3 TS systems is presented by Singh et al.; in [3] Qasem et al. present a type-3 logic fuzzy system that was optimized using a Kalman filter with adaptive fuzzy kernel size; in [26] Wang et al. present a non-singleton type-3 fuzzy approach for flowmeter fault detection for the gas industry; in [27] Alattas et al. present a new data-driven control system for gyroscopes: using type-3 fuzzy systems; in [1] Cao et al. analyze a deep-learned recurrent type-3 fuzzy system with application for renewable energy prediction; in [28] Tian et al. design a deep-learned type-3 fuzzy system and describe its application in modeling problems; in [5] Mohammadzadeh et al. describe an interval type-3 fuzzy system and a new online fractional-order learning algorithm; and in [29] Ma et al. use an optimal type-3 fuzzy system for solving singular equations.

The field of control is an area in which there is a wide and deep number of problems where IT3FLSs may prove to have good performance. The following works focus their studies on showing that an IT3FLS is an excellent tool in control, based on their results. A stabilization of deep type-3 fuzzy control is presented by Gheisarnejad et al. in [30]; an interval type-3 control for solar systems is developed by Liu et al. in [6]; a type-3 controller for gyroscopes is studied by Vafaie et al. in [31]; interval type-3 control for navigation of autonomous vehicles is presented by Tian et al. in [32]; a fractional-order type-3 fuzzy control is implemented by Mohammadzadeh et al. in [33]; an interesting model-predictive type-3 controller for power converters is presented by Gheisarnejad et al. in [34]; a predictive type-3 control for multi-agents is presented by Taghieh et al. in [35]; an event-triggered type-3 controller for multi-agent systems is presented by Yan et al. in [36]; and a type-3 fuzzy voltage management is applied in battery systems by Nabipour et al. in [37]. As can be noted from the discussion of previous works on type-3 fuzzy logic, the particular application that is being considered in this article has not been tackled before with interval type-3 fuzzy models, and this was part of the motivation for carrying out this work. In addition, from a practical point of view, we are presenting a working prototype to the industrial workers in a manufacturing plant in Tijuana, Mexico (as they provided the experts to give us their empirical knowledge on tuning the imaging system). Additionally, on the theoretical side, we were able to extend concepts from type-1 and type-2 to the level of type-3 [38], that could be useful for other problems. In summary, the objective of this research work was to extend the theory and methodology for designing type-2 fuzzy to interval type-3 fuzzy, and also to test this theory and methodology with a challenging application that allows us to make a comparative study of type-3 versus type-2 and type-1 in tuning the imaging systems of televisions.

The key contribution is the utilization of interval type-3 fuzzy theory for achieving an efficient tuning during the production of televisions. This has not been previously reported in the literature, which is evidence of the innovative nature of this research work. In addition, we show that interval type-3 outperforms type-2 and type-1 fuzzy in handling the uncertainty in the decision-making process involved in the evaluation of image quality. There is also innovation on the application side of this work. It is worth noting that the utilization of type-3 fuzzy in the image-tuning application has not been described previously in the literature, which indicates of the novelty of the study. There are only applications of type-2 and type-1 to manufacturing problems reported at this time [23]. In this sense, the approach presented here could be generalized to other problems related to the manufacturing of similar, products, such as sound speakers, sound systems, and others. These problems also involve the tuning of images or sound in a similar way, and the approach proposed here could be adapted to solve them.

The rest of the paper is described as follows: Section 2 highlights the concepts of interval type-3. Section 3 outlines the basic terminology involved in Mamdani type-3 fuzzy systems. Then, Section 4 describes how to use type-3 fuzzy techniques for automating the tuning of televisions and illustrates its validity with simulations. At the end, Section 5 outlines the conclusions.

2. Interval Type-3 Fuzzy Theory

We begin by formulating type-3 terminology.

Definition 1. *A type-3 fuzzy set (T3 FS) [2,4,5,38], denoted by $A^{(3)}$, is represented by the plot of a function called MF of $A^{(3)}$ in the Cartesian product $X \times [0,1] \times [0,1]$ in $[0,1]$, where X is the primary variable universe of $A^{(3)}$, x.*

In this case, u is the membership function of x, and v is the membership function of u. The MF of $\mu_{A^{(3)}}$ is formulated by $\mu_{A^{(3)}}(x,u,v)$ (or $\mu_{A^{(3)}}$ for short) and it is labeled a type-3 MF (T3 MF). In other words,

$$\mu_{A^{(3)}} : X \times [0,1] \times [0,1] \rightarrow [0,1]$$

$$A^{(3)} = \left\{ \left(x, u(x), v(x,u), \mu_{A^{(3)}}(x,u,v)\right) \mid x \in X,\ u \in U \subseteq [0,1], v \in V \subseteq [0,1] \right\} \quad (1)$$

where U is the universe for the secondary variable u and V is the universe for tertiary variable v. A T3FS, $A^{(3)}$ can be formulated as:

$$A^{(3)} = \int_{x\in X} \int_{u\in[0,1]} \int_{v\in[0,1]} \mu_{A^{(3)}}(x,u,v)/(x,u,v) \quad (2)$$

$$A^{(3)} = \int_{x\in X} \left[\int_{u\in[0,1]} \left[\int_{v\in[0,1]} \mu_{A^{(3)}}(x,u,v)/v \right] /u \right] /x \quad (3)$$

where $\iiint$ is notation for the union over all the admissible x, u, v values.

Equation (3) is formulated as a T3 FS MF mapping with the expressions:

$$A^{(3)} = \int_{x\in X} \mu_{A_x^{(3)}}(u,v)/x \quad (4)$$

$$\mu_{A_x^{(3)}}(u,v) = \int_{u\in[0,1]} \mu_{A_{(x,u)}^{(3)}}(v)/u \quad (5)$$

$$\mu_{A_{(x,u)}^{(3)}}(v) = \int_{v\in[0,1]} \mu_{A^{(3)}}(x,u,v)/v \quad (6)$$

where $\mu_{A_x^{(3)}}(u,v)$ is the primary MF, $\mu_{A_N^{(3)}}(u,v)$ is the secondary membership function, and $\mu_{A_{(x,u)}^{(3)}}(v)$ is the tertiary MF of the T3 FS.

If $\mu_{A^{(3)}}(x,u,v) = 1$ for all $x \in X$, $u \in U$, $v \in V$, the T3 FS, $A^{(3)}$, is simplified to an interval type-3 fuzzy set (IT3 FS) with the notation $\mathbb{A}$, postulated by expression (7):

$$\mathbb{A} = \int_{x\in X} \left[\int_{u\in[0,1]} \left[\int_{v\in[\underline{\mu}_{\mathbb{A}}(x,u),\ \overline{\mu}_{\mathbb{A}}(x,u)} 1/v \right] /u \right] /x \quad (7)$$

where

$$\mu_{\mathbb{A}(x,u)}(v) = \int_{v\in[\underline{\mu}_{\mathbb{A}}(x,u),\ \overline{\mu}_{\mathbb{A}}(x,u)} 1/v \quad (8)$$

$$\mu_{\mathbb{A}(x)}(u,v) = \int_{u\in[0,1]} \left[\int_{v\in[\underline{\mu}_{\mathbb{A}}(x,u),\ \overline{\mu}_{\mathbb{A}}(x,u)} 1/v \right] /u \quad (9)$$

$$\mathbb{A} = \int_{x\in X} \mu_{\mathbb{A}_{(x)}}(u,v)/x \quad (10)$$

Assuming that $v \in \left[\underline{\mu}_{\mathbb{A}}(x,u),\ \overline{\mu}_{\mathbb{A}}(x,u)\right]$ and the lower and upper MFs $\underline{\mu}_{\mathbb{A}}(x,u)$, $\overline{\mu}_{\mathbb{A}}(x,u)$ are general type-2 MFs (T2 MFs) on the plane (x,u), Equation (4) can be simplified to an interval type-3 MF (IT3 MF), $\widetilde{\mu}_{\mathbb{A}}(x,u) \in \left[\underline{\mu}_{\mathbb{A}}(x,u),\ \overline{\mu}_{\mathbb{A}}(x,u)\right]$, defined by Equation (11):

$$\mathbb{A} = \int_{x\in X}\int_{u\in[0,1]} \widetilde{\mu}_{\mathbb{A}}(x,u)/(x,u) \tag{11}$$

where the lower T2 MF $\underline{\mu}_{\mathbb{A}}(x,u)$, is contained in the upper T2 MF $\overline{\mu}_{\mathbb{A}}(x,u)$, that is, $\underline{\mu}_{\mathbb{A}}(x,u) \subseteq \overline{\mu}_{\mathbb{A}}(x,u)$, then $\underline{\mu}_{\mathbb{A}}(x,u) \leq \overline{\mu}_{\mathbb{A}}(x,u)$, and as a consequence an IT3 FS is expressed by two T2 FSs, one inferior $\underline{A}$ with T2 MF $\underline{\mu}_{\mathbb{A}}(x,u)$, and another superior $\overline{A}$, with T2 MF $\overline{\mu}_{\mathbb{A}}(x,u)$, expressed by Equations (12) and (13) (see Figure 1):

$$\underline{A} = \int_{x\in X}\int_{u\in[0,1]} \underline{\mu}_{\mathbb{A}}(x,u)/(x,u) = \int_{x\in X}\left[\int_{u\in[0,1]} \underline{f}_x(u)/u\right]/x \tag{12}$$

$$\overline{A} = \int_{x\in X}\int_{u\in[0,1]} \overline{\mu}_{\mathbb{A}}(x,u)/(x,u) = \int_{x\in X}\left[\int_{u\in[0,1]} \overline{f}_x(u)/u\right]/x \tag{13}$$

where the secondary MFs of $\underline{A}$ and $\overline{A}$ are T1 MFs of T1FS expressed by Equations (14) and (15):

$$\mu_{\underline{A}(x)}(u) = \int_{u\in J_x} \underline{f}_x(u)/u \tag{14}$$

$$\mu_{\overline{A}(x)}(u) = \int_{u\in J_x} \overline{f}_x(u)/u \tag{15}$$

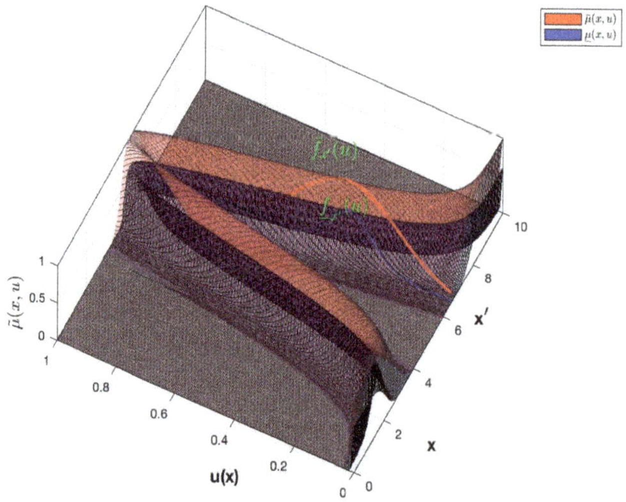

Figure 1. IT3 FS with IT3MF $\widetilde{\mu}(x,u)$ where $\underline{\mu}(x,u)$ is the LMF and $\overline{\mu}(x,u)$ is the UMF.

In this case, we utilize interval type-3 MFs that are scaled Gaussians in the primary and secondary variables, respectively. This function can be represented as $\widetilde{\mu}_{\mathbb{A}}(x,u)$, with Gaussian footprint of uncertainty $FOU(\mathbb{A})$, characterized with parameters $[\sigma, m]$ (UpperParameters) for the upper membership function UMF, and for the lower membership function LMF the parameters λ (LowerScale) and ℓ (LowerLag), to form the $DOU = [\underline{\mu}(x), \overline{\mu}(x)]$. The vertical cuts $\mathbb{A}_{(x)}(u)$ characterize the $FOU(\mathbb{A})$, and are IT2 FSs with Gaussian IT2 MFs, $\mu_{\mathbb{A}(x)}(u)$ with parameters $[\sigma_u, m(x)]$ for the UMF and LMF λ (LowerScale), ℓ (LowerLag).

The IT3 MF, $\tilde{\mu}_{\mathbb{A}}(x,u)$ = ScaleGaussScaleGaussIT3MF (x, $[\sigma, m]$, λ, ℓ) is described with the following equations:

$$\overline{u}(x) = exp\left[-\frac{1}{2}\left(\frac{x-m}{\sigma}\right)^2\right] \tag{16}$$

$$\underline{u}(x) = \lambda \cdot exp\left[-\frac{1}{2}\left(\frac{x-m}{\sigma^*}\right)^2\right] \tag{17}$$

where $\sigma^* = \sigma\sqrt{\frac{\ln(\ell)}{\ln(\varepsilon)}}$ and ε is the machine epsilon. If $\ell = 0$, then $\sigma^* = \sigma$. In this case, $\overline{u}(x)$ and $\underline{u}(x)$ are the upper and lower limits of the domain of uncertainty (DOU). The range, $\delta(x)$ and radius, σ_x of the FOU are:

$$\delta(x) = \overline{u}(x) - \underline{u}(x) \tag{18}$$

$$\sigma_x = \frac{\delta(x)}{2\sqrt{3}} + \varepsilon \tag{19}$$

The apex or core, $m(x)$, of the IT3 MF $\tilde{\mu}(x,u)$, is defined by the expression:

$$m(x) = exp\left[-\frac{1}{2}\left(\frac{x-m}{\rho}\right)^2\right] \tag{20}$$

where $\rho = (\sigma + \sigma^*)/2$. Then, the vertical cuts with IT2 MF, $\mu_{\mathbb{A}(x)}(u) = \left[\underline{\mu}_{\mathbb{A}(x)}(u), \overline{\mu}_{\mathbb{A}(x)}(u)\right]$, are described by the equations:

$$\overline{\mu}_{\mathbb{A}(x)}(u) = exp\left[-\frac{1}{2}\left(\frac{u-u(x)}{\sigma_x}\right)^2\right] \tag{21}$$

$$\underline{\mu}_{\mathbb{A}(x)}(u) = \lambda \cdot exp\left[-\frac{1}{2}\left(\frac{u-u(x)}{\sigma_x^*}\right)^2\right] \tag{22}$$

where $\sigma_x^* = \sigma_x\sqrt{\frac{\ln(\ell)}{\ln(\varepsilon)}}$. If $\ell = 0$, then $\sigma_u^* = \sigma_u$. Then, $\overline{\mu}_{\mathbb{A}(x)}(u)$ and $\underline{\mu}_{\mathbb{A}(x)}(u)$ are the UMF and LMF of the IT2 FSs of the vertical cuts of the secondary IT2MF of the IT3 FS.

3. Mamdani Type-3 Fuzzy Models

The IT3 FLS structure contains the same main components (fuzzifier, rule base, inference machine and, in the final stage, an output processing unit) as its analogous T2 FLSs. While in the case of T2 FLSs the final stage consists of a process of type reduction to T1 FS + defuzzification, in the case of an IT3 FLS, the output process consists of type reduction to an IT2 FS + defuzzification. The fuzzy operators of the inference machine of an IT3 FLS and the type-reduction methods are equivalent to a T2 FLS, except that in the inputs and outputs we have IT3 FSs in an IT3 FLS. The interval type-3 fuzzy operators of union ($\cup$) and intersection ($\cap$), are related to the join ($\sqcup$) and *meet* ($\sqcap$) operators, respectively. The Cartesian product ($\times$) and the implication ($\rightarrow$) are intersection operations. We first define the type-3 fuzzy operators, as follows: consider two IT3 FSs, $\mathbb{A}$ and $\mathbb{B}$, that are expressed utilizing the representation of horizontal cuts, as in [38]:

$$\mathbb{A} = \int_{x\in X} \mu_{\mathbb{A}(x)}(u)/x = \int_{x\in X}\left[\sup_{\alpha\in[0,1]} \alpha/\ \mathbb{A}_\alpha(x)\right]/x = \int_{x\in X}\left[\sup_{\alpha\in[0,1]} \alpha/\left[\underline{\mathbf{A}}_\alpha(x), \overline{\mathbf{A}}_\alpha(x)\right]\right]/x \tag{23}$$

where

$$\underline{\mathbf{A}}_\alpha(x) = [\underline{a}_\alpha(x), \underline{b}_\alpha(x)]$$

$$\underline{a}_\alpha(x) = inf\left\{u \,\middle|\, u \in [0,1],\ \underline{\mu}_{\mathbb{A}}(x,u) \geq \alpha\right\}$$

$$\underline{b}_\alpha(x) = sup\left\{u \,\middle|\, u \in [0,1]\,,\ \underline{\mu}_{\mathbb{A}}(x,u) \geq \alpha\right\}$$
$$\overline{\boldsymbol{A}}_\alpha(x) = \left[\overline{a}_\alpha(x), \overline{b}_\alpha(x)\right]$$
$$\overline{a}_\alpha(x) = inf\{u\ |u \in [0,1]\,,\ \overline{\mu}_{\mathbb{A}}(x,u) \geq \alpha\}$$
$$\overline{b}_\alpha(x) = sup\{u\ |u \in [0,1]\,,\ \overline{\mu}_{\mathbb{A}}(x,u) \geq \alpha\}$$

$$\mathbb{B} = \int_{x\in X} \mu_{\mathbb{B}(x)}(u)/x = \int_{x\in X} \left[\underset{\alpha\in[0,1]}{sup}\ \alpha/\ \mathbb{B}_\alpha(x)\right]/x = \int_{x\in X} \left[\underset{\alpha\in[0,1]}{sup}\ \alpha/\left[\ \underline{\boldsymbol{B}}_\alpha(x), \overline{\boldsymbol{B}}_\alpha(x)\right]\right]/x \tag{24}$$

where

$$\underline{\boldsymbol{B}}_\alpha(x) = [\underline{c}_\alpha(x), \underline{d}_\alpha(x)]$$
$$\underline{c}_\alpha(x) = inf\left\{u \,\middle|\, u \in [0,1]\,,\ \underline{\mu}_{\mathbb{B}}(x,u) \geq \alpha\right\}$$
$$\underline{d}_\alpha(x) = sup\left\{u \,\middle|\, u \in [0,1]\,,\ \underline{\mu}_{\mathbb{B}}(x,u) \geq \alpha\right\}$$
$$\overline{\boldsymbol{B}}_\alpha(x) = \left[\overline{c}_\alpha(x), \overline{d}_\alpha(x)\right]$$
$$\overline{c}_\alpha(x) = inf\{u\ |u \in [0,1]\,,\ \overline{\mu}_{\mathbb{B}}(x,u) \geq \alpha\}$$
$$\overline{d}_\alpha(x) = sup\{u\ |u \in [0,1]\,,\ \overline{\mu}_{\mathbb{B}}(x,u) \geq \alpha\}$$

Union of IT3 FSs

The union of two IT3FSs, $\mathbb{A} \cup \mathbb{B}$, is calculated using horizontal cuts as:

$$\mathbb{A} \cup \mathbb{B} = \int_{x\in X} \mu_{(\mathbb{A}\cup\mathbb{B})_x}(u)/x = \int_{x\in X} \left[\underbrace{sup}_{\alpha\in[0,1]}\ \alpha/(\mathbb{A}_\alpha \cup \mathbb{B}_\alpha)\right]/x = \int_{x\in X} \left[\underset{\alpha\in[0,1]}{sup}\ \alpha/\ \left[\ \underline{\boldsymbol{A}}_\alpha(x) \cup \underline{\boldsymbol{B}}_\alpha(x), \overline{\boldsymbol{A}}_\alpha(x) \cup \overline{\boldsymbol{B}}_\alpha(x)\right]\right]/x \tag{25}$$

where

$$\underline{\boldsymbol{A}}_\alpha(x) \cup \underline{\boldsymbol{B}}_\alpha(x) = [\underline{a}_\alpha(x) \vee \underline{c}_\alpha(x), \underline{b}_\alpha(x) \vee \underline{d}_\alpha(x)]$$

and

$$\overline{\boldsymbol{A}}_\alpha(x) \cup \overline{\boldsymbol{B}}_\alpha(x) = \left[\overline{a}_\alpha(x) \vee\ \overline{c}_\alpha(x),\ \overline{b}_\alpha(x) \vee \overline{d}_\alpha(x)\right]$$

Intersection of IT3 FSs

The intersection of two IT3FSs, $\mathbb{A} \bigcap \mathbb{B}$, is calculated using horizontal cuts as:

$$\mathbb{A} \bigcap \mathbb{B} = \int_{x\in X} \mu_{(\mathbb{A}\cap\mathbb{B})_x}(u)/x = \int_{x\in X} \left[\underset{\alpha\in[0,1]}{sup}\ \alpha/\left(\mathbb{A}_\alpha \bigcap \mathbb{B}_\alpha\right)\right]/x = \int_{x\in X} \left[\underset{\alpha\in[0,1]}{sup}\ \alpha/\ \left[\underline{\boldsymbol{A}}_\alpha(x) \bigcap \underline{\boldsymbol{B}}_\alpha(x), \overline{\boldsymbol{A}}_\alpha(x) \bigcap \overline{\boldsymbol{B}}_\alpha(x)\right]\right]/x \tag{26}$$

where

$$\underline{\boldsymbol{A}}_\alpha(x) \bigcap \underline{\boldsymbol{B}}_\alpha(x) = [\underline{a}_\alpha(x) \wedge \underline{c}_\alpha(x), \underline{b}_\alpha(x) \wedge \underline{d}_\alpha(x)]$$
$$\overline{\boldsymbol{A}}_\alpha(x) \bigcap \overline{\boldsymbol{B}}_\alpha(x) = \left[\overline{a}_\alpha(x) \wedge\ \overline{c}_\alpha(x),\ \overline{b}_\alpha(x) \wedge \overline{d}_\alpha(x)\right]$$

Complement of IT3 FSs

The complement of an IT3 FS, $\overline{\mathbb{A}}$, is calculated using horizontal cuts as:

$$\overline{\mathbb{A}} = \int_{x\in X} \mu_{(\overline{\mathbb{A}})_x}(v)/x = \int_{x\in X} \left[\underbrace{sup}_{\alpha\in[0,1]}\ \alpha/\neg\mu_{\mathbb{A}_\alpha(x)}\right]/x = \int_{x\in X} \left[\underbrace{sup}_{\alpha\in[0,1]}\ \alpha/\left[\neg\underline{\boldsymbol{A}}_\alpha(x), \neg\overline{\boldsymbol{A}}_\alpha(x)\right]\right]/x \tag{27}$$

$$\neg\underline{\boldsymbol{A}}_\alpha(x) = [1 - \underline{b}_\alpha(x), 1 - \underline{a}_\alpha(x)]$$
$$\neg\overline{\boldsymbol{A}}_\alpha(x) = \left[1 - \overline{b}_\alpha(x), 1 - \overline{a}_\alpha(x)\right]$$

Definition 2. *The structure of the Mamdani if–then rule is:*

R_Z^k : *IF* x_1 *is* $\mathbb{F}_1^k$ *and ... and* x_i *is* $\mathbb{F}_i^k$ *and ... and* x_n *is* $\mathbb{F}_n^k$ *THEN* y_1 *is* $\mathbb{G}_1^k$, ..., y_j *is* $\mathbb{G}_j^k$, ..., y_m *is* $\mathbb{G}_m^k$

where i = 1 ... , n (number of inputs), j = 1 ... , m (number of outputs) and k = 1 ... , r (number of rules).

To initiate the explanation, we represent the antecedents of the rules with a fuzzy relation $\mathbb{A}^k = \mathbb{F}_1^k \times \ldots \times \mathbb{F}_n^k$, utilizing the Cartesian product, $\times$, with interval type-3 fuzzy sets (IT3 FS), $\mathbb{F}_i^k$, and the implication for the consequent of the j-th output is also an IT3 FS, $\mathbb{G}_j^k$; then, the fuzzy relation of the rule $\mathbb{R}_j^k$ can be formulated as:

$$\mathbb{R}_j^k = \mathbb{A}^k \rightarrow \mathbb{G}_j^k \tag{28}$$

The n-dimensional input is given by a type-2 fuzzy relation, $\mathbb{A}_{\mathbb{X}'}$, with T2MF as:

$$\mathbb{A}_{\mathbb{X}'} = \mathbb{X}_1 \times \ldots \times \mathbb{X}_n \tag{29}$$

Each relation of the rule $\mathbb{R}_j^k$ establishes a fuzzy set of the consequent of the rule $\mathbb{B}_j^k = \mathbb{A}_{\mathbb{X}'} \circ \mathbb{R}_j^k$ in $\boldsymbol{Y}$ such that:

$$\mathbb{B}_j^k = \left[\mathbb{X}_1 \circ \left(\mathbb{F}_1^k \times \mathbb{G}_j^k\right)\right] \times \ldots \times \left[\mathbb{X}_n \circ \left(\mathbb{F}_n^k \times \mathbb{G}_j^k\right)\right] = \times_{i=1}^n \left[\mathbb{X}_i \circ \left(\mathbb{F}_i^k \times \mathbb{G}_j^k\right)\right] \tag{30}$$

where the *level of activation of the rule* is an IT3 FS, $\mathbb{B}_j^k$. By aggregating all the sets, $\mathbb{B}_j^k$ that represent the levels of activation of the rules, we obtain the aggregated set $\mathbb{B}_j$ for the outputs $j = 1 \ldots, m$.

$$\mathbb{B}_j = \mathbb{B}_j^1 \cup \ldots \cup \mathbb{B}_j^k \cup \ldots \cup \mathbb{B}_j^r = \cup_{k=1}^r \mathbb{B}_j^k \tag{31}$$

The abstract model of $\hat{y}_j = f(\boldsymbol{x})$ is a fuzzy model IT3 (y_j *is* $\mathbb{B}_j$), where the sets $\mathbb{B}_j^k$ are submodels of $\mathbb{B}_j$.

Equation (32) is obtained by the MF of IT3 fuzzy relation, $\mu_{\mathbb{B}_j^k}(y_j|\boldsymbol{x}')$, and is:

$$\mu_{\mathbb{B}_j^k}(y_j|\boldsymbol{x}') = \mu_{\mathbb{A}_{\mathbb{X}'} \circ \mathbb{R}_j^k}(y_j|\boldsymbol{x}') = \underbrace{sup}_{x \in X}\left[\mu_{\mathbb{A}_{\mathbb{X}'}}(\boldsymbol{x}) \sqcap \mu_{\mathbb{A}^k \rightarrow \mathbb{G}_j^k}(\boldsymbol{x}, y_j)\right], \ \boldsymbol{y} \in \boldsymbol{Y} \tag{32}$$

where $\mu_{\mathbb{B}_j^k}(y_j|\boldsymbol{x}')$ is the input–output relation between the fuzzy set that fires the inference of a rule (reasoning) and the output fuzzy set. The composition ($\circ$) is a nonlinear mapping from input $\boldsymbol{x}'$ to an IT3 FS with MF, $\mu_{\mathbb{B}_j^k}(y_j|\boldsymbol{x}')$ ($y_j \in \boldsymbol{Y}$) of the output y_j. The reasoning is a mechanism that transforms fuzzy sets into fuzzy sets by the composition operator (basically a max–min operator). Simplifying Equation (32), we obtain:

$$\mu_{\mathbb{B}_j^k}(y_j|\boldsymbol{x}') = \tilde{\Phi}^k(\boldsymbol{x}') \sqcap \mu_{\mathbb{G}_j^k}(y_j) \tag{33}$$

where

$$\tilde{\Phi}^k(\boldsymbol{x}') = \sqcap_{i=1}^n \left[\underbrace{sup}_{x_i \in X_i} \mu_{\mathbb{Q}_i^k}(x_i|x_i')\right] \tag{34}$$

$$\mu_{\mathbb{Q}_i^k}(x_i|x_i') = \mu_{\mathbb{X}_i}(x_i|x_i') \sqcap \mu_{\mathbb{F}_i^k}(x_i) \tag{35}$$

Maximizing function $\mu_{\mathbb{Q}_i^k}(x_i|x_i')$, we obtain the supremum value in $x = x_{k,i}^{max}$:

$$x_{k,i}^{max} \equiv \underbrace{\text{argmax}}_{x_i}\left\{\underbrace{sup}_{x_i \in X_i}\ \mu_{\mathbb{Q}_i^k}(x_i|x_i')\right\} \tag{36}$$

The *firing strength* $\widetilde{\Phi}^k(x')$, is the membership of the t-norm operation, $\sqcap$, of all the supreme membership values $\mu_{\mathbb{Q}_i^k}\left(x_{k,i}^{max}\middle|x_i'\right)$ of the intersection of each input $\mu_{\mathbb{X}_i}(x_i|x_i')$ with its antecedent $\mu_{\mathbb{F}_i^k}(x_i)$ that contributes to the rule level of activation, i.e.:

$$\widetilde{\Phi}^k(x') = \sqcap_{i=1}^{n}\mu_{\mathbb{Q}_i^k}\left(x_{k,i}^{max}\middle|x_i'\right) \tag{37}$$

The *level of activation of the rule* is the membership $\mu_{\mathbb{B}_j^k}(y_j|x')$ resulting from the operation $\sqcap$ of the firing strength $\widetilde{\Phi}^k(x')$ and the membership of the consequent of the rule $\mu_{\mathbb{G}_j^k}(y_j)$, that is, the composition operation ($\circ$) of the facts and the knowledge base rules that describe the relational function, $\mathbb{B}_j^k = \mathbb{A}_{X'} \circ \mathbb{R}_j^k$.

Equation (27) for the MF of the fuzzy relation IT3, $\mu_{\widetilde{\mathbb{B}}_j}(y_j|x')$, is the aggregation of all the rules for each output j= 1 ..., m, using the operator *join* ($\sqcap$)-fuzzy union-. The combining of the rules using the *join* ($\sqcup$) operator for calculating the aggregation of the values of $\mu_{\mathbb{B}_j^k}(y_j|x')$ is described by the equation:

$$\mu_{\mathbb{B}_j}(y_j|x') = \mu_{\mathbb{B}_j^1}(y_j|x') \sqcup \ldots \sqcup \mu_{\mathbb{B}_j^k}(y_j|x') \sqcup \ldots \sqcup \mu_{\mathbb{B}_j^r}(y_j|x') = \sqcup_{k=1}^{r}\ \mu_{\mathbb{B}_j^k}(y_j|x') \tag{38}$$

or

$$\mu_{\mathbb{B}_j}(y_j|x') = \sqcup_{k=1}^{r}\left[\widetilde{\Phi}^k(x') \sqcap \mu_{\mathbb{G}_j^k}(y_j)\right] \tag{39}$$

For applications that require a numeric output, $\mu_{\mathbb{B}_j}(y_j|x')$ is reduced to an IT2 FS or interval, and this is then reduced to a numeric value $\hat{y}_j$. The type reduction methods are the same as the ones used in T2 FS theory.

$$\hat{y}_j = typeReduction\left(y_j, \mu_{\mathbb{B}_j}(y_j|x')\right) \tag{40}$$

In Figure 2, we illustrate the inference in a type-3 system for a particular value of x = 4, and in Figure 3 the type reduction process.

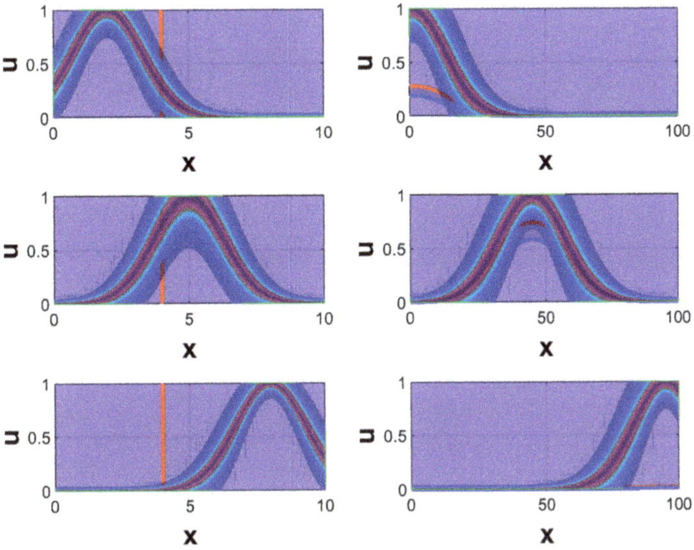

Figure 2. Illustration of the inference process for a value of x = 4.

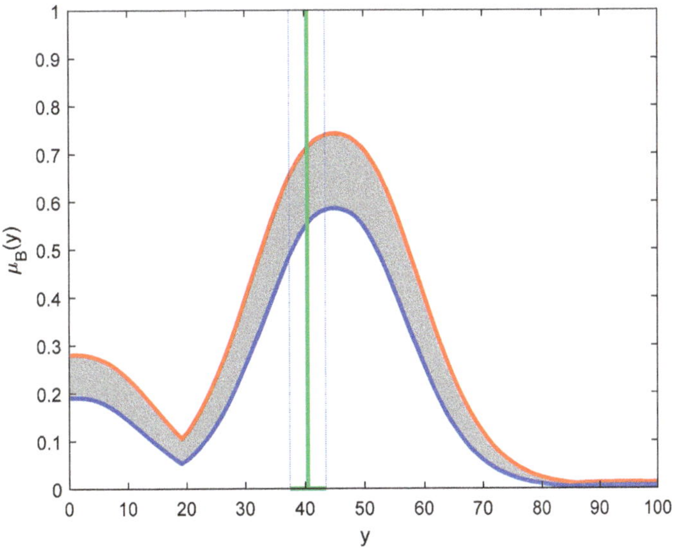

Figure 3. Illustration of the type reduction process for a value of x = 4.

In Figure 4, we illustrate the inference in a type-3 fuzzy system for another value of x = 6, and in Figure 5, the corresponding type reduction process.

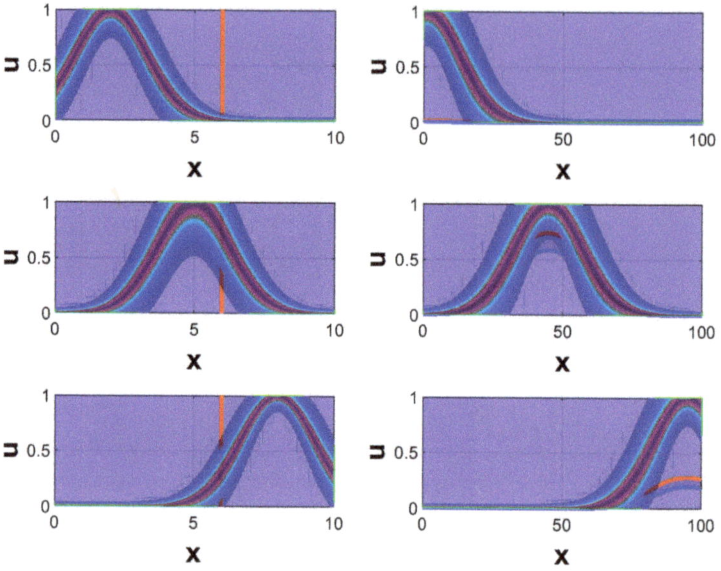

Figure 4. Illustration of the inference process for a value of x = 6.

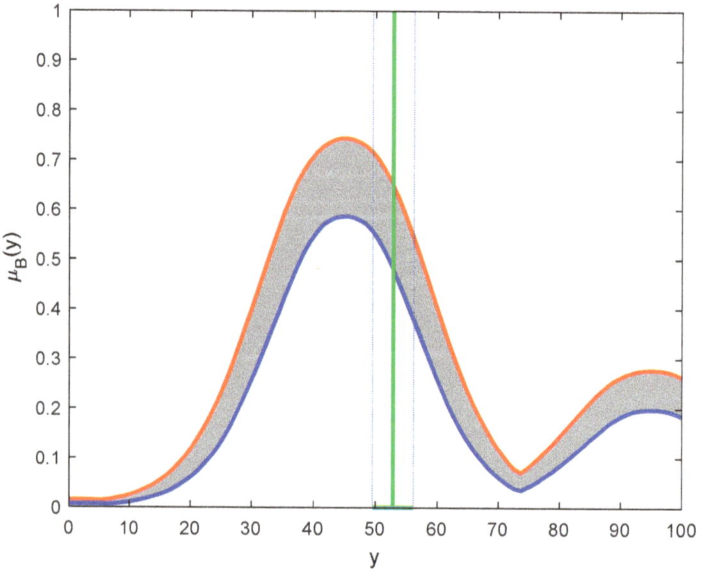

Figure 5. Illustration of the type reduction process for a value of x = 6.

For more details on the type reduction process for type-3 fuzzy sets the reader can check a more detailed (step by step) explanation in a recent reference work on type-3 fuzzy systems [38]. Of course, this type reduction is similar to the process that is performed for type-2 fuzzy sets [10,11].

The structure of an interval type-3 system is almost the same as for type-2 and type-1, and it is composed of a fuzzifier, rules, inference, type reduction and defuzzifier [38]. In Figure 6 we show the structure of an interval IT3 system [4,6].

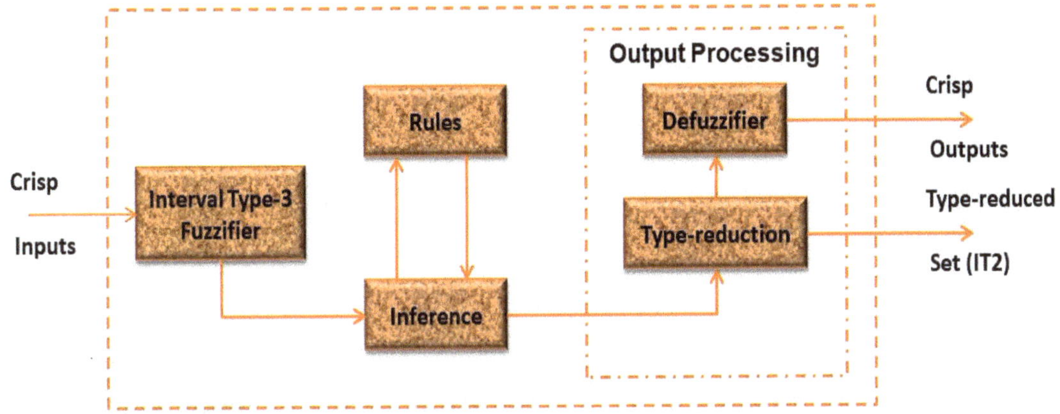

Figure 6. Structure of an interval type-3 system.

In the next section, we explain the usefulness of interval type-3 fuzzy as we illustrate the design method and also show the improvements in results compared to type-1 and type-2 systems.

4. Simulation Results

We developed our own toolbox for type-3 fuzzy systems to implement the fuzzy rules for automated tuning of televisions. A fuzzy system with three inputs and one output was utilized. The inputs are the voltage, current intensity, and time, and the output is the image quality. We use the Mamdani inference and Gaussian MFs. The fuzzy system was designed by reducing the knowledge of human experts to a system of 14 rules. The block diagram of the system is illustrated in Figure 7.

We show in Table 1 the rule base for automated tuning of televisions that encapsulates the knowledge of the experts in image tuning. In Table 2, the parameters of the MFs utilized in the inputs and output are presented. The parameters shown in Table 2 were determined by empirical knowledge of experts combined with a trial-and-error approach, but in the future, these could be optimized to improve results even more. At this stage of the research we considered three membership functions for several reasons: (1) according to experts this was reasonable for them and the fuzzy model was also understandable for them, (2) previous implementations of the fuzzy tuning (type-2 and type-1) of imaging systems have been carried out with three membership functions [23], so for comparative purposes we also needed to have three membership functions, and (3) in future work, we plan to consider changing and optimizing the number of membership functions, so that we investigate this issue more precisely.

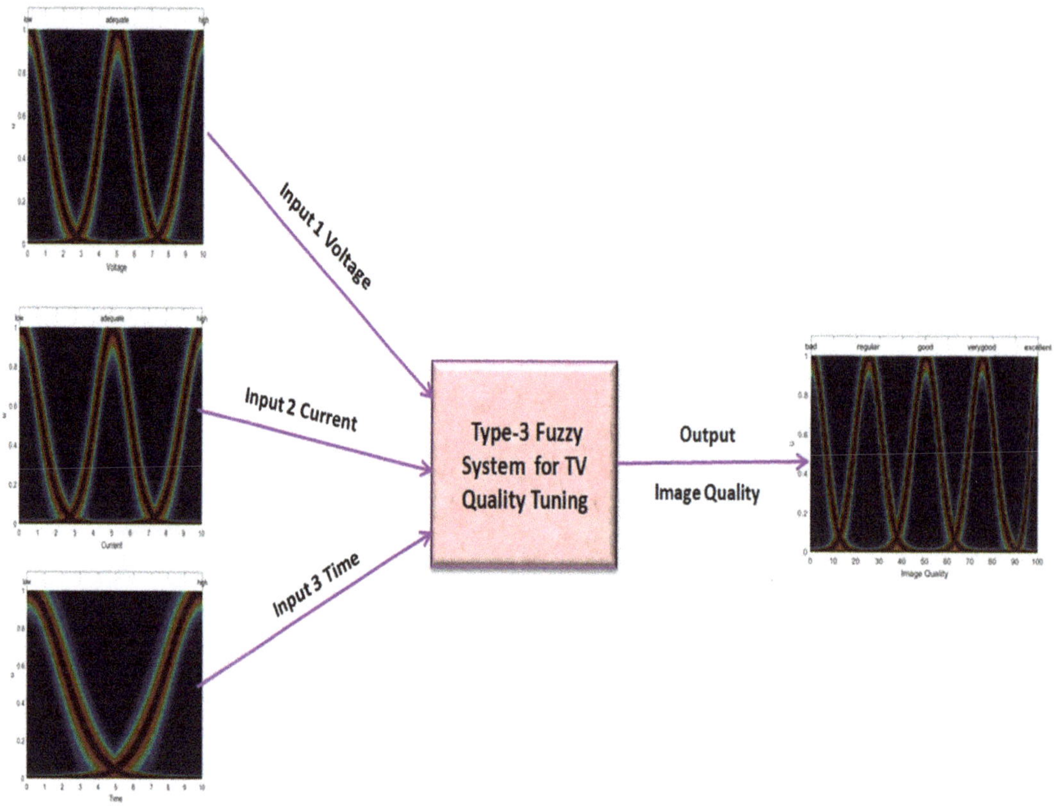

Figure 7. Structure of interval type-3 fuzzy for TV image quality tuning.

Table 1. Fuzzy rules for tuning control.

Number	IF	AND	AND	THEN
	Voltage	**Current Intensity**	**Time**	**Image Quality**
1	High	Adequate	Low	Very Good
2	Adequate	High	Low	Very Good
3	High	High	Low	Regular
4	Low	Adequate	Low	Regular
5	Adequate	Low	Low	Regular
6	Low	Low	Low	Bad
7	Adequate	Adequate	High	Very Good
8	High	Adequate	High	Good
9	Adequate	High	High	Good
10	Adequate	Adequate	High	Regular
11	Low	Adequate	High	Bad
12	Adequate	Adequate	Low	Excellent

Table 2. Parameter values for the Gaussian MFs used in the linguistic values.

Variable	Membership Function	σ	m
Input 1	low	1.30	0.00
Input 1	adequate	1.10	5.00
Input 1	high	1.30	10.00
Input 2	low	1.30	0.00
Input 2	adequate	1.10	5.00
Input 2	high	1.30	10.00
Input 3	low	2.50	0.00
Input 3	high	2.60	10.00
Output	bad	7.00	0.00
Output	regular	7.00	25.00
Output	good	7.00	50.00
Output	very good	6.50	75.00
Output	excellent	4.10	100.00

A sample of the simulation results for 11 cases is shown in Table 3, where we can see that the results from the fuzzy system are close to the real values provided by the experts (in this case two experts were consulted because of the availability of experts at the real plant). In Figures 8–10, the MFs of the inputs (voltage, current intensity and time) are presented. We depict in Figure 11 the MFs for the output of the system. The design of the membership functions was based on the original definitions that were utilized for type-1 and type-2 in [23]. Finally, we illustrate, in Figures 12 and 13, two views of the surface of the fuzzy model.

Table 3. Simulation results for a sample of cases.

Voltage	Current	Time	Image Quality with T1 Fuzzy (%)	Image Quality with IT2 Fuzzy (%)	Image Quality with GT2 Fuzzy (%)	Image Quality with IT3 Fuzzy (%)	Expert Evaluation (%)
9.03	7.47	2.53	37.2215	38.5492	39.1266	39.6137	40.50
5.01	5.02	3.10	84.3312	85.4573	86.8751	87.9177	88.25
4.91	5.10	5.10	50.7735	51.4486	51.9168	52.2079	53.00
8.75	4.95	5.03	55.4532	56.6396	57.2788	58.5392	57.75
5.20	4.85	8.70	48.1782	48.3319	48.8429	49.1119	50.75
2.25	6.33	7.20	24.9891	24.5638	24.0734	21.9642	23.25
5.10	4.99	5.20	48.7865	49.5543	50.7942	51.8969	51.50
6.20	3.17	5.15	48.6734	49.5112	50.7333	51.8500	52.25
5.31	5.21	4.80	53.1853	53.7693	54.2964	55.8204	56.50
3.99	6.25	5.10	49.0231	49.9732	51.2754	52.1439	53.25
5.00	5.00	0.20	89.9638	90.9367	91.7652	94.3397	95.50

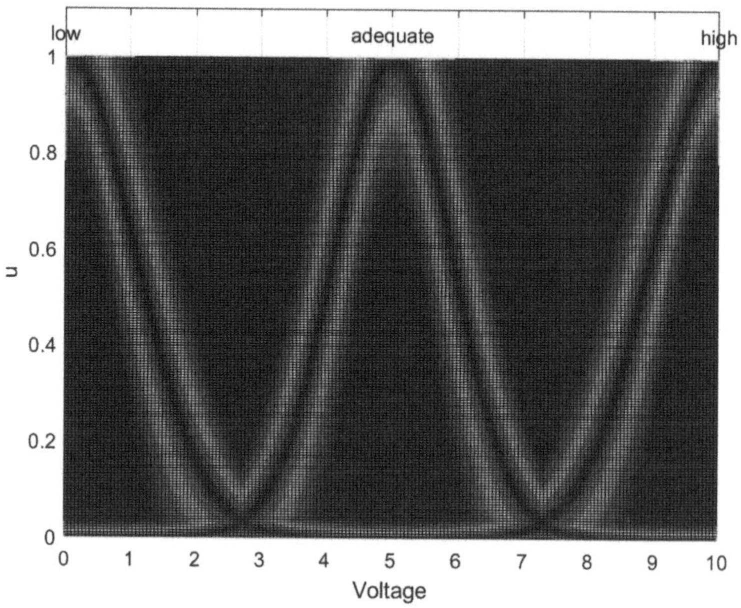

Figure 8. Input MFs of the electric voltage variable.

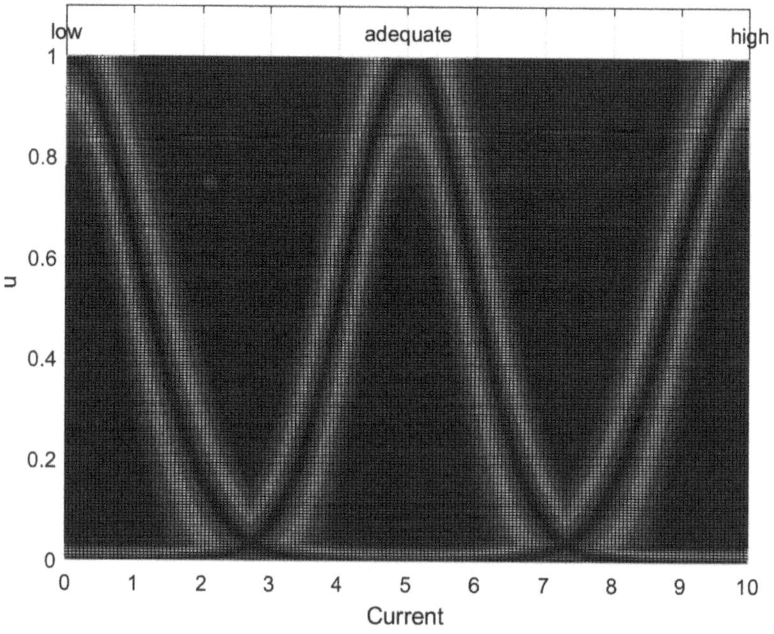

Figure 9. Input MFs of the electric current intensity variable.

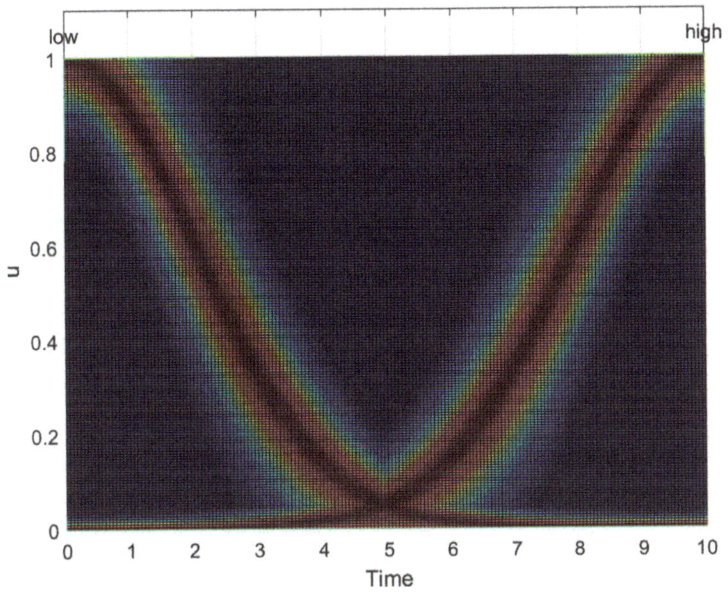

Figure 10. Input MFs of the time linguistic variable.

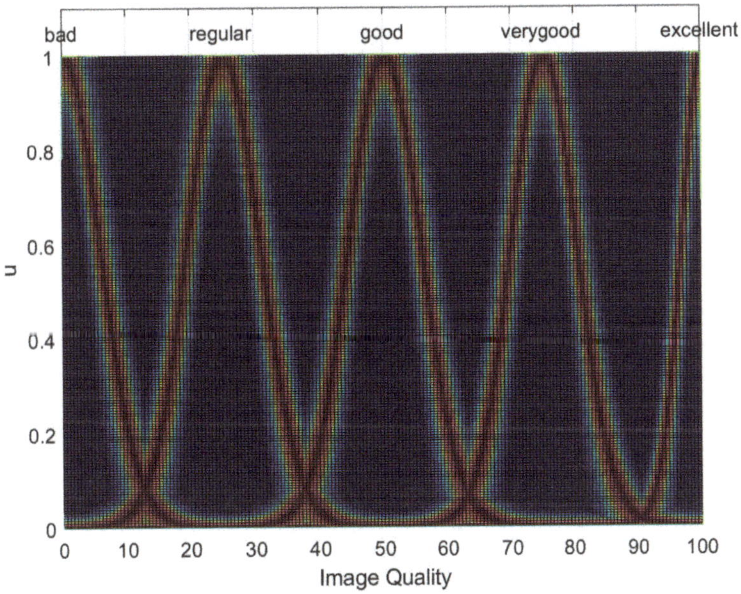

Figure 11. Output MFs of the image quality variable.

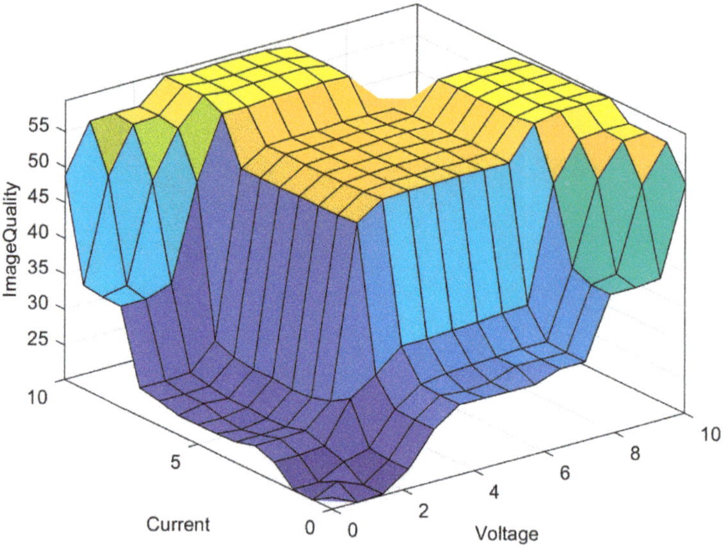

Figure 12. 3-D view of the model surface with respect to current intensity and voltage.

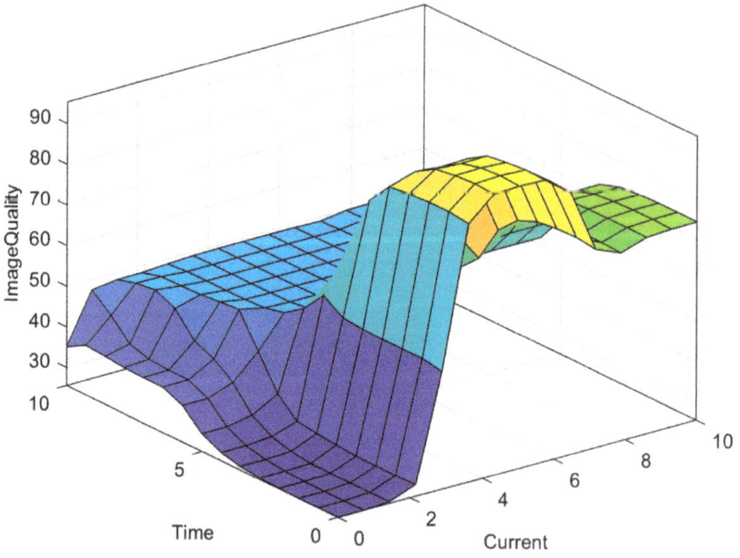

Figure 13. 3-D view of the model surface with respect to current intensity and time.

From Table 3 we can notice that the image quality achieved with type-3 fuzzy is closer to the expert evaluation when compared to general type-2 (GT2), interval type-2 (IT2) and type-1 (T1).

Figures 12 and 13 provide a graphical representation of the fuzzy model. Two figures are needed because we have, in total, four variables, so we need to show two different views of the model. In Figure 12, we can appreciate the influence of current intensity and voltage on the image quality, and this can be viewed as showing all possible image quality outputs for different combinations of the input values. In Figure 13, we also show, in a similar way, the influence of time and current intensity on the image quality.

5. Conclusions

We have described in this article an intelligent system utilizing type-3 fuzzy logic for the tuning of the imaging system of televisions. We have shown in Section 2 the concepts of interval type-3. Then, in Section 3 the basic terminology involved in Mamdani type-3 fuzzy systems was presented. Section 4 then described how to use type-3 fuzzy techniques for automating the tuning of televisions and illustrated its validity with simulations. The tuning problem can be defined as controlling the imaging system of the television to meet quality standards. Previously, this process has been carried out by experts, by manually adjusting the imaging system of televisions on production lines. In the approach proposed here, we utilize an interval type-3 fuzzy system to automate this tuning process. The fuzzy system was designed to control the tuning, so that the imaging system meets quality requirements. An intelligent system was implemented based on type-3 fuzzy control and produced good simulation results. The validation of the type-3 fuzzy approach was made by comparing its results with those of human experts in the process of electrical tuning of televisions. In most of the tests, the interval type-3 fuzzy system provided results closer to the human experts, when compared to type-2 and type-1 fuzzy approaches. We believe that these results are due to the fact that type-3 is able to handle in a better way the uncertainty involved in the tuning process of the imaging system. The main contribution of the article has been the application of the new concepts of interval type-3 to an interesting problem with relevance to the television manufacturing process. The main advantage of the proposal is the relative simplicity of building the fuzzy model based on expert knowledge, though this could be a disadvantage if there were a lack of experts concerning other problems or case studies. In future works, we plan to optimize the MFs of the system by using metaheuristic optimization techniques, in this way improving the results even more. In addition, the proposed type-3 decision-making approach could be applied and tested in similar quality control problems [23] and classification systems [39,40].

Author Contributions: Conceptualization, creation of main idea, writing—review and editing, O.C.; formal analysis, J.R.C.; methodology and validation, P.M. All authors have read and agreed to the published version of the manuscript.

Funding: This research received no external funding.

Institutional Review Board Statement: Not Applicable.

Informed Consent Statement: Not Applicable.

Data Availability Statement: Not applicable.

Acknowledgments: We would like to thank TecNM and Conacyt for their support during the realization of this research.

Conflicts of Interest: The authors declare no conflict of interest.

References

1. Cao, Y.; Raise, A.; Mohammadzadeh, A.; Rathinasamy, S.; Band, S.S.; Mosavi, A. Deep learned recurrent type-3 fuzzy system: Application for renewable energy modeling/prediction. *Energy Rep.* **2021**, *7*, 8115–8127. [CrossRef]
2. Turksen, I.B. From Type 1 to Full Type N Fuzzy System Models. *J. Mult. Valued Log. Soft Comput.* **2014**, *22*, 543–560.
3. Qasem, S.N.; Ahmadian, A.; Mohammadzadeh, A.; Rathinasamy, S.; Pahlevanzadeh, B. A type-3 logic fuzzy system: Optimized by a correntropy based Kalman filter with adaptive fuzzy kernel size. *Inform. Sci.* **2021**, *572*, 424–443. [CrossRef]
4. Rickard, J.T.; Aisbett, J.; Gibbon, G. Fuzzy Subsethood for Fuzzy Sets of Type-2 and Generalized Type-*n*. *IEEE Trans. Fuzzy Syst.* **2008**, *17*, 50–60. [CrossRef]
5. Mohammadzadeh, A.; Sabzalian, M.H.; Zhang, W. An Interval Type-3 Fuzzy System and a New Online Fractional-Order Learning Algorithm: Theory and Practice. *IEEE Trans. Fuzzy Syst.* **2019**, *28*, 1940–1950. [CrossRef]
6. Liu, Z.; Mohammadzadeh, A.; Turabieh, H.; Mafarja, M.; Band, S.S.; Mosavi, A. A New Online Learned Interval Type-3 Fuzzy Control System for Solar Energy Management Systems. *IEEE Access* **2021**, *9*, 10498–10508. [CrossRef]
7. Zadeh, L.A. The Concept of a Linguistic Variable and its Application to Approximate Reasoning. *Inf. Sci.* **1975**, *8*, 43–80. [CrossRef]
8. Zadeh, L.A. Knowledge representation in Fuzzy Logic. *IEEE Trans. Knowl. Data Eng.* **1989**, *1*, 89. [CrossRef]

9. Zadeh, L.A. Fuzzy Logic. *Computer* **1998**, *1*, 83–93.
10. Mendel, J.M. *Uncertain Rule-Based Fuzzy Logic Systems: Introduction and New Directions*; Prentice-Hall: Upper-Saddle River, NJ, USA, 2001.
11. Mendel, J.M. *Uncertain Rule-Based Fuzzy Logic Systems: Introduction and New Directions*, 2nd ed.; Springer: Berlin/Heidelberg, Germany, 2017.
12. Karnik, N.N.; Mendel, J.M. Operations on Type-2 Fuzzy Sets. *Fuzzy Sets Syst.* **2001**, *122*, 327–348. [CrossRef]
13. Moreno, J.E.; Sanchez, M.A.; Mendoza, O.; Rodríguez-Díaz, A.; Castillo, O.; Melin, P.; Castro, J.R. Design of an interval Type-2 fuzzy model with justifiable uncertainty. *Inf. Sci.* **2020**, *513*, 206–221. [CrossRef]
14. Mendel, J.M.; Hagras, H.; Tan, W.-W.; Melek, W.W.; Ying, H. *Introduction to Type-2 Fuzzy Logic Control*; Wiley and IEEE Press: Hoboken, NJ, USA, 2014.
15. Olivas, F.; Valdez, F.; Castillo, O.; Melin, P. Dynamic parameter adaptation in particle swarm optimization using interval type-2 fuzzy logic. *Soft Comput.* **2016**, *20*, 1057–1070. [CrossRef]
16. Sakalli, A.; Kumbasar, T.; Mendel, J.M. Towards Systematic Design of General Type-2 Fuzzy Logic Controllers: Analysis, Interpretation, and Tuning. *IEEE Trans. Fuzzy Syst.* **2021**, *29*, 226–239. [CrossRef]
17. Ontiveros, E.; Melin, P.; Castillo, O. High order α-planes integration: A new approach to computational cost reduction of General Type-2 Fuzzy Systems. *Eng. Appl. Artif. Intell.* **2018**, *74*, 186–197. [CrossRef]
18. Castillo, O.; Amador-Angulo, L. A generalized type-2 fuzzy logic approach for dynamic parameter adaptation in bee colony optimization applied to fuzzy controller design. *Inf. Sci.* **2018**, *460-461*, 476–496. [CrossRef]
19. Precup, R.-E.; Preitl, S.; Petriu, E.; Bojan-Dragos, C.-A.; Szedlak-Stinean, A.-I.; Roman, R.-C.; Hedrea, E.-L. Model-based fuzzy control results for networked control systems. *Rep. Mech. Eng.* **2020**, *1*, 10–25. [CrossRef]
20. Precup, R.-E.; Preitl, S.; Petriu, E.M.; Roman, R.-C.; Bojan-Dragos, C.-A.; Hedrea, E.-L.; Szedlak-Stinean, A.-I. A center manifold theory-based approach to the stability analysis of state feedback takagi-sugeno-kang fuzzy control systems. *Facta Univ. Ser. Mech. Eng.* **2020**, *18*, 189. [CrossRef]
21. Vilela, M.; Oluyemi, G.; Andrei, P. A holistic approach to assessment of value of information (VOI) with fuzzy data and decision criteria. *Decis. Mak. Appl. Manag. Eng.* **2020**, *3*, 97–118. [CrossRef]
22. Castillo, O. Towards Finding the Optimal n in Designing Type-n Fuzzy Systems for Particular Classes of Problems: A Review. *Appl. Comput. Math.* **2018**, *17*, 3–9.
23. Castillo, O.; Melin, P. *Soft Computing and Fractal Theory for Intelligent Manufacturing*; Springer: Heidelberg, Germany, 2003. [CrossRef]
24. Rickard, J.T.; Aisbett, J.; Gibbon, G.; Morgenthaler, D. Fuzzy subsethood for type-n fuzzy sets. In Proceedings of the NAFIPS 2008—2008 Annual Meeting of the North American Fuzzy Information Processing Society, New York, NY, USA, 19–22 May 2008; pp. 1–6.
25. Singh, D.; Verma, N.K.; Ghosh, A.K.; Malagaudanavar, A.K. An Approach Towards the Design of Interval Type-3 T-S Fuzzy System. *IEEE Trans. Fuzzy Syst.* **2021**. [CrossRef]
26. Wang, J.-H.; Tavoosi, J.; Mohammadzadeh, A.; Mobayen, S.; Asad, J.H.; Assawinchaichote, W.; Vu, M.T.; Skruch, P. Non-Singleton Type-3 Fuzzy Approach for Flowmeter Fault Detection: Experimental Study in a Gas Industry. *Sensors* **2021**, *21*, 7419. [CrossRef] [PubMed]
27. Alattas, K.A.; Mohammadzadeh, A.; Mobayen, S.; Aly, A.A.; Felemban, B.F.; Vu, M.T. A New Data-Driven Control System for MEMSs Gyroscopes: Dynamics Estimation by Type-3 Fuzzy Systems. *Micromachines* **2021**, *12*, 1390. [CrossRef] [PubMed]
28. Tian, M.-W.; Mohammadzadeh, A.; Tavoosi, J.; Mobayen, S.; Asad, J.H.; Castillo, O.; Várkonyi-Kóczy, A.R. A Deep-learned Type-3 Fuzzy System and Its Application in Modeling Problems. *Acta Polytech. Hung.* **2022**, *19*, 151–172. [CrossRef]
29. Ma, C.; Mohammadzadeh, A.; Turabieh, H.; Mafarja, M.; Band, S.S.; Mosavi, A. Optimal Type-3 Fuzzy System for Solving Singular Multi-Pantograph Equations. *IEEE Access* **2020**, *8*, 225692–225702. [CrossRef]
30. Gheisarnejad, M.; Mohammadzadeh, A.; Farsizadeh, H.; Khooban, M.-H. Stabilization of 5G Telecom Converter-Based Deep Type-3 Fuzzy Machine Learning Control for Telecom Applications. *IEEE Trans. Circuits Syst. II Express Briefs* **2021**, *69*, 544–548. [CrossRef]
31. Vafaie, R.H.; Mohammadzadeh, A.; Piran, J. A new type-3 fuzzy predictive controller for MEMS gyroscopes. *Nonlinear Dyn.* **2021**, *106*, 381–403. [CrossRef]
32. Tian, M.-W.; Yan, S.-R.; Mohammadzadeh, A.; Tavoosi, J.; Mobayen, S.; Safdar, R.; Assawinchaichote, W.; Vu, M.T.; Zhilenkov, A. Stability of Interval Type-3 Fuzzy Controllers for Autonomous Vehicles. *Mathematics* **2021**, *9*, 2742. [CrossRef]
33. Mohammadzadeh, A.; Castillo, O.; Band, S.S.; Mosavi, A. A Novel Fractional-Order Multiple-Model Type-3 Fuzzy Control for Nonlinear Systems with Unmodeled Dynamics. *Int. J. Fuzzy Syst.* **2021**, *23*, 1633–1651. [CrossRef]
34. Gheisarnejad, M.; Mohammadzadeh, A.; Khooban, M. Model Predictive Control-Based Type-3 Fuzzy Estimator for Voltage Stabilization of DC Power Converters. *IEEE Trans. Ind. Electron.* **2021**. [CrossRef]
35. Taghieh, A.; Aly, A.A.; Felemban, B.F.; Althobaiti, A.; Mohammadzadeh, A.; Bartoszewicz, A. A Hybrid Predictive Type-3 Fuzzy Control for Time-Delay Multi-Agent Systems. *Electronics* **2021**, *11*, 63. [CrossRef]
36. Yan, S.; Aly, A.A.; Felemban, B.F.; Gheisarnejad, M.; Tian, M.; Khooban, M.H.; Mohammadzadeh, A.; Mobayen, S. A New Event-Triggered Type-3 Fuzzy Control System for Multi-Agent Systems: Optimal Economic Efficient Approach for Actuator Activating. *Electronics* **2021**, *10*, 3122. [CrossRef]

37. Nabipour, N.; Qasem, S.N.; Jermsittiparsert, K. Type-3 fuzzy voltage management in PV/Hydrogen fuel cell/battery hybrid systems. *Int. J. Hydrogen Energy* **2020**, *45*, 32478–32492. [CrossRef]
38. Castillo, O.; Castro, J.R.; Melin, P. *Interval Type-3 Fuzzy Systems: Theory and Design*; Springer: Berlin/Heidelberg, Germany, 2022. [CrossRef]
39. Naderipour, M.; Zarandi, M.H.F.; Bastani, S. A fuzzy cluster-validity index based on the topology structure and node attribute in complex networks. *Expert Syst. Appl.* **2021**, *187*, 115913. [CrossRef]
40. Kalhori, M.R.N.; Zarandi, M.H.F. A new interval type-2 fuzzy reasoning method for classification systems based on normal forms of a possibility-based fuzzy measure. *Inf. Sci.* **2021**, *581*, 567–586. [CrossRef]

axioms

MDPI

Article

Analysis of Interval-Valued Intuitionistic Fuzzy Aczel–Alsina Geometric Aggregation Operators and Their Application to Multiple Attribute Decision-Making

Tapan Senapati [1,2], Radko Mesiar [3,4], Vladimir Simic [5], Aiyared Iampan [6,*], Ronnason Chinram [7] and Rifaqat Ali [8]

1 Department of Mathematics, Padima Janakalyan Banipith, Kukrakhupi 721517, India; math.tapan@gmail.com
2 School of Mathematics and Statistics, Southwest University, Beibei, Chongqing 400715, China
3 Faculty of Civil Engineering, Slovak University of Technology, Radlinského 11, Sk-810 05 Bratislava, Slovakia; radko.mesiar@stuba.sk
4 Department Algebra & Geometry, Faculty of Science, Palacky University Olomouc, 17 Listopadu 12, 77146 Olomouc, Czech Republic
5 Department of Transport and Traffic Engineering, University of Belgrade, Vojvode Stepe 305, 11010 Belgrade, Serbia; vsima@sf.bg.ac.rs
6 Department of Mathematics, School of Science, University of Phayao, Mae Ka, Mueang, Phayao 56000, Thailand
7 Division of Computational Science, Faculty of Science, Prince of Songkla University, Hat Yai, Songkhla 90110, Thailand; ronnason.c@psu.ac.th
8 Department of Mathematics, College of Science and Arts, Muhayil, King Khalid University, Abha 61413, Saudi Arabia; rrafat@kku.edu.sa
* Correspondence: aiyared.ia@up.ac.th

Abstract: When dealing with the haziness that is intrinsic in decision analysis-driven decision making procedures, interval-valued intuitionistic fuzzy sets (IVIFSs) can be quite effective. Our approach to solving the multiple attribute decision making (MADM) difficulties, where all of the evidence provided by the decision-makers is demonstrated as interval-valued intuitionistic fuzzy (IVIF) decision matrices, in which all of the components are distinguished by an IVIF number (IVIFN), is based on Aczel–Alsina operational processes. We begin by introducing novel IVIFN operations including the Aczel–Alsina sum, product, scalar multiplication, and exponential. We may then create IVIF aggregation operators, such as the IVIF Aczel–Alsina weighted geometric operator, the IVIF Aczel–Alsina ordered weighted geometric operator, and the IVIF Aczel–Alsina hybrid geometric operator, among others. We present a MADM approach that relies on the IVIF aggregation operators that have been developed. A case study is used to demonstrate the practical applicability of the strategies proposed in this paper. By contrasting the newly developed technique with existing techniques, the method is capable of demonstrating the advantages of the newly developed approach. A key result of this work is the discovery that some of the current IVIF aggregation operators are subsets of the operators reported in this article.

Keywords: MADM; Aczel–Alsina operations; IVIFNs; IVIF Aczel–Alsina geometric aggregation operators

MSC: 90B50; 47S40

Citation: Senapati, T.; Mesiar, R.; Simic, V.; Iampan, A.; Chinram, R.; Ali, R. Analysis of Interval-Valued Intuitionistic Fuzzy Aczel–Alsina Geometric Aggregation Operators and Their Application to Multiple Attribute Decision-Making. *Axioms* **2022**, *11*, 258. https://doi.org/10.3390/axioms11060258

Academic Editor: Oscar Castillo

Received: 30 January 2022
Accepted: 24 May 2022
Published: 29 May 2022

1. Introduction

The intuitionistic fuzzy set [1] was extended by Atanassov and Gargov to the IVIFS [2], which is represented by membership and non-membership functions whose values are intervals rather than real numbers. Due to the advantages of IVIFS, several researchers have attempted to incorporate IVIF information generated by different kinds of operators to generate judgments [3,4]. For instance, Xu [5] constructed several aggregation operators for IVIFNs, including the IVIF weighted averaging (IVIFWA) operator and the IVIF hybrid averaging (IVIFHA) operator. Liu [6] presented two IVIF operators based on the power average and Heronian mean operators and then integrated IVIF information using them. Zhao and Xu [7] provided several novel IVIF aggregation operations. Yu et al. [8] created the IVIF prioritized weighted averaging/geometric operator. Chen and Han [9,10] provided a MADM approach that was built on the multiplication of IVIF values, in addition to the LP and NLP methodologies. The influenced IVIF weighted and ordered weighted geometric operators were invented by Wei et al. [11]. Li [12] suggested a MADM technique using IVIFSs based on TOPSIS-based nonlinear programming (NLP). Xu and Gou [13] discussed the IVIF aggregation operator in detail. Chen et al. [14] developed a variety of MADM techniques based on IVIFSs. The influenced IVIF hybrid Choquet integral operators developed by Meng et al. [15] were used in decision-making issues. Wang and Liu [16,17] recommended the IVIF Einstein weighted averaging and geometric operators. IVIF MADM has already been widely applied in a variety of fields, including hotel location selection [18], air quality evaluation [19], solid waste management [20], hotel location selection [18], sustainable supplier selection [21], potential partner selection [22], and weapon-group target analysis [23].

Schweizer and Sklar pioneered the idea of triangular norms in their theory of empirical metric spaces [24]. As it develops out, t-norms and their associated t-conorms are vital operations in fuzzification and other evolutionary computing, for instance, Lukasiewicz t-norm and t-conorm [25], Hamacher t-norm and t-conorm [26], Einstein t-norm and t-conorm [17], general continuous Archimedean t-norm, t-conorm [27], etc. Klement et al. [28] conducted a thorough examination of the characteristics and concept implications of triangular norms in the latest years.

1.1. Motivation of the Study

Generalizing the ideas of Menger [29] from 1942, Schweizer and Sklar [24] proposed in 1960 the concept of triangular norms, or t-norms. While their methodology was developed within the context of probabilistic metric spaces for the purpose of making generalizations the triangular inequality of metrics, however, within some years they have been considered in several other branches, most notably fuzzy set theory (there, t-norms generate the fuzzy conjunctions, generalizing the original proposal of Zadeh [30] considering the min operation when introducing the intersection of fuzzy sets). Already in the framework of probabilistic metric spaces, but later also to cover the fuzzy disjunctions, the dual operations to t-norms, namely t-conorms were considered [31]. Later, t-norms and t-conorms have been considered in several generalizations of the fuzzy set theory, including intuitionistic fuzzy set theory [1], interval-valued fuzzy set theory and fuzzy type-2 theory [32], IVIFS theory [2], etc. For more details concerning t-norms and t-conorms we highly suggest the monograph [28] due to Klement et al.

Let $F : [0,1]^2 \to [0,1]$ be a commutative, associative and monotone function. Then, if $e = 1$ is its neutral element, $F(x,1) = F(1,x) = x$ for all $x \in [0,1]$, F is called a triangular norm (t-norm in short). Similarly, if $e = 0$ is its neutral element, i.e., $F(x,0) = F(0,x) = x$ for all $x \in [0,1]$, then F is called a triangular t-conorm (t-conorm, in short).

To have a clear distinction for t-norms and t-conorms in notation, we will consider the traditional notation T for t-norms and S for t-conorms. Note that these two classes are dual, i.e., for any t-norm T, the function $S : [0,1]^2 \to [0,1]$ given by $S(x,y) = 1 - T(1-x, 1-y)$ is a t-conorm (also called a t-conorm dual to T), and for any t-conorm S, the function $T : [0,1]^2 \to [0,1]$ determined by $T(x,y) = 1 - S(1-x, 1-y)$ is a t-norm (t-norm dual to S).

It is not difficult to see that the strongest (greatest) t-norm is $T_M(x,y) = min(x,y)$ following the notation from [28], while the smallest t-norm is the drastic product T_D which is vanishing on $[0,1]^2$ (clearly, if $max(x,y) = 1$ then for any t-norm we have $T(x,y) = min(x,y)$). Two prototypical t-norms playing an important role both in theory and applications are the product t-norm T_P (standard product of reals), and the Lukasiewicz

t-norm T_L given by $T_L(x,y) = max(0, x+y-1)$. One of the most distinguished subclasses of the class of all t-norms is formed by the continuous Archimedean t-norms, i.e., t-norms generated by a continuous additive generator. Their importance is clearly visible when n-ary extensions of t-norms are considered. For deeper results and more details see [28]. In our paper, we will deal with some specially generated t-norms, namely with strict t-norms which are isomorphic to the product t-norm, and which are generated by decreasing bijective additive generators $t : [0,1] \to [0,\infty]$. In such a case, $T(x,y) = t^{-1}(t(x)+t(y))$, and, considering the n-array extension (which is unique due to the associativity of t-norms), $T(x_1,\ldots,x_n) = t^{-1}(\sum_{i=1}^{n} t(x_i))$. Recall that both extremal t-norms T_M and T_D, as well as the product t-norm T_P commute with the power functions, i.e., for any $\lambda > 0$, they satisfy the equality $T(x^\lambda, y^\lambda) = T(x,y)^\lambda$. Aczel and Alsina in the early 1980s [33] have characterized all other t-norm solutions of the above functional equation, showing that these are just strict t-norms generated by additive generators $t_{\eth}$, $\eth \in]0,\infty[$, given by $t_{\eth}(x) = (-logx)^{\eth}$. The related t-norms are denoted as $T_A^{\eth}$ and called (strict) Aczel–Alsina t-norms, and given by

$$T_A^{\eth}(x,y) = \begin{cases} T_D(x,y), & \text{if } \eth = 0 \\ \min(x,y), & \text{if } \eth = \infty \\ e^{-((-\log x)^{\eth}+(-\log y)^{\eth})^{1/\eth}}, & \text{otherwise.} \end{cases}$$

Observe that including the extremal t-norms, we obtain their Aczel–Alsina family $(T_A^{\eth})$, $\eth \in [0,\infty]$ of t-norms, which is strictly increasing and continuous in parameter $\eth$.

Due to the duality, similar notes and examples can be introduced for t-conorms. There, the smallest t-conorms is $S_M = max$ (dual to T_M), and the greatest t-conorm is the drastic product S_D, which is constant 1 on $[0,1]^2$. For any t-conorm S, if $min(x,y) = 0$, then $S(x,y) = max(x,y)$. Dual t-conorm S_L to T_L(Lukasiewicz t-conorm, also called a truncated sum) is given by $S_L(x,y) = min(1, x+y)$, and the dual t-conorm S_P to the product T_P (called a probabilistic sum) is given by $S_P(x,y) = x+y-xy$. Continuous Archimedean t-conorms are also generated by additive generators (which are increasing), and if S is dual to a continuous Archimedean t-norm T generated by an additive generator t, then S is generated by an additive generator s given by $s(x) = t(1-x)$. In particular, dual t-conorms $S_A^{\eth}$ to strict Aczel–Alsina t-noms $T_A^{\eth}$ are generated by additive generators $s_{\eth}(x) = (-log(1-x))^{\eth}$, and they are given by

$$S_A^{\eth}(x,y) = \begin{cases} S_D(x,y), & \text{if } \eth = 0 \\ \max(x,y), & \text{if } \eth = \infty \\ 1 - e^{-((-\log(1-x))^{\eth}+(-\log(1-y))^{\eth})^{1/\eth}}, & \text{otherwise.} \end{cases}$$

Observe that including the extremal t-conorms, we obtain their Aczel–Alsina family $(S_A^{\eth})$, $\eth \in [0,\infty]$ of t-conorms, which is strictly decreasing and continuous in parameter $\eth$.

Aczel-Alsina [33] came up with two new operations called Aczel–Alsina t-norm and Aczel-Alsina t-conorm. These operations have a good relationship with the deployment of parameters. Wang et al. [34] used the Aczel-Alsina triangular norm (AA t-norm) to come up with a score level convolution neural network that increases the distance between imposters and legitimate at the same time. Senapati et al. [35–38] came up with Aczel—Alsina operations depending on intuitionistic fuzzy, IVIF, hesitant fuzzy, picture fuzzy aggregation operators, and they used them to solve MADM problems. The primary objective of this insightful article is to illustrate several geometric aggregation operators using IVIF data, known to as IVIF Aczel–Alsina geometric aggregations, for the purpose of identifying the successfully guide of decisions made utilizing decision-making techniques. Unaware of the previously existing unique ways that have been developed in this domain, we have fully examined every possibility to exhibit our proposed approach, in order for it to exceed all past attempts to apprehend the system assessment problem.

1.2. Structure of This Study

The framework of the study is presented in Figure 1. The following details are presented: The next section discusses several basic concepts relating to IVIFSs. Section 3 discusses the Aczel–Alsina operational laws governing the IVIFNs. Section 4 discusses the IVIF Aczel–Alsina weighted geometric (IVIFAAWG) operator, the IVIF Aczel–Alsina order weighted geometric (IVIFAAOWG) operator, and the IVIF Aczel–Alsina hybrid geometric (IVIFAAHG) operator, as well as a few particular instances. In Section 5, we demonstrate how to use the IVIFAAWG operator to construct particular approaches for resolving multiple attribute decision-making challenges in which support and understanding are represented as IVIF values. Section 6 shows the overall methodology with a genuine scenario. Section 7 investigates the effect of a parameter on the outcome of decision-making. Section 8 provides a comparison investigation of alternative important strategies to substantiate the suggested technique's sufficiency. Section 9 concludes this analysis and identifies potential future concerns.

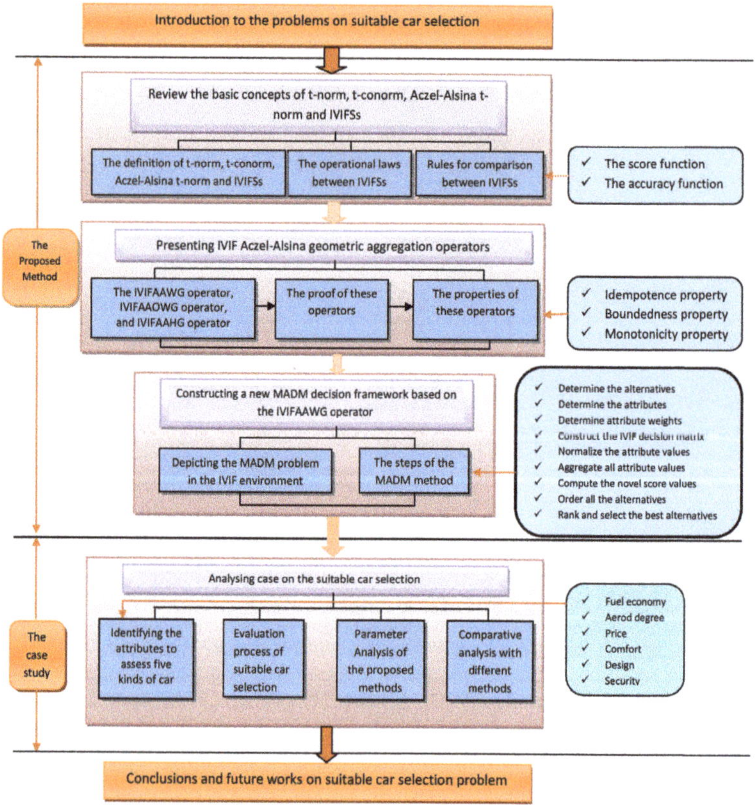

Figure 1. The framework of the study.

2. Preliminaries

This section will summarize some major themes that will be discussed throughout the remainder of this work.

Definition 1 ([2]). *Assuming F is a recognized universe of discourse, an IVIFS in F is an expression $\tilde{E}$ given by*

$$\tilde{E} = \{\langle f, \tilde{\beta}_E(f), \tilde{\delta}_E(f)\rangle : f \in F\} \quad (1)$$

where $\tilde{\beta}_E(f) : F \to D[0,1]$, $\tilde{\delta}_E(f) : F \to D[0,1]$ *and* $D[0,1]$ *is the set of all subintervals of* $[0,1]$. *The intervals* $\tilde{\beta}_E(f)$ *and* $\tilde{\delta}_E(f)$ *denote the intervals of the degree of membership and degree of non-membership of the element* f *in the set* $\tilde{E}$, *where* $\tilde{\beta}_E(f) = [\beta_E^L(f), \beta_E^U(f)]$ *and* $\tilde{\delta}_E(f) = [\delta_E^L(f), \delta_E^U(f)]$, *for all* $f \in F$, *including the condition* $0 \le \beta_E^U(f) + \delta_E^U(f) \le 1$. $\pi_E(f) = [\pi_E^L(f), \pi_E^U(f)]$ *denotes the indeterminacy degree of element* f *that belongs to* $\tilde{E}$, *where* $\pi_E^L(f) = 1 - \beta_E^U(f) - \delta_E^U(f)$ *and* $\pi_E^U(f) = 1 - \beta_E^L(f) - \delta_E^L(f)$.

Assume that $\tilde{E} = \{\langle f, \tilde{\beta}_E(f), \tilde{\delta}_E(f)\rangle : f \in F\}$ and $\tilde{W} = \{\langle f, \tilde{\beta}_W(f), \tilde{\delta}_W(f)\rangle : f \in F\}$ are two IFSs over the universe F. The next relations and operations concerning two IVIFSs were described as follows [2,25]:

(i) $\tilde{E} \subseteq \tilde{W}$, if $\beta_E^L(f) \le \beta_W^L(f)$, $\beta_E^U(f) \le \beta_W^U(f)$, $\delta_E^L(f) \ge \delta_W^L(f)$, and $\delta_E^U(f) \ge \delta_W^U(f)$ for all $f \in F$;

(ii) $\tilde{E} = \tilde{W}$ iff $\tilde{E} \subseteq \tilde{W}$ and $\tilde{W} \subseteq \tilde{E}$;

(iii) $\tilde{E}^C = \{\langle f, \tilde{\delta}_E(f), \tilde{\beta}_E(f)\rangle | f \in F\}$ for all $f \in F$;

(iv) $\tilde{E} \cap_{T,S} \tilde{W} = \{\langle f, [T\{\beta_E^L(f), \beta_W^L(f)\}, T\{\beta_E^U(f), \beta_W^U(f)\}], [S\{\delta_E^L(f), \delta_W^L(f)\}, S\{\delta_E^U(f), \delta_W^U (f)\}]\rangle | f \in F\}$;

(v) $\tilde{E} \cup_{S,T} \tilde{W} = \{\langle f, [S\{\beta_E^L(f), \beta_W^L(f)\}, S\{\beta_E^U(f), \beta_W^U(f)\}], [T\{\delta_E^L(f), \delta_W^L(f)\}, T\{\delta_E^U(f), \delta_W^U (f)\}]\rangle | f \in F\}$;

where any pair (T, S) can be utilized, T indicates a t-norm and S a so-called t-conorm dual to the t-norm T, characterized by $S(x,y) = 1 - T(1-x, 1-y)$.

For convenience, Xu [5] called $\tilde{\eth} = ([\beta_{\eth}^L, \beta_{\eth}^U], [\delta_{\eth}^L, \delta_{\eth}^U])$ an IVIFN, where $[\beta_{\eth}^L, \beta_{\eth}^U] \in D[0,1]$, $[\delta_{\eth}^L, \delta_{\eth}^U] \in D[0,1]$ and $\beta_{\eth}^U + \delta_{\eth}^U \le 1$.

For any three IVIFNs $\tilde{\eth} = ([\beta_{\eth}^L, \beta_{\eth}^U], [\delta_{\eth}^L, \delta_{\eth}^U])$, $\tilde{\eth}_1 = ([\beta_{\eth_1}^L, \beta_{\eth_1}^U], [\delta_{\eth_1}^L, \delta_{\eth_1}^U])$ and $\tilde{\eth}_2 = ([\beta_{\eth_2}^L, \beta_{\eth_2}^U], [\delta_{\eth_2}^L, \delta_{\eth_2}^U])$, Xu [5] and Xu and Chen [39] stated a few operations as follows:

(i) $\tilde{\eth}_1 \cap \tilde{\eth}_2 = ([\min\{\beta_{\eth_1}^L, \beta_{\eth_2}^L\}, \min\{\beta_{\eth_1}^U, \beta_{\eth_2}^U\}], [\max\{\delta_{\eth_1}^L, \delta_{\eth_2}^L\}, \max\{\delta_{\eth_1}^U, \delta_{\eth_2}^U\}])$;

(ii) $\tilde{\eth}_1 \cup \tilde{\eth}_2 = ([\max\{\beta_{\eth_1}^L, \beta_{\eth_2}^L\}, \max\{\beta_{\eth_1}^U, \beta_{\eth_2}^U\}], [\min\{\delta_{\eth_1}^L, \delta_{\eth_2}^L\}, \min\{\delta_{\eth_1}^U, \delta_{\eth_2}^U\}])$;

(iii) $\tilde{\eth}_1 \oplus \tilde{\eth}_2 = ([\beta_{\eth_1}^L + \beta_{\eth_2}^L - \beta_{\eth_1}^L\beta_{\eth_2}^L, \beta_{\eth_1}^U + \beta_{\eth_2}^U - \beta_{\eth_1}^U\beta_{\eth_2}^U], [\delta_{\eth_1}^L\delta_{\eth_2}^L, \delta_{\eth_1}^U\delta_{\eth_2}^U])$;

(iv) $\tilde{\eth}_1 \otimes \tilde{\eth}_2 = ([\beta_{\eth_1}^L\beta_{\eth_2}^L, \beta_{\eth_1}^U\beta_{\eth_2}^U], [\delta_{\eth_1}^L + \delta_{\eth_2}^L - \delta_{\eth_1}^L\delta_{\eth_2}^L, \delta_{\eth_1}^U + \delta_{\eth_2}^U - \delta_{\eth_1}^U\delta_{\eth_2}])$;

(v) $\varphi \cdot \tilde{\eth} = ([1 - (1-\beta_{\eth}^L)^{\varphi}, 1 - (1-\beta_{\eth}^U)^{\varphi}], [(\delta_{\eth}^L)^{\varphi}, (\delta_{\eth}^U)^{\varphi}])$, $\varphi > 0$;

(vi) $\tilde{\eth}^{\varphi} = ([(\beta_{\eth}^L)^{\varphi}, (\beta_{\eth}^U)^{\varphi}], [1 - (1-\delta_{\eth}^L)^{\varphi}, 1 - (1-\delta_{\eth}^U)^{\varphi}])$, $\varphi > 0$.

Several indices [5,40] were used to characterize IVIFN.

Definition 2 ([40]). *For any IVIFN* $\tilde{\eth} = ([\beta_{\eth}^L, \beta_{\eth}^U], [\delta_{\eth}^L, \delta_{\eth}^U])$, *the score function* $Sco(\tilde{\eth})$, *accuracy function* $Acc(\tilde{\eth})$, *membership uncertainty index* $Mui(\tilde{\eth})$ *and hesitation uncertainty index* $Hui(\tilde{\eth})$ *of* $\eth$ *be defined as follows:*

$$Sco(\tilde{\eth}) = \frac{1}{2}(\beta_{\eth}^L + \beta_{\eth}^U - \delta_{\eth}^L - \delta_{\eth}^U), \tag{2}$$

$$Acc(\tilde{\eth}) = \frac{1}{2}(\beta_{\eth}^L + \beta_{\eth}^U + \delta_{\eth}^L + \delta_{\eth}^U), \tag{3}$$

$$Mui(\tilde{\eth}) = \beta_{\eth}^U + \delta_{\eth}^L - \beta_{\eth}^L - \delta_{\eth}^U, \tag{4}$$

$$Hui(\tilde{\eth}) = \beta_{\eth}^U + \delta_{\eth}^U - \beta_{\eth}^L - \delta_{\eth}^L. \tag{5}$$

Based on these indices of IVIFNs, the total ordering [40] on IVIFNs was defined as follows.

Definition 3. *Let* $\tilde{\eth}_1 = ([\beta_{\eth_1}^L, \beta_{\eth_1}^U], [\delta_{\eth_1}^L, \delta_{\eth_1}^U])$ *and* $\tilde{\eth}_2 = ([\beta_{\eth_2}^L, \beta_{\eth_2}^U], [\delta_{\eth_2}^L, \delta_{\eth_2}^U])$ *be two IVIFNs, then*

(1) *if* $Sco(\tilde{\eth}_1) < Sco(\tilde{\eth}_2)$, *then* $\tilde{\eth}_1 < \tilde{\eth}_2$,

(2) *if* $Sco(\tilde{\eth}_1) = Sco(\tilde{\eth}_2)$, *then*

   (a) *if* $Acc(\tilde{\eth}_1) < Acc(\tilde{\eth}_2)$, *then* $\tilde{\eth}_1 < \tilde{\eth}_2$,

   (b) *if* $Acc(\tilde{\eth}_1) = Acc(\tilde{\eth}_2)$, *then*

(I) *if* $Mui(\tilde{\eth}_1) < Mui(\tilde{\eth}_2)$, *then* $\tilde{\eth}_1 < \tilde{\eth}_2$,
(II) *if* $Mui(\tilde{\eth}_1) = Mui(\tilde{\eth}_2)$, *then*
  (i) *if* $Hui(\tilde{\eth}_1) < Hui(\tilde{\eth}_2)$, *then* $\tilde{\eth}_1 < \tilde{\eth}_2$,
  (ii) *if* $Hui(\tilde{\eth}_1) = Hui(\tilde{\eth}_2)$, *then* $\tilde{\eth}_1$ *and* $\tilde{\eth}_2$ *are same, i.e.,* $\beta^L_{\eth_1} = \beta^L_{\eth_2}$, $\beta^U_{\eth_1} = \beta^U_{\eth_2}$, $\delta^L_{\eth_1} = \delta^L_{\eth_2}$ *and* $\delta^U_{\eth_1} = \delta^U_{\eth_2}$, *denoted by* $\tilde{\eth}_1 = \tilde{\eth}_2$.

Definition 3 defines a way to compare two IVIFNs by prioritizing the functions of score, accuracy, membership uncertainty index, and hesitation uncertainty index. Because once two IVIFNs are analyzed, the sequencing is examined in the following order: general belonging degree, accuracy or hesitation level, membership uncertainty index, and hesitation uncertainty index. This comparative procedure is repeated unless one of the four functions defined in Definition 3 recognizes the two IVIFNs. When these two IVIFNs are distinguished at a particular level of severity, the computation is completed and functions with lower value levels are not computed.

Deschrijver et al. [41] designed the concept of the notion of non-empty intervals. They denoted by L the lattice of non-empty intervals $L = \{[m,n] | (m,n) \in [0,1]^2, m \leq n\}$ with the partial order $\leq_L$ determined as $[m,n] \leq_L [p,q] \Leftrightarrow m \leq p$ and $n \leq q$. The inferior and superior elements are denoted by the symbol $0_L = [0,0]$ and $1_L = [1,1]$, respectively.

In this specific situation, Wang and Liu [16,17] meant by $L^\star$ the lattice of non-empty IVIFNs $L^\star = \{\langle[m,n],[p,q]\rangle | [m,n],[p,q] \in D[0,1], n+q \leq 1\}$ with the partial order $\leq_{L^\star}$ characterized as $\langle[m_1,n_1],[p_1,q_1]\rangle \leq_{L^\star} \langle[m_2,n_2],[p_2,q_2]\rangle \Leftrightarrow [m_1,n_1] \leq_L [m_2,n_2] \& [p_2,q_2] \leq_L [p_1,q_1] \Leftrightarrow m_1 \leq m_2, n_1 \leq n_2, p_1 \geq p_2$ and $q_1 \geq q_2$, where the inferior and superior elements are $0_{L^\star} = \langle 0_L, 1_L\rangle = \langle[0,0],[1,1]\rangle$ and $1_{L^\star} = \langle 1_L, 0_L\rangle = \langle[1,1],[0,0]\rangle$, respectively.

Remark 1. *If* $\alpha \leq_{L^\star} \nu$, *then* $\alpha \leq \nu$, *i.e., the total order consists of the standard partial order on* $L^\star$.

Definition 4. $g_{L^\star} : (L^\star)^\hbar \to L^\star$ *is an aggregation function if it is monotone with respect to* $\leq_{L^\star}$ *and satisfies* $g_{L^\star}(0_{L^\star},\ldots,0_{L^\star}) = 0_{L^\star}$ *and* $g_{L^\star}(1_{L^\star},\ldots,1_{L^\star}) = 1_{L^\star}$.

Currently, a wide number of operators are now being developed for accumulating IVIF data in $L^\star$ [42,43]. The IVIF weighted geometric (IVIFWG) operator and the IVIF ordered weighted geometric (IVIFOWG) operator are probably the most frequently acknowledged operators for accumulating inputs, and they are discussed in details in the following.

Definition 5. *Let* $\tilde{\eth}_\zeta = ([\beta^L_{\eth_\zeta}, \beta^U_{\eth_\zeta}], [\delta^L_{\eth_\zeta}, \delta^U_{\eth_\zeta}])$ $(\zeta = 1,2,\ldots,\hbar)$ *be an accumulation of IVIFNs and* $\xi = (\xi_1, \xi_2, \ldots, \xi_\hbar)^T$ *is the weight vector of* $\eth_\zeta$ $(\zeta = 1,2,\ldots,\hbar)$ *so as* $\xi_\zeta \in [0,1]$, $\zeta = 1,2,\ldots,\hbar$ *and* $\sum_{\zeta=1}^{\hbar} \xi_\zeta = 1$. *Therefore, the IVIF weighted geometric (IVIFWG) operator of dimension* $\hbar$ *is a function* $IVIFWG : (L^\star)^\hbar \to L^\star$ *and* $IVIFWG(\tilde{\eth}_1, \tilde{\eth}_2, \ldots, \tilde{\eth}_\hbar) = \bigotimes_{\zeta=1}^{\hbar} (\tilde{\eth}_\zeta)^{\xi_\zeta}$

$$= \left(\left[\prod_{\zeta=1}^{\hbar} (\beta^L_{\eth_\zeta})^{\xi_\zeta}, \prod_{\zeta=1}^{\hbar} (\beta^U_{\eth_\zeta})^{\xi_\zeta}\right], \left[1 - \prod_{\zeta=1}^{\hbar} (1 - \delta^L_{\eth_\zeta})^{\xi_\zeta}, 1 - \prod_{\zeta=1}^{\hbar} (1 - \delta^U_{\eth_\zeta})^{\xi_\zeta}\right]\right).$$

Definition 6. *Let* $\tilde{\eth}_\zeta = ([\beta^L_{\eth_\zeta}, \beta^U_{\eth_\zeta}], [\delta^L_{\eth_\zeta}, \delta^U_{\eth_\zeta}])$ $(\zeta = 1,2,\ldots,\hbar)$ *be a collection of IVIFNs and* $\xi = (\xi_1, \xi_2, \ldots, \xi_\hbar)^T$ *is the weight vector of* $\eth_\zeta$ $(\zeta = 1,2,\ldots,\hbar)$ *so as* $\xi_\zeta \in [0,1]$, $\zeta = 1,2,\ldots,\hbar$ *and* $\sum_{\zeta=1}^{\hbar} \xi_\zeta = 1$. *Then, the IVIF ordered weighted geometric (IVIFOWG) operator of dimension* $\hbar$ *is a function* $IVIFOWG : (L^\star)^\hbar \to L^\star$ *and* $IVIFOWG(\tilde{\eth}_1, \tilde{\eth}_2, \ldots, \tilde{\eth}_\hbar) = \bigotimes_{\zeta=1}^{\hbar} (\tilde{\eth}_{\varrho(j)})^{\xi_\zeta}$

$$= \left(\left[\prod_{\zeta=1}^{\hbar} (\beta^L_{\eth_{\varrho(j)}})^{\xi_\zeta}, \prod_{\zeta=1}^{\hbar} (\beta^U_{\eth_{\varrho(j)}})^{\xi_\zeta}\right], \left[1 - \prod_{\zeta=1}^{\hbar} (1 - \delta^L_{\eth_{\varrho(j)}})^{\xi_\zeta}, 1 - \prod_{\zeta=1}^{\hbar} (1 - \delta^U_{\eth_{\varrho(j)}})^{\xi_\zeta}\right]\right).$$

3. Aczel–Alsina Operations of IVIFNs

This section will introduce the Aczel–Alsina operations on IVIFNs and discuss some of its fundamental properties.

If you let the t-norm T be the Aczel–Alsina product T_A and the t-conorm S be the Aczel–Alsina sum S_A, the generalized intersection and union over two IVIFNs E and W are the Aczel–Alsina product $(E \otimes W)$ and Aczel–Alsina sum $(E \oplus W)$ over two IVIFNs E and W, respectively, which can be seen:

$$\begin{aligned} E \otimes W &= \left\langle \left[T_A\{\beta_E^L, \beta_W^L\}, T_A\{\beta_E^U, \beta_W^U\}\right], \left[S_A\{\delta_E^L, \delta_W^L\}, S_A\{\delta_E^U, \delta_W^U\}\right] \right\rangle \\ E \oplus W &= \left\langle \left[S_A\{\beta_E^L, \beta_W^L\}, S_A\{\beta_E^U, \beta_W^U\}\right], \left[T_A\{\delta_E^L, \delta_W^L\}, T_A\{\delta_E^U, \delta_W^U\}\right] \right\rangle. \end{aligned}$$

Proposition 1. *Let* $\tilde{\eth}_1 = ([\beta_{\tilde{\eth}_1}^L, \beta_{\tilde{\eth}_1}^U], [\delta_{\tilde{\eth}_1}^L, \delta_{\tilde{\eth}_1}^U])$ *and* $\tilde{\eth}_2 = ([\beta_{\tilde{\eth}_2}^L, \beta_{\tilde{\eth}_2}^U], [\delta_{\tilde{\eth}_2}^L, \delta_{\tilde{\eth}_2}^U])$ *be two IVIFNs,* $\eth \in [0, \infty]$ *and* $\varphi > 0$. *Then, the Aczel–Alsina t-norm and t-conorm operations of IVIFNs are assigned as:*

(i) $\tilde{\eth}_1 \oplus \tilde{\eth}_2 = \left\langle \left[1 - e^{-((-\log(1-\beta_{\tilde{\eth}_1}^L))^{\eth} + (-\log(1-\beta_{\tilde{\eth}_2}^L))^{\eth})^{1/\eth}}, 1 - e^{-((-\log(1-\beta_{\tilde{\eth}_1}^U))^{\eth} + (-\log(1-\beta_{\tilde{\eth}_2}^U))^{\eth})^{1/\eth}}\right], \left[e^{-((-\log \delta_{\tilde{\eth}_1}^L)^{\eth} + (-\log \delta_{\tilde{\eth}_2}^L)^{\eth})^{1/\eth}}, e^{-((-\log \delta_{\tilde{\eth}_1}^U)^{\eth} + (-\log \delta_{\tilde{\eth}_2}^U)^{\eth})^{1/\eth}}\right] \right\rangle,$

(ii) $\tilde{\eth}_1 \otimes \tilde{\eth}_2 = \left\langle \left[e^{-((-\log \beta_{\tilde{\eth}_1}^L)^{\eth} + (-\log \beta_{\tilde{\eth}_2}^L)^{\eth})^{1/\eth}}, e^{-((-\log \beta_{\tilde{\eth}_1}^U)^{\eth} + (-\log \beta_{\tilde{\eth}_2}^U)^{\eth})^{1/\eth}}\right], \left[1 - e^{-((-\log(1-\delta_{\tilde{\eth}_1}^L))^{\eth} + (-\log(1-\delta_{\tilde{\eth}_2}^L))^{\eth})^{1/\eth}}, 1 - e^{-((-\log(1-\delta_{\tilde{\eth}_1}^U))^{\eth} + (-\log(1-\delta_{\tilde{\eth}_2}^U))^{\eth})^{1/\eth}}\right] \right\rangle,$

Definition 7. *Let* $\tilde{\eth} = ([\beta_{\tilde{\eth}}^L, \beta_{\tilde{\eth}}^U], [\delta_{\tilde{\eth}}^L, \beta_{\tilde{\eth}}^U])$ *be a IVIFN,* $\eth \in [0, \infty]$ *and* $\varphi > 0$. *Then, the following two operations of IVIFNs are defined as:*

(i) $\varphi\tilde{\eth} = \left\langle \left[1 - e^{-(\varphi(-\log(1-\beta_{\tilde{\eth}}^L))^{\eth})^{1/\eth}}, 1 - e^{-(\varphi(-\log(1-\beta_{\tilde{\eth}}^U))^{\eth})^{1/\eth}}\right], \left[e^{-(\varphi(-\log \delta_{\tilde{\eth}}^L)^{\eth})^{1/\eth}}, e^{-(\varphi(-\log \delta_{\tilde{\eth}}^U)^{\eth})^{1/\eth}}\right] \right\rangle,$

(ii) $\tilde{\eth}^{\varphi} = \left\langle \left[e^{-(\varphi(-\log \beta_{\tilde{\eth}}^L)^{\eth})^{1/\eth}}, e^{-(\varphi(-\log \beta_{\tilde{\eth}}^U)^{\eth})^{1/\eth}}\right], \left[1 - e^{-(\varphi(-\log(1-\delta_{\tilde{\eth}}^L))^{\eth})^{1/\eth}}, 1 - e^{-(\varphi(-\log(1-\delta_{\tilde{\eth}}^U))^{\eth})^{1/\eth}} \right\rangle.$

Example 1. *Let* $\tilde{\eth} = ([0.55, 0.60], [0.35, 0.40])$, $\tilde{\eth}_1 = ([0.75, 0.80], [0.15, 0.20])$ *and* $\tilde{\eth}_2 = ([0.35, 0.45], [0.45, 0.50])$ *be three IVIFNs, then applying Aczel–Alsina operation on IVIFNs as specified in Proposition 1 and Definition 7 for* $\eth = 3$ *and* $\varphi = 2$, *we get*

(i) $\tilde{\eth}_1 \oplus \tilde{\eth}_2 = \left\langle \left[1 - e^{-((-\log(1-0.75))^3 + (-\log(1-0.35))^3)^{1/3}}, 1 - e^{-((-\log(1-0.80))^3 + (-\log(1-0.45))^3)^{1/3}}\right], \left[e^{-((-\log 0.15)^3 + (-\log 0.45)^3)^{1/3}}, e^{-((-\log 0.20)^3 + (-\log 0.50)^3)^{1/3}}\right] \right\rangle = ([0.75341, 0.80534], [0.14325, 0.19182]).$

(ii) $\tilde{\eth}_1 \otimes \tilde{\eth}_2 = \left\langle \left[e^{-((-\log 0.75)^3 + (-\log 0.35)^3)^{1/3}}, e^{-((-\log 0.80)^3 + (-\log 0.45)^3)^{1/3}}\right], \left[1 - e^{-((-\log(1-0.15))^3 + (-\log(1-0.45))^3)^{1/3}}, 1 - e^{-((-\log(1-0.20))^3 + (-\log(1-0.50))^3)^{1/3}}\right] \right\rangle = ([0.34751, 0.44741], [0.45218, 0.50380]).$

(iii) $2\tilde{\eth} = \left\langle \left[1 - e^{-(2(-\log(1-0.55))^3)^{1/3}}, 1 - e^{-(2(-\log(1-0.60))^3)^{1/3}}\right], \left[e^{-(2(-\log 0.35)^3)^{1/3}}, e^{-(2(-\log 0.40)^3)^{1/3}}\right] \right\rangle = ([0.63434, 0.68477], [0.26642, 0.31523]).$

(iv) $\tilde{\eth}^2 = \left\langle \left[e^{-(2(-\log 0.55)^3)^{1/3}}, e^{-(2(-\log 0.60)^3)^{1/3}}\right], \left[1 - e^{-(2(-\log(1-0.35))^3)^{1/3}}, 1 - e^{-(2(-\log(1-0.40))^3)^{1/3}}\right] \right\rangle = ([0.47084, 0.52540], [0.41885, 0.47460]).$

Theorem 1. *Let* $\tilde{\eth} = ([\beta^L_{\eth}, \beta^U_{\eth}], [\delta^L_{\eth}, \beta^U_{\eth}])$, $\tilde{\eth}_1 = ([\beta^L_{\eth_1}, \beta^U_{\eth_1}], [\delta^L_{\eth_1}, \delta^U_{\eth_1}])$, *and* $\tilde{\eth}_2 = ([\beta^L_{\eth_2}, \beta^U_{\eth_2}], [\delta^L_{\eth_2}, \delta^U_{\eth_2}])$ *be three IVIFNs, then we have*

(i) $\tilde{\eth}_1 \oplus \tilde{\eth}_2 = \tilde{\eth}_2 \oplus \tilde{\eth}_1$;
(ii) $\tilde{\eth}_1 \otimes \tilde{\eth}_2 = \tilde{\eth}_2 \otimes \tilde{\eth}_1$;
(iii) $\varphi(\tilde{\eth}_1 \oplus \tilde{\eth}_2) = \varphi\tilde{\eth}_1 \oplus \varphi\tilde{\eth}_2$, $\varphi > 0$;
(iv) $(\varphi_1 + \varphi_2)\tilde{\eth} = \varphi_1\tilde{\eth} \oplus \varphi_2\tilde{\eth}$, $\varphi_1, \varphi_2 > 0$;
(v) $(\tilde{\eth}_1 \otimes \tilde{\eth}_2)^{\varphi} = \tilde{\eth}_1^{\varphi} \otimes \tilde{\eth}_2^{\varphi}$, $\varphi > 0$;
(vi) $\tilde{\eth}^{\varphi_1} \otimes \tilde{\eth}^{\varphi_2} = \tilde{\eth}^{(\varphi_1+\varphi_2)}$, $\varphi_1, \varphi_2 > 0$.

Proof. For the three IVIFNs $\tilde{\eth}$, $\tilde{\eth}_1$ and $\tilde{\eth}_2$, $\eth \in [0, \infty]$, and $\varphi, \varphi_1, \varphi_2 > 0$, as stated in Proposition 1 and Definition 7, we can get

(i) $\tilde{\eth}_1 \oplus \tilde{\eth}_2 = \Big\langle \Big[1 - e^{-((-\log(1-\beta^L_{\eth_1}))^{\eth} + (-\log(1-\beta^L_{\eth_2}))^{\eth})^{1/\eth}}, 1 - e^{-((-\log(1-\beta^U_{\eth_1}))^{\eth} + (-\log(1-\beta^U_{\eth_2}))^{\eth})^{1/\eth}}\Big], \Big[e^{-((-\log \delta^L_{\eth_1})^{\eth} + (-\log \delta^L_{\eth_2})^{\eth})^{1/\eth}}, e^{-((-\log \delta^U_{\eth_1})^{\eth} + (-\log \delta^U_{\eth_2})^{\eth})^{1/\eth}}\Big]\Big\rangle = \Big\langle \Big[1 - e^{-((-\log(1-\beta^L_{\eth_2}))^{\eth} + (-\log(1-\beta^L_{\eth_1}))^{\eth})^{1/\eth}}, 1 - e^{-((-\log(1-\beta^U_{\eth_2}))^{\eth} + (-\log(1-\beta^U_{\eth_1}))^{\eth})^{1/\eth}}\Big], \Big[e^{-((-\log \delta^L_{\eth_2})^{\eth} + (-\log \delta^L_{\eth_1})^{\eth})^{1/\eth}}, e^{-((-\log \delta^U_{\eth_2})^{\eth} + (-\log \delta^U_{\eth_1})^{\eth})^{1/\eth}}\Big]\Big\rangle = \tilde{\eth}_2 \oplus \tilde{\eth}_1$.

(ii) It is simple.

(iii) Let $t = 1 - e^{-((-\log(1-\beta^L_{\eth_1}))^{\eth} + (-\log(1-\beta^L_{\eth_2}))^{\eth})^{1/\eth}}$.
Then, $\log(1-t) = -((-\log(1-\beta^L_{\eth_1}))^{\eth} + (-\log(1-\beta^L_{\eth_2}))^{\eth})^{1/\eth}$.
Using this, we get $\varphi(\tilde{\eth}_1 \oplus \tilde{\eth}_2) = \varphi\Big\langle \Big[1 - e^{-((-\log(1-\beta^L_{\eth_1}))^{\eth} + (-\log(1-\beta^L_{\eth_2}))^{\eth})^{1/\eth}}, 1 - e^{-((-\log(1-\beta^U_{\eth_1}))^{\eth} + (-\log(1-\beta^U_{\eth_2}))^{\eth})^{1/\eth}}\Big], \Big[e^{-((-\log \delta^L_{\eth_1})^{\eth} + (-\log \delta^L_{\eth_2})^{\eth})^{1/\eth}}, e^{-((-\log \delta^U_{\eth_1})^{\eth} + (-\log \delta^U_{\eth_2})^{\eth})^{1/\eth}}\Big]\Big\rangle = \Big\langle \Big[1 - e^{-(\varphi((-\log(1-\beta^L_{\eth_1}))^{\eth} + (-\log(1-\beta^L_{\eth_2}))^{\eth})^{1/\eth}}, 1 - e^{-(\varphi((-\log(1-\beta^U_{\eth_1}))^{\eth} + (-\log(1-\beta^U_{\eth_2}))^{\eth})^{1/\eth}}\Big], \Big[e^{-(\varphi((-\log \delta^L_{\eth_1})^{\eth} + (-\log \delta^L_{\eth_2})^{\eth}))^{1/\eth}}, e^{-(\varphi((-\log \delta^U_{\eth_1})^{\eth} + (-\log \delta^U_{\eth_2})^{\eth}))^{1/\eth}}\Big]\Big\rangle = \Big\langle \Big[1 - e^{-(\varphi(-\log(1-\beta^L_{\eth_1}))^{\eth})^{1/\eth}}, 1 - e^{-(\varphi(-\log(1-\beta^U_{\eth_1}))^{\eth})^{1/\eth}}\Big], \Big[e^{-(\varphi(-\log \delta^L_{\eth_1})^{\eth})^{1/\eth}}, e^{-(\varphi(-\log \delta^U_{\eth_1})^{\eth})^{1/\eth}}\Big]\Big\rangle \oplus \Big\langle \Big[1 - e^{-(\varphi(-\log(1-\beta^L_{\eth_2}))^{\eth})^{1/\eth}}, 1 - e^{-(\varphi(-\log(1-\beta^U_{\eth_2}))^{\eth})^{1/\eth}}\Big], \Big[e^{-(\varphi(-\log \delta^L_{\eth_2})^{\eth})^{1/\eth}}, e^{-(\varphi(-\log \delta^U_{\eth_2})^{\eth})^{1/\eth}}\Big]\Big\rangle = \varphi\tilde{\eth}_1 \oplus \varphi\tilde{\eth}_2$.

(iv) $\varphi_1\tilde{\eth} \oplus \varphi_2\tilde{\eth} = \Big\langle \Big[1 - e^{-(\varphi_1(-\log(1-\beta^L_{\eth}))^{\eth})^{1/\eth}}, 1 - e^{-(\varphi_1(-\log(1-\beta^U_{\eth}))^{\eth})^{1/\eth}}\Big], \Big[e^{-(\varphi_1(-\log \delta^L_{\eth})^{\eth})^{1/\eth}}, e^{-(\varphi_1(-\log \delta^U_{\eth})^{\eth})^{1/\eth}}\Big]\Big\rangle \oplus \Big\langle \Big[1 - e^{-(\varphi_2(-\log(1-\beta^L_{\eth}))^{\eth})^{1/\eth}}, 1 - e^{-(\varphi_2(-\log(1-\beta^U_{\eth}))^{\eth})^{1/\eth}}\Big], \Big[e^{-(\varphi_2(-\log \delta^L_{\eth})^{\eth})^{1/\eth}}, e^{-(\varphi_2(-\log \delta^U_{\eth})^{\eth})^{1/\eth}}\Big]\Big\rangle$
$= \Big\langle \Big[1 - e^{-((\varphi_1+\varphi_2)(-\log(1-\beta^L_{\eth}))^{\eth})^{1/\eth}}, 1 - e^{-((\varphi_1+\varphi_2)(-\log(1-\beta^U_{\eth}))^{\eth})^{1/\eth}}\Big], \Big[e^{-((\varphi_1+\varphi_2)(-\log \delta^L_{\eth})^{\eth})^{1/\eth}}, e^{-((\varphi_1+\varphi_2)(-\log \delta^U_{\eth})^{\eth})^{1/\eth}}\Big]\Big\rangle = (\varphi_1 + \varphi_2)\tilde{\eth}$.

(v) $(\tilde{\eth}_1 \otimes \tilde{\eth}_2)^{\varphi} = \Big\langle \Big[e^{-((-\log \beta^L_{\eth_1})^{\eth} + (-\log \beta^L_{\eth_2})^{\eth})^{1/\eth}}, e^{-((-\log \beta^U_{\eth_1})^{\eth} + (-\log \beta^U_{\eth_2})^{\eth})^{1/\eth}}\Big], \Big[1 - e^{-((-\log(1-\delta^L_{\eth_1}))^{\eth} + (-\log(1-\delta^L_{\eth_2}))^{\eth})^{1/\eth}}, 1 - e^{-((-\log(1-\delta^U_{\eth_1}))^{\eth} + (-\log(1-\delta^U_{\eth_2}))^{\eth})^{1/\eth}}\Big]\Big\rangle^{\varphi} = \Big\langle \Big[e^{-(\varphi((-\log \beta^L_{\eth_1})^{\eth} + (-\log \beta^L_{\eth_2})^{\eth}))^{1/\eth}}, e^{-(\varphi((-\log \beta^U_{\eth_1})^{\eth} + (-\log \beta^U_{\eth_2})^{\eth}))^{1/\eth}}\Big], \Big[1 - e^{-(\varphi((-\log(1-\delta^L_{\eth_1}))^{\eth} + (-\log(1-\delta^L_{\eth_2}))^{\eth})^{1/\eth}}, 1 - e^{-(\varphi((-\log(1-\delta^U_{\eth_1}))^{\eth} + (-\log(1-\delta^U_{\eth_2}))^{\eth})^{1/\eth}}\Big]\Big\rangle = \Big\langle \Big[e^{-(\varphi(-\log \beta^L_{\eth_1})^{\eth})^{1/\eth}},$

$$e^{-(\varphi(-\log\beta^{U}_{\eth_1})^{\eth})^{1/\eth}}\Big],\Big[1-e^{-(\varphi(-\log(1-\delta^{L}_{\eth_1}))^{\eth})^{1/\eth}},1-e^{-(\varphi(-\log(1-\delta^{U}_{\eth_1}))^{\eth})^{1/\eth}}\Big]\Big\rangle$$
$$\oplus\Big\langle\Big[e^{-(\varphi(-\log\beta^{L}_{\eth_2})^{\eth})^{1/\eth}},e^{-(\varphi(-\log\beta^{U}_{\eth_2})^{\eth})^{1/\eth}}\Big],\Big[1-e^{-(\varphi(-\log(1-\delta^{L}_{\eth_2}))^{\eth})^{1/\eth}},$$
$$1-e^{-(\varphi(-\log(1-\delta^{U}_{\eth_2}))^{\eth})^{1/\eth}}\Big]\Big\rangle=\tilde{\eth}_1^{\varphi}\otimes\tilde{\eth}_2^{\varphi}.$$

(vi) $$\tilde{\eth}^{\varphi_1}\otimes\tilde{\eth}^{\varphi_2}=\Big\langle\Big[e^{-(\varphi_1(-\log\beta^{L}_{\eth})^{\eth})^{1/\eth}},e^{-(\varphi_1(-\log\beta^{U}_{\eth})^{\eth})^{1/\eth}}\Big],\Big[1-$$
$$e^{-(\varphi_1(-\log(1-\delta^{L}_{\eth}))^{\eth})^{1/\eth}},1-e^{-(\varphi_1(-\log(1-\delta^{U}_{\eth}))^{\eth})^{1/\eth}}\Big]\Big\rangle\otimes\Big\langle\Big[e^{-(\varphi_2(-\log\beta^{L}_{\eth})^{\eth})^{1/\eth}},$$
$$e^{-(\varphi_2(-\log\beta^{U}_{\eth})^{\eth})^{1/\eth}}\Big],\Big[1-e^{-(\varphi_2(-\log(1-\delta^{L}_{\eth}))^{\eth})^{1/\eth}},1-e^{-(\varphi_2(-\log(1-\delta^{U}_{\eth}))^{\eth})^{1/\eth}}\Big]\Big\rangle$$
$$=\Big\langle\Big[e^{-((\varphi_1+\varphi_2)(-\log\beta^{L}_{\eth})^{\eth})^{1/\eth}},e^{-((\varphi_1+\varphi_2)(-\log\beta^{U}_{\eth})^{\eth})^{1/\eth}}\Big],\Big[1-$$
$$e^{-((\varphi_1+\varphi_2)(-\log(1-\delta^{L}_{\eth}))^{\eth})^{1/\eth}},1-e^{-((\varphi_1+\varphi_2)(-\log(1-\delta^{U}_{\eth}))^{\eth})^{1/\eth}}\Big]\Big\rangle=\tilde{\eth}^{(\varphi_1+\varphi_2)}.$$

□

4. IVIF Aczel–Alsina Geometric Aggregation Operators

We demonstrate some IVIF geometric aggregation operators throughout this section using the Aczel–Alsina operations.

Definition 8. *Let* $\tilde{\eth}_\zeta=([\beta^{L}_{\eth_\zeta},\beta^{U}_{\eth_\zeta}],[\delta^{L}_{\eth_\zeta},\delta^{U}_{\eth_\zeta}])$ $(\zeta=1,2,\ldots,\hbar)$ *be an accumulation of IVIFNs and* $\xi=(\xi_1,\xi_2,\ldots,\xi_\hbar)^T$ *be the weight vector associated with* $\eth_\zeta$ $(\zeta=1,2,\ldots,\hbar)$*, along with* $\xi_\zeta\in[0,1]$ *and* $\sum_{\zeta=1}^{\hbar}\xi_\zeta=1$*. In that case an IVIF Aczel–Alsina weighted geometric (IVIFAAWG) operator can be described as function* $IVIFAAWG:(L^\star)^\hbar\to L^\star$*, in which*

$$IVIFAAWG_\xi(\tilde{\eth}_1,\tilde{\eth}_2,\ldots,\tilde{\eth}_\hbar)=\bigotimes_{\zeta=1}^{\hbar}(\tilde{\eth}_\zeta)^{\xi_\zeta}=(\tilde{\eth}_1)^{\xi_1}\bigotimes(\tilde{\eth}_2)^{\xi_2}\bigotimes\cdots\bigotimes(\tilde{\eth}_\hbar)^{\xi_\hbar}.$$

Following that, we prove the associated theorem for the Aczel–Alsina operations on IVIFNs.

Theorem 2. *Let* $\tilde{\eth}_\zeta=([\beta^{L}_{\eth_\zeta},\beta^{U}_{\eth_\zeta}],[\delta^{L}_{\eth_\zeta},\delta^{U}_{\eth_\zeta}])$ $(\zeta=1,2,\ldots,\hbar)$ *be an accumulation of IVIFNs and* $\eth\in[0,\infty]$*, then aggregated value of them utilizing the IVIFAAWG operator is also a IVIFNs, and*

$$IVIFAAWG_\xi(\tilde{\eth}_1,\tilde{\eth}_2,\ldots,\tilde{\eth}_\hbar)=\bigotimes_{\zeta=1}^{\hbar}(\tilde{\eth}_\zeta)^{\xi_\zeta}$$
$$=\Bigg\langle\Bigg[e^{-\left(\sum_{\zeta=1}^{\hbar}\xi_\zeta(-\log\beta^{L}_{\eth_\zeta})^{\eth}\right)^{1/\eth}},e^{-\left(\sum_{\zeta=1}^{\hbar}\xi_\zeta(-\log\beta^{U}_{\eth_\zeta})^{\eth}\right)^{1/\eth}}\Bigg],\tag{6}$$
$$\Bigg[1-e^{-\left(\sum_{\zeta=1}^{\hbar}\xi_\zeta(-\log(1-\delta^{L}_{\eth_\zeta}))^{\eth}\right)^{1/\eth}},1-e^{-\left(\sum_{\zeta=1}^{\hbar}\xi_\zeta(-\log(1-\delta^{U}_{\eth_\zeta}))^{\eth}\right)^{1/\eth}}\Bigg]\Bigg\rangle$$

where $\xi=(\xi_1,\xi_2,\ldots,\xi_\hbar)$ *function as weight vector associated with* $\tilde{\eth}_\zeta$ $(\zeta=1,2,\ldots,\hbar)$ *so that* $\xi_\zeta\in[0,1]$*, and* $\sum_{\zeta=1}^{\hbar}\xi_\zeta=1$.

Proof. We may prove Theorem 2 using the following mathematical induction method:
(i) When $\hbar = 2$, rely upon Aczel–Alsina operations of IVIFNs, we acquire

$$\begin{aligned}(\tilde{\eth}_1)^{\xi_1} &= \left\langle \left[e^{-(\xi_1(-\log \beta^L_{\eth_1})^{\eth})^{1/\eth}}, e^{-(\xi_1(-\log \beta^U_{\eth_1})^{\eth})^{1/\eth}} \right], \right. \\ &\left. \left[1 - e^{-(\xi_1(-\log(1-\delta^L_{\eth_1}))^{\eth})^{1/\eth}}, 1 - e^{-(\xi_1(-\log(1-\delta^U_{\eth_1}))^{\eth})^{1/\eth}} \right] \right\rangle, \\ (\tilde{\eth}_2)^{\xi_2} &= \left\langle \left[e^{-(\xi_2(-\log \beta^L_{\eth_2})^{\eth})^{1/\eth}}, e^{-(\xi_2(-\log \beta^U_{\eth_2})^{\eth})^{1/\eth}} \right], \right. \\ &\left. \left[1 - e^{-(\xi_2(-\log(1-\delta^L_{\eth_2}))^{\eth})^{1/\eth}}, 1 - e^{-(\xi_2(-\log(1-\delta^U_{\eth_2}))^{\eth})^{1/\eth}} \right] \right\rangle.\end{aligned}$$

Depending on Definition 7 and Proposition 1, we get

$$IVIFAAWG_{\xi}(\tilde{\eth}_1, \tilde{\eth}_2) = (\tilde{\eth}_1)^{\xi_1} \otimes (\tilde{\eth}_2)^{\xi_2} = \left\langle \left[e^{-(\xi_1(-\log \beta^L_{\eth_1})^{\eth})^{1/\eth}}, e^{-(\xi_1(-\log \beta^U_{\eth_1})^{\eth})^{1/\eth}} \right], \left[1 - e^{-(\xi_1(-\log(1-\delta^L_{\eth_1}))^{\eth})^{1/\eth}}, 1 - e^{-(\xi_1(-\log(1-\delta^U_{\eth_1}))^{\eth})^{1/\eth}} \right] \right\rangle \otimes \left\langle \left[e^{-(\xi_2(-\log \beta^L_{\eth_2})^{\eth})^{1/\eth}}, e^{-(\xi_2(-\log \beta^U_{\eth_2})^{\eth})^{1/\eth}} \right], \left[1 - e^{-(\xi_2(-\log(1-\delta^L_{\eth_2}))^{\eth})^{1/\eth}}, 1 - e^{-(\xi_2(-\log(1-\delta^U_{\eth_2}))^{\eth})^{1/\eth}} \right] \right\rangle$$

$$= \left\langle \left[e^{-\left(\xi_1(-\log \beta^L_{\eth_1})^{\eth} + \xi_2(-\log \beta^L_{\eth_2})^{\eth}\right)^{1/\eth}}, e^{-\left(\xi_1(-\log \beta^U_{\eth_1})^{\eth} + \xi_2(-\log \beta^U_{\eth_2})^{\eth}\right)^{1/\eth}} \right], \left[1 - e^{-\left(\xi_1(-\log(1-\delta^L_{\eth_1}))^{\eth} + \xi_2(-\log(1-\delta^L_{\eth_2}))^{\eth}\right)^{1/\eth}}, 1 - e^{-\left(\xi_1(-\log(1-\delta^U_{\eth_1}))^{\eth} + \xi_2(-\log(1-\delta^U_{\eth_2}))^{\eth}\right)^{1/\eth}} \right] \right\rangle$$

$$= \left\langle \left[e^{-\left(\sum_{\zeta=1}^{2} \xi_\zeta(-\log \beta^L_{\eth_\zeta})^{\eth}\right)^{1/\eth}}, e^{-\left(\sum_{\zeta=1}^{2} \xi_\zeta(-\log \beta^U_{\eth_\zeta})^{\eth}\right)^{1/\eth}} \right], \left[1 - e^{-\left(\sum_{\zeta=1}^{2} \xi_\zeta(-\log(1-\delta^L_{\eth_\zeta}))^{\eth}\right)^{1/\eth}}, 1 - e^{-\left(\sum_{\zeta=1}^{2} \xi_\zeta(-\log(1-\delta^U_{\eth_\zeta}))^{\eth}\right)^{1/\eth}} \right] \right\rangle.$$

Hence, (6) is true for $\hbar = 2$.
(ii) Assume that (6) is true for $\hbar = k$, then we have

$$IVIFAAWG_{\xi}(\tilde{\eth}_1, \tilde{\eth}_2, \ldots, \tilde{\eth}_k) = \bigotimes_{\zeta=1}^{k} (\tilde{\eth}_\zeta)^{\xi_\zeta}$$

$$= \left\langle \left[e^{-\left(\sum_{\zeta=1}^{k} \xi_\zeta(-\log \beta^L_{\eth_\zeta})^{\eth}\right)^{1/\eth}}, e^{-\left(\sum_{\zeta=1}^{k} \xi_\zeta(-\log \beta^U_{\eth_\zeta})^{\eth}\right)^{1/\eth}} \right], \left[1 - e^{-\left(\sum_{\zeta=1}^{k} \xi_\zeta(-\log(1-\delta^L_{\eth_\zeta}))^{\eth}\right)^{1/\eth}}, 1 - e^{-\left(\sum_{\zeta=1}^{k} \xi_\zeta(-\log(1-\delta^U_{\eth_\zeta}))^{\eth}\right)^{1/\eth}} \right] \right\rangle.$$

Now for $\hbar = k + 1$, then

$$IVIFAAWG_{\xi}(\tilde{\eth}_1, \tilde{\eth}_2, \ldots, \tilde{\eth}_k, \tilde{\eth}_{k+1}) = \bigotimes_{\zeta=1}^{k} (\tilde{\eth}_\zeta)^{\xi_\zeta} \otimes (\tilde{\eth}_{k+1})^{\xi_{k+1}}$$

$$= \left\langle \left[e^{-\left(\sum_{\zeta=1}^{k} \xi_\zeta(-\log \beta^L_{\eth_\zeta})^{\eth}\right)^{1/\eth}}, e^{-\left(\sum_{\zeta=1}^{k} \xi_\zeta(-\log \beta^U_{\eth_\zeta})^{\eth}\right)^{1/\eth}} \right], \left[1 - e^{-\left(\sum_{\zeta=1}^{k} \xi_\zeta(-\log(1-\delta^L_{\eth_\zeta}))^{\eth}\right)^{1/\eth}}, 1 - e^{-\left(\sum_{\zeta=1}^{k} \xi_\zeta(-\log(1-\delta^U_{\eth_\zeta}))^{\eth}\right)^{1/\eth}} \right] \right\rangle$$

$$\otimes \left\langle \left[e^{-\left(\xi_{k+1}(-\log \beta^L_{\eth_{k+1}})^{\eth}\right)^{1/\eth}}, e^{-\left(\xi_{k+1}(-\log \beta^U_{\eth_{k+1}})^{\eth}\right)^{1/\eth}} \right], \right.$$

$$\left[1-e^{-\left(\xi_{k+1}(-\log(1-\delta^L_{\eth_{k+1}}))^{\eth}\right)^{1/\eth}},1-e^{-\left(\xi_{k+1}(-\log(1-\delta^U_{\eth_{k+1}}))^{\eth}\right)^{1/\eth}}\right]\Bigg\rangle$$

$$=\left\langle\left[e^{-\left(\sum_{\zeta=1}^{k+1}\xi_\zeta(-\log\beta^L_{\eth_\zeta})^{\eth}\right)^{1/\eth}},e^{-\left(\sum_{\zeta=1}^{k+1}\xi_\zeta(-\log\beta^U_{\eth_\zeta})^{\eth}\right)^{1/\eth}}\right],\right.$$

$$\left.\left[1-e^{-\left(\sum_{\zeta=1}^{k+1}\xi_\zeta(-\log(1-\delta^L_{\eth_\zeta}))^{\eth}\right)^{1/\eth}},1-e^{-\left(\sum_{\zeta=1}^{k+1}\xi_\zeta(-\log(1-\delta^U_{\eth_\zeta}))^{\eth}\right)^{1/\eth}}\right]\right\rangle.$$

Thus, (6) is true for $\hbar=k+1$.

Therefore, from (i) and (ii), we may conclude that (6) holds for any $\hbar$. □

Theorem 3. *(Idempotency) If all* $\tilde{\eth}_\zeta=([\beta^L_{\tilde{\eth}_\zeta},\beta^U_{\tilde{\eth}_\zeta}],[\delta^L_{\tilde{\eth}_\zeta},\delta^U_{\tilde{\eth}_\zeta}])$ $(\zeta=1,2,\ldots,\hbar)$ *are equal, i.e.,* $\tilde{\eth}_\zeta=\tilde{\eth}$ *for all* ζ*, then* $IVIFAAWG_\xi(\tilde{\eth}_1,\tilde{\eth}_2,\ldots,\tilde{\eth}_\hbar)=\tilde{\eth}$.

Proof. Since $\tilde{\eth}_\zeta=([\beta^L_{\tilde{\eth}_\zeta},\beta^U_{\tilde{\eth}_\zeta}],[\delta^L_{\tilde{\eth}_\zeta},\delta^U_{\tilde{\eth}_\zeta}])$ $(\zeta=1,2,\ldots,\hbar)$, then we have by Equation (6),

$$IVIFAAWG_\xi(\tilde{\eth}_1,\tilde{\eth}_2,\ldots,\tilde{\eth}_\hbar)=\bigotimes_{\zeta=1}^{\hbar}(\tilde{\eth}_\zeta)^{\xi_\zeta}=\left\langle\left[e^{-\left(\sum_{\zeta=1}^{\hbar}\xi_\zeta(-\log\beta^L_{\tilde{\eth}_\zeta})^{\eth}\right)^{1/\eth}},\right.\right.$$

$$\left.\left.e^{-\left(\sum_{\zeta=1}^{\hbar}\xi_\zeta(-\log\beta^U_{\tilde{\eth}_\zeta})^{\eth}\right)^{1/\eth}}\right],\left[1-e^{-\left(\sum_{\zeta=1}^{\hbar}\xi_\zeta(-\log(1-\delta^L_{\tilde{\eth}_\zeta}))^{\eth}\right)^{1/\eth}},1-e^{-\left(\sum_{\zeta=1}^{\hbar}\xi_\zeta(-\log(1-\delta^U_{\tilde{\eth}_\zeta}))^{\eth}\right)^{1/\eth}}\right]\right\rangle$$

$$=\left\langle\left[e^{-\left((-\log\beta^L_{\tilde{\eth}})^{\eth}\right)^{1/\eth}},e^{-\left((-\log\beta^U_{\tilde{\eth}})^{\eth}\right)^{1/\eth}}\right],\left[1-e^{-\left((-\log(1-\delta^L_{\tilde{\eth}}))^{\eth}\right)^{1/\eth}},1-\right.\right.$$

$$\left.\left.e^{-\left((-\log(1-\delta^U_{\tilde{\eth}}))^{\eth}\right)^{1/\eth}}\right]\right\rangle=\left\langle\left[e^{\log\beta^L_{\tilde{\eth}}},e^{\log\beta^U_{\tilde{\eth}}}\right],\left[1-e^{\log(1-\delta^L_{\tilde{\eth}})},1-e^{\log(1-\delta^U_{\tilde{\eth}})}\right]\right\rangle$$

$=([\beta^L_{\tilde{\eth}},\beta^U_{\tilde{\eth}}],[\delta^L_{\tilde{\eth}},\delta^U_{\tilde{\eth}}])=\tilde{\eth}$. Thus, $IVIFAAWG_\xi(\tilde{\eth}_1,\tilde{\eth}_2,\ldots,\tilde{\eth}_\hbar)=\tilde{\eth}$ holds. □

Theorem 4. *(Boundedness) Let* $\tilde{\eth}_\zeta=([\beta^L_{\tilde{\eth}_\zeta},\beta^U_{\tilde{\eth}_\zeta}],[\delta^L_{\tilde{\eth}_\zeta},\delta^U_{\tilde{\eth}_\zeta}])$ $(\zeta=1,2,\ldots,\hbar)$ *be an accumulation of IVIFNs. Let* $\tilde{\eth}^-=\min(\tilde{\eth}_1,\tilde{\eth}_2,\ldots,\tilde{\eth}_\hbar)$ *and* $\tilde{\eth}^+=\max(\tilde{\eth}_1,\tilde{\eth}_2,\ldots,\tilde{\eth}_\hbar)$*. Then,* $\tilde{\eth}^-\leq IVIFAAWG_\xi(\tilde{\eth}_1,\tilde{\eth}_2,\ldots,\tilde{\eth}_\hbar)\leq\tilde{\eth}^+$.

Proof. Let $\tilde{\eth}_\zeta=([\beta^L_{\tilde{\eth}_\zeta},\beta^U_{\tilde{\eth}_\zeta}],[\delta^L_{\tilde{\eth}_\zeta},\delta^U_{\tilde{\eth}_\zeta}])$ $(\zeta=1,2,\ldots,\hbar)$ be an accumulation of IVIFNs. Let $\tilde{\eth}^-=\min(\tilde{\eth}_1,\tilde{\eth}_2,\ldots,\tilde{\eth}_\hbar)=([\beta^{L-}_{\tilde{\eth}},\beta^{U-}_{\tilde{\eth}}],[\delta^{L-}_{\tilde{\eth}},\delta^{U-}_{\tilde{\eth}}])$ and $\tilde{\eth}^+=\max(\tilde{\eth}_1,\tilde{\eth}_2,\ldots,\tilde{\eth}_\hbar)=([\beta^{L+}_{\tilde{\eth}},\beta^{U+}_{\tilde{\eth}}],[\delta^{L+}_{\tilde{\eth}},\delta^{U+}_{\tilde{\eth}}])$. We have, $\beta^{L-}_{\tilde{\eth}}=\min_\zeta\{\beta^L_{\tilde{\eth}_\zeta}\}$, $\beta^{U-}_{\tilde{\eth}}=\min_\zeta\{\beta^U_{\tilde{\eth}_\zeta}\}$, $\delta^{L-}_{\tilde{\eth}}=\max_\zeta\{\delta^L_{\tilde{\eth}_\zeta}\}$, $\delta^{U-}_{\tilde{\eth}}=\max_\zeta\{\delta^U_{\tilde{\eth}_\zeta}\}$, $\beta^{L+}_{\tilde{\eth}}=\max_\zeta\{\beta^L_{\tilde{\eth}_\zeta}\}$, $\beta^{U+}_{\tilde{\eth}}=\max_\zeta\{\beta^U_{\tilde{\eth}_\zeta}\}$, $\delta^{L+}_{\tilde{\eth}}=\min_\zeta\{\delta^L_{\tilde{\eth}_\zeta}\}$, and $\delta^{U+}_{\tilde{\eth}}=\min_\zeta\{\delta^U_{\tilde{\eth}_\zeta}\}$. Hence, there have the subsequent inequalities,

$$e^{-\left(\sum\limits_{\zeta=1}^{\hbar}\xi_{\zeta}(-\log\beta_{\partial}^{L-})^{\tilde{\partial}}\right)^{1/\tilde{\partial}}}\le e^{-\left(\sum\limits_{\zeta=1}^{\hbar}\xi_{\zeta}(-\log\beta_{\partial_{\zeta}}^{L})^{\tilde{\partial}}\right)^{1/\tilde{\partial}}}\le e^{-\left(\sum\limits_{\zeta=1}^{\hbar}\xi_{\zeta}(-\log\beta_{\partial}^{L+})^{\tilde{\partial}}\right)^{1/\tilde{\partial}}},$$

$$e^{-\left(\sum\limits_{\zeta=1}^{\hbar}\xi_{\zeta}(-\log\beta_{\partial}^{U-})^{\tilde{\partial}}\right)^{1/\tilde{\partial}}}\le e^{-\left(\sum\limits_{\zeta=1}^{\hbar}\xi_{\zeta}(-\log\beta_{\partial_{\zeta}}^{U})^{\tilde{\partial}}\right)^{1/\tilde{\partial}}}\le e^{-\left(\sum\limits_{\zeta=1}^{\hbar}\xi_{\zeta}(-\log\beta_{\partial}^{U+})^{\tilde{\partial}}\right)^{1/\tilde{\partial}}},$$

$$\begin{aligned}1-e^{-\left(\sum\limits_{\zeta=1}^{\hbar}\xi_{\zeta}(-\log(1-\delta_{\partial}^{L+}))^{\tilde{\partial}}\right)^{1/\tilde{\partial}}}&\le 1-e^{-\left(\sum\limits_{\zeta=1}^{\hbar}\xi_{\zeta}(-\log(1-\delta_{\partial_{\zeta}}^{L}))^{\tilde{\partial}}\right)^{1/\tilde{\partial}}}\\&\le 1-e^{-\left(\sum\limits_{\zeta=1}^{\hbar}\xi_{\zeta}(-\log(1-\delta_{\partial}^{L-}))^{\tilde{\partial}}\right)^{1/\tilde{\partial}}},\\1-e^{-\left(\sum\limits_{\zeta=1}^{\hbar}\xi_{\zeta}(-\log(1-\delta_{\partial}^{U+}))^{\tilde{\partial}}\right)^{1/\tilde{\partial}}}&\le 1-e^{-\left(\sum\limits_{\zeta=1}^{\hbar}\xi_{\zeta}(-\log(1-\delta_{\partial_{\zeta}}^{U}))^{\tilde{\partial}}\right)^{1/\tilde{\partial}}}\\&\le 1-e^{-\left(\sum\limits_{\zeta=1}^{\hbar}\xi_{\zeta}(-\log(1-\delta_{\partial}^{U-}))^{\tilde{\partial}}\right)^{1/\tilde{\partial}}}.\end{aligned}$$

Therefore, $\tilde{\partial}^{-}\le IVIFAAWG_{\xi}(\tilde{\partial}_1,\tilde{\partial}_2,\ldots,\tilde{\partial}_{\hbar})\le\tilde{\partial}^{+}$. □

Theorem 5. *(Monotonicity) Let $\tilde{\partial}_{\zeta}$ and $\tilde{\partial}'_{\zeta}$ $(\zeta=1,2,\ldots,\hbar)$ be two sets of IVIFNs, if $\tilde{\partial}_{\zeta}\le\tilde{\partial}'_{\zeta}$ for all ζ, then $IVIFAAWG_{\xi}(\tilde{\partial}_1,\tilde{\partial}_2,\ldots,\tilde{\partial}_{\hbar})\le IVIFAA\text{-}WG_{\xi}(\tilde{\partial}'_1,\tilde{\partial}'_2,\ldots,\tilde{\partial}'_{\hbar})$.*

Proof. The proof is straightforward. □

Now, we present IVIF Aczel–Alsina ordered weighted geometric (IVIFAAOWG) operator.

Definition 9. *Let $\tilde{\partial}_{\zeta}=([\beta_{\partial_{\zeta}}^{L},\beta_{\partial_{\zeta}}^{U}],[\delta_{\partial_{\zeta}}^{L},\delta_{\partial_{\zeta}}^{U}])$ $(\zeta=1,2,\ldots,\hbar)$ be an accumulation of IVIFNs. An IVIF Aczel–Alsina ordered weighted geometric (IVIFAAOWG) operator of dimension $\hbar$ is a mapping $IVIFAAOWG:(L^{\star})^{\hbar}\to L^{\star}$ with the corresponding vector $\xi=(\xi_1,\xi_2,\ldots,\xi_{\hbar})^T$ such that $\xi_{\zeta}\in[0,1]$, and $\sum\limits_{\zeta=1}^{\hbar}\xi_{\zeta}=1$, as*

$$\begin{aligned}IVIFAAOWG_{\xi}(\tilde{\partial}_1,\tilde{\partial}_2,\ldots,\tilde{\partial}_{\hbar})&=\bigotimes_{\zeta=1}^{\hbar}(\tilde{\partial}_{\varrho(\zeta)})^{\xi_{\zeta}}\\&=(\tilde{\partial}_{\varrho(1)})^{\xi_1}\bigotimes(\tilde{\partial}_{\varrho(2)})^{\xi_2}\bigotimes\cdots\bigotimes(\tilde{\partial}_{\varrho(\hbar)})^{\xi_{\hbar}},\end{aligned}$$

where $(\varrho(1),\varrho(2),\ldots,\varrho(\hbar))$ are the permutation of $(\zeta=1,2,\ldots,\hbar)$, for which $\tilde{\partial}_{\varrho(\zeta-1)}\ge\tilde{\partial}_{\varrho(\zeta)}$ for all $\zeta=1,2,\ldots,\hbar$.

We generate the following theorem on IVIFNs based on the Aczel–Alsina product.

Theorem 6. *Let $\tilde{\partial}_{\zeta}=([\beta_{\partial_{\zeta}}^{L},\beta_{\partial_{\zeta}}^{U}],[\delta_{\partial_{\zeta}}^{L},\delta_{\partial_{\zeta}}^{U}])$ $(\zeta=1,2,\ldots,\hbar)$ be an accumulation of IVIFNs. An IVIF Aczel–Alsina ordered weighted geometric (IVIFAAOWG) operator of dimension $\hbar$ is a mapping $IVIFAAOWG:(L^{\star})^{\hbar}\to L^{\star}$ with the associated vector $\vartheta=(\vartheta_1,\vartheta_2,\ldots,\vartheta_{\hbar})^T$ such that $\vartheta_{\zeta}\in[0,1]$, and $\sum\limits_{\zeta=1}^{\hbar}\vartheta_{\zeta}=1$. Then,*

$$IVIFAAOWG_{\vartheta}(\tilde{\eth}_1,\tilde{\eth}_2,\ldots,\tilde{\eth}_{\hbar}) = \bigotimes_{\zeta=1}^{\hbar}(\tilde{\eth}_{\varrho(\zeta)})^{\vartheta_\zeta}$$

$$= \left\langle \left[e^{-\left(\sum_{\zeta=1}^{\hbar}\vartheta_\zeta\left(-\log \beta^L_{\tilde{\eth}_{\varrho(\zeta)}}\right)^{\eth}\right)^{1/\eth}}, e^{-\left(\sum_{\zeta=1}^{\hbar}\vartheta_\zeta\left(-\log \beta^U_{\tilde{\eth}_{\varrho(\zeta)}}\right)^{\eth}\right)^{1/\eth}} \right], \left[1 - e^{-\left(\sum_{\zeta=1}^{\hbar}\vartheta_\zeta\left(-\log\left(1-\delta^L_{\tilde{\eth}_{\varrho(\zeta)}}\right)\right)^{\eth}\right)^{1/\eth}}, 1 - e^{-\left(\sum_{\zeta=1}^{\hbar}\vartheta_\zeta\left(-\log\left(1-\delta^U_{\tilde{\eth}_{\varrho(\zeta)}}\right)\right)^{\eth}\right)^{1/\eth}} \right] \right\rangle$$

where $(\varrho(1),\varrho(2),\ldots,\varrho(\hbar))$ *are the permutation of* $(\zeta = 1,2,\ldots,\hbar)$, *for which* $\tilde{\eth}_{\varrho(\zeta-1)} \geq \tilde{\eth}_{\varrho(\zeta)}$ *for all* $\zeta = 1,2,\ldots,\hbar$.

Proof. Like Theorem 2, Theorem 6 is simply obtained. □

The following characteristics can be proven well by employing the IVIFAAOWG operator.

Property 1. *(Idempotency) If* $\tilde{\eth}_\zeta$ $(\zeta = 1,2,\ldots,\hbar)$ *are identical, i.e.,* $\tilde{\eth}_\zeta = \tilde{\eth}$ *for every* ζ, *then* $IVIFAAOWG_{\vartheta}(\tilde{\eth}_1,\tilde{\eth}_2,\ldots,\tilde{\eth}_{\hbar}) = \tilde{\eth}$.

Property 2. *(Boundedness) Let* $\tilde{\eth}_\zeta$ $(\zeta = 1,2,\ldots,\hbar)$ *be an accumulation of IVIFNs. Let* $\tilde{\eth}^- = \min_s \tilde{\eth}_\zeta$, $\tilde{\eth}^+ = \max_s \tilde{\eth}_\zeta$. *Then,* $\tilde{\eth}^- \leq IVIFAAOWG_{\vartheta}(\tilde{\eth}_1,\tilde{\eth}_2,\ldots,\tilde{\eth}_{\hbar}) \leq \tilde{\eth}^+$.

Property 3. *(Monotonicity) Suppose that* $\tilde{\eth}_\zeta$ *and* $\tilde{\eth}'_\zeta$ $(\zeta = 1,2,\ldots,\hbar)$ *are two sets of IVIFNs and* $\tilde{\eth}_\zeta \leq \tilde{\eth}'_\zeta$ *for every* ζ, *then* $IVIFAAOWG_{\vartheta}(\tilde{\eth}_1,\tilde{\eth}_2,\ldots,\tilde{\eth}_{\hbar}) \leq IVIFAAOWG_{\vartheta}(\tilde{\eth}'_1,\tilde{\eth}'_2,\ldots,\tilde{\eth}'_{\hbar})$.

Property 4. *(Commutativity) Let* $\tilde{\eth}_\zeta$ *and* $\tilde{\eth}'_\zeta$ $(\zeta = 1,2,\ldots,\hbar)$ *be two sets of IVIFNs, then* $IVIFAAOWG_{\vartheta}(\tilde{\eth}_1,\tilde{\eth}_2,\ldots,\tilde{\eth}_{\hbar}) = IVIFAAOWG_{\vartheta}(\tilde{\eth}'_1,\tilde{\eth}'_2,\ldots,\tilde{\eth}'_{\hbar})$ *where* $\tilde{\eth}'_\zeta$ $(\zeta = 1,2,\ldots,\hbar)$ *is any permutation of* $\tilde{\eth}_\zeta$ $(\zeta = 1,2,\ldots,\hbar)$.

As defined in Definition 8, the IVIFAAWG operator measures only the IVIFNs, and as defined in Definition 9, the IVIFAAOWG operator measures only the IVIFNs' consistent positions. Following that, weights represent different aspects of both the IVIFAAWG and IVIFAAOWG operators. Nevertheless, both the operators think about just one of them. To overcome this disadvantage, in the following we will exhibit IVIF Aczel–Alsina hybrid geometric (IVIFAAHG) operator, which weights both the given IVIFN and its ordered position.

Definition 10. *Let* $\tilde{\eth}_\zeta$ $(\zeta = 1,2,\ldots,\hbar)$ *be an accumulation of IVIFNs. An IVIFAAHG operator of dimension* $\hbar$ *is a function* $IVIFAAHG : (L^*)^{\hbar} \to L^*$, *such that*

$$\begin{aligned} IVIFAAHG_{\xi,\vartheta}(\tilde{\eth}_1,\tilde{\eth}_2,\ldots,\tilde{\eth}_{\hbar}) &= \bigotimes_{\zeta=1}^{\hbar}(\dot{\tilde{\eth}}_{\varrho(\zeta)})^{\vartheta_\zeta} \\ &= (\dot{\tilde{\eth}}_{\varrho(1)})^{\vartheta_1} \bigotimes (\dot{\tilde{\eth}}_{\varrho(2)})^{\vartheta_2} \bigotimes \cdots \bigotimes (\dot{\tilde{\eth}}_{\varrho(\hbar)})^{\vartheta_{\hbar}} \end{aligned}$$

where $\vartheta = (\vartheta_1,\vartheta_2,\ldots,\vartheta_{\hbar})^T$ *is the weighting vector associated with the IVIFAAHG operator, with* $\vartheta_\zeta \in [0,1]$ $(\zeta = 1,2,\ldots,\hbar)$ *and* $\sum_{\zeta=1}^{\hbar}\vartheta_\zeta = 1$; $\dot{\tilde{\eth}}_\zeta = \tilde{\eth}_\zeta^{\hbar\xi_\zeta}$, $\zeta = 1,2,\ldots,\hbar$, $(\dot{\tilde{\eth}}_{\varrho(1)},\dot{\tilde{\eth}}_{\varrho(2)},\ldots,\dot{\tilde{\eth}}_{\varrho(\hbar)})$ *is any permutation of a collection of the weighted IVIFNs* $(\tilde{\eth}_1,\tilde{\eth}_2,\ldots,\tilde{\eth}_{\hbar})$, *such that* $\dot{\tilde{\eth}}_{\varrho(\zeta-1)} \geq \dot{\tilde{\eth}}_{\varrho(\zeta)}$ $(\zeta = 1,2,\ldots,\hbar)$; $\xi = (\xi_1,\xi_2,\ldots,\xi_{\hbar})^T$ *is the weight vector of* $\tilde{\eth}_\zeta$ $(\zeta = 1,2,\ldots,\hbar)$, *with* $\xi_\zeta \in [0,1]$ $(\zeta = 1,2,\ldots,\hbar)$ *and* $\sum_{\zeta=1}^{\hbar}\xi_\zeta = 1$, *and* $\hbar$ *is the balancing coefficient, which plays a role of balance.*

The following theorem can be deduced using Aczel–Alsina operations on IVIFNs information.

Theorem 7. *Let* $\tilde{\eth}_\zeta = ([\beta^L_{\eth_\zeta}, \beta^U_{\eth_\zeta}], [\delta^L_{\eth_\zeta}, \delta^U_{\eth_\zeta}])$ $(\zeta = 1, 2, \ldots, \hbar)$ *be an accumulation of IVIFNs and* $\eth \in [0, \infty]$. *Their aggregated value by IVIFAAHG operator is still a IVIFN, and*

$$IVIFAAHG_\xi(\tilde{\eth}_1, \tilde{\eth}_2, \ldots, \tilde{\eth}_\hbar) = \bigotimes_{\zeta=1}^{\hbar} (\dot{\tilde{\eth}}_{\varrho(\zeta)})^{\xi_\zeta} =$$

$$\left\langle \left[e^{-\left(\sum_{\zeta=1}^{\hbar} \xi_\zeta \left(-\log \dot{\beta}^L_{\eth_{\varrho(\zeta)}}\right)^{\eth}\right)^{1/\eth}}, e^{-\left(\sum_{\zeta=1}^{\hbar} \xi_\zeta \left(-\log \dot{\beta}^U_{\eth_{\varrho(\zeta)}}\right)^{\eth}\right)^{1/\eth}} \right], \left[1 - e^{-\left(\sum_{\zeta=1}^{\hbar} \xi_\zeta \left(-\log \left(1-\dot{\delta}^L_{\eth_{\varrho(\zeta)}}\right)\right)^{\eth}\right)^{1/\eth}}, 1 - e^{-\left(\sum_{\zeta=1}^{\hbar} \xi_\zeta \left(-\log \left(1-\dot{\delta}^U_{\eth_{\varrho(\zeta)}}\right)\right)^{\eth}\right)^{1/\eth}} \right] \right\rangle$$

where $\vartheta = (\vartheta_1, \vartheta_2, \ldots, \vartheta_\hbar)^T$ *is the weighting vector associated with the IVIFAAHG operator, with* $\vartheta_\zeta \in [0, 1]$ $(\zeta = 1, 2, \ldots, \hbar)$ *and* $\sum_{\zeta=1}^{\hbar} \vartheta_\zeta = 1$; $\dot{\tilde{\eth}}_\zeta = \tilde{\eth}_\zeta^{\hbar\xi_\zeta}$, $\zeta = 1, 2, \ldots, \hbar$, $(\dot{\tilde{\eth}}_{\varrho(1)}, \dot{\tilde{\eth}}_{\varrho(2)}, \ldots, \dot{\tilde{\eth}}_{\varrho(\hbar)})$ *is any permutation of a collection of the weighted IVIFNs* $(\dot{\tilde{\eth}}_1, \dot{\tilde{\eth}}_2, \ldots, \dot{\tilde{\eth}}_\hbar)$, *such that* $\dot{\tilde{\eth}}_{\varrho(\zeta-1)} \geq \dot{\tilde{\eth}}_{\varrho(\zeta)}$ $(\zeta = 1, 2, \ldots, \hbar)$; $\xi = (\xi_1, \xi_2, \ldots, \xi_\hbar)^T$ *is the weight vector of* $\tilde{\eth}_\zeta$ $(\zeta = 1, 2, \ldots, \hbar)$, *with* $\xi_\zeta \in [0, 1]$ $(\zeta = 1, 2, \ldots, \hbar)$ *and* $\sum_{\zeta=1}^{\hbar} \xi_\zeta = 1$, *and* $\hbar$ *is the balancing coefficient, which plays a role of balance.*

Proof. Like Theorem 2, Theorem 7 is simply obtained. □

Theorem 8. *The IVIFAAWG and IVIFAAOWG operators are both variants of the IVIFAAHG operator.*

Proof. (1) Assume $\vartheta = (1/\hbar, 1/\hbar, \ldots, 1/\hbar)^T$. Then,

$$\begin{aligned} IVIFAAHG_{\xi,\vartheta}(\tilde{\eth}_1, \tilde{\eth}_2, \ldots, \tilde{\eth}_\hbar) &= (\dot{\tilde{\eth}}_{\varrho(1)})^{\vartheta_1} \bigotimes (\dot{\tilde{\eth}}_{\varrho(2)})^{\vartheta_2} \bigotimes \cdots \bigotimes (\dot{\tilde{\eth}}_{\varrho(\hbar)})^{\vartheta_\hbar} \\ &= (\dot{\tilde{\eth}}_{\varrho(1)})^{(1/\hbar)} \bigotimes (\dot{\tilde{\eth}}_{\varrho(2)})^{(1/\hbar)} \bigotimes \cdots \bigotimes (\dot{\tilde{\eth}}_{\varrho(\hbar)})^{(1/\hbar)} \\ &= (\tilde{\eth}_1)^{\xi_1} \bigotimes (\tilde{\eth}_2)^{\xi_2} \bigotimes \cdots \bigotimes (\tilde{\eth}_\hbar)^{\xi_\hbar} \\ &= IVIFAAWG_\xi(\tilde{\eth}_1, \tilde{\eth}_2, \ldots, \tilde{\eth}_\hbar), \end{aligned}$$

(2) Let $\xi = (1/\hbar, 1/\hbar, \ldots, 1/\hbar)^T$. Then, $\dot{\tilde{\eth}}_\zeta = \tilde{\eth}_\zeta$ $(\zeta = 1, 2, \ldots, \hbar)$ and

$$\begin{aligned} IVIFAAHG_{\xi,\vartheta}(\tilde{\eth}_1, \tilde{\eth}_2, \ldots, \tilde{\eth}_\hbar) &= (\dot{\tilde{\eth}}_{\varrho(1)})^{\vartheta_1} \bigotimes (\dot{\tilde{\eth}}_{\varrho(2)})^{\vartheta_2} \bigotimes \cdots \bigotimes (\dot{\tilde{\eth}}_{\varrho(\hbar)})^{\vartheta_\hbar} \\ &= (\tilde{\eth}_{\varrho(1)})^{\vartheta_1} \bigotimes (\tilde{\eth}_{\varrho(2)})^{\vartheta_2} \bigotimes \cdots \bigotimes (\tilde{\eth}_{\varrho(\hbar)})^{\vartheta_\hbar} \\ &= IVIFAAOWG_\vartheta(\tilde{\eth}_1, \tilde{\eth}_2, \ldots, \tilde{\eth}_\hbar), \end{aligned}$$

which completes the proof. □

5. MADM Methods Influenced by IVIFAAWG Operator

In this section, we shall take advantage of the IVIFAAWG operator to create a way for addressing MADM difficulties with IVIF information.

For a MADM issue, let $\Phi = \{\Phi_1, \Phi_2, \ldots, \Phi_\psi\}$ function as the set of alternatives and $J = \{J_1, J_2, \ldots, J_\hbar\}$ function as the set of attributes, and attributes weight vector is $\xi = (\xi_1, \xi_2, \ldots, \xi_\hbar)^T$, fulfilling $\xi_\zeta \in [0, 1]$ and $\sum_{\zeta=1}^{\hbar} \xi_\zeta = 1$. We explicit the assessment information of the alternative $\Phi_\wp$ concerning the criterion J_ζ by $\widetilde{Y}_{\wp\zeta} = ([\beta^L_{\eth_{\wp\zeta}}, \beta^U_{\eth_{\wp\zeta}}], [\delta^L_{\eth_{\wp\zeta}}, \delta^U_{\eth_{\wp\zeta}}])$, and $\Gamma = \left(\widetilde{Y}_{\wp\zeta}\right)_{\psi\times\hbar}$ is definitely an IVIF decision matrix. Hence, the MADM issue with IVIFNs may be discussed in the following matrix form, acknowledged by Equation (7).

$$\Gamma = \left(\widetilde{Y}_{\wp\zeta}\right)_{\psi\times\hbar} = \begin{matrix} \\ \Phi_1 \\ \Phi_2 \\ \vdots \\ \Phi_\psi \end{matrix} \begin{matrix} J_1 \quad J_2 \cdots J_\hbar \\ \begin{pmatrix} ([\beta^L_{\eth_{11}},\beta^U_{\eth_{11}}],[\delta^L_{\eth_{11}},\delta^U_{\eth_{11}}]) & ([\beta^L_{\eth_{12}},\beta^U_{\eth_{12}}],[\delta^L_{\eth_{12}},\delta^U_{\eth_{12}}]) & \cdots & ([\beta^L_{\eth_{1\hbar}},\beta^U_{\eth_{1\hbar}}],[\delta^L_{\eth_{1\hbar}},\delta^U_{\eth_{1\hbar}}]) \\ ([\beta^L_{\eth_{21}},\beta^U_{\eth_{21}}],[\delta^L_{\eth_{21}},\delta^U_{\eth_{21}}]) & ([\beta^L_{\eth_{22}},\beta^U_{\eth_{22}}],[\delta^L_{\eth_{22}},\delta^U_{\eth_{22}}]) & \cdots & ([\beta^L_{\eth_{2\hbar}},\beta^U_{\eth_{2\hbar}}],[\delta^L_{\eth_{2\hbar}},\delta^U_{\eth_{2\hbar}}]) \\ \vdots & \vdots & \ddots & \vdots \\ ([\beta^L_{\eth_{\psi1}},\beta^U_{\eth_{\psi1}}],[\delta^L_{\eth_{\psi1}},\delta^U_{\eth_{\psi1}}]) & ([\beta^L_{\eth_{\psi2}},\beta^U_{\eth_{\psi2}}],[\delta^L_{\eth_{\psi2}},\delta^U_{\eth_{\psi2}}]) & \cdots & ([\beta^L_{\eth_{\psi\hbar}},\beta^U_{\eth_{\psi\hbar}}],[\delta^L_{\eth_{\psi\hbar}},\delta^U_{\eth_{\psi\hbar}}]) \end{pmatrix} \end{matrix} \quad (7)$$

where every one of the components $\widetilde{Y}_{\wp\zeta} = ([\beta^L_{\eth_{\wp\zeta}},\beta^U_{\eth_{\wp\zeta}}],[\delta^L_{\eth_{\wp\zeta}},\delta^U_{\eth_{\wp\zeta}}])$ is certainly an IVIFN, where $[\beta^L_{\eth_{\wp\zeta}},\beta^U_{\eth_{\wp\zeta}}]$ is the positive membership degree because of which alternative $\Phi_\wp$ fulfills the attribute J_ζ that has been appropriated by the decision-makers, and $[\delta^L_{\eth_{\wp\zeta}},\delta^U_{\eth_{\wp\zeta}}]$ gave the degree that the alternative $\Phi_\wp$ does not fulfill the attribute J_ζ that has been distributed by the decision-maker, where $[\beta^L_{\eth_{\wp\zeta}},\beta^U_{\eth_{\wp\zeta}}] \subset D[0,1]$, $[\delta^L_{\eth_{\wp\zeta}},\delta^U_{\eth_{\wp\zeta}}] \subset D[0,1]$ and $0 \le \beta^U_{\eth_{\wp\zeta}} + \delta^U_{\eth_{\wp\zeta}} \le 1$, $(\wp = 1,2,\ldots,\psi)$.

The methodology dependent on IVIFAAWG operator to find out the MADM difficulties with IVIF data explicitly incorporates these steps:

Step 1. Modify decision matrix $\Gamma = \left(\widetilde{Y}_{\wp\zeta}\right)_{\psi\times\hbar}$ into the normalization matrix $\overline{\Gamma} = \left(\overline{\widetilde{Y}}_{\wp\zeta}\right)_{\psi\times\hbar}$.

$$\overline{\widetilde{Y}}_{\wp\zeta} = \begin{cases} \widetilde{Y}_{\wp\zeta} \text{ for benefit attribute } J_\zeta \\ (\widetilde{Y}_{\wp\zeta})^c \text{ for cost attribute } J_\zeta \end{cases} \quad (8)$$

where $(\widetilde{Y}_{\wp\zeta})^c$ is the complement of $\widetilde{Y}_{\wp\zeta}$, such that $(\widetilde{Y}_{\wp\zeta})^c = ([\delta^L_{\eth_{\wp\zeta}},\delta^U_{\eth_{\wp\zeta}}],[\beta^L_{\eth_{\wp\zeta}},\beta^U_{\eth_{\wp\zeta}}])$.

In fact, if all the attributes J_ζ $(\zeta = 1,2,\ldots,\hbar)$ are the same type, then there is no need to normalize them, but if it is found that there are two types of attributes then we will convert cost attributes to benefit attributes. Then, $\Gamma = \left(\widetilde{Y}_{\wp\zeta}\right)_{\psi\times\hbar}$ will be transformed into IVIF decision matrix $\overline{\Gamma} = \left(\overline{\widetilde{Y}}_{\wp\zeta}\right)_{\psi\times\hbar}$.

Step 2. Make use of the decision data expressed in matrix Γ, and the operator IVIFAAWG to get the overall preference values $\widetilde{Y}_\wp$ $(\wp = 1,2,\ldots,\psi)$ of the alternative $\Phi_\wp$, i.e.,

$$\widetilde{Y}_\wp = IVIFAAWG_\xi(\widetilde{Y}_{\wp1},\widetilde{Y}_{\wp2},\ldots,\widetilde{Y}_{\wp\hbar}) = \bigotimes_{\zeta=1}^{\hbar} (\widetilde{Y}_{\wp\zeta})^{\xi_\zeta}$$

$$= \left\langle \left[e^{-\left(\sum_{\zeta=1}^{\hbar} \xi_\zeta(-\log\beta^L_{\eth_\zeta})^\eth\right)^{1/\eth}}, e^{-\left(\sum_{\zeta=1}^{\hbar} \xi_\zeta(-\log\beta^U_{\eth_\zeta})^\eth\right)^{1/\eth}} \right], \left[1 - e^{-\left(\sum_{\zeta=1}^{\hbar} \xi_\zeta(-\log(1-\delta^L_{\eth_\zeta}))^\eth\right)^{1/\eth}}, 1 - e^{-\left(\sum_{\zeta=1}^{\hbar} \xi_\zeta(-\log(1-\delta^U_{\eth_\zeta}))^\eth\right)^{1/\eth}} \right] \right\rangle. \quad (9)$$

Step 3. Rank all of the alternatives in order of preference. Make use of the method in Definition 3 to rank the entire rating values $\widetilde{Y}_\wp$ $(\wp = 1,2,\ldots,\psi)$ and rank all the alternatives $\Phi_\wp$ $(\wp = 1,2,\ldots,\psi)$ as per ~$\widetilde{Y}_\wp$ $(\wp = 1,2,\ldots,\psi)$ in descending order. Lastly, we choose the advantageous alternative(s) with the highest rating value.

Step 4. End.

6. Numerical Example

This section contains an interesting explanation demonstrating the systematic methodology for choosing an appropriate car.

6.1. Problem Description

Consider a consumer who is considering purchasing a car. There are five distinct types of cars (alternatives) $\Phi_\wp$ ($\wp = 1,2,\ldots,5$). The consumer considers six attributes while deciding which vehicle to buy (adapted from Herrera and Martinez [44]): J_1: Fuel economy; J_2: Aerod degree; J_3: Price; J_4: Comfort; J_5: Design; and J_6: Security. The weight vector of the attributes J_ζ ($\zeta = 1,2,\ldots,6$) is $\xi = (0.15, 0.25, 0.14, 0.16, 0.20, 0.10)^T$. Expect that the features of the alternatives $\Phi_\wp$ ($\wp = 1,2,\ldots,5$) are addressed by the IVIFNs, as demonstrated in the IVIF decision matrix $\Gamma = \left(\widetilde{Y}_{\wp\zeta}\right)_{6\times 5}$ (Table 1).

Table 1. IVIF decision matrix.

	Φ_1	Φ_2	Φ_3	Φ_4	Φ_5
J_1	([0.56,0.66],[0.26,0.31])	([0.38,0.47],[0.34,0.44])	([0.56,0.63],[0.23,0.32])	([0.64,0.73],[0.16,0.27])	([0.48,0.63],[0.26,0.36])
J_2	([0.78,0.88],[0.07,0.12])	([0.47,0.56],[0.27,0.37])	([0.51,0.57],[0.16,0.26])	([0.65,0.75],[0.13,0.20])	([0.64,0.69],[0.21,0.31])
J_3	([0.61,0.82],[0.11,0.18])	([0.79,0.84],[0.11,0.16])	([0.51,0.56],[0.36,0.44])	([0.54,0.64],[0.25,0.36])	([0.79,0.84],[0.08,0.16])
J_4	([0.82,0.91],[0.02,0.07])	([0.55,0.65],[0.22,0.32])	([0.63,0.74],[0.21,0.25])	([0.65,0.75],[0.20,0.25])	([0.60,0.73],[0.17,0.27])
J_5	([0.44,0.56],[0.32,0.42])	([0.68,0.78],[0.17,0.22])	([0.35,0.45],[0.35,0.45])	([0.59,0.69],[0.25,0.30])	([0.45,0.54],[0.35,0.45])
J_6	([0.70,0.83],[0.08,0.17])	([0.53,0.58],[0.31,0.36])	([0.76,0.83],[0.07,0.17])	([0.41,0.51],[0.36,0.42])	([0.56,0.66],[0.22,0.32])

6.2. The IFAAWG Operator-Based Technique

To determine one of most perfect car $\Phi_\wp$ ($\wp = 1,2,\ldots,5$), we employ the IFAAWG operator to construct a MADM theory using intuitionistic fuzzy information, which is frequently evaluated as follows:

- **Step 1.** Because the attributes are classified into two types, we begin by converting the attribute of the cost type into the attribute of the benefit type by employing Equation (8). At that point, $\Gamma = \left(\widetilde{Y}_{\wp\zeta}\right)_{6\times 5}$ is changed into the normalized decision matrix $\overline{\Gamma} = \left(\overline{\widetilde{Y}}_{\wp\zeta}\right)_{6\times 5}$ (Table 2).
- Step 2. Assume that $\eth = 1$. The IVIFAAWG operator is used to know the overall alternative values $\widetilde{Y}_\wp$ for five alternatives $\Phi_\wp$ ($\wp = 1,2,\ldots,5$),
$\widetilde{Y}_1 = ([0.637689, 0.762041], [0.154922, 0.224767])$,
$\widetilde{Y}_2 = ([0.547075, 0.633999], [0.237723, 0.318131])$,
$\widetilde{Y}_3 = ([0.516381, 0.595996], [0.241492, 0.328694])$,
$\widetilde{Y}_4 = ([0.591841, 0.691298], [0.212673, 0.286312])$,
$\widetilde{Y}_5 = ([0.574598, 0.669233], [0.226311, 0.324705])$.
- Step 3. We evaluate the score values $\hat{K}(\widetilde{Y}_\wp)$ ($\wp = 1,2,\ldots,5$) of the universal IVIFNs $\widetilde{Y}_\wp$ ($\wp = 1,2,\ldots,5$) utilizing Equation (2) as $\hat{K}(\widetilde{Y}_1) = 0.510021$, $\hat{K}(\widetilde{Y}_2) = 0.312610$, $\hat{K}(\widetilde{Y}_3) = 0.271095$, $\hat{K}(\widetilde{Y}_4) = 0.392077$, $\hat{K}(\widetilde{Y}_5) = 0.346408$.
- Step 4. Ranking these five alternatives $\Phi_\wp$ ($\wp = 1,2,\ldots,5$) according to the score values $\hat{K}(\widetilde{Y}_\wp)$ ($\wp = 1,2,\ldots,5$) of the overall IVIFNs as $\Phi_1 \succ \Phi_4 \succ \Phi_5 \succ \Phi_2 \succ \Phi_3$.
- Step 5. Thus, the best car is Φ_1.

Table 2. Normalized IVIF decision matrix.

	Φ_1	Φ_2	Φ_3	Φ_4	Φ_5
J_1	([0.56,0.66],[0.26,0.31])	([0.38,0.47],[0.34,0.44])	([0.56,0.63],[0.23,0.32])	([0.64,0.73],[0.16,0.27])	([0.48,0.63],[0.26,0.36])
J_2	([0.78,0.88],[0.07,0.12])	([0.47,0.56],[0.27,0.37])	([0.51,0.57],[0.16,0.26])	([0.65,0.75],[0.13,0.20])	([0.64,0.69],[0.21,0.31])
J_3	([0.61,0.82],[0.11,0.18])	([0.79,0.84],[0.11,0.16])	([0.51,0.56],[0.36,0.44])	([0.54,0.64],[0.25,0.36])	([0.79,0.84],[0.08,0.16])
J_4	([0.82,0.91],[0.02,0.07])	([0.55,0.65],[0.22,0.32])	([0.63,0.74],[0.21,0.25])	([0.65,0.75],[0.20,0.25])	([0.60,0.73],[0.17,0.27])
J_5	([0.44,0.56],[0.32,0.42])	([0.68,0.78],[0.17,0.22])	([0.35,0.45],[0.35,0.45])	([0.59,0.69],[0.25,0.30])	([0.45,0.54],[0.35,0.45])
J_6	([0.70,0.83],[0.08,0.17])	([0.53,0.58],[0.31,0.36])	([0.76,0.83],[0.07,0.17])	([0.41,0.51],[0.36,0.42])	([0.56,0.66],[0.22,0.32])

7. The Impact of the Parameter ð in This Technique

To show how the different values of the parameter ð affect the alternatives, we use different values of the parameter ð to categorize the alternatives. The IVIFAAWG operator is used to rank the alternatives $\Phi_{\wp}$ $(t = 1,2\ldots,5)$, and they are shown in Table 3 and shown in Figure 2. Clearly, when the value of ð for IVIFAAWG operator starts growing, the score values of the possible alternatives decrease, but the ranking stays the same: $\Phi_1 \succ \Phi_4 \succ \Phi_5 \succ \Phi_2 \succ \Phi_3$. Thus, the most important alternative is Φ_1.

Table 3. Ranking order of the alternatives with various parameter ð by IVIFAAWG operator.

ð	$\hat{K}(\tilde{Y}_1)$	$\hat{K}(\tilde{Y}_2)$	$\hat{K}(\tilde{Y}_3)$	$\hat{K}(\tilde{Y}_4)$	$\hat{K}(\tilde{Y}_5)$	Ranking Order
1	0.510021	0.312610	0.271095	0.392077	0.346408	$\Phi_1 \succ \Phi_4 \succ \Phi_5 \succ \Phi_2 \succ \Phi_3$
2	0.432522	0.274768	0.232654	0.369262	0.315391	$\Phi_1 \succ \Phi_4 \succ \Phi_5 \succ \Phi_2 \succ \Phi_3$
3	0.374209	0.245251	0.200569	0.344796	0.289366	$\Phi_1 \succ \Phi_4 \succ \Phi_5 \succ \Phi_2 \succ \Phi_3$
4	0.332473	0.222023	0.174023	0.319924	0.267292	$\Phi_1 \succ \Phi_4 \succ \Phi_5 \succ \Phi_2 \succ \Phi_3$
5	0.302133	0.203274	0.152149	0.295960	0.248489	$\Phi_1 \succ \Phi_4 \succ \Phi_5 \succ \Phi_2 \succ \Phi_3$
6	0.279331	0.187738	0.134129	0.273905	0.232478	$\Phi_1 \succ \Phi_4 \succ \Phi_5 \succ \Phi_2 \succ \Phi_3$
7	0.261630	0.174584	0.119238	0.254265	0.218860	$\Phi_1 \succ \Phi_4 \succ \Phi_5 \succ \Phi_2 \succ \Phi_3$
8	0.247512	0.163268	0.106868	0.237122	0.207273	$\Phi_1 \succ \Phi_4 \succ \Phi_5 \succ \Phi_2 \succ \Phi_3$
9	0.236003	0.153420	0.096520	0.222303	0.197390	$\Phi_1 \succ \Phi_4 \succ \Phi_5 \succ \Phi_2 \succ \Phi_3$
10	0.226454	0.144778	0.087797	0.209530	0.188927	$\Phi_1 \succ \Phi_4 \succ \Phi_5 \succ \Phi_2 \succ \Phi_3$

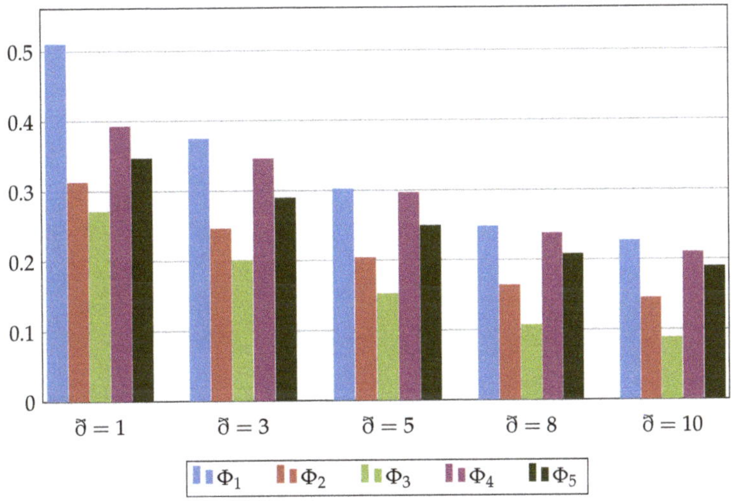

Figure 2. Score values belonging to the alternatives for various values ð by IVIFAAWG operator.

Additionally, Figure 2 reveals that when the value of ð is changed in the example, the ranking results remain identical, demonstrating the resilience of the IVIFAAWG operators.

8. Sensitivity Analysis (SA) of Criteria Weights

To investigate the effect of criteria weights on ranking order, we present a sensitivity investigation. This is done using 24 different weight sets, namely—$Q1, Q2, \ldots, Q24$ (Table 4) formed by considering all possible combinations of the criteria weights $\eta_1 = 0.15$, $\eta_2 = 0.25$, $\eta_3 = 0.14$, $\eta_4 = 0.16$, $\eta_5 = 0.20$, and $\eta_6 = 0.10$. This is especially valuable for achieving a more broad scope of criteria weights for taking a gander at the affectability of the created model. The scores of alternatives are accumulated in Figure 3, and their respective ranking orders are indexed in Table 5. Upon examining the ranking order of alternatives, it is seen that Φ_1 holds the first rank in 100% of the scenarios when the IVIFWG operator (taking

$\eth = 2$) is applied. Hence, the priority of alternatives acquired by utilizing our developed method is credible.

Table 4. Various weight sets of criteria.

Weight Sets	η_1	η_2	η_3	η_4	η_5	η_6	Weight Sets	η_1	η_2	η_3	η_4	η_5	η_6
Q1	0.15	0.25	0.14	0.16	0.20	0.10	Q13	0.16	0.20	0.25	0.15	0.14	0.10
Q2	0.15	0.14	0.16	0.20	0.10	0.25	Q14	0.16	0.25	0.15	0.14	0.10	0.20
Q3	0.15	0.16	0.20	0.10	0.25	0.14	Q15	0.16	0.15	0.14	0.10	0.20	0.25
Q4	0.15	0.20	0.10	0.25	0.14	0.16	Q16	0.16	0.14	0.10	0.20	0.25	0.15
Q5	0.25	0.15	0.14	0.20	0.10	0.16	Q17	0.20	0.25	0.10	0.14	0.15	0.16
Q6	0.25	0.14	0.20	0.10	0.16	0.15	Q18	0.20	0.10	0.14	0.15	0.16	0.25
Q7	0.25	0.20	0.10	0.16	0.15	0.14	Q19	0.20	0.14	0.15	0.16	0.25	0.10
Q8	0.25	0.10	0.16	0.15	0.14	0.20	Q20	0.20	0.15	0.16	0.25	0.10	0.14
Q9	0.14	0.16	0.15	0.20	0.10	0.25	Q21	0.10	0.14	0.15	0.16	0.20	0.25
Q10	0.14	0.15	0.20	0.10	0.25	0.16	Q22	0.10	0.15	0.16	0.20	0.25	0.14
Q11	0.14	0.20	0.10	0.25	0.16	0.15	Q23	0.10	0.16	0.20	0.25	0.14	0.15
Q12	0.14	0.10	0.25	0.16	0.15	0.20	Q24	0.10	0.20	0.25	0.14	0.15	0.16

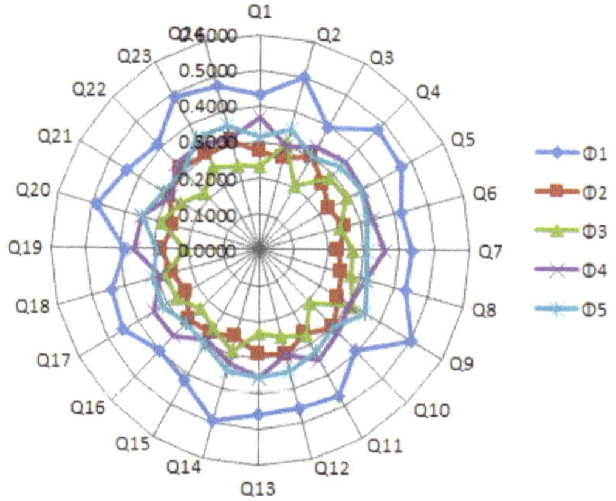

Figure 3. Utility values of alternatives for distinct sets of weighted criteria.

Table 5. Priority order of alternatives for diverse weight sets.

	Ranking Order		Ranking Order		Ranking Order
Q1	$\Phi_1 \succ \Phi_4 \succ \Phi_5 \succ \Phi_2 \succ \Phi_3$	Q9	$\Phi_1 \succ \Phi_5 \succ \Phi_3 \succ \Phi_4 \succ \Phi_2$	Q17	$\Phi_1 \succ \Phi_4 \succ \Phi_5 \succ \Phi_3 \succ \Phi_2$
Q2	$\Phi_1 \succ \Phi_5 \succ \Phi_3 \succ \Phi_4 \succ \Phi_2$	Q10	$\Phi_1 \succ \Phi_4 \succ \Phi_2 \succ \Phi_5 \succ \Phi_3$	Q18	$\Phi_1 \succ \Phi_5 \succ \Phi_4 \succ \Phi_3 \succ \Phi_2$
Q3	$\Phi_1 \succ \Phi_4 \succ \Phi_5 \succ \Phi_2 \succ \Phi_3$	Q11	$\Phi_1 \succ \Phi_4 \succ \Phi_5 \succ \Phi_3 \succ \Phi_2$	Q19	$\Phi_1 \succ \Phi_4 \succ \Phi_5 \succ \Phi_2 \succ \Phi_3$
Q4	$\Phi_1 \succ \Phi_4 \succ \Phi_5 \succ \Phi_3 \succ \Phi_2$	Q12	$\Phi_1 \succ \Phi_5 \succ \Phi_2 \succ \Phi_4 \succ \Phi_3$	Q20	$\Phi_1 \succ \Phi_5 \succ \Phi_4 \succ \Phi_3 \succ \Phi_2$
Q5	$\Phi_1 \succ \Phi_4 \succ \Phi_5 \succ \Phi_3 \succ \Phi_2$	Q13	$\Phi_1 \succ \Phi_5 \succ \Phi_4 \succ \Phi_2 \succ \Phi_3$	Q21	$\Phi_1 \succ \Phi_5 \succ \Phi_2 \succ \Phi_4 \succ \Phi_3$
Q6	$\Phi_1 \succ \Phi_4 \succ \Phi_5 \succ \Phi_2 \succ \Phi_3$	Q14	$\Phi_1 \succ \Phi_5 \succ \Phi_4 \succ \Phi_3 \succ \Phi_2$	Q22	$\Phi_1 \succ \Phi_4 \succ \Phi_2 \succ \Phi_5 \succ \Phi_3$
Q7	$\Phi_1 \succ \Phi_4 \succ \Phi_5 \succ \Phi_3 \succ \Phi_2$	Q15	$\Phi_1 \succ \Phi_5 \succ \Phi_4 \succ \Phi_2 \succ \Phi_3$	Q23	$\Phi_1 \succ \Phi_5 \succ \Phi_4 \succ \Phi_2 \succ \Phi_3$
Q8	$\Phi_1 \succ \Phi_5 \succ \Phi_4 \succ \Phi_3 \succ \Phi_2$	Q16	$\Phi_1 \succ \Phi_4 \succ \Phi_5 \succ \Phi_2 \succ \Phi_3$	Q24	$\Phi_1 \succ \Phi_5 \succ \Phi_4 \succ \Phi_2 \succ \Phi_3$

9. Comparison Study

Following that, we will compare and contrast our proposed approach with some other conventional methods such as the IVIF weighted averaging (IVIFWA) operator [5], the IVIF weighted geometric (IVIFWG) operator [39], the IVIF Einstein weighted geometric ($IVIFWG^{\varepsilon}$) operator [16], and the IVIF Einstein weighted averaging ($IVIFWA^{\varepsilon}$) operator [17]. The comparison findings are given in Tables 6 and 7, and they are depicted in

Figure 4 visually. If you look at Tables 3 and 6, you can see that the IVIFWG operator is a special case of the IVIFAAWG operator, and that this happens when $\eth = 1$.

As a consequence, our recommended procedures for resolving IVIF MADM problems are frequently more extensive and adaptable than some of the techniques now in use.

Table 6. Comparative assessment using a few popular methodologies.

Techniques	$\hat{K}(\widetilde{Y}_1)$	$\hat{K}(\widetilde{Y}_2)$	$\hat{K}(\widetilde{Y}_3)$	$\hat{K}(\widetilde{Y}_4)$	$\hat{K}(\widetilde{Y}_5)$	Preference Order
Xu [5]	0.605185	0.370086	0.326785	0.375578	0.391143	$\Phi_1 \succ \Phi_5 \succ \Phi_4 \succ \Phi_2 \succ \Phi_3$
Xu & Chen [39]	0.510021	0.312610	0.271095	0.392077	0.346408	$\Phi_1 \succ \Phi_4 \succ \Phi_5 \succ \Phi_2 \succ \Phi_3$
Wang & Liu [16]	0.523568	0.321157	0.279447	0.396147	0.352904	$\Phi_1 \succ \Phi_4 \succ \Phi_5 \succ \Phi_2 \succ \Phi_3$
Wang & Liu [17]	0.597400	0.362337	0.319370	0.413345	0.385472	$\Phi_1 \succ \Phi_4 \succ \Phi_5 \succ \Phi_2 \succ \Phi_3$
Proposed method	0.226454	0.144778	0.087797	0.209530	0.188927	$\Phi_1 \succ \Phi_4 \succ \Phi_5 \succ \Phi_2 \succ \Phi_3$

Table 7. Qualitative evaluations of the current methods.

Techniques	Whether It Is More Straightforward to Express Ambiguous Data	Whether It Should Make Information Aggregation More Parameter-Adjustable
Xu [5]	Yes	No
Xu & Chen [39]	Yes	No
Wang & Liu [16]	Yes	No
Wang & Liu [17]	Yes	No
Proposed method	Yes	Yes

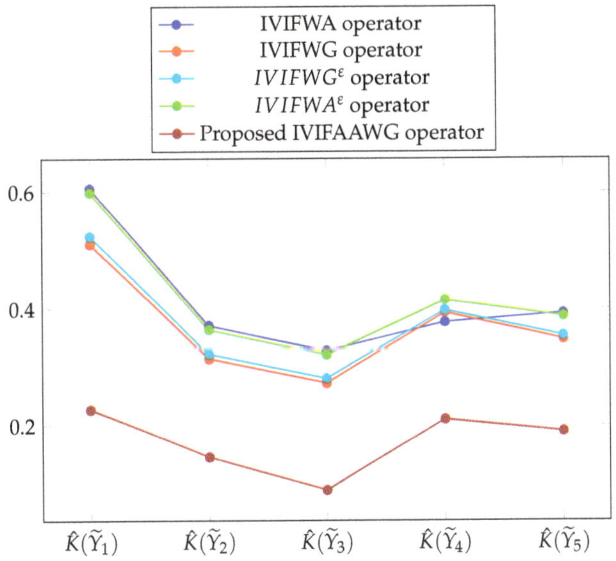

Figure 4. Comparison analysis with a few prevailing techniques.

10. Conclusions

We began this study by extending the Aczel–Alsina t-norm and t-conorm to IVIF scenarios, defining and examining a few additional working principles for IVIFNs. Then, in light of these new operating laws, different new aggregation operators, such as the IVIFAAWG operator, the IVIFAAOWG operator, and the IVIFAAHG operator, were devised to accommodate situations in which the specified assertions are IVIFNs. The fundamental characteristics of the recommended operators are examined, as well as their specific situations. We provide a realistic approach to MADM difficulties with IVIFNs depending on the IFAAWG operator. Furthermore, an exemplary scenario of choosing suitable cars is utilized to demonstrate the developed model, and a comparative study with some other methods is undertaken to show the recommended operators' distinct advantages. In future studies, we plan to extend the challenge further by introducing new characteristics, including the use of probabilistic aggregations. Additionally, we will discuss additional decision-making aspects like cluster analysis, performance analysis [45], sustainable city logistics [46], risk investment assessment [47], Wireless Sensor Networks [48], capital budgeting techniques [49], home buying process [50], and other domains in uncertain environment [51–58].

Author Contributions: Conceptualization, T.S. and R.M.; methodology, T.S. and V.S.; validation, V.S.; formal analysis, V.S. and R.A.; investigation, R.M.; data curation, R.C.; writing—original draft preparation, T.S. and A.I.; writing—review and editing, T.S. and R.C.; supervision, R.M.; project administration, V.S.; funding acquisition, A.I. and R.C. All authors have read and agreed to the published version of the manuscript.

Funding: The author, Rifaqat Ali, extends his appreciation to Deanship of Scientific Research at King Khalid University, for funding this work through General Research Project under grant number (GRP/93/43). The author, Aiyared Iampan, is thankful to the revenue budget in 2022, School of Science, University of Phayao, for supporting this research. The author, Radko Mesiar, is thankful to the Slovak Research and Development Agency for supporting this research through Grant Number APVV-18-0052.

Data Availability Statement: Not applicable.

Conflicts of Interest: The authors declare no conflict of interest.

List of Abbreviations

The following abbreviations are used in this manuscript:

IVIF	interval-valued intuitionistic fuzzy
IVIFS	interval-valued intuitionistic fuzzy set
IVIFN	interval-valued intuitionistic fuzzy number
MADM	multiple attribute decision making
IVIFWA	IVIF weighted averaging
IVIFHA	IVIF hybrid averaging
$IVIFWA^{\varepsilon}$	IVIF Einstein weighted averaging
$IVIFWG^{\varepsilon}$	IVIF Einstein weighted geometric
IVIFAAWG	IVIF Aczel-Alsina weighted geometric
IVIFAAOWG	IVIF Aczel-Alsina order weighted geometric
IVIFAAHG	IVIF Aczel-Alsina hybrid geometric

References

1. Attanassov, K.T. Intuitionistic fuzzy sets. *Fuzzy Sets Syst.* **1986**, *20*, 87–96. [CrossRef]
2. Atanassov, K.T.; Gargov, G. Interval valued intuitionistic fuzzy sets. *Fuzzy Sets Syst.* **1989**, *31*, 343–349. [CrossRef]
3. Beliakov, G.; Bustince, H.; James, S.; Calvo, T.; Fernandez, J. Aggregation for Atanassov's intuitionistic and interval valued fuzzy sets: The median operator. *IEEE Trans. Fuzzy Syst.* **2012**, *20*, 487–498. [CrossRef]
4. Chen, T.Y.; Wang, H.P.; Lu, Y.Y. A multicriteria group decision-making approach based on interval-valued intuitionistic fuzzy sets: A comparative perspective. *Expert Syst. Appl.* **2011**, *38*, 7647–7658. [CrossRef]
5. Xu, Z. Methods for aggregating interval-valued intuitionistic fuzzy information and their application to decision making. *Control Decis.* **2007**, *22*, 215–219.
6. Liu, P. Multiple attribute group decision making method based on interval-valued intuitionistic fuzzy power Heronian aggregation operators. *Comput. Ind. Eng.* **2017**, *108*, 199–212. [CrossRef]
7. Zhao, H.; Xu, Z. Group decision making with density-based aggregation operators under interval-valued intuitionistic fuzzy environments. *J. Intell. Fuzzy Syst.* **2014**, *27*, 1021–1033. [CrossRef]
8. Yu, D.; Wu, Y.; Lu, T. Interval-valued intuitionistic fuzzy prioritized operators and their application in group decision making. *Know-Based Syst.* **2012**, *30*, 57–66. [CrossRef]

9. Chen, S.M.; Han, W.H. A new multiattribute decision making method based on multiplication operations of interval-valued intuitionistic fuzzy values and linear programming methodology. *Inf. Sci.* **2018**, *429*, 421–432. [CrossRef]
10. Chen, S.M.; Han, W.H. Multiattribute decision making based on nonlinear programming methodology, particle swarm optimization techniques and interval-valued intuitionistic fuzzy values. *Inf. Sci.* **2019**, *471*, 252–268. [CrossRef]
11. Wei, G.; Wang, X. Some geometric aggregation operators based on interval-valued intuitionistic fuzzy sets and their application to group decision making. In Proceedings of the 2007 International Conference on Computational Intelligence and Security (CIS 2007), Harbin, China, 15–19 December 2007; pp. 495–499.
12. Li, D.F. TOPSIS-based nonlinear-programming methodology for multiattribute decision making with interval-valued intuitionistic fuzzy sets. *IEEE Trans. Fuzzy Syst.* **2010**, *18*, 299–311. [CrossRef]
13. Xu, Z.; Gou, X. An overview of interval-valued intuitionistic fuzzy information aggregations and applications. *Granul. Comput.* **2017**, *2*, 13–39. [CrossRef]
14. Chen, S.M.; Kuo, L.W.; Zou, X.Y. Multiattribute decision making based on Shannon's information entropy, non-linear programming methodology, and interval-valued intuitionistic fuzzy values. *Inf. Sci.* **2018**, *465*, 404–424. [CrossRef]
15. Meng, F.Y.; Cheng, H.; Zhang, Q. Induced Atanassov's inter-valvalued intuitionistic fuzzy hybrid Choquet integral operators and their application in decision making. *Int. J. Comput. Intell. Syst.* **2014**, *7*, 524–542. [CrossRef]
16. Wang, W.; Liu, X. The multi-attribute decision making method based on interval-valued intuitionistic fuzzy Einstein hybrid weighted geometric operator. *Comput. Math. Appl.* **2013**, *66*, 1845–1856. [CrossRef]
17. Wang, W.; Liu, X. Interval-valued intuitionistic fuzzy hybrid weighted averaging operator based on Einstein operation and its application to decision making. *J. Intell. Fuzzy Syst.* **2013**, *25*, 279–290. [CrossRef]
18. Cheng, S.H. Autocratic multiattribute group decision making for hotel location selection based on interval-valued intuitionistic fuzzy sets. *Inf. Sci.* **2018**, *427*, 77–87. [CrossRef]
19. Chen, S.M.; Cheng, S.H.; Tsai, W.H. Multiple attribute group decision making based on interval-valued intuitionistic fuzzy aggregation operators and transformation techniques of interval-valued intuitionistic fuzzy values. *Inf. Sci.* **2016**, *367–368*, 418–442. [CrossRef]
20. Abdullah, L.; Zulkifli, N.; Liao, H.; Herrera-Viedma, E.; Al-Barakati, A. An interval-valued intuitionistic fuzzy DEMATEL method combined with Choquet integral for sustainable solid waste management. *Eng. Appl. Artif. Intel.* **2019**, *82*, 207–215. [CrossRef]
21. Liu, H.C.; Quan, M.Y.; Li, Z.W.; Wang, Z.L. A new integrated MCDM model for sustainable supplier selection under interval-valued intuitionistic uncertain linguistic environment. *Inf. Sci.* **2019**, *486*, 254–270. [CrossRef]
22. Meng, F.; Tang, J.; Wang, P.; Chen, X. A programming-based algorithm for interval-valued intuitionistic fuzzy group decision making. *Knowl. Based Syst.* **2018**, *144*, 122–143. [CrossRef]
23. Kong, D.; Chang, T.; Pan, J.; Hao, N.; Yang, G. A decision variable-based combinatorial optimization approach for interval-valued intuitionistic fuzzy MAGDM. *Inf. Sci.* **2019**, *484*, 197–218. [CrossRef]
24. Schweizer, B.; Sklar, A. Statistical metric spaces. *Pacific J. Math.* **1960**, *10*, 313–334. [CrossRef]
25. Deschrijver, G.; Cornelis, C.; Kerre, E.E. On the representation of intuitionistic fuzzy t-norms and t-conorms. *IEEE Trans. Fuzzy Syst.* **2004**, *12*, 45–61. [CrossRef]
26. Liu, P. Some Hamacher aggregation operators based on the interval-valued intuitionistic fuzzy numbers and their application to group decision making. *IEEE Trans. Fuzzy Syst.* **2014**, *22*, 83–97. [CrossRef]
27. Yu, D. Group decision making under interval-valued multiplicative intuitionistic fuzzy environment based on Archimedean t-conorm and t-norm. *Int. J. Intell. Syst.* **2015**, *30*, 590–616. [CrossRef]
28. Klement, E.P.; Mesiar, R.; Pap, E. *Triangular Norms*; Kluwer Academic Publishers: Dordrecht, The Netherlands, 2000.
29. Menger, K. Statistical metrics. *Proc. Natl. Acad. Sci. USA* **1942**, *8*, 535–537. [CrossRef]
30. Zadeh, L.A. Fuzzy sets. *Inform. Control* **1965**, *8*, 338–353. [CrossRef]
31. Schweizer, B.; Sklar, A. Associative functions and statistical triangle inequalities. *Publ. Math. Debrecen* **1961**, *8*, 169–186.
32. Goguen, J.A. L-fuzzy sets. *J. Math. Anal. Appl.* **1967**, *8*, 145–174. [CrossRef]
33. Aczel, J.; Alsina, C. Characterization of some classes of quasilinear functions with applications to triangular norms and to synthesizing judgements. *Aequationes Math.* **1982**, *25*, 313–315. [CrossRef]
34. Wang, N.; Li, Q.; El-Latif, A.A.A.; Yan, X.; Niu, X. A Novel Hybrid Multibiometrics Based on the Fusion of Dual Iris, Visible and Thermal Face Images. In Proceedings of the 2013 International Symposium on Biometrics and Security Technologies, Chengdu, China, 2–5 July 2013; pp. 217–223. [CrossRef]
35. Senapati, T.; Chen, G.; Yager, R.R. Aczel-Alsina aggregation operators and their application to intuitionistic fuzzy multiple attribute decision making. *Int. J. Intell. Syst.* **2022**, *37*, 1529–1551. [CrossRef]
36. Senapati, T.; Chen, G.; Mesiar, R.; Yager, R.R. Novel Aczel–Alsina operations-based interval-valued intuitionistic fuzzy aggregation operatorsandtheir applications in multiple attribute decision-making process. *Int. J. Intell. Syst.* **2021**, 1–23. [CrossRef]
37. Senapati, T.; Chen, G.; Mesiar, R.; Yager, R.R.; Saha, A. Novel Aczel-Alsina operations-based hesitant fuzzy aggregation operators and their applications in cyclone disaster assessment. *Int. J. Gen. Syst.* **2022**, 1–39. [CrossRef]
38. Senapati, T. Approaches to multi-attribute decision-making based on picture fuzzy Aczel–Alsina average aggregation operators. *Comp. Appl. Math.* **2022**, *41*, 40. [CrossRef]

39. Xu, Z.; Chen, J. On geometric aggregation over interval-valued intuitionistic fuzzy information. In Proceedings of the Fourth International Conference on Fuzzy Systems and Knowledge Discovery (FSKD 07), Haikou, China, 24–27 August 2007; Volume 2, pp. 466–471. [CrossRef]
40. Wang, Z.; Li, K.W.; Wang, W. An approach to multiattribute decision making with interval-valued intuitionistic fuzzy assessments and incomplete weights. *Inf. Sci.* **2009**, *179*, 3026–3040.
41. Deschrijver, G.; Kerre, E. On the relationship between some extensions of fuzzy set theory. *Fuzzy Sets Syst.* **2003**, *133*, 227–235. [CrossRef]
42. Miguel, D.L.; Bustince, H.; Fernandez, J.; Indurain, E.; Kolesarova, A.; Mesiar, R. Construction of admissible linear orders for interval-valued Atanassov intuitionistic fuzzy sets with an application to decisionmaking. *Inf. Fusion* **2016**, *27*, 189–197. [CrossRef]
43. De Miguel, L.; Bustince, H.; Pekala, B.; Bentkowska, U.; Da Silva, I.; Bedregal, B.; Mesiar, R.; Ochoa, G. Interval-valued Atanassov intuitionistic OWA aggregations using admissible linear orders and their application to decision making. *IEEE Trans. Fuzzy Syst.* **2016**, *24*, 1586–1597. [CrossRef]
44. Herrera, E.; Martinez, L. An approach for combining linguistic and numerical information based on 2-tuple fuzzy linguistic representation model in decision-making. *Int. J. Uncertain. Fuzziness Knowl. Based Syst.* **2000**, *8*, 539–562. [CrossRef]
45. Beg, I.; Rashid, T. Group decision making using intuitionistic hesitant fuzzy sets. *Int. J. Fuzzy Log. Intell.* **2014**, *14*, 181–187. [CrossRef]
46. Saha, A.; Simic, V.; Senapati, T.; Dabic-Miletic, S.; Ala, A. A dual hesitant fuzzy sets-based methodology for advantage prioritization of zero-emission last-mile delivery solutions for sustainable city logistics. *IEEE Trans. Fuzzy Syst.* **2022**. [CrossRef]
47. Tan, J.; Liu, Y.; Senapati, T.; Garg, H.; Rong, Y. An extended MABAC method based on prospect theory with unknown weight information under Fermatean fuzzy environment for risk investment assessment in B&R. *J. Ambient. Intell. Humaniz. Comput.* **2022**. [CrossRef]
48. Sahoo, L.; Sen, S.; Tiwary, K.; Samanta, S.; Senapati, T. Modified Floyd-Warshall's algorithm for maximum connectivity in Wireless Sensor Networks under uncertainty. *Discrete Dyn. Nat. Soc.* **2022**, *2022*, 5973433. [CrossRef]
49. Sergi, D.; Sari, I.U.; Senapati, T. Extension of capital budgeting techniques using interval-valued Fermatean fuzzy sets. *J. Intell. Fuzzy Syst.* **2022**, *42*, 365–376. [CrossRef]
50. Ibrar, M.; Khan, A.; Khan, S.; Abbas, F. Fuzzy parameterized bipolar fuzzy soft expert set and its application in decision making. *Int. J. Fuzzy Log. Intell.* **2019**, *19*, 234–241. [CrossRef]
51. Saha, A.; Senapati, T.; Yager, R.R. Hybridizations of generalized Dombi operators and Bonferroni mean operators under dual probabilistic linguistic environment for group decision-making. *Int. J. Intell. Syst.* **2021**, *36*, 6645–6679. [CrossRef]
52. Senapati, T.; Yager, R.R. Fermatean fuzzy weighted averaging/geometric operators and its application in multi-criteria decision-making methods. *Eng. Appl. Artif. Intel.* **2019**, *85*, 112–121. [CrossRef]
53. Senapati, T.; Yager, R.R. Some new operations over Fermatean fuzzy numbers and application of Fermatean fuzzy WPM in multiple criteria decision making. *Informatica* **2019**, *30*, 391–412. [CrossRef]
54. Senapati, T.; Yager, R.R. Fermatean fuzzy sets. *J. Ambient. Intell. Humaniz. Comput.* **2020**, *11*, 663–674. [CrossRef]
55. Mesiar, R.; Kolesarova, A.; Senapati, T. Aggregation on lattices isomorphic to the lattice of closed subintervals of the real unit interval. *Fuzzy Sets Syst.* **2022**. [CrossRef]
56. Senapati, T.; Chen, G. Picture fuzzy WASPAS technique and its application in multi-criteria decision-making. *Soft Comput.* **2022**. [CrossRef]
57. Senapati, T.; Chen, G. Some novel interval-valued Pythagorean fuzzy aggregation operator based on Hamacher triangular norms and their application in MADM issues. *Comp. Appl. Math.* **2021**, *40*, 109. [CrossRef]
58. Senapati, T.; Yager, R.R.; Chen, G. Cubic intuitionistic WASPAS technique and its application in multi-criteria decision-making. *J. Ambient. Intell. Humaniz. Comput.* **2021**, *12*, 8823–8833. [CrossRef]

axioms MDPI

Article

New Fuzzy Extensions on Binomial Distribution

Gia Sirbiladze [1,*], Janusz Kacprzyk [2], Teimuraz Manjafarashvili [1], Bidzina Midodashvili [1] and Bidzina Matsaberidze [1]

[1] Department of Computer Sciences, Faculty of Exact and Natural Sciences, Ivane Javakhishvili Tbilisi State University, University St. 13, Tbilisi 0186, Georgia; teimuraz.manjafarashvili@tsu.ge (T.M.); bidzina.midodashvili@tsu.ge (B.M.); b.matsaberidze@gmail.com (B.M.)

[2] Intelligent Systems Laboratory, Systems Research Institute, Polish Academy of Sciences, Ul. Newelska 6, 01-447 Warsaw, Poland; janusz.kacprzyk@ibspan.waw.pl

* Correspondence: gia.sirbiladze@tsu.ge

Abstract: The use of discrete probabilistic distributions is relevant to many practical tasks, especially in present-day situations where the data on distribution are insufficient and expert knowledge and evaluations are the only instruments for the restoration of probability distributions. However, in such cases, uncertainty arises, and it becomes necessary to build suitable approaches to overcome it. In this direction, this paper discusses a new approach of fuzzy binomial distributions (BDs) and their extensions. Four cases are considered: (1) When the elementary events are fuzzy. Based on this information, the probabilistic distribution of the corresponding fuzzy-random binomial variable is calculated. The conditions of restrictions on this distribution are obtained, and it is shown that these conditions depend on the ratio of success and failure of membership levels. The formulas for the generating function (GF) of the constructed distribution and the first and second order moments are also obtained. The Poisson distribution is calculated as the limit case of a fuzzy-random binomial experiment. (2) When the number of successes is of a fuzzy nature and is represented as a fuzzy subset of the set of possible success numbers. The formula for calculating the probability of convolution of binomial dependent fuzzy events is obtained, and the corresponding GF is built. As a result, the scheme for calculating the mathematical expectation of the number of fuzzy successes is defined. (3) When the spectrum of the extended distribution is fuzzy. The discussion is based on the concepts of a fuzzy-random event and its probability, as well as the notion of fuzzy random events independence. The fuzzy binomial upper distribution is specifically considered. In this case the fuzziness is represented by the membership levels of the binomial and non-binomial events of the complete failure complex. The GF of the constructed distribution and the first-order moment of the distribution are also calculated. Sufficient conditions for the existence of a limit distribution and a Poisson distribution are also obtained. (4) As is known, based on the analysis of lexical material, the linguistic spectrum of the statistical process of word-formation becomes two-component when switching to vocabulary. For this, two variants of the hybrid fuzzy-probabilistic process are constructed, which can be used in the analysis of the linguistic spectrum of the statistical process of word-formation. A fuzzy extension of standard Fuchs distribution is also presented, where the fuzziness is reflected in the growing numbers of failures. For better representation of the results, the examples of fuzzy BD are illustrated in each section.

Keywords: fuzzy-sets; fuzzy-random variables; distribution generating function; fuzzy binomial distribution; Fuchs distribution

MSC: 03E72; 60A86

Citation: Sirbiladze, G.; Kacprzyk, J.; Manjafarashvili, T.; Midodashvili, B.; Matsaberidze, B. New Fuzzy Extensions on Binomial Distribution. *Axioms* **2022**, *11*, 220. https://doi.org/10.3390/axioms11050220

Academic Editor: Humberto Bustince

Received: 13 April 2022
Accepted: 5 May 2022
Published: 9 May 2022

1. Introduction

In current practice, and especially in the creation of new technologies, the use of extensions of classical probabilistic distributions based on expert data and evaluations is becoming more and more common. Particularly, the fuzzy extensions of discrete distributions are attracting attention, and the use of fuzzy-stochastic distributions or fuzzy-stochastic processes often have no alternative in dealing with incomplete objective-experimental data [1–8]. Based on these considerations, the aim of our research was to develop a new approach to the extension of the BD under the fuzzy uncertainty environment. In the introduction, we first review the existing research directions on the fuzzy BD extensions and then present the main principle of our approach.

Briefly, regarding the basic works studying fuzzy BD and its application in the different problems, practices, and research, the addition of two fuzzy Bernoulli distributions and the sum of subsequent fuzzy BDs have been discussed in [9]. Extensions of these ideas would be of use to study fuzzy randomness and the concept of measure. In [10], the authors assume that the probability of "success" p is not known exactly and is to be estimated from a random sample or from expert opinion. For the fuzzy BD, a fuzzy number $\widetilde{p}$ instead of p is substituted. In [11], discrete probability distributions, where some of the probability values are uncertain, are considered. These uncertainties are modeled using fuzzy numbers. The basic laws of fuzzy probability theory are derived. Applications to the binomial probability distribution and queuing theory are considered. In [12], essential properties of fuzzy probability are derived to present the measurement of fuzzy conditional probability, fuzzy independency, and fuzzy Bayes theorem. Fuzzy discrete distributions, fuzzy binomials, and fuzzy Poisson distributions are introduced with different examples. Among intelligent techniques, the authors in [13] focus on the application of the fuzzy set theory in the acceptance sampling. Multi-objective mathematical models for fuzzy single and fuzzy double acceptance sampling plans with illustrative examples are proposed. The study illustrates how an acceptance sampling plan should be designed under fuzzy BD. The fuzzy set theory can be successfully used to cope with the vagueness in these linguistic expressions for acceptance sampling. In [14], the main distributions of acceptance sampling plans are handled with fuzzy parameters, and their acceptance probability functions are derived. Then, the characteristic curves of acceptance sampling are examined under fuzziness. Illustrative examples are given with binomial and other fuzzy distributions. In [15], the authors intend to generate some properties of negative BD under imprecise measurement. These properties include fuzzy mean, fuzzy variance, fuzzy moments, and fuzzy GF. The uncertainty in the observations may not be addressed with the classical approach to probability distribution; therefore, the fuzzy set theory helps to modify the classical approach. In [16], the authors discuss the single acceptance sampling plan, when the proportion of nonconforming products is a fuzzy number. They showed that the operating characteristic (OC) curve of the plan is a band with high and low bounds and that for a fixed sample size and acceptance number, the width of the band depends on the ambiguity proportion parameter in the lot. Illustrative examples are given with binomial and other fuzzy distributions. In [17], the portfolio consists of only options traded in the financial market. One of the most famous models of option pricing is the Binomial Cox-Ross-Rubinstein (CRR) Model. Using Fuzzy Binomial CRR procedure, the price of option is an interval with a specific membership degree, by which the investors are allowed to adjust their portfolios. We make a portfolio dynamically adjusted periodically, in which the membership degree of an option price determines the decision of buying or selling the option in the simulation. Classifiers based on the BD can be found in the scientific literature, but due to the uncertainty of the epidemiological data, a fuzzy approach may be interesting. Reference [18] presents a new classifier named fuzzy binomial naive Bayes (FBiNB). The theoretical development is presented as well as the results of its application on simulated multidimensional data. A brief comparison among FBiNB, a classical binomial naive Bayes classifier, and a naive Bayes classifier is performed. The results obtained showed that the FBiNB provided the best performance, according to the Kappa coefficient. In [19], two main distributions of acceptance sampling plans are considered, which are binomial and Poisson distributions with fuzzy parameters, and they derived their acceptance probability functions. Then, fuzzy acceptance sampling plans were developed based on these distributions. In [20] the authors study the determination of the Quick Switching Single Double Sampling System using fuzzy BD, where the acceptance number tightening method is used. In [21], the fuzzy representations of a real-valued random variable are introduced for capturing relevant information on the distribution of the variable through the corresponding fuzzy-valued mean value. Specifically, characteristic fuzzy representations of a random variable allow us to capture the whole information on its distribution. As a result, the tests about fuzzy means of fuzzy random variables can be applied to develop goodness-of-fit tests. In this work, empirical comparisons of goodness-of-fit tests based on some convenient fuzzy representations with well-known procedures in case the null hypothesis relates to some specified BDs are presented. As is known [22], the optimal hypothesis tests for the BD and some other discrete distributions are uniformly most powerful (UMP) one-tailed and UMP unbiased (UMPU) two-tailed randomized tests. Therefore, conventional confidence intervals are not dual to randomized tests and perform badly on discrete data at small and moderate sample sizes. In this work, a new confidence interval notion, called fuzzy confidence intervals, that is dual to and inherits the exactness and optimality of UMP and UMPU tests is introduced. A new P-value notion, called fuzzy P-values or abstract randomized P-values, that also inherits the same exactness and optimality is also introduced. In [15], the generating procedure of some properties of negative BD under imprecise measurement is developed. These properties include fuzzy mean, fuzzy variance, fuzzy moments, and fuzzy moments GF.

It should be noted that in almost all of the studies presented here, the use of binomial distribution (BD) in an uncertain environment may result in fuzziness for only one reason: the value-realization of a binomial value in an uncertain environment cannot be the result of exact measurements or calculations, and it must be represented by fuzzy variables [9–22]. In other words, we are dealing with a binomial experiment when the possible results are presented in fuzzy values, more often in triangular or trapezoidal fuzzy numbers [23]—i.e., the binomial distribution is a descriptor of a *random-fuzzy experiment* whose realizations or characteristic parameters are represented in fuzzy values. The problem presented in this article is different from those presented in the studies above. It refers to a generalization of binomial distribution when the results or characteristics of an experiment are described by fuzzy variables. These variables are defined on the universe of all the results of the experiment and not on a certain subset of real numbers, as discussed in the studies presented above—i.e., we are dealing with a *fuzzy-random experiment*, where the binomial variable is a fuzzy-random variable. It has both a probability distribution and a membership function on the universe of all results of the experiment. Of course, the use of such binomial models is in great demand. This was the main motivation for us, the authors, to explore some of the new fuzzy extensions of binomial distribution.

In this work, we present a new approach to the extension of a classical BD under different fuzzy environments. In contrast to the above approaches to the study of fuzzy BDs, a completely new approach is developed in this paper. Section 2 presents the fuzzy extension of the BD, where the Bernoulli fuzzy-random variable is considered instead of the Bernoulli random variable. Success and failure events have both probabilistic distributions and their implementation possibility in the form of compatibility levels. Based on this information, the probabilistic distribution of the corresponding binomial fuzzy-random variable is calculated. The conditions of restrictions on this distribution are obtained. The Poisson distribution is calculated as a limit case of the constructed binomial fuzzy-random experiment. Section 3 considers the fuzzy extension of a BD, where the number of successes, unlike the previous case, is of a fuzzy nature and is represented as a fuzzy subset of the set of possible success numbers. A formula for calculating the probability of the occurrence of binomial dependent fuzzy events is obtained. The formula for calculating the probability of the convolution of binomial dependent fuzzy events is obtained. The invariance principle of exponential distribution is applied, and the corresponding GF is constructed. As a result, a scheme for calculating the mathematical expectation of the number of fuzzy successes is created. Section 4 considers the fuzzy extension of the binomial upper distribution, where the fuzziness is represented in the compatibility levels of the binomial and non-binomial events of the complete failure complex. The GF of the constructed distribution and the first-order moment of the distribution are also calculated. Sufficient conditions for the existence of a corresponding limit distribution and the Poisson distribution are also obtained. Section 5 presents the fuzzy extension of the classical Fuchs distribution, where fuzziness is reflected in the number of increasing failures. The built distribution function and the first and second order moments of the distribution are also calculated. Sufficient conditions for the existence of a corresponding limit distribution and the Poisson distribution are obtained. For better representation of the results, the examples of fuzzy BD are illustrated in each section. Section 6 presents the main results obtained and prospects for future research. A sequential scheme of the key facts and obtained results is presented by Scheme 1.

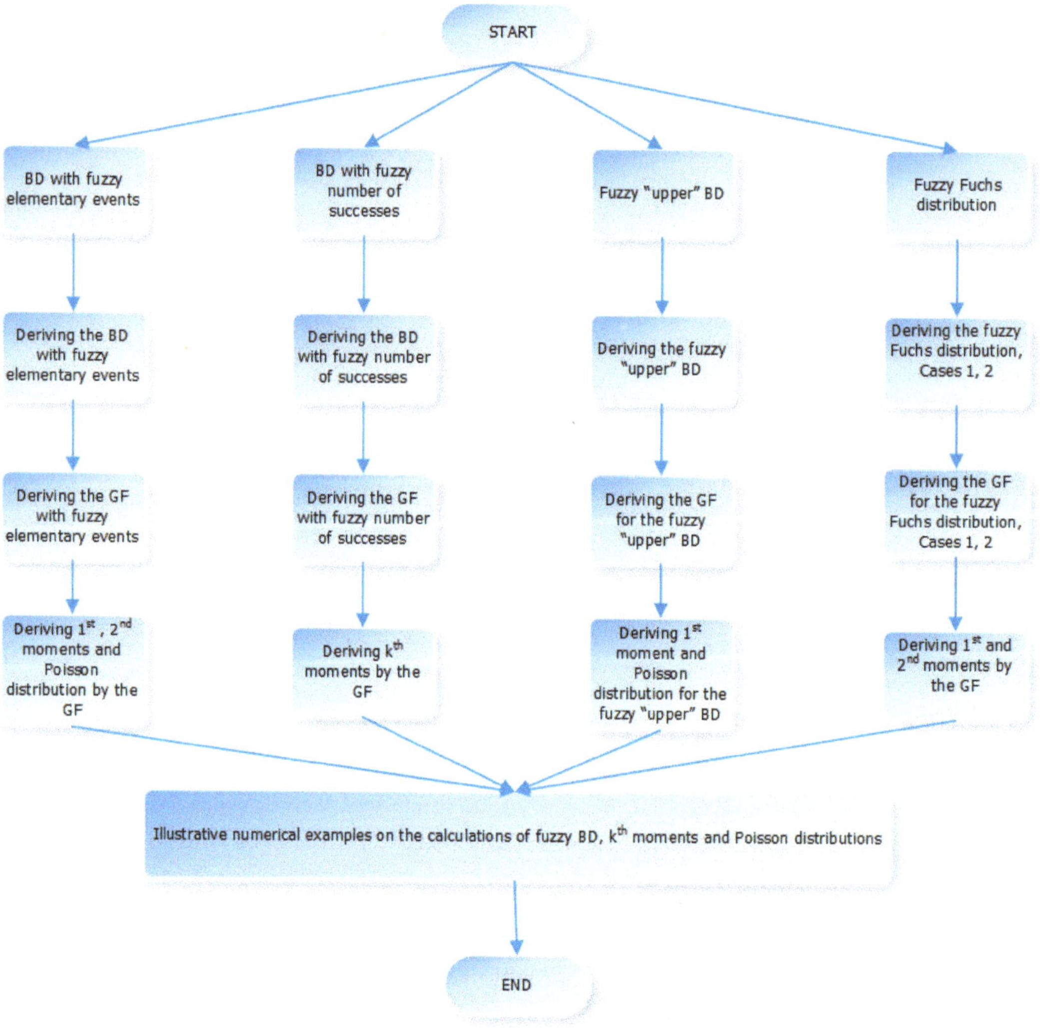

Scheme 1. Sequential scheme of key facts and obtained results.

2. BD by Fuzzy Elementary Events

Consider P_1 and $P_0 = 1 - P_1$ as elementary a priori probabilities of success ("1") and failure ("0") events, respectively. Let us also consider the membership levels μ_1 and μ_2 for (1) and (0), respectively. Therefore, we created a fuzzy-random variable of Bernoulli -$\widetilde{\mathcal{X}} \sim \begin{pmatrix} values & 1 & 0 \\ probabilities & P_1 & P_0 \\ membership\, levels & \mu_1 & \mu_2 \end{pmatrix}$. Then, the probabilities of the fuzzy events $\widetilde{1}$ and $\widetilde{0}$ according to [24,25] can be calculated by the formulas:

$$\mathcal{P}(\widetilde{1}) = \mu_1 P_1 \text{ and } \mathcal{P}(\widetilde{0}) = \mu_2 P_0 \tag{1}$$

For a sequence of n repetitive ordinary (non-fuzzy) trials in a binomial experiment, we introduce the notations

$$\begin{array}{c} C_1 \equiv (1,\ldots,1), \quad C_2 \equiv (1,\ldots,1,0),\ldots, \\ C_{2^n-1} \equiv (0,\ldots,0,1), \quad C_{2^n} \equiv (0,\ldots,0), \end{array} \tag{2}$$

as there exist 2^n possible results by the combination of (1) and (0). For describing the "n repetitive fuzzy elementary experiments"

$$\widetilde{C}_1 \equiv (\widetilde{1},\ldots,\widetilde{1}),\ldots,\widetilde{C}_{2^n} \equiv (\widetilde{0},\ldots,\widetilde{0}) \tag{3}$$

We refer to the notion of a fuzzy variable introduced in [24]. Suppose we have a fuzzy Bernoulli variable $\widetilde{\mathcal{X}} \equiv (X, U, \widetilde{R}(x,u))$, where X is a fuzzy elementary event, $U = \{0,1\}$ is a universal set, and the restriction $\widetilde{R}(x,u) \subset U$ means that

$$\widetilde{R}(x,u) \equiv \widetilde{R}(\widetilde{\mathcal{X}}) \equiv \widetilde{0} \cup \widetilde{1} \equiv \left\{\widetilde{0},\widetilde{1}\right\}, \tag{4}$$

Consider an ordered set of n such variables $(\widetilde{\mathcal{X}}_1,\ldots,\widetilde{\mathcal{X}}_n)$ as a fuzzy binomial experiment. According to [24], the universal set of such a compound fuzzy variable is the Cartesian product $U_1 \times \ldots \times U_n$. Now, suppose that $\widetilde{\mathcal{X}}_1,\ldots,\widetilde{\mathcal{X}}_n$ are the same non-interactive variables, i.e.,

$$\widetilde{R}(\widetilde{\mathcal{X}}_1,\ldots,\widetilde{\mathcal{X}}_n) = \overline{\widetilde{R}}(\widetilde{\mathcal{X}}_1) \cap \ldots \cap \overline{\widetilde{R}}(\widetilde{\mathcal{X}}_n) \tag{5}$$

where $\overline{\widetilde{R}}(\widetilde{\mathcal{X}}_i)$ is a cylindrical continuation of a marginal constraint $\widetilde{R}(\widetilde{\mathcal{X}}_i),\ i = 1,\ldots,n$. We refer to the sequence of "n repetitive fuzzy elementary experiments" as a fuzzy point $\widetilde{R}(\widetilde{\mathcal{X}}_1,\ldots,\widetilde{\mathcal{X}}_n)$. According to (5), we have:

$$\begin{array}{l} \mu_{\widetilde{C}_1} = \min\{\mu_1,\ldots,\mu_1\},\ \mu_{\widetilde{C}_{2^n}} = \min\{\mu_2,\ldots,\mu_2\}, \\ \mu_{\widetilde{C}_i} = \min\{(\mu_1\, or\, \mu_2) \wedge \ldots \wedge (\mu_1\, or\, \mu_2)\} = \mu_1 \wedge \mu_2,\ i = 2,3,\ldots,\ 2^n - 1. \end{array} \tag{6}$$

If we use the formula for calculating a fuzzy event probability, we obtain the following probabilities:

$$\begin{array}{l} \mathcal{P}\left(\widetilde{C}_1\right) \equiv \mathcal{P}(\widetilde{1},\ldots,\widetilde{1},\widetilde{1}) = \mu_1 P(1,\ldots,1,1) \\ \mathcal{P}\left(\widetilde{C}_2\right) \equiv \mathcal{P}(\widetilde{1},\ldots,\widetilde{1},\widetilde{0}) = (\mu_1 \wedge \mu_2) P(1,\ldots,1,0),\ldots, \\ \mathcal{P}\left(\widetilde{C}_{2^n-1}\right) \equiv \mathcal{P}(\widetilde{0},\ldots,\widetilde{0},\widetilde{1}) = (\mu_1 \wedge \mu_2) P(0,\ldots,0,1) \\ \mathcal{P}\left(\widetilde{C}_{2^n}\right) \equiv \mathcal{P}(\widetilde{0},\ldots,\widetilde{0},\widetilde{0}) = \mu_2 P(0,\ldots,0,0). \end{array} \tag{7}$$

As is well known, the projection of a relation on a given set of variables is a marginal sub-relation of that relation which applies only on these variables. It is considered on the

Cartesian product of the universes of these variables. If we sum the distribution (7) by the projection of relation (5)

$$\underset{U_{i_1}\times\ldots\times U_{i_{n-1}}}{\text{Proj}}\left\langle \widetilde{\text{R}}(\widetilde{\mathcal{X}}_1,\ldots,\widetilde{\mathcal{X}}_n)\right\rangle = \widetilde{R}_q\left(\widetilde{\mathcal{X}}_{i_1},\ldots,\widetilde{\mathcal{X}}_{i_{n-1}}\right),\quad q\equiv(i_1,\ldots,i_{n-1}), \tag{8}$$

we receive only normed fuzzy probabilities of $\widetilde{1}$ and $\widetilde{0}$

$$\mathcal{P}(\widetilde{1}) = \frac{\mu_1 P_1}{\sum_{i=1}^{2^n}\mathcal{P}\left(\widetilde{C}_i\right)}, \tag{9}$$

$$\mathcal{P}(\widetilde{0}) = 1-\mathcal{P}(\widetilde{1}) = \frac{\mu_1 P_0 + (\mu_2-\mu_1)P(0,\ldots,0)}{\sum_{i=1}^{2^n}\mathcal{P}\left(\widetilde{C}_i\right)}.$$

After substituting (7) and (9) in the BD formula, we receive:

$$\mathcal{P}(\widetilde{C}_{(k)}) = \frac{P_1^k}{\left[1+\left(\frac{\mu_2}{\mu_1}-1\right)P(0,\ldots,0)\right]^{n-1}}\left[1+\left(\frac{\mu_2}{\mu_1}-1\right)P(0,\ldots,0)-P_1\right]^{n-k}, \tag{10}$$
$$k=1,\ldots,n.$$

where common notation $\widetilde{C}_{(k)}$ is introduced for those $\widetilde{C}_i$ to which the same number k of successes correspond, since the probabilities of such $\widetilde{C}_i$ are equal. Note that

$$\sum_{i=1}^{2^n}\mathcal{P}(\widetilde{C}_i) = \mu_1 + (\mu_2-\mu_1)P(0,\ldots,0), \tag{11}$$

It is clear from (9) and (10) that if $\mu_1=\mu_2$, then the conditions for the independence of fuzzy events degenerate to the corresponding conditions for ordinary events.

The constraint (7) for probabilities $\mathcal{P}(\widetilde{C}_{(k)})$ leads to the relationship

$$\frac{\mu_2}{\mu_1} = \left[1+\frac{1-P_1\cdot\sqrt[n-1]{\frac{P_1}{P(1,\ldots,1)}}}{P(1,\ldots,1)\left(\sqrt[n-1]{\frac{P_1}{P(1,\ldots,1)}}-1\right)^n}\right]^{-1}. \tag{12}$$

By putting Formula (12) into (11) and assuming that $\mu_2\geq\mu_1$ and $\mathcal{P}\left(\widetilde{C}_i\right)\geq 0$, we get a system of conditions

$$\mathcal{P}\left(\widetilde{C}_{(k)}\right) = P(1,\ldots,1)\left[\sqrt[n-1]{\frac{P_1}{P(1,\ldots,1)}}-1\right]^{n-k}, k=1,\ldots,n; \tag{13}$$

$$0\leq\frac{P_1\cdot\sqrt[n-1]{\frac{P_1}{P(1,\ldots,1)}}-1}{P(1,\ldots,1)\left[\sqrt[n-1]{\frac{P_1}{P(1,\ldots,1)}}-1\right]^n}<1;\ \frac{\mu_2}{\mu_1}=1+\frac{-1+P_1\cdot\sqrt[n-1]{\frac{P_1}{P(1,\ldots,1)}}}{P(0,\ldots,0)}. \tag{14}$$

The probabilities of considering fuzzy events, normalized in $\widetilde{\text{R}}(\widetilde{\mathcal{X}}_1,\ldots,\widetilde{\mathcal{X}}_n) = \bigcup_{i=1}^{2^n}\widetilde{C}_i$, are calculated by the formula

$$\mathcal{P}'(\widetilde{C}_i) = \frac{\mathcal{P}(\widetilde{C}_i)}{\sum_{j=1}^{2^n}\mathcal{P}(\widetilde{C}_j)},\quad i=1,\ldots,2^n. \tag{15}$$

In deriving the BD with fuzzy elementary events, we will proceed from the notion of the independence of fuzzy events [23], which is not equivalent to the ordinary independence. This leads to the certain conditions of independence, which we discuss below. For the purpose of clarity, let $\mu_1 \leq \mu_2$; then, we obtain the fuzzy binomial distribution:

$$\mathcal{P}'\left(\widetilde{C}_1\right) = \left[\mathcal{P}'(\widetilde{1})\right]^n, \ldots, \mathcal{P}'\left(\widetilde{C}_{2^n}\right) = \left[\mathcal{P}'(\widetilde{0})\right]^n$$

Thus, conditions (13)–(15) are equivalent to the existence of the n-ar fuzzy-random variable, which is a sequence of n repetitive, fuzzy, non-interacting, and independent elementary events whose distribution is described by the BD with fuzzy elementary events

$$\begin{gathered}\mathcal{P}'\left(\widetilde{\mathcal{B}}_n^k\right) = C_n^k\left[\mathcal{P}'(\widetilde{1})\right]^k\left[\mathcal{P}'(\widetilde{0})\right]^{n-k} = C_n^k \frac{\mu_1^k P_1^k [\mu_1 P_0 + (\mu_2-\mu_1)P(0\ldots,0)]^{n-k}}{[\mu_1+(\mu_2-\mu_1)P(0,\ldots 0)]^n} = \\ C_n^k \frac{P_1^k\left[P_0+\left(\frac{\mu_2}{\mu_1}-1\right)P(0,\ldots,0)\right]^{n-k}}{\left[1+\left(\frac{\mu_2}{\mu_1}-1_1\right)P(0,\ldots 0)\right]^n},\end{gathered} \tag{16}$$

where

$$\widetilde{\mathcal{B}}_n^k = \bigcup_{\forall j \text{ with } k \text{ successes}} \widetilde{C}_j.$$

If $\mu_2 < \mu_1$, for the calculation of $\mathcal{P}'\left(\widetilde{\mathcal{B}}_n^k\right)$, it is necessary to make the following changes in the ending part of Equation (16). Instead of $\frac{\mu_2}{\mu_1}$, we write $\frac{\mu_1}{\mu_2}$, and instead of $P(0,\ldots,0)$, we write $P(1,\ldots,1)$:

$$\frac{\mu_2}{\mu_1} \leftarrow \frac{\mu_1}{\mu_2}, \qquad P(0,\ldots,0) \leftarrow P(1,\ldots,1).$$

To be more precise, we receive

$$\begin{gathered}\mathcal{P}'\left(\widetilde{\mathcal{B}}_n^k\right) = C_n^k \frac{[\mu_2 P_1+(\mu_1-\mu_2)P(1,\ldots,1)]^k \mu_2^{n-k} P_0^{n-k}}{[\mu_2+(\mu_1-\mu_2)P(1,\ldots,1)]^n}, \\ C_n^k \frac{P_0^{n-k}\left[P_1+\left(\frac{\mu_1}{\mu_2}-1\right)P(1,\ldots,1)\right]^{n-k}}{\left[1+\left(\frac{\mu_1}{\mu_2}-1\right)P(1,\ldots,1)\right]^n}.\end{gathered} \tag{17}$$

Note that in both cases, if $\mu_2 = \mu_1$, then (16) and (17) transform to the usual BD.

From Formulas (16) and (17), we see that $\mathcal{P}'\left(\widetilde{\mathcal{B}}_n^k\right)$ depends on the ratio $\frac{\mu_2}{\mu_1}$ if $\mu_2 > \mu_1$, and on the ratio $\frac{\mu_1}{\mu_2}$ if $\mu_2 < \mu_1$, while the condition of independence and non-interaction (14) allows us to express the normalized probability $\mathcal{P}'\left(\widetilde{\mathcal{B}}_n^k\right)$ with the probabilities of the corresponding non-fuzzy events. Indeed, it is not difficult to show that

$$\mathcal{P}'(\widetilde{1}) = \begin{cases} \sqrt[n-1]{P_1(\overbrace{1,\ldots,1}^{n-1})}, & \mu_1 < \mu_2 \\ \sqrt[n-1]{P_0(\overbrace{1,\ldots,1}^{n-1})}, & \mu_1 > \mu_2 \end{cases}, \quad \mathcal{P}'(\widetilde{0}) = \begin{cases} \sqrt[n-1]{P_1(\overbrace{0,\ldots,0}^{n-1})}, & \mu_1 < \mu_2 \\ \sqrt[n-1]{P_0(\overbrace{0,\ldots,0}^{n-1})}, & \mu_1 > \mu_2 \end{cases} \tag{18}$$

If we enter the values from Formula (18) to Formulas (16) and (17), we get

$$\mathcal{P}'\left(\widetilde{\mathcal{B}}_n^k\right) = \begin{cases} C_n^k \left[P_1(\overbrace{1,\ldots,1}^{n-1})\right]^{\frac{k}{n-1}} \left[P_1(\overbrace{0,\ldots,0}^{n-1})\right]^{\frac{n-k}{n-1}}, \mu_1 < \mu_2, \\ C_n^k \left[P_0(\overbrace{1,\ldots,1}^{n-1})\right]^{\frac{k}{n-1}} \left[P_0(\overbrace{0,\ldots,0}^{n-1})\right]^{\frac{n-k}{n-1}}, \mu_1 > \mu_2. \end{cases} \tag{19}$$

Using the notion of a discrete distribution moment generating function, we analytically obtain the formula of the GF of the BD with fuzzy elementary events (two cases are considered as presented above).

$$G_{\mathcal{P}'(\mathfrak{B}_n^k)}(y) = \begin{cases} \frac{[\mu_1 P_0+\mu_1 P_1 y+(\mu_2-\mu_1)P(0,\ldots,0)]^n}{[\mu_1+(\mu_2-\mu_1)P(0,\ldots,0)]^n}, \mu_1 < \mu_2, \\ \frac{[\mu_2 P_1 y+(\mu_1-\mu_2)P(1,\ldots,1)y+\mu_2 P_0]^n}{[\mu_2+(\mu_1-\mu_2)P(1,\ldots,1)]^n}, \mu_1 > \mu_2. \end{cases} \tag{20}$$

As is well known, distribution moments are easily calculated from the generating function. Without presenting a long process of calculation, we give the analytical form of the first and second order moments of the BD with fuzzy elementary events

$$\bar{k} = \begin{cases} \frac{n\mu_1 P_1}{\mu_1+(\mu_2-\mu_1)P(0,\ldots,0)}, & \mu_1 < \mu_2, \\ \frac{n[\mu_2 P_1+(\mu_1-\mu_2)P(1,\ldots,1)]}{\mu_2+(\mu_1-\mu_2)P(1,\ldots,1)}, & \mu_1 > \mu_2. \end{cases} = \begin{cases} \frac{nP_1}{1+\left(\frac{\mu_2}{\mu_1}-1\right)P(0,\ldots,0)}, & \mu_1 < \mu_2, \\ \frac{n\left[P_1+\left(\frac{\mu_1}{\mu_2}-1\right)P(1,\ldots,1)\right]}{1+\left(\frac{\mu_1}{\mu_2}-1\right)P(1,\ldots,1)}, & \mu_1 > \mu_2. \end{cases} \tag{21}$$

$$\bar{k}^2 = \bar{k}(1+\frac{n-1}{n}\bar{k}) = \begin{cases} \frac{n\mu_1 P_1}{\mu_1+(\mu_2-\mu_1)P(0,\ldots,0)}\left[1+\frac{(n-1)\mu_1 P_1}{\mu_1+(\mu_2-\mu_1)P(0,\ldots,0)}\right], & \mu_1 < \mu_2, \\ \frac{n[\mu_2 P_1+(\mu_1-\mu_2)P(1,\ldots,1)]}{\mu_2+(\mu_1-\mu_2)P(1,\ldots,1)}\left[1+\frac{(n-1)[\mu_2 P_1+(\mu_1-\mu_2)P(1,\ldots,1)]}{\mu_2+(\mu_1-\mu_2)P(1,\ldots,1)}\right], & \mu_1 > \mu_2. \end{cases}$$

$$= \begin{cases} \frac{nP_1}{1+\left(\frac{\mu_2}{\mu_1}-1\right)P(0,\ldots,0)}\left[1+\frac{(n-1)P_1}{1+\left(\frac{\mu_2}{\mu_1}-1\right)P(0,\ldots,0)}\right], & \mu_1 < \mu_2, \\ \frac{n\left[P_1+\left(\frac{\mu_1}{\mu_2}-1\right)P(1,\ldots,1)\right]}{1+\left(\frac{\mu_1}{\mu_2}-1\right)P(1,\ldots,1)}\left[1+\frac{(n-1)P_1+\left(\frac{\mu_1}{\mu_2}-1\right)P(1,\ldots,1)]}{1+\left(\frac{\mu_1}{\mu_2}-1\right)P(1,\ldots,1)}\right], & \mu_1 > \mu_2. \end{cases} \tag{22}$$

Expressions (16), (17), and (21) allow us to prove the existence of Poisson limits for BD with fuzzy elementary events. It is not difficult to calculate the limits below if we use a well-known numerical sequence limit calculation technique. There are some possible cases:

(1). $\bar{k} = const$. In this case, we obviously have

$$\lim_{\substack{n\to\infty \\ \bar{k}=const}} \mathcal{P}'\left(\widetilde{\mathcal{B}}_n^k\right) = e^{-\bar{k}}\frac{\bar{k}^k}{k!}, \quad k = 0,1,\ldots \tag{23}$$

(2). μ_1 and μ_2 are fixed and $nP_1 = const$. It is easy to show that:

$$\lim_{\substack{n\to\infty \\ nP_1=\lambda=const \\ P_1\to 0}} \mathcal{P}'\left(\widetilde{\mathcal{B}}_n^k\right) = \begin{cases} e^{-c'}\frac{(c')^k}{k!}, & c' = \frac{\lambda}{1+\left(\frac{\mu_2}{\mu_1}-1\right)[P(\overbrace{0,\ldots,0}^{n})]}, \mu_1 < \mu_2, \\ e^{-c''}\frac{(c'')^k}{k!} & c'' = \lambda+\left(\frac{\mu_1}{\mu_2}-1\right)[P(\overbrace{1,\ldots,1}^{n})], \mu_1 > \mu_2. \end{cases} \tag{24}$$

Example 1. *Let the fuzzy Bernoulli distribution be given* $\widetilde{\mathcal{X}} \sim \begin{pmatrix} values & 1 & 0 \\ probabilities & 0.3 & 0.7 \\ membership\ levels & 0.5 & 0.6 \end{pmatrix}$. *Based on Formula (19), construct fuzzy BD for the $n = 5$. Use Formulas (21) and (22) and calculate the moments of the first and second order $\bar{k}$ and $\bar{k}^2$. Calculate the standard deviation of distribution $SD = \sqrt{\bar{k}^2 - (\bar{k})^2}$. Using the Poisson distribution Formula (24), calculate the distribution values for $k = 0,1,\ldots,7$ when $nP_1 \simeq const = 6$.*

Solution of Example 1. It is clear that for the calculations $P_1 = 0.3$ and $P_0 = 0.7$, $\mu_1 = 0.5$ and $\mu_2 = 0.6$, $n = 5$, $k = 0,1,2,3,4,5$. In our case, $\mu_1 < \mu_2$. Let us assume that $P_1(\overbrace{0,\ldots,0}^{n-1}) = P_1(\overbrace{0,\ldots,0}^{4}) = (0.7)^4$ and $P_1(\overbrace{1,\ldots,1}^{n-1}) = P_1(\overbrace{1,\ldots,1}^{4}) = (0.3)^4$. We receive (Table 1).

Table 1. Conditional fuzzy binomial probability distribution.

k	0	1	2	3	4	5
$\mathcal{P}'\left(\widetilde{\mathcal{B}}_n^k\right)$	0.1681	0.3601	0.3087	0.1323	0.0283	0.0024

Using Formulas (21) and (22), we receive $\overline{k} = 1.4512$, $\overline{k}^2 = 3.1360$, and $SD = \sqrt{\overline{k}^2 - (\overline{k})^2} = 1.0149$. For the Poisson distribution, if $nP_1 \simeq const = 6$, then, for $k = 0, 1, 2, 3, 4, 5$, we receive (Table 2).

Table 2. Fragment of Poisson distribution.

k	0	1	2	3	4	5	6	7
$\lim_{\substack{n \to \infty \\ nP_1 = const}} \mathcal{P}'\left(\widetilde{\mathcal{B}}_n^k\right)$	0.0029	0.0170	0.0497	0.0967	0.1411	0.1647	0.1603	0.1336

3. BDs with a Fuzzy Number of Successes

Consider a set $\mathcal{A}_n \equiv \{0, 1, \ldots, n\}$. Let $\widetilde{k}$, $\widetilde{k} \subset \mathcal{A}_n$ be the fuzzy subset in $\mathcal{A}_n$, $\widetilde{k} =$ *"approximately k number"* with some membership function $\mu_{\widetilde{k}} : \mathcal{A}_n \to [0,1]$ and $\widetilde{k} = \bigcup_{l=0}^{n} \left[\mu_{\widetilde{k}}(l)/l\right]$ [23,24].

If $\mathcal{A}_n$ is a set of numbers of possible successes in n trials of the binomial scheme, then it is well known that to each element of $\mathcal{A}_n$ corresponds the probability $P(\mathcal{B}_{n;p}^k) = C_n^k p^k q^{n-k}$. Therefore, according to [24,25], for the BD with the fuzzy success number, we obtain the formula

$$\mathcal{P}\left(\mathcal{B}_{n;p}^{\widetilde{k}}\right) = \sum_{l=0}^{n} \mu_{\widetilde{k}}(l) P\left(\mathcal{B}_{n;p}^{l}\right) \tag{25}$$

Here, $\mathcal{P}\left(\widetilde{\mathcal{B}}_{n;p}^k\right)$ is the probability measure of a fuzzy event $\mathcal{B}_{n;p}^{\widetilde{k}}$ or the fuzzy subset $\widetilde{k}$.

Note that in this scheme under consideration, the fuzzy events $\mathcal{B}_{n;p}^{\widetilde{k}}$ are not mutually exclusive events. Therefore, according to the additivity property of a probability measure of a fuzzy event [24,25], we have

$$\mathcal{P}\left(\bigcup_{k=0}^{n} \mathcal{B}_{n;p}^{\widetilde{k}}\right) = \sum_{k=0}^{n} \mathcal{P}\left(\mathcal{B}_{n;p}^{\widetilde{k}}\right) - \sum_{k,k'} \mathcal{P}\left(\mathcal{B}_{n;p}^{\widetilde{k}} \cap \mathcal{B}_{n;p}^{\widetilde{k'}}\right) + \sum_{k,k',k''} \mathcal{P}\left(\mathcal{B}_{n;p}^{\widetilde{k}} \cap \mathcal{B}_{n;p}^{\widetilde{k'}} \cap \mathcal{B}_{n;p}^{\widetilde{k''}}\right) + \ldots$$
$$+(-1)^n \mathcal{P}\left(\mathcal{B}_{n;p}^{\widetilde{0}} \cap \ldots \cap \mathcal{B}_{n;p}^{\widetilde{n}}\right). \tag{26}$$

Let $0 < p_i < 1$, $i = 1, 2$ be two numbers. An important feature of the distribution (25) is that the law of composition is satisfied

$$\mathcal{P}\left(\mathcal{B}_{n;p_1p_2}^{\widetilde{k}}\right) = \sum_{m=0}^{n} P\left(\mathcal{B}_{n;p_1}^{m}\right) \mathcal{P}\left(\mathcal{B}_{m,p_2}^{\widetilde{k}}\right) \tag{27}$$

which is easily verified by the simple calculations

$$\mathcal{P}\left(\mathcal{B}_{n;p_1p_2}^{\widetilde{k}}\right) = \sum_{l=0}^{n} \mu_{\widetilde{k}}(l) P\left(\mathcal{B}_{n;p_1p_2}^{l}\right) = \sum_{l=0}^{n} \mu_{\widetilde{k}}(l) C_n^k (p_1p_2)^l (1 - p_1p_2)^{n-l}$$

and

$$\sum_{m=0}^{n} P\left(\mathcal{B}_{n;p_1}^{m}\right)\mathcal{P}\left(\mathcal{B}_{m,p_2}^{\widetilde{k}}\right) = \sum_{m=0}^{n} P\left(\mathcal{B}_{n;p_1}^{m}\right)\sum_{l=0}^{n} \mu_{\widetilde{k}}(l)P\left(\mathcal{B}_{n;p_2}^{l}\right) =$$
$$\sum_{l=0}^{n} \mu_{\widetilde{k}}(l)\sum_{m=0}^{n} C_n^m C_m^l p_1^m (1-p_1)^{n-m} p_2^l (1-p_2)^{m-l} = \sum_{l=0}^{n} \mu_{\widetilde{k}}(l)\frac{n!}{l!(n-l)!}(p_1p_2)^l(1-p_1p_2)^{n-l}$$
$$\times \sum_{m=0}^{n} \frac{(n-l)!}{(n-m)!(m-l)!}\frac{p_1^{m-l}(1-p_1)^{n-m}(1-p_2)^{m-l}}{(1-p_1p_2)^{n-l}} = \sum_{l=0}^{n} \mu_{\widetilde{k}}(l)\frac{n!}{l!(n-l)!}p_1p_2^l(1-p_1p_2)^{n-l}$$
$$\times \sum_{j=0}^{n-l} \frac{(n-l)!}{j!(n-l-j)!}\frac{p_1^j(1-p_1)^{n-l-j}(1-p_2)^j}{(1-p_1p_2)^{n-l}} = \sum_{l=0}^{n} \mu_{\widetilde{k}}(l)P\left(\mathcal{B}_{n;p_1p_2}^{l}\right).$$

Based on the property of the invariability of the exponential distribution, let us extend the fuzzy subset $\widetilde{k}$ from the set $\mathcal{A}_n$ to the non-negative integer numbers set $N \cup \{0\}$. In this case, the extended membership function $\mu_{\widetilde{k}}(l),\ l \in N \cup \{0\}$ will be a mapping of a set of natural numbers $\mathbb{N}$ into $[0,1]$. Consider the expression of the moments' generating function of fuzzy BD.

Consider the expression of the moments' GF of the fuzzy BD

$$G(\widetilde{k}) = \sum_{n=0}^{\infty} \mathcal{P}\left(\mathcal{B}_{n;p}^{\widetilde{k}}\right) f_n(u), \tag{28}$$

where $f_n(u) = (1-u)u^n,\ 0 < u < 1$.

If we denote $v = \frac{pu}{1-u+pu}$ and $g_l(v) = (1-v)v^l$, then

$$G(\widetilde{k}) = \sum_{l=0}^{\infty} \mu_{\widetilde{k}}(l) g_l(v). \tag{29}$$

Indeed,

$$G(\widetilde{k}) = \sum_{n=0}^{\infty} f_n(u)\mathcal{P}\left(\mathcal{B}_{n;p}^{\widetilde{k}}\right) = \sum_{n=0}^{\infty} f_n(u)\sum_{l=0}^{n} \mu_{\widetilde{k}}(l)P\left(\mathcal{B}_{n;p}^{l}\right) = f_0(u)\sum_{l=0}^{0} \mu_{\widetilde{k}}(l)P\left(\mathcal{B}_{0;p}^{l}\right)$$
$$+f_1(u)\sum_{l=0}^{1} \mu_{\widetilde{k}}(l)P\left(\mathcal{B}_{1;p}^{l}\right) + f_2(u)\sum_{l=0}^{2} \mu_{\widetilde{k}}(l)P\left(\mathcal{B}_{2;p}^{l}\right) + \ldots$$
$$= \mu_{\widetilde{k}}(0)\left[f_0(u)P\left(\mathcal{B}_{0;p}^{0}\right) + f_1(u)P\left(\mathcal{B}_{1;p}^{0}\right) + f_2(u)P\left(\mathcal{B}_{2;p}^{0}\right) + \ldots\right] +$$
$$\mu_{\widetilde{k}}(1)\left[f_1(u)P\left(\mathcal{B}_{1;p}^{1}\right) + f_2(u)P\left(\mathcal{B}_{2;p}^{1}\right) + \ldots\right]$$
$$+\mu_{\widetilde{k}}(2)\left[f_2(u)P\left(\mathcal{B}_{2;p}^{2}\right) + f_3(u)P\left(\mathcal{B}_{3;p}^{2}\right) + \ldots\right] + \ldots$$

Given that for $r < s$ $P\left(\mathcal{B}_{r;p}^{s}\right) = 0$, then

$$G\left(\widetilde{k}\right) = \sum_{n=0}^{\infty} \mu_{\widetilde{k}}(n)\sum_{l=0}^{\infty} f_l(u)P\left(\mathcal{B}_{l;p}^{n}\right)$$
$$= \sum_{n=0}^{\infty} \mu_{\widetilde{k}}(n)\sum_{l=0}^{\infty} \frac{l!}{n!(n-l)!}p^n(1-p)^{l-n}(1-u)u^l$$
$$= \sum_{n=0}^{\infty} \mu_{\widetilde{k}}(n)(1-u)(pu)^n\sum_{l=0}^{\infty} \frac{l!}{n!(n-l)!}[(1-p)u]^{l-n} =$$
$$\sum_{n=0}^{\infty} \mu_{\widetilde{k}}(n)(1-u)(pu)^n\sum_{j=0}^{\infty} \frac{(n+j)!}{n!j!}[(1-p)u]^j\ .$$

The last sum is a decomposition of the function $[1-(1-p)u]^{-n+1}$ into series by degrees of $(1-p)u$. Considering the connection between u and v, we finally obtain the expression of (29)

$$G\left(\widetilde{k}\right) = \sum_{n=0}^{\infty} \mu_{\widetilde{k}}(l)\frac{1-u}{1-(1-p)u}\left[\frac{pu}{1-(1-p)u}\right]^n.$$

To determine the mean value of a success fuzzy number "with probability measure $\mathcal{P}$", let us do the following. Consider a set of ordinary (nonfuzzy) events $\mathcal{A} \subset \mathcal{A}_n$. Define the function of a set $E(.)$ in such a way that, for any subset $\mathcal{A}$, this function corresponds to the conditional mean, i.e., if $\mathcal{A} \subset \mathcal{A}_n$, then $E(\mathcal{A}) = \overline{k}_{\mathcal{A}}$. According to the principle of generalization [23], the domain of definition $E(.)$ can be extended to fuzzy subsets as well. Suppose we have a fuzzy subset $\widetilde{k}$ of $\mathcal{A}_n$, and $\widetilde{k}$ is represented as

$$\widetilde{k} = \underset{\alpha}{\cup}\mathcal{A}_\alpha, \qquad \alpha \in [0,1], \tag{30}$$

where $\mathcal{A}_\alpha$ denotes a cut set of level α. Then,

$$E(\widetilde{k}) = \bigcup_\alpha E(\mathcal{A}_\alpha) = \bigcup_\alpha \overline{k}_{\mathcal{A}_\alpha}. \tag{31}$$

Here, $E(\widetilde{k})$ is a fuzzy subset on the set of all conditional mean values $\mathcal{E}$. Relationships (30) and (31) define the calculation rule for the values of the characteristic functions of fuzzy subsets on the set of all conditional means $\mu\left(\overline{k}_{\mathcal{A}}\right)$ corresponding to ordinary subsets $\mathcal{A}_n$ over $\mu_{\widetilde{k}}(l)$.

Define the mean value of the fuzzy success number as a convex combination [23] of the fuzzy subsets $E(\widetilde{k})$ with the following weights: $W_n(\widetilde{k}) = \frac{\mathcal{P}\left(B^{\widetilde{k}}_{n;p}\right)}{\sum_l \mathcal{P}\left(B^{l}_{n;p}\right)}$. We define a fuzzy subset with the following membership function

$$\mu_{\widetilde{k}_p}\left(l_{\mathcal{A}}\right) = \sum_{\widetilde{k}\in\mathcal{A}_n} W_n(\widetilde{k})\mu_{E(\widetilde{k})}\left(\overline{l}_{\mathcal{A}}\right), \overline{l}_{\mathcal{A}} \in \mathcal{E} \tag{32}$$

Note that when $\mu_{\widetilde{u}}(l) \to \delta_{l\,k}$, $\delta_{l\,k} = \begin{cases} 1, \; if\; l = k, \\ 0, \; if\; l \neq k \end{cases}$, that is, when moving $\widetilde{k}$ to the ordinary set $\{k\}$, "the average by the measure $\mathcal{P}$" tends to the mathematical expectation of the number of successes of the BD, $\widetilde{k}_{\mathcal{P}} \to np$. The method given here can be used for the calculation of any order fuzzy moments $\widetilde{k}^r_{\mathcal{P}}$, but when calculating high-order moments, it is necessary to use a certain rule for multiplying fuzzy numbers. Most importantly, we present a rule that is derived from the principle of generalization [23].

The discussion of the Poisson and Normal approximations for (25) is reduced to the substitution of the corresponding approximate values of $P\left(B^{l}_{n;p}\right)$ in this formula.

Example 2. *Let the Bernoulli distribution be given* $\mathcal{X} \sim \begin{pmatrix} values & 1 & 0 \\ propbabilities & 0.3 & 0.7 \end{pmatrix}$ *and let a binomial experiment be created based on this Bernoulli experiment for* $n = 6$*. Let be given the following fuzzy subsets "approximately k successes"* ($k = 0, \ldots, 6$) *(Table 3).*

Table 3. Fuzzy subsets "approximately k successes" ($k = 0, 1, 2, 3, 4, 5, 6$).

$\widetilde{k}\backslash k$	0	1	2	3	4	5	6
$\widetilde{0}$	1.0	0.8	0.6	0.5	0.3	0.2	0.1
$\widetilde{1}$	0.9	1.0	0.8	0.6	0.5	0.3	0.1
$\widetilde{2}$	0.7	0.8	1.0	0.9	0.6	0.4	0.2
$\widetilde{3}$	0.4	0.6	0.8	1.0	0.9	0.7	0.5
$\widetilde{4}$	0.2	0.3	0.5	0.8	1.0	0.8	0.6
$\widetilde{5}$	0.1	0.3	0.5	0.7	0.9	1.0	0.8
$\widetilde{6}$	0.1	0.2	0.3	0.5	0.7	0.9	1.0

Use the results of this Section to calculate the numerical values of BD with fuzzy success numbers.

Solution of Example 2. Note that $p = 0.3$. Using expression (25) and the data of Table 3, we calculate the BD values presented in Table 4.

Table 4. Numerical values of BD with fuzzy success numbers—$\mathcal{P}\left(\mathcal{B}_{n;p}^{\widetilde{k}}\right)$.

$\widetilde{k}$	$\widetilde{0}$	$\widetilde{1}$	$\widetilde{2}$	$\widetilde{3}$	$\widetilde{4}$	$\widetilde{5}$	$\widetilde{6}$
$\mathcal{P}\left(\mathcal{B}_{n;p}^{\widetilde{k}}\right)$	0.6667	0.8118	0.8552	0.7342	0.4927	0.4586	0.3137

4. Fuzzy "Upper" BD

As is well known, the discussion on the (non-fuzzy) "upper" BD is based on a model of the superposition of two processes: the binomial process $\mathcal{B}_{n;p}^{k}$ and the process of "increasing the total number of failures" $\mathcal{B}_0$-denoted by $\mathcal{B}_0 \circ \mathcal{B}_{n;p}^{k}$, characterized by a priori probability $P(\mathcal{B}_0) = 1 - \gamma$ [26], where p is the elementary event probability of ("1"). Let μ_0 and μ_0' be the values of the membership function that correspond to the complex events $\overbrace{(0,\ldots,0)}^{n}$ at attempting to distinguish the binomial and non-binomial origin events. Then, as it is easy to verify, the probability of k successes in n trials of the binomial "upper" fuzzy experiment—denoted by $\widetilde{\mathcal{B}}_0 \circ \mathcal{B}_{n;p}^{k}$ will have the form

$$\mathcal{P}\left(\widetilde{\mathcal{B}}_0 \circ \mathcal{B}_{n;p}^{k}\right) = \frac{1}{Z}\begin{cases} \mu_0 P(\mathcal{B}_0) + \mu_0' P\left(\mathcal{B}_0\right) P\left(\mathcal{B}_{n;p}^{0}\right), & k = 0, \\ P\left(\mathcal{B}_0\right) P\left(\mathcal{B}_{n;p}^{k}\right), & k = 1,\ldots,n, \end{cases} = \frac{1}{Z}\begin{cases} \mu_0(1-\gamma) + \mu_0'\gamma(1-p)^n, & k = 0, \\ \gamma C_n^k p^k (1-p)^{n-k}, & k = 1,\ldots,n \end{cases} \tag{33}$$

where Z is a constant that is determined by the normalization condition $\sum_k \mathcal{P}\left(\widetilde{\mathcal{B}}_0 \circ \mathcal{B}_{n;p}^{k}\right) = 1$ and

$$Z = \mu_0(1-\gamma) + \mu_0'\gamma(1-p)^n + \gamma\left[1 - (1-p)^n\right]. \tag{34}$$

The corresponding GF and the first moment of this probabilistic distribution are as follows:

$$G_{\mathcal{P}(\widetilde{\mathcal{B}}_0 \circ \mathcal{B}_{n,p}^{k})}(y) = \frac{1}{Z}[\mu_0(1-\gamma) + \mu_0\gamma(1-p)^n + \gamma((1-p+py)^n - (1-p)^n)], \tag{35}$$

and $\overline{k} = Z^{-1}\gamma np$.

Poisson's limit $(np \to c > 0,\ n \to \infty,\ p \to 0)$ is

$$P_{Poiss}(k) = \frac{1}{Z}\begin{cases} \mu_0(1-\gamma) + \mu_0'\gamma e^{-c}, & k = 0, \\ \gamma e^{-c}\frac{c^k}{k!}, & k = 1,\ 2,\ \ldots\ . \end{cases} \tag{36}$$

$\overline{k}$ and c are related by the ratio

$$\overline{k} = \left[\mu_0(1-\gamma) + \mu_0'\gamma e^{-c} + \gamma\left(1 - e^{-c}\right)\right]^{-1}\gamma c. \tag{37}$$

By the integration of Formula (36) with respect to membership levels $0 \le \mu_0 \le 1,\ 0 \le \mu'_0 \le 1$, we obtain the Poisson distribution

$$\overline{P}_{Poiss}(k) = \begin{cases} 1 - (1-e^{-c})\xi, & k = 0, \\ \xi e^{-c}\frac{c^k}{k!}, & k = 1,2,\ldots, \end{cases} \tag{38}$$

where

$$\xi = \iint\limits_{0 \le \mu_0, \mu_0' \le 1} \gamma Z^{-1} d\mu_0 d\mu_0'. \tag{39}$$

It is easy to show that GF G_{Poiss} looks like as follows:

$$G_{Poiss}(y) = 1 - (1 - ec)\,\xi + \xi e^{-c}(e^{cy} - 1), \tag{40}$$

and in this case, $\overline{\overline{k}} = \xi c$. Therefore, we finally receive

$$\overline{P}_{Poiss}(k) = \begin{cases} 1 - \left(1 - e^{-\frac{\overline{\overline{k}}}{\xi}}\right)\xi, & k = 0, \\ \xi e^{-\frac{\overline{\overline{k}}}{\xi}} \frac{\left(\frac{\overline{\overline{k}}}{\xi}\right)^k}{k!}, & k = 1, 2, \ldots. \end{cases} \tag{41}$$

Example 3. *Let the binomial experiment by the same data presented in Example 2 be given: $p = 0.3,\ q = 0.7,\ n = 6$. For the creation of the (non-fuzzy) "upper" BD $\mathcal{B}_0 \circ \mathcal{B}^k_{n;p}$ as a model of the superposition of two processes—the binomial process $\mathcal{B}^k_{n;p}$ and the process of "increasing the total number of failures" $\mathcal{B}_0$—we enter the a priori probability value $P(\mathcal{B}_0) = 1 - \gamma = 0.65$ [13] and the elementary event probability of ("1")—$p = 0.3$. Let $\mu_0 = 0.8$ and $\mu_0' = 0.4$ be the levels of the membership function that correspond to the complex events $\overbrace{(0, \ldots, 0)}^{n}$ when we want to distinguish the binomial and non-binomial origin events. Calculate: 1. the probability distribution of k success of the fuzzy "upper" binomial experiment—denoted by $\widetilde{\mathcal{B}}_0 \circ \mathcal{B}^k_{n;p}$; 2. the Poisson distribution—$P_{Poiss}(k)$; 3. the Poisson distribution $\overline{P}_{Poiss}(k)$.*

Solution of Example 3. Case 1. Using Formula (33), we receive the numerical values of the probability distribution of k success of the fuzzy "upper" binomial experiment—denoted by $\widetilde{\mathcal{B}}_0 \circ \mathcal{B}^k_{n;p}$. $p = 0.3,\ q = 0.7,\ n = 6$ (Table 5).

Table 5. The values of probabilities of the fuzzy "upper" BD $\widetilde{\mathcal{B}}_0 \circ \mathcal{B}^k_{n;p}$.

k	0	1	2	3	4	5	6
$\mathcal{P}\left(\widetilde{\mathcal{B}}_0 \circ \mathcal{B}^k_{n,p}\right)$	0.6347	0.1253	0.1342	0.0767	0.0247	0.0042	0.0002

Case 2. By Formula (36), we calculated the values of the Poisson distribution—$P_{Poiss}(k)$ for the $k = 0, 1 \ldots, 6$ success (Table 6).

Table 6. The probabilities of k success of the Poisson distribution—$P_{Poiss}(k)$.

k	0	1	2	3	4	5	6
$P_{Poiss}(k)$	0.6445	0.1242	0.1129	0.0685	0.0319	0.0128	0.0052

Case 3. Using Formula (37), we numerically calculated the value of the first order moment of distribution—$\overline{k}$. Therefore, we analytically received expression of the functions Z (Formula (34)) and GF $G_{\mathcal{P}(\widetilde{\mathcal{B}}_0 \circ \mathcal{B}^k_{n;p})}(y)$. After this, we numerically calculated the value of the integral ξ. Finally, we calculated the values of the Poisson distribution $\overline{P}_{Poiss}(k)$ for the $k = 0, 1 \ldots, 6$ success (Table 7).

Table 7. The probabilities of k success of the Poisson distribution $\overline{P}_{Poiss}(k)$.

k	0	1	2	3	4	5	6
$P_{Poiss}(k)$	0.5100	0.1747	0.1572	0.0943	0.0424	0.0153	0.0061

5. Fuzzy Fuchs Distribution

Let us consider a hybrid fuzzy-random process where the fuzzy process is pre-distributed while the random process is ordinary. Based on the analysis of lexical material, it has been established that the linguistic spectrum of the statistical process of word-formation (which is in conversation) becomes two-component when switching to vocabulary. This has been explained for several languages [24]. In this section, we construct two variants of such a process, which can be used in the analysis of the linguistic spectrum of the statistical process of word-formation. It is well known that, as in the case of the binomial "upper" distribution, all variants of the Fuchs distribution are based on a two-process superposition model, which, in the case under consideration, is interpreted as "determined" and binomial, $\Phi^k_{n;v;p} = \mathcal{B}_v \circ \mathcal{B}^k_{n-v;p}$ [24].

The derivation of the Fuchs probability distribution function for the most characteristic cases discussed below actually coincides with the corresponding (non-fuzzy) probability distribution. Therefore, we will present only the final results. In addition, we use the Fuchs model and terminology [26]. We consider two cases:

Case 1. The pre-placement process is non-fuzzy, while the fuzziness of the binomial process is conditioned by the fuzziness of the elementary events. In this case, the fuzzy elemental event is characterized by a probability that depends on the number of pre-placed elements. As in Section 1, we consider a basic fuzzy-random variable of Bernoulli $\widetilde{\mathcal{B}} \sim \begin{pmatrix} values & 1 & 0 \\ probabilities & P_1 & P_0 \\ membership\ levels & \mu_1 & \mu_2 \end{pmatrix}$ and a sequence of fuzzy-random variables of Bernoulli $\widetilde{\mathcal{B}}_v \sim \begin{pmatrix} values & 1 & 0 \\ probabilities & P_1^{(v)} & P_0^{(v)} \\ membership\ levels for\ (v) & \mu_1^{(v)} & \mu_2^{(v)} \end{pmatrix}$, $v = 0, \ldots, n$ for the creation of a fuzzy Fuchs probability distribution. In this case, the Fuchs probabilistic distribution is as follows:

$$\mathcal{P}'\left(\widetilde{\mathcal{B}}_v \circ \widetilde{\mathcal{B}}^k_{n-v;p}\right) = \sum_{v=0}^{n} \rho_v C^{k-v}_{n-v}\left[\mathcal{P}'_{n-v}(\widetilde{1})\right]^{k-v}\left[\mathcal{P}'_{n-v}(\widetilde{0})\right]^{n-k}, \tag{42}$$

where ρ_v are the proportions of those cells in which the v elements are pre-placed (according to (15)) for $v = 0,\ 1,\ \ldots$ and must meet the conditions $\mu_1^{(v)} < \mu_2^{(v)},\ v = 0, \ldots n$, and

$$\mathcal{P}^{(v)}\left(\widetilde{C}_{(k)}\right) = \overbrace{P_1^{(v)}(1,\ldots,1)}^{n-v}\left[\sqrt[n-v-1]{\frac{P_1^{(v)}}{\overbrace{P_1^{(v)}(1,\ldots,1)}^{n-v}}} - 1\right]^{n-k}, \quad k = 1, \ldots, \tag{43}$$

$$\mathcal{P}^{(v)}\left(\widetilde{C}_{2^{n-v}}\right) = \overbrace{P_1^{(v)}(1,\ldots,1)}^{n-v} \cdot \left[\sqrt[n-v-1)]{\frac{P_1^{(v)}}{\overbrace{P_1^{(v)}(1,\ldots,1)}^{n-v}}} - 1\right]^{n-v} + 1 - P_1^{(v)} \cdot \sqrt[n-v-1]{\frac{P_1^{(v)}}{\overbrace{P_1^{(v)}(1,\ldots,1)}^{n-v}}},$$

$$0 \leq \frac{P_1^{(v)} \times \sqrt[n-v-1]{\frac{P_1^{(v)}}{\overbrace{P_1^{(v)}(1,\ldots,1)}^{n-v}}}}{\overbrace{P_1^{(v)}(1,\ldots,1)}^{n-v}\left[\sqrt[n-v-1]{\frac{P_1^{(v)}}{\overbrace{P_1^{(v)}(1,\ldots,1)}^{n-v}}} - 1\right]^{n-v}} < 1,$$

$$\frac{\mu_2^{(\nu)}}{\mu_1^{(v)}} = 1 + [\overbrace{P_1^{(\nu)}(0,\ldots,0)}^{n-\nu}]^{-1}\left[-1 + \sqrt[n-\nu-1]{\frac{P_1^{(\nu)}}{\underbrace{P_1^{(\nu)}(1,\ldots,1)}_{n-\nu}}}\right].$$

The corresponding GF of the distribution (42) and the first two moments are as follows:

$$G_{\mathcal{P}'(\tilde{B}_v \circ \tilde{B}^k_{n-v;p})}(y) = \sum_{v=0} \rho_v y^v \frac{[\mu_1 P_0 + \mu_1 P_1 y + (\mu_2-\mu_1)[\overbrace{P_1^{(v)}(0,\ldots,0)}^{n-v}]^{n-v}}{[\mu_1 + (\mu_2-\mu_1)[\underbrace{P_1^{(v)}(0,\ldots,0)}_{n-v}]^{n-v}},$$
$$\bar{k} = nP_1 + (1-P_0)\left(\sum_{v=0}^n \mu_1^{(v)} \rho_v\right)^{-1}\left(\sum_{v=0}^n \mu_2^{(v)} \rho_v\right) \tag{44}$$

$$\bar{k}^2 = \left(\sum_{v=0}^n \mu_1^{(\nu)} \rho_\nu\right)^{-1}\left[\sum_{v=0}^n \mu_2^{(\nu)} \rho_\nu + P_1 \sum_{v=0}^n (n-\nu)(2\nu+1+P_1(n-\nu-1))\mu_2^{(\nu)} \rho_\nu\right]. \tag{45}$$

We can obtain the similar expressions for $G_{\mathcal{P}'(\tilde{B}_v \circ \tilde{B}^k_{n-v;p})}(y)$, $\bar{k}$, and $\bar{k}^2$ in the case $\mu_1^{(\nu)} > \mu_2^{(\nu)}$, $\nu = 0,\ldots,n$, (omitted here).

Case 2. The pre-placement process is fuzzy, while the Binomial process is non-fuzzy—$\tilde{\Phi}^k_{n;\nu;p} = \tilde{B}_\nu \circ B^k_{n-\nu;p}$. Analogously to the previous case, we receive

$$\mathcal{P}'(\tilde{B}_v \circ B^k_{n-v;p}) = \sum_{v=0}^n \frac{\rho_v p_v}{\sum_{s=0}^n \rho_s p_s} P\left(B^k_{n-v;p}\right), \tag{46}$$

where (ν, ρ_ν, p_ν), $\nu = 0,1,\ldots,n$ is some fuzzy-random variable of the pre-placement process in the Fuchs distribution.

Given the subjective nature of the spectral probabilities in the Fuchs distribution, we can argue that, in this case, the non-fuzzy and fuzzy distributions coincide.

Example 4. *Case 1. Calculate the first and second moments of the Fuchs distribution if, in the role of fuzzy Bernoulli distribution, we selected* $\tilde{B} \sim \begin{pmatrix} values & 1 & 0 \\ probabilities & P_1 = 0.3 & P_0 = 0.7 \\ membership\ levels & \mu_1 = 0.5 & \mu_2 = 0.6 \end{pmatrix}$, *and the sequence of the membership levels of* $\tilde{B}_\nu$ *is given by Table 8.*

Table 8. Sequence of the membership levels of $\tilde{B}_\nu$.

Values	**1**	**0**
Probabilities	$P_1 = 0.3$	$P_0 = 0.7$
Membership levels	$\mu_1 = 0.6$	$\mu_2 = 0.8$
Membership levels for $\nu = 0$	$\mu_1^{(0)} = 0.5$	$\mu_2^{(0)} = 0.6$
Membership levels for $\nu = 1$	$\mu_1^{(1)} = 0.4$	$\mu_2^{(1)} = 0.7$
Membership levels for $\nu = 2$	$\mu_1^{(2)} = 0.3$	$\mu_2^{(2)} = 0.6$
Membership levels for $\nu = 3$	$\mu_1^{(3)} = 0.5$	$\mu_2^{(3)} = 0.8$
Membership levels for $\nu = 4$	$\mu_1^{(4)} = 0.3$	$\mu_2^{(4)} = 0.6$
Membership levels for $\nu = 5$	$\mu_1^{(5)} = 0.5$	$\mu_2^{(5)} = 0.9$
Membership levels for $\nu = 6$	$\mu_1^{(0)} = 0.6$	$\mu_2^{(0)} = 0.7$

Calculate the values of $\bar{k}$ and $\bar{k}^2$.

Case 2. Let the fuzzy binomial experiment and the fuzzy random variable on all possible success values be given $\{0,1,2,3,4,5,6\}$ (Table 9).

Table 9. The fuzzy random variable.

ν	0	1	2	3	4	5	6
p_ν	0.05	0.1	0.2	0.3	0.2	0.1	0.05
ρ_ν	0.15	0.25	0.45	0.75	0.55	0.35	0.25

Let the fuzzy Bernoulli variable also be given $\widetilde{\mathcal{X}} \sim \begin{pmatrix} values & 1 & 0 \\ probabilities & P_1 = 0.3 & P_0 = 0.7 \\ membership\, levels & \mu_1 = 0.5 & \mu_2 = 0.6 \end{pmatrix}$. Calculate the numerical value of the Fuchs distribution.

Solution of the Example 4.

In Case 1, the fuzzy character of the binomial process is conditioned by the fuzzy character of the elementary events. Therefore, we received an expression of the corresponding GF. After this, we calculated the values of $\widetilde{k} = 2.3100$ and $\widetilde{k^2} = 10.7470$ (Formulas (44) and (45)).

In Case 2, when in the Fuchs experiment there is a fuzzy pre-placement process while the binomial process is non fuzzy—$\widetilde{\Phi}^k_{n;\nu;p} = \widetilde{\mathcal{B}}_\nu \circ \mathcal{B}^k_{n-\nu;p}$, for obtaining the numerical values of the Fuchs fuzzy distribution, we used Table 9 and Formula (46), where $P(\mathcal{B}^l_{n-\nu;p}) = C^l_{n-\nu} p^l (1-p)^{n-\nu-l}$, $p = P_1 = 0.3$, $C^l_{n-\nu} = 0$ if $l > n - \nu$. The results are given by Table 10.

Table 10. Values of the Fuchs fuzzy distribution.

k	0	1	2	3	4	5	6
$\mathcal{P}'(\widetilde{\mathcal{B}}_v \circ \mathcal{B}^k_{n-v;p})$	0.1157	0.4044	0.5702	0.3867	0.1382	0.0336	0.0045

6. Conclusions

The research presented in this paper is relevant today in terms of its applicability. Experimental, objective data are often not sufficient to build discrete distributions in the study, analysis, and synthesis of difficult and complex phenomena. Often, such data do not exist at all. Modern modeling, and in particular simulation modeling, is unthinkable outside of the solution of the problems of restoring discrete distributions. The research presented in this paper is different from the existing studies. It refers to a generalization of binomial distribution where the results of an experiment are described by fuzzy variables. These variables are defined in the universe of all the results of the experiment. We are dealing with a binomial fuzzy-random variable. It has both a probability distribution and a membership function in the universe of all results of the experiment. This paper discusses four new and different cases of BD fuzzy extensions. *Case 1*: The fuzzy extension of the BD is presented when the Bernoulli fuzzy-random variable is considered instead of the Bernoulli random variable—i.e., the success and failure events have both probabilistic distributions and their implementation capabilities in the form of compatibility levels. Based on this information, the probabilistic distribution of the corresponding binomial fuzzy-random variable is calculated. The conditions of restrictions on this distribution are obtained. It is shown that these conditions depend on the ratio of success and failure compatibility levels. The formulas for the GF of the built distribution and the first and second order moments are also obtained. The Poisson distribution is calculated as a limit case of a constructed binomial fuzzy-random experiment. *Case 2*: The fuzzy extension of the BD is considered, where the number of successes, in contrast to the previous case, is of a fuzzy nature and is represented as a fuzzy subset of the set of possible success numbers. A formula for calculating the probability of the convolution of binomial dependent fuzzy events is obtained. Using the principle of the invariancy of an exponential distribution, the corresponding GF is built. As a result, the scheme for calculating the mathematical expectation of the number of fuzzy successes is defined. It becomes possible in future studies to obtain Poisson and normal distributions as marginal cases of the fuzzy BDs constructed here. *Case 3*: The fuzzy extension of the "upper" BD is considered, where the fuzziness is represented by the compatibility levels of the binomial and non-binomial events of the complete failure complex. The GF and the first-order moment of the built distribution are calculated. Sufficient conditions for the existence of an appropriate marginal distribution, a Poisson distribution, are also obtained. *Case 4*: The fuzzy extension of the classical Fuchs distribution is presented, where the fuzziness is reflected in the growing number of failures. The built distribution function and the first and second order moments of the distribution are also calculated. In each section of the paper, for illustration of the obtained results, examples of the built fuzzy BD are considered. It becomes possible in future studies to obtain Poisson and normal distributions as marginal cases of the fuzzy Fuchs distribution. Of course, the practical application of the hybrid fuzzy-binomial models studied here is in great demand. This is the main motivation to continue research in this direction in the future. The main gradient of the research will be directed to the solution of applied problems, where the distributions built in this paper, or their modifications and generalizations, will be used.

Author Contributions: Conceptualization, G.S. and B.M. (Bidzina Midodashvili); Formal analysis, T.M.; Methodology, J.K.; Software, B.M. (Bidzina Matsaberidze). The authors contributed equally in this work. All authors have read and agreed to the published version of the manuscript.

Funding: This research was funded by the Shota Rustaveli National Scientific Foundation of Georgia (SRNSF), grant number [FR-21-2015].

Institutional Review Board Statement: Not applicable.

Informed Consent Statement: Not applicable.

Data Availability Statement: The paper is original and, therefore, no data were used.

Acknowledgments: We would like to mention our deceased colleague Tamaz Gachechiladze, whose ideas were very helpful to us in this work. The authors are grateful to the anonymous reviewers for their valuable comments and suggestions in improving the quality of the paper.

Conflicts of Interest: The authors declare no conflict of interest.

References

1. Kacprzyk, J.; Kondratenko, Y.P.; Merigó, J.M.; Hormazabal, J.H.; Sirbiladze, G.; Gil-Lafuente, A.M. A Status Quo Biased Multistage Decision Model for Regional Agricultural Socioeconomic Planning Under Fuzzy Information, Advanced Control Techniques in Complex Engineering Systems: Theory and Applications. In *Studies in Systems, Decision and Control*; Springer: Cham, Switzerland, 2019; Volume 203, pp. 201–226.
2. Sirbiladze, G. Extremal Fuzzy Dynamic Systems. Theory and Applications. In *IFSR International Series on Systems Science and Engineering*; Springer: New York, NY, USA; Heidelberg, Germany; Dordrecht, The Netherlands; London, UK, 2013; p. 28.
3. Sirbiladze, G.; Ghvaberidze, I.K.B. Multistage decision-making fuzzy methodology for optimal investments based on experts' evaluations. *Eur. J. Oper. Res.* **2014**, *232*, 169–177. [CrossRef]
4. Sirbiladze, G. Associated Probabilities' Aggregations in Interactive MADM for q-Rung Orthopair Fuzzy Discrimination Environment. *Int. J. Intell. Syst.* **2020**, *35*, 335–372. [CrossRef]
5. Garg, H.; Sirbiladze, G.; Ali, Z.; Mahmood, T. Hamy Mean Operators Based on Complex q-Rung Orthopair Fuzzy Setting and Their Application in Multi-Attribute Decision Making. *Mathematics* **2021**, *9*, 2312. [CrossRef]
6. Sirbiladze, G. Associated Probabilities in Interactive MADM under Discrimination q-Rung Picture Linguistic Environment. *Mathematics* **2021**, *9*, 2337. [CrossRef]
7. Sirbiladze, G. An Identification Model for a Fuzzy Time Based Stationary Discrete Process. *Iran. J. Fuzzy Syst.* **2022**, *19*, 169–186.
8. Sirbiladze, G.; Manjafarashvil, T.T. Connections between Campos-Bolanos and Murofushi–Sugeno Representations of a Fuzzy Measure. *Mathematics* **2022**, *10*, 516. [CrossRef]
9. Goswami, P.; Baruah, H.K. Fuzzy Discrete Distribution: The Binomial Case. 2008. Available online: https://Www.Researchgate.Net/Publication/235006838_Fuzzy_Discrete_Distributions (accessed on 10 April 2022).

10. Buckley, J.J. Discrete Fuzzy Random Variables. In *Fuzzy Probabilities. New Approach and Applications, Studies in Fuzziness and Soft Computing*; Springer: Berlin, Germany, 2003; Volume 115, pp. 51–54.
11. Buckley, J.J.; Eslami, E. Uncertain probabilities I: The discrete case. *Soft Comput.* **2003**, *7*, 500–505. [CrossRef]
12. Parlak, I.B.; Tolga, A.C. Fuzzy Probability Theory I: Discrete Case. In *Fuzzy Statistical Decision-Making, Studies in Fuzziness and Soft Computing*; Kahraman, C., Kabak, Ö., Eds.; Springer: Berlin, Germany, 2016; Volume 343, pp. 13–31.
13. Kahraman, C.; Bekar, E.T.; Senvar, O. A Fuzzy Design of Single and Double Acceptance Sampling Plans. In *Intelligent Systems Reference Library*; Kahraman, C., Yanık, S., Eds.; Springer: Berlin, Germany, 2016; Volume 97, pp. 179–211.
14. Turanoğlu, E.; Kaya, İ.; Kahraman, C. Fuzzy Acceptance Sampling and Characteristic Curves. *Int. J. Comput. Intell. Syst.* **2012**, *5*, 13–29. [CrossRef]
15. Adepoju, A.A.; Mohammed, U.; Sani, S.S.; Adamu, K.; Tukur, K.; Ishaq, A.I. Statistical properties of negative binomial distribution under imprecise observation. *J. Niger. Stat. Assoc.* **2019**, *31*, 1–8.
16. Jamkhaneh, E.B.; Gildeh, B.S.; Yari, G. Acceptance Single Sampling Plan with Fuzzy Parameter. *Iran. J. Fuzzy Syst.* **2011**, *8*, 47–55.
17. Sumarti, N.; Nadya, P. A Dynamic Portfolio of American Option using Fuzzy Binomial Method. *J. Innov. Technol. Educ.* **2016**, *3*, 85–92. [CrossRef]
18. Moraes, R.M.; Machado, L.S. A Fuzzy Binomial Naive Bayes Classifier for Epidemiological Data. In Proceedings of the 2016 IEEE International Conference on Fuzzy Systems (FUZZ), Vancouver, BC, Canada, 24–29 July 2016; pp. 745–749.
19. Kahraman, C.; Kaya, I. Fuzzy acceptance sampling plans. *Stud. Fuzziness Soft Comput.* **2010**, *252*, 457–481.
20. Uma, G.; Nandhinievi, R. Determination of QSS by single–normal and double tightened plan using fuzzy binomial distribution. *Int. J. Res. Advent Technol.* **2018**, *6*, 27–43.
21. Colubi, A.; Gil, M.A.; González-Rodríguez, G.; López, M.T. Empirical comparisons of goodness-of-fit tests for binomial distributions based on fuzzy representations. In *Advances in Soft Computing*; Dubois, D., Lubiano, M.A., Prade, H., Gil, M.Á., Grzegorzewski, P., Hryniewicz, O., Eds.; Soft Methods for Handling Variability and Imprecision; Springer: Berlin/Heidelberg, Germany, 2008; Volume 48. [CrossRef]
22. Charles, J.G.; Glen, D.M. Fuzzy and randomized confidence intervals and P-values. *Stat. Sci.* **2005**, *20*, 358–366.
23. Zadeh, L.A. The concept of a linguistic variable and its application to approximate reasoning—II. *Inf. Sci.* **1975**, *8*, 301–357. [CrossRef]
24. Manjafarashvili, T. On determining the probability of fuzzy events. *AN GSSR* **1980**, *97*, 23–34.
25. Zadeh, L.A. Probability measures of fuzzy events. *J. Math. Anal. Appl.* **1968**, *23*, 421–427. [CrossRef]
26. Fuk, D.H. Certain probabilistic inequalities for martingales. *Sib. Math. J.* **1971**, *14*, 131–137. [CrossRef]

MDPI
St. Alban-Anlage 66
4052 Basel
Switzerland
Tel. +41 61 683 77 34
Fax +41 61 302 89 18
www.mdpi.com

Axioms Editorial Office
E-mail: axioms@mdpi.com
www.mdpi.com/journal/axioms

MDPI